EVERYMAN'S LIBRARY
EDITED BY ERNEST RHYS

REFERENCE

A DICTIONARY OF DATES
BROUGHT DOWN TO
THE PRESENT DAY

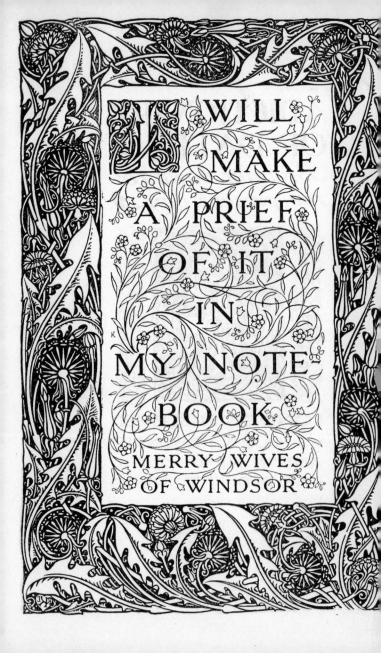

I WILL MAKE A PRIEF OF IT IN MY NOTE BOOK

MERRY WIVES OF WINDSOR

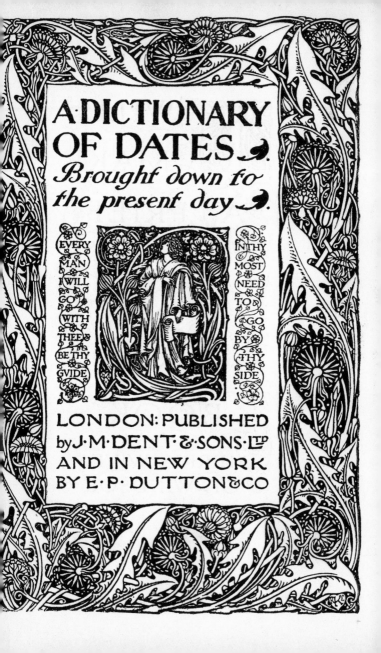

A DICTIONARY OF DATES

Brought down to the present day

EVERY MAN I WILL GO WITH THEE BE THY GVIDE

IN THY MOST NEED TO GO BY THY SIDE

LONDON: PUBLISHED
by J·M·DENT·&·SONS·Lᵀᴰ
AND IN NEW YORK
BY E·P·DUTTON&CO

PREFACE

THE aim of the compilers of this volume has been to give every date likely to be of service to the general reader, while getting rid of the superfluities which make the typical date-book too bulky for easy use. It is not intended to be in any way a substitute for dictionaries of biography or the books of information on special subjects, which are otherwise accounted for in the series. It only supplies the names of personages, for instance, where they mark a distinct point in time—as Caxton, Ket of Ket's Rebellion, or Wagner—or where they enter into a chronological group, such as the Kings, Popes, Archbishops, Authors, etc., who mark the record. That is, it is a book to save memory on the side which most requires economy and gains least by unusual effort; one to annihilate as far as possible that confusion of successive events and relative epochs to which we are all liable. Those who have on occasion been at a loss to remember the exact concurrence of Louis the Fourteenth in France and Charles the Second in England, or the months between the Battle of Minden and the Battle of Pfaffendorf, or the temporal gap between Descartes and Hegel, will find chronology made easy by a working acquaintance with these pages. Take the case of London alone: the Bishops, the Bridge, the City, the County; the date of the first Lord Mayor, the Fire, the Plague, the Treaties and the University—all these have their reference; while Westminster demands some half-dozen separate entries. Even as it is, the necessity of drawing the line between the indispensable and the seldom used date has in some pages, it may be, led to a doubtful omission or insertion.

The publishers are only too conscious that this first

attempt to issue a useful dictionary of dates for the use of readers of "Everyman's Library" is not by any means perfect, but they hope that, as in the natural course of time the book will require revision, they will have many practical and useful suggestions from their readers, which they hope to incorporate in future editions.

BEDFORD STREET,
    September 1911.

LIST OF ABBREVIATIONS USED THROUGHOUT THIS WORK

art.	article	incorp.	incorporated
b.	battle	instit.	instituted
b.	born	intro.	introduced
d.	died	orig.	originally
estab.	established	res.	restored
fd.	founded	U.S.A.	United States of America
fl.	flourished	W.	war

A

DICTIONARY OF DATES

A

Aarau, Treaty of. Religious wars of Switzerland were ended by this treaty, Aug. 11, 1712.

Abancay (Peru). River on banks of which Alvarado was taken prisoner on July 12, 1537, by Spanish commander Almagro.

Abbaye. Military prison close to the church of St. Germain des Prés. During French Rev. (Sept. 2 and 3, 1792) it was the scene of a terrible massacre. [Refer Carlyle, *French Revolution*.]

Abbeville (France). Treaties of A. (1) between Henry III. of England and Louis IX. of France, signed May 20, 1259 [refer Pearson, *Hist. of England during Early and Middle Ages*]; (2) between Henry VIII., represented by Cardinal Wolsey, and Francis I., signed at A. Aug. 18, 1527. Occupied by German troops, Feb. 6, 1871.

Abbeys. *See* Monasteries.

Abdications of Sovereigns (including forced abdications and " desertions ") :—

Sulla, Roman dictator	. . . .	B.C.	79
Diocletian, Roman emperor	. . .	A.D.	305
Stephen II. of Hungary	. . .	,,	1131
Albert the Bear of Brandenburg	. .	,,	1142
Lescov V. of Poland	. . .	,,	1200
Ladislaus III. of Poland	. . .	,,	1206
Pope Celestine V. (forced)	. . .	Dec. 13,	1294
John Balliol of Scotland	. . .		1296
Otho (of Bavaria) of Hungary	. .		1309
Edward II. of England (forced)	. .		1327
Richard II. of England (forced)	. .	Sept. 29,	1399
Eric VII. of Denmark	. . .	,,	1439
Pope Felix V.	. . .	,,	1449
Charles V. as emperor of Germany	. .	Oct. 25,	1555
,, as king of Spain	. .	Jan. 16,	1556
Mary Queen of Scots (forced)	. .	July 24,	1567
Christina of Sweden	. . .	June 16,	1654
John Casimir of Poland (forced)	. .		1668
James II. of England (fled)	. .	Dec. 11,	1688
Frederick Augustus II. of Poland	. .		1704
Philip V. of Spain (resumed)	. .		1724
Victor Amadeus of Sardinia	. .		1730
Charles of Naples	. . .		1759

ABDICATIONS OF SOVEREIGNS (*continued*)—

Stanislaus II. of Poland (forced)	1795
Charles Emmanuel IV. of Sardinia	June 4, 1802
Francis II. of Germany, who became Emperor of Austria	Aug. 11, 1804
Charles IV. of Spain, in favour of his son	Mar. 19, 1808
,, ,, ,, in favour of Bonaparte (*see* Spain)	May 1, 1808
Joseph Bonaparte of Naples (for Spain)	June 1, 1808
Gustavus IV. of Sweden	Mar. 29, 1809
Louis **Bonaparte** of Holland	July 1, 1810
Jerome of Westphalia	Oct. 20, 1813
Napoleon I. of France	April 5, 1814
Victor Emmanuel of Sardinia	Mar. 13, 1821
Pedro IV. of Portugal	May 2, 1826
Charles X. of France	Aug. 2, 1830
Pedro I. of Brazil	April 7, 1831
Dom Miguel of Portugal (fled)	May 26, 1834
William I. of Holland	Oct. 8, 1840
Louis Philippe of France	Feb. 24, 1848
Louis Charles of Bavaria	Mar. 21, 1848
Ferdinand of Austria	Dec. 2, 1848
Charles Albert of Sardinia	Mar. 23, 1849
Leopold II. of Tuscany	July 21, 1859
Bernhard of Saxe-Meiningen	Sept. 20, 1866
Isabella II. of Spain	June 25, 1870
Amadeus II. of Spain	Feb. 11, 1873
Prince Alexander of Bulgaria (forced)	Sept. 7, 1886
Milan, King of Servia	Mar. 3, 1889
Oscar, King of Norway and Sweden, recognised Norway as separate state	Oct. 27, 1905
Abdul Hamid II., Sultan of Turkey (forced)	April 27, 1909
Manoel of Portugal (forced)	Oct. 4, 1910

Abelard. Scholastic philosopher, and lover of Heloise, whom he seduced about 1119; author with H. of famous letters. Their ashes interred in Père la Chaise.

Aberdeen (N. Scotland). City built A.D. 893; made a royal burgh by William the Lion, 1179. Charter granted by Robert Bruce 1319. Burned by English 1336. St. Machar's Cathedral (1357-1527) res. 1869. King's College fd. by Bishop Elphinstone 1494. University erected 1500-6. [Refer Watt, *History of Aberdeen.*]

Aberdeen Administration. Named after Lord Aberdeen (1784-1860), First Lord of the Treasury; called Coalition Ministry. Formed after resignation of Derby Administration; sworn in, Dec. 1852; resigned, Jan. 1855; succeeded by Palmerston Administration (*q.v.*). [Refer *Letters of Queen Victoria.*]

Aberdeen Doctors. The name given to six clergymen who between 1638-9 opposed the administration of the oath to preserve the Solemn League and Covenant (*q.v.*). [Refer Burton, *History of Scotland.*]

Aberration of Light, theory of, discovered by James Bradley 1727.

Aberystwyth (W. Wales). Castle fd. by Gilbert de Strongbow, 1109; Town incorp. by Edward I.; University College of Wales, 1872; Welsh Nat. Library 1911.

Aberystwyth University. *See* Universities.

Abhorrers. The elections of 1679 proved unfavourable to the court of Charles II., and parliament did not meet. Court party known as Abhorrers. [Refer Macaulay, *History of England.*]

Abingdon (Berks). Seat of a monastery fd. in A.D. 675 by Cissa, which was burnt by the Danes 866-871. In 1645 Lord Essex held A. against Charles I. Defenders put prisoners to death without trial, hence term Abingdon law. [Refer Townsend, *History of Abingdon.*]

Abiogenesis. Term used by Huxley, in 1870, to express theory that living organisms can be produced by spontaneous generation; disproved by Tyndall.

Abo. Peace of, Sweden ceded portion of Finland to Russia, Aug. 18, 1743.

Abolitionists. Party in U.S.A. (Northern States) opposed to slavery. Congress 1774. Small society formed 1832, which became in time a party of great political power, attaining its object in the Civil War of 1861-4. [Refer Harper, *Encyclopædia U.S. History.*]

Aboukir (Egypt). Nelson defeated French in Bay of A. Aug. 1, 1798. Napoleon defeated Turkish army at A. 1799. Sir Ralph Abercromby took town from French, Mar. 8, 1801.

Abrantes, Treaty of. Signed Nov. 29, 1807. Ratified at Madrid and sometimes named after the latter city.

Absenteeism. First statute passed in English Parliament 1379, " ordering all proprietors who were absentees to contribute two-thirds of their means to the defence of Ireland." Tax levied on all moneys paid out of Ireland 1729. [Refer art. in Low and Pulling, *Dicty. of Eng. Hist.*]

Abu Klea (Soudan). Stewart defeated Mahdi, Jan. 17, 1885.

Abyssinia. First known to Europe through Portuguese missionaries in 15th century, but it has a place in history long before. Christianity known in A. in the 4th century. A. is rescued from Mahommed Granyé by Portuguese 1543. Theodore, King of A., applies to Queen Victoria for aid against the invading Egyptians 1863. His letter is unaccountably neglected, and Theodore, feeling slighted, imprisons the English consul and missionaries. Lord Stanley issues ultimatum April 1867, ordering delivery of prisoners within three months. No notice taken of this, so Sir Robert Napier starts for A. with an army, which reaches Magdala (*q.v.*) April 10, 1868, and defeats Abyssinian army. Theodore kills himself in this battle. Kassai of Tigré crowns himself emperor 1872; Italians occupy Massowah 1885; death of Kassai 1889; Menelek, his successor, defeats Italians near Adowa, Feb. 1896; treaty which follows acknowledges independence of A. Sir Rennell Rodd's mission 1897; dispute concerning frontier of Western Protectorate is settled by agreement between Britain and A. 1905; international agreement concerning A. 1907.

Academies, from Academia, a grove outside Athens (bequeathed to Academus). Plato first taught philosophy here 398 B.C. Ptolemy founds an A. at Alexandria 314 B.C. First philosophical A. in France fd. by Père Mersenne at Paris 1635. The following are the principal A. with the dates when they were founded. The A. of Great Britain are under their various titles.

Ancona, A. of the *Caliginosi,* 1642.

Berlin, Akademie der Wissenschaften, 1700; Architecture, 1799.

Bologna, Ecclesiastical, 1687; Mathematics, 1690; Sciences and Arts, 1712.

Brescia, Brescia A., 1801; of the *Erranti,* 1626.

Brest and Toulon, Military, 1682.

Brussels, *Belles Lettres,* 1773.

Caen, *Belles Lettres,* 1705.

Chicago, U.S.A., Sciences, 1865.

Constantinople, A. of, 1851.

Copenhagen, Sciences, 1743.

Cortona, Antiquities, 1726.

Dublin, Royal Irish A., 1782.

Erfurt, Saxony, Sciences, 1754.

Faenza, the *Philoponi,* 1612.

Florence, Fine Arts, 1270; Platonica, 1474 (dissolved 1521); Della Crusca, 1582; Del Cimento, 1657; Dei Georgofli, 1752 (agricultural); Antiquities, 1807.

Geneva, Medical, 1715.

Genoa, Painting, etc., 1751; Sciences, 1783.

Göttingen, Gesellschaft der Wissenschaften, 1752.

Haarlem, The Sciences, 1760.

Helsingfors, Societas Scientiarum.

Leipzig, A. of, 1768.

Lisbon, Portuguese A., 1779.

London, Royal Society, 1662; Royal Academy of Arts, 1768; Royal Academy of Music, 1822.

Lyons, Sciences, 1700.

Madrid, Royal Spanish, 1713; History, 1730; Painting and the Arts, 1753.

Mannheim, Sculpture, 1775.

Mantua, the *Vigilanti* (Sciences), 1704.

Marseilles, *Belles Lettres,* 1726.

Massachusetts, Arts and Sciences, 1780.

Milan, A. of, 1838; Architecture, 1380; Sciences, 1719.

Modena, Società Italiana delle Scienze.

Munich, Arts and Sciences, 1759.

Naples, *Rossana,* 1540; *Secretorum Naturæ,* 1560; Sciences, 1695; *Herculaneum,* 1755.

Newhaven, U.S.A., Connecticut A. of Arts and Sciences, 1799.

New York, Literature and Philosophy, 1814; of Sciences, 1818; National A., 1863.

Nîmes, Royal A., 1682.

Padua, Poetry, 1610; Sciences, 1792; A. of, 1779.

Palermo, Medical, 1645; Fine Arts, 1300.

Paris, A. Royale de Peinture et Sculpture, 1648; A. Royale d'Architecture, 1671; A. Française, 1637; A. des Inscriptions, 1663; A. Royale des Sciences, 1666; A. de Peinture, 1648. All these A. at Paris were suppressed 1793, and in 1795 one large one, the *Institut National*, was fd. This in 1816 was split up in four classes by Louis XVIII.: (*a*) L'Académie Française; (*b*) L'Académie des Inscriptions et Belles Lettres; (*c*) L'Académie des Sciences; (*d*) L'Académie des Beaux-Arts, and in 1832 L'Académie des Sciences, Morales et Politiques.

Parma, the *Innominati*, 1550.

Pennsylvania, A. of Fine Arts, 1805.

Perugia, *Insensati*, 1561; *Filirgiti*, 1574.

Philadelphia, U.S.A., Arts and Sciences, 1749.

Rome, *Umoristi*, 1611; *Fantastici*, 1625; *Infecondi*, 1653; Painting, 1656; *Degli Arcadi*, 1656; English 1752; *De' Nuovi Lincei*, 1847.

St. Petersburg, Imperial, 1728.

Salem, Mass., Peabody A. of Sciences.

Stockholm, Sciences, 1741; *Belles Lettres*, 1753; Agriculture, 1781.

Toulon, Military, 1682.

Turin, Sciences, 1757; Fine Arts, 1778.

Upsala, Royal Society, 1720.

Venice, Medical, 1701.

Verona, Music, 1543; Sciences, 1780.

Vienna, Sculpture and Arts, 1705; Surgery, 1783; Oriental, 1810.

Warsaw, Languages and History, 1753.

Academy, The. Literary journal established by Murray 1869.

Acarnania (N. Greece). People of A. engage in Peloponnesian War 432 B.C. against Ambracians. Acarnanians conquered by Lacedæmonians 390 B.C.; defeated by Romans 197 B.C.; subjugated 145 B.C. [Refer Thucydides, *Peloponnesian War*.]

Acclimatisation. Society of Great Britain estab. 1860. French Society fd. 1854. Jardin Zoologique d'Acclimatation opened at Paris 1860. Garden of A. for the rearing of English Birds and Fishes opened at Melbourne, Australia, Feb. 1861.

Accountant-General in Chancery Office. Instit. 1726, abolished 1872.

Accountants, Chartered Institute of, of England and Wales. Fd. 1880; ditto of Scotland, fd. 1854.

Accountants' Institute. Estab. July 30, 1870.

Accountants' Society. Estab. 1872.

Acoustics. The science of sounds. Explained by Pythagoras *cir.* 500 B.C., by Aristotle 330 B.C. Galileo's important discoveries A.D. 1600. Velocity of sound dis. by Newton 1698. Dr. Brook Taylor's practical demonstrations of Galileo's theories 1714. Tyndall's experiments, July 1873. Stroh's experiments, April 27, 1882. Mersenne's discovery in 1636 explained by Helmholtz 1862. Recent experiments carried out by Rudolf König of Paris and Prof. Mayer of Hoboken. [Refer Rayleigh's *Theory of Sound*.]

Acre, St. Jean d'. The *Acco* of Old Test. and *Ptolemaïs* of New Test. Taken by Crusaders 1104, by Saladin 1187, by Richard I., after two years' siege, 1191; retaken by Saracens 1291 [refer De Joinville, *Chronicles of the Crusades*], by Turks 1517, by Ibrahim Pasha 1832. Napoleon besieged it unsuccessfully in 1799. Stormed and taken by Sir Robert Stopford on Nov. 3, 1840. *See* Crusades.

Acropolis (of Athens). Begun 468 B.C., partially destroyed A.D. 1687; taken from Turks by Greeks, June 21, 1822; retaken, May 17, 1827. [Refer Smith, *Classical Dicty*. (new ed. Everyman's Lib. 1910).]

Act of Parliament or Statute. Written law which has received royal assent. Earliest mentioned, Statute of Merton 1235; earliest existing statute roll 6 Edward I., of Gloucester. Magna Charta 1215; Bill of Rights 1628; abolished dispensing power of Crown 1689; Test Act 1673, repealed 1828; Act of Union of Scotland and England 1707; with Ireland 1800; Septennial Act 1716; Stamp Act 1765; abolition of slave trade 1807; Corn Laws, Peel's, 1846; all duties abolished 1869; Ballot Act 1872; Licensing Act 1904. Lords cannot originate money-bills, but can protest against measures they dislike; Nov. 30, 1909, exercised veto in rejecting Lloyd-George's budget.

Act of Settlement. Passed 1662. Secured possession of forfeited estates of Irish rebels; repealed 1689, res. 1690. [Refer Macaulay, *Hist. of Eng.*]

Act of Supremacy. Henry VIII.'s Act declaring himself head of the English Church 1534. Formally assumed title, Jan. 15, 1535. Denial of Act declared by Edward VI. to be treasonable 1547. Repealed by Philip and Mary 1554; restored by Elizabeth, 1559. [Refer Froude, *Henry VIII*.]

Act of Toleration, for relief of Dissenters, May 24, 1689; confirmed 1711. Roman Catholics included in the Act, April 13, 1829. *See* Nonconformists. [Refer Macaulay, *Hist. of Eng.*]

Act of Uniformity, ordering use of Prayer Book, Jan. 15, 1549; confirmed 1552; repealed by Queen Mary 1553; res. by Elizabeth 1559. Formed basis of the Act under Charles II., which contained stringent regulations with regard to the Book of Common Prayer. Came into operation Aug. 24, 1662. [Refer Macaulay, *Hist. of Eng.*]

Acts of Sederunt (Scotland), empowering judges to make rules and ordinances necessary for the regulation of the courts, granted by James V. 1532, ratified 1540. [Refer art. in *Chambers's Encyclopædia*.

Actinometer. Instrument for measurement of solar rays invented by Sir John Herschel about 1820. For a long description of the A. refer to *Edinburgh Journal of Science* for 1825. The Pyrheliometer has now taken its place.

Actuary, from Actuarius. Name given in ancient Rome to certain clerks and officers. Institute of Actuaries fd. 1848. International Congress 1898. Faculty of A. in Scotland estab. Edinburgh 1856. A. Society of America assembled April 24, 1890. [Refer art. in *Encyclopædia Brit.*]

Adamites. A sect which rose in A.D. 130 to imitate Adam's condition before the fall, introduced into Germany about A.D. 1415, suppressed 1420. [Refer Strong and McClintock, *Dicty. Eccles. Lit.*]

Addington Administration. Formed after Pitt's resignation, Mar. 17, 1801; terminated May 12, 1804. Henry Addington, First Lord of the Treasury.

Addled Parliament met Tuesday, April 5, 1614; dismissed by James I., June 7 of the same year.

Adelaide (S. Australia). Fd. by Col. Light, who arrived July 27, 1836. Free port 1845.

Aden (Arabia). Mentioned in Marco Polo's travels. Taken by Portuguese in 1513, and captured by Turks 1538. After 1730 an independent state until bombarded and taken by East India Company's troops, Jan. 19, 1839.

Administrations (Great Britain) since the accession of George I.:—

> *George I. :*
>
> > Charles Townshend, Viscount Townshend, Sept. 1714.
> > James Stanhope, Lord Stanhope, April 1717.
> > James Stanhope, Lord Stanhope, Mar. 1718.
> > Robert Walpole, 1721.
>
> *George II. :*
>
> > Sir Robert Walpole, 1727.
> > John Carteret, Lord Carteret, Feb. 1742.
> > Hon. Henry Pelham, Nov. 1744.
> > William Pulteney, Earl of Bath, Feb. 10-12, 1746.
> > Hon. Henry Pelham, Feb. 1746.
> > Thomas Pelham Holles, Duke of Newcastle, April 1754.
> > William Pitt, Nov. 1756.
> > Thomas Pelham Holles, Duke of Newcastle, and William Pitt
> > > as Secretary of State, known as the Coalition Ministry, June 19, 1757.
>
> *George III. :*
>
> > Thomas Pelham Holles, Duke of Newcastle, 1760.
> > Earl of Bute, May 1762.

ADMINISTRATIONS (*continued*)—

George III. (continued) :

George Grenville, May 1763.
Marquis of Rockingham, 1765.
Earl of Chatham, Aug. 1766.
Duke of Grafton, Dec. 1767.
Frederick, Lord North, Jan. 1770.
Marquis of Rockingham, Mar. 1782.
Earl of Shelburne, July 1782.
Duke of Portland, Lord North, and Charles James Fox, known as Coalition Ministry, April 1783.
William Pitt, Dec. 1783.
Henry Addington, Mar. 1801.
William Pitt, May 1804.
Lord Grenville (" All the Talents " Ministry), Feb. 1806.
Duke of Portland, Mar. 1807.
Spencer Perceval, Oct. 1809.
Earl of Liverpool, June 1812.

George IV. :

Earl of Liverpool, Jan. 1820.
George Canning, April 1827.
Viscount Goderich, Sept. 1827.
Duke of Wellington, Jan. 1828.

William IV. :

Earl Grey, Nov. 1830.
Viscount Melbourne, July 1834.
Provisional government during absence of Sir Robert Peel, Nov. 1834.
Sir Robert Peel, Dec. 1834.
Viscount Melbourne, April 1835.

Victoria :

Viscount Melbourne, June 1837.
Sir Robert Peel, Sept. 1841.
Lord John Russell, July 1846.
Earl of Derby, Feb. 1852.
Earl of Aberdeen, Dec. 1852.
Viscount Palmerston, Feb. 1855.
Earl of Derby, Feb. 1858.
Viscount Palmerston, June 1859 (Palmerston *d.* Oct. 1865), succeeded by Lord John Russell.
Earl of Derby, June 1866 (Derby retired Feb. 1868), succeeded by Benjamin Disraeli.
W. E. Gladstone, Dec. 1868.
Benjamin Disraeli, Earl of Beaconsfield, Feb. 1874.
W. E. Gladstone, April 1880.
Marquis of Salisbury, July 1885.
W. E. Gladstone, Feb. 1886.
Marquis of Salisbury, Aug. 1886.
W. E. Gladstone, Aug. 1892 (Gladstone resigned Feb. 1894), succeeded by Earl of Rosebery.

Victoria (continued) :
Marquis of Salisbury, June 1895.
Marquis of Salisbury, Nov. 1900.

Edward VII. :
A. J. Balfour, July 12, 1902.
Sir Henry Campbell-Bannerman, Dec. 5, 1905.
H. H. Asquith, April 16, 1908.

George V. :
H. H. Asquith, Dec. 1910.

[Refer Hunt and Poole, *Political History of England,* 12 vols.]

Admiral (for origin of word refer Gibbon, *Rome,* ch. liii.).
Edward I. in 1294 appointed William Leyburne " captain of all the
postmen," and in 1306 three admirals over the eastern, western,
and southern coasts. First Lord High Admiral appointed 1360.
The last was William, Duke of Clarence, 1827-8; since then the same
powers have been vested in the Lords Commissioners of the Admiralty. [Refer art. in Low and Pulling, *Dicty. of Eng. Hist.*] In the
U.S.A. the admiral was declared the ranking officer in the navy,
Mar. 2, 1867. Rank abolished, Jan. 24, 1873, but revived in 1899,
when Admiral Dewey was appointed.

Admiralty, High Court of. Estab. as a civil court by Edward III.
1360. By Judicature Act of 1873 the Admiralty Court was united
with the Court of Probate and Divorce and the whole known as the
Supreme Court of Judicature.

Admiralty Office. Henry VIII. appointed commissioners in 1512
to inspect his war-ships. This was the beginning of the present
office.

" Admonition to the Parliament." Pamphlet demanding complete abolition of episcopacy. Presented to House of Commons
by extreme Puritans in 1572. A second one also drawn up and
suppressed, June 11, 1573. [Refer Low and Pulling, *Dicty. Eng.
Hist.*]

Adoptianists. A sect fd. A.D. 787 reviving the Oriental heresy of
Nestorianism (*q.v.*). Condemned at the following Church Councils:
Narbonne, June 27, 791; Friuli 791; also at Diet and Council of
Ratisbon, Aug. 792, and Council of Frankfort-on-Maine 794.
[Refer Strong and McClintock, *Dicty. Eccles. and Biblical Lit.*]

Adowa or **Adua** (N. Abyssinia). Abyssinians inflicted crushing
defeat on Italians, Mar. 1, 1896.

Adrianople (Turkey). Old town enlarged by the Emperor Adrian
(*d.* A.D. 138). Constantine defeated Licinius near, July 3, 323; Valens
defeated and slain by Goths 378; seized by Turks under Amurath
1361; their capital until 1453; captured by Russians, Aug. 20,
1829; res. Sept. 14, 1829; occupied by Russians, Jan. 20, 1878.
[Refer art. *Encyclopædia Britannica.*]

Adrianople, Peace of. Ended Russo-Turkish War ; signed
Sept. 14, 1829.

Adventists. A religious sect with several branches. The Evangelical Adventists were the followers of William Miller (1781-1849). They believed in the speedy coming of the end of the world, and fixed the day on Oct. 22, 1844, but continually altered it. [Refer Strong and McClintock, *Dicty. Eccles. Lit.*]

Adventure Bay (S.E. Van Diemen's Land). Discovered by Capt. Furneaux 1773; visited by Capt. Cook, Jan. 26, 1777.

Advertisements. The earliest A. in England are found in *Perfect Occurrences of Every Daie* 1647, in *Mercurius Elencticus* 1648, and in the parliamentary newspaper *Mercurius Politicus* 1652. Duty on A. 1712; reduced, June 28, 1833; abolished, Aug. 4, 1853. *See* Newspapers.

Advertisements. The name given to a book of discipline published in 1565 by Archbishop Parker. The full title of the book was: *Advertisements partly for due order in the public administration of Common Prayer and using of the Holy Sacraments, and partly for the apparel of all persons ecclesiastical, by virtue of the Queen's Majesty's letter commanding the same.* It brought about a tremendous controversy, and marked the commencement of the Puritan persecutions. [Refer art. in Low and Pulling, *Dicty. of Eng. Hist.*]

Advocate, The Lord, also **King's** or **Queen's.** Chief law officer of the Crown in Scotland. First mentioned as Lord in 1587, but the office had existed then for over a hundred years.

Advocate-General, or **King's Advocate.** Chief law officer of the Crown in Admiralty and Ecclesiastical Courts and in Doctors' Commons. The office has not been held since 1872.

Advocates' College or **Doctors' Commons** (*q.v.*).

Advocates' Library (Edinburgh) Estab. 1682 by Sir George Mackenzie of Rosehaugh.

Ædiles. Roman magistrates who superintended trade, money-market, streets, sanitation, games, etc.; first appointed 494 B.C.

Ægina. Greek island in Saronic Gulf. Became independent in 6th century B.C. Once chief seat of Grecian art.

Aeronautical Society of Great Britain. Estab. Jan. 12, 1866.

Aeronautics. *See* Balloons and Aviation.

Aeroplanes. *See* Aviation.

Afghanistan (Asia). Defeated by Alexander the Great, 330 B.C. Annexed by Romans 305 B.C. Independent 255 B.C. Tartar dynasty A.D. 997. Part of Great Mogul Empire 1525. Under Persian subjection 1737. Present kingdom fd. 1747. Revolt of Afghans 1720; subdued 1738. *See* Afghan War.

Afghan War (1st). Lord Auckland declared war in favour of Shah Shuja, Oct. 1, 1838. Towns captured, Kandahar, April 20, 1839; Ghazni, July 23; Kabul, Aug. 7; massacre of British officers at Kabul, Nov. 2, 1841. Massacre of British army in Khyber Pass on their march to Jelalabad 1842. Avenging army captures Kabul, Sept. 16, 1842. [Refer Kaye, *War in Afghanistan*, 2nd ed.]

Afghan War (2nd). British mission with military escort stopped at Khyber Pass, Sept. 22, 1878. British ultimatum sent, Oct. 25, 1878. Gen. Roberts annexes Kuram district to India, Dec. 26, 1878. Afghans left Kandahar, Jan. 6, 1879. Gen. Roberts defeated Mangals near Matoon, and occupied Kandahar, Jan. 7, 1879. British march towards Kabul, Sept. 6, 1879. Dakka occupied, Sept. 29, 1879. Battle of Char-asiab, Oct. 6, 1879; Kabul occupied by Gen. Roberts, Oct. 12, 1879. Universal amnesty proclaimed by Gen. Roberts, Jan. 6, 1880. Kandahar besieged, July 27, 1880, and held by British; relieved by Gen. Roberts, Aug. 31, 1880. Tranquillity at Kabul announced, Nov. 1880. [Refer Holdich, *The Indian Borderland*.]

Africa. Part of A. known as Carthage subdued by Romans 146 B.C. North A. conquered by Vandals A.D. 429-35. Saracens subdue North 637-709 [refer Gibbon, *Rome*]. Portuguese settlements begun 1450. English merchants visited Guinea 1550 (*see* African Company). Bruce's travels (*q.v.*) commenced 1768. Sierra Leone settled by English 1787. Mungo Park's voyages: (1) May 22, 1795; (2) Jan. 30, 1805. Great Niger expedition subsidised by parliament for colonising 1841. Richardson's explorations in Sahara 1845-6 and 1849. *See also* Livingstone, Zululand, Transvaal War, Boers, Cape Colony, etc., etc.

African Company. Patents granted by Elizabeth 1588. Companies formed also in reigns of James I. and Charles I. Royal Africa or Guinea Co. of Merchants fd. under Charles II. Sept. 27, 1672; abolished, May 7, 1821, when the Crown took possession of all settlements, etc.

African, South, War. *See* South African War, Transvaal War.

Agen (France). Came into English possession 1151. Captured by French 1322; regained 1322; again lost and res. to England by Treaty of Bretigny, May 8, 1360. Incorporated with France 1453. Taken by Huguenots 1561; lost by them 1562; regained 1591; surrendered to Henry of Navarre 1592.

Agincourt. *See* under Battles.

Agra (India). Taj Mahal built 1632. Seat of Mogul government until 1647. Captured by Baber 1526, when the Koh-i-noor was among the booty; by Lord Lake, Oct. 17, 1803. Principal buildings destroyed during Indian Mutiny 1857. Native troops disarmed, June 1, 1857. Rebels defeated, Oct. 10, 1857. *See* Indian Mutiny.

Agricultural Hall, Islington, London. Opened June 24, 1862.

Agricultural Holdings Act (Great Britain) grants compensation for unexhausted improvements to agricultural tenant in Scotland on quitting his holding; passed 1883, amended 1900. [Refer art. in *Chambers's Encyclopædia*.]

Ahmedabad or **Ahmadabad** (India). Fd. 1411; subjugated by Akbar 1572; stormed and captured by British 1780; res. again, but finally possessed by British, Nov. 6, 1817. Earthquakes at, 1819, 1868.

Ahmednagar (India). Seized by the Mahrattas 1707; remained in latter's possession till 1797, when it was captured by Scindra. Taken by Wellington, Aug. 12, 1803. Annexed to British possessions, June 13, 1817.

Aigues-Mortes (France). Crusades embark from, Aug. 25, 1248, and July 4, 1270 [refer De Joinville, *Chronicles of the Crusades*]. Interview between Charles V. and Francis I. at 1538.

Air. Oxygen discovered in, by Dr. Priestley 1774. Before this date it was believed to be an element. First vacuum made by Torricelli about 1646. First air pump made by Otto von Guericke about 1650. *See* Oxygen, etc.

Aire (France). Captured from Spaniards by French 1641. The Spaniards retook it shortly afterwards. Ceded to France by Treaty of Utrecht 1713. Captured by British under Lord Hill, Mar. 2, 1814.

Aix (France). Destroyed by Saracens and rebuilt in A.D. 796; captured by Charles V. 1535. Church Councils at, in 1112, 1374, 1409, 1416, 1585, 1612.

Aix-la-Chapelle (Aachen) (Prussia). Fd. by Romans A.D. 125. Charlemagne made it his capital 795, and also died here and was buried 814 [refer Gibbon, *Rome*]. Treaties signed at: May 2, 1668, between France and Spain; 1748, at close of W. of Austrian Succession. Congress to regulate affairs of Europe after restoration of Bourbons, Sept. 29—Nov. 21, 1818.

Akkerman (Bessarabia). Taken by Russians 1770; res. 1774; ceded to Russia by Turkey 1812. Treaty signed here between Russia and Turkey, Sept. 4, 1826.

Alabama (U.S.A.). Orig. settled by French 1702. Ceded to Great Britain by Treaty of Paris 1763. The whole district ceded to U.S.A. 1819. Admitted to Union as a state 1819. [Refer Harper, *Encyclopædia of U.S. History.*]

Alabama, The. An armed vessel belonging to the Confederate States secretly built at Birkenhead, England, in 1862. It did great damage to the Northern States' ships. It was sunk by the U.S. steamer *Kearsage*, June 19, 1864. The U.S. Government claimed the amount of the damage done by the *Alabama* from the British Government, and in 1871 a court of arbitration decided against Great Britain, who had to pay heavy damages. [Refer Harper, *Encyclopædia of U.S. History.*]

Alaska Territory (N.W. district of U.S.A.). Orig. called Russian America. First visited by Behring 1741. Controlled by Russian-American Co. 1799. U.S. purchases territory from Russia 1867. [Refer Harper, *Encyclopædia of U.S. History.*]

Albans, St. (Herts, England). Ancient town near site of Roman town Verulam, called after British martyr, St. Alban, supposed to have been martyred A.D. 286. Monastery erected about 795; dissolved 1539. Battles fought at during Wars of the Roses: (1) May 22, 1455; (2) Feb. 17, 1461.

Albert Medal. Granted for saving life from shipwreck; instituted by Queen Victoria, Mar. 12, 1866.

Albert Memorials. Albert Hall, London, opened by Queen Victoria, Mar. 29, 1871. Memorial in Hyde Park, London, commenced May 13, 1864; opened July 3, 1872. Albert Memorial Chapel, Windsor, opened Dec. 1, 1875. Albert Bridge, Chelsea, opened Aug. 28, 1873.

Alcantara, Order of. Military confraternity fd. 1156. Alexander III. (pope) forms it into a religious order of knighthood 1177. Grandmastership vested in Spanish Crown 1494 by Pope Alexander VI. [Refer art. in *Chambers's Encyclopædia*.]

Alchemy. *See* Chemistry.

Aldersgate (London). One of the four old gates in the city wall. Rebuilt 1616; destroyed 1761.

Aldershot Camp (Hants, Eng.). Formed by government April 1854; enlarged 1856. Queen Victoria reviewed Crimean troops at, July 1856.

Aldine Press. Instit. by Aldo Manuzio (Aldus Manutius) 1494. Italics first used in 1501. Aldus *d.* 1515. The Press continued for 100 years and printed 908 different works. *See* Printing. [Refer art. in *Chambers's Encyclopædia*.]

Alençon (France). In 1026 a castle was erected round which A. was formed. Seized by William the Conqueror 1048; by Henry II. 1135; res. to France 1219. Captured by English 1424, who were expelled 1450. Occupied by German army, Jan. 17, 1871.

Alessandria (Italy). Fd. 1168, orig. called Cæsarea. Ceded to French 1800, who held it until 1814. Headquarters of Piedmontese during Lombardo-Venetian rebellion 1848-9.

Alexander the Great. *b.* 356 B.C. Fought in first battle at Chæroneia 338 B.C.; ascended throne 336 B.C.; first campaign (against Persians) 334 B.C.; battle of Issus 333 B.C.; founded city of Alexandria 331 B.C.; battle of Arbela 331 B.C.; married Roxana and commenced Indian campaign 327 B.C.; *d.* Babylon 323 B.C. [Refer Grote, *Greece;* Smith, *Classical Dicty.* (Everyman's Lib.), etc.]

Alexandria (mouth of Nile). Fd. by Alexander the Great 332 B.C. The capital of Egypt under the Ptolemies. Taken by Julius Cæsar 47 B.C. Res. by Adrian A.D. 122. Captured by Persians 616; by Pagans 640. Recovered and retaken 644. Plundered by Crusaders 1365. Captured by French, July 1798. Recaptured by English under Gen. Abercromby 1801. Taken by British under Fraser 1807. Bombardment of, July 1882. [Refer Smith, *Classical Dicty.* (Everyman's Lib.); Grote, *Greece*, etc.]

Alexandrian Codex. A manuscript of the Scriptures in Greek probably dating from the 5th century. Presented by the Patriarch of Constantinople to Charles I. of England 1628. Now in the British Museum.

Alexandrian Library. Commenced by Ptolemy Soter about 298 B.C. Burnt partly when Alexandria was attacked by Julius Cæsar 47 B.C.; also by Theophilus A.D. 391. Almost totally destroyed by Omar and the Saracens A.D. 641.

Algebra. Said to have been invented by Diophantus of Alexandria about A.D. 330-67 (?) [refer Gibbon, *Rome*, ch. lii.]; came into general use 1590.

Algeciras (Spain). Taken by Moors 711; by Spaniards under Alphonso XI. 1344. Naval engagements: (1) English and Spanish fleets defeated by French, July 6, 1801; (2) result reversed, July 12, 1801. Conference at concerning Moroccan affairs, Jan.-April 1906.

Algeria (Africa). Moors and Jews settle in A. after their exile from Spain 1492. Possessed by France 1830, and now practically belongs to that country. *See also* Algiers. [Refer Playfair, *Handbook for Algeria.*]

Algiers (Algeria). Conquered by Romans 46 B.C.; by Vandals A.D. 439; recovered for empire 534; subdued by Arabs 690; taken by Ferdinand of Spain 1509. Bombarded by British fleet, Aug. 27, 1816; surrendered to French, July 5, 1830. War with French 1830-57. Again besieged, Aug. 15, 1870—June 24, 1871; now under French protection. *See* Algeria.

Algoa Bay (Cape Colony). First British colonists landed at 1820.

Alhambra (Granada). Palace of Moorish kings. Surrounding wall built probably 1019; palace 1248; captured by Christians 1491. [Refer Irving, *Conquest of Granada.*]

Alicante (Spain). Besieged by Moors 1331; by French 1709; bombarded by Carthagenian insurgents, Oct. 1, 1873.

Aliens Act. Passed Jan. 1793; Act to register A. 1795. Aliens Bill passed, Aug. 11, 1905; came into force, Jan. 1, 1906. Bill to amend rejected by Lords, May 17, 1906. [Refer art. in Low and Pulling, *Dicty. of Eng. Hist.*]

Alkmaar (Holland). Captured by British during Duke of York's Dutch campaign, Oct. 2, 1799. [Refer Alison, *History of Europe.*]

Allahabad (India). Ceded to English 1765. Massacre during Mutiny 1857. Made capital of N.W. Provinces, Nov. 1861.

Allegiance, Oath of. Statutes requiring: Elizabeth 1558, William and Mary 1689, Anne 1701 [refer Macaulay, *Hist. of England*], combined with Oaths of Supremacy (*q.v.*) and Abjuration (*q.v.*), Victoria, July 23, 1858. Power to modify the oath to enable Jews to sit in parliament, July 23, 1858; amended, Aug. 6, 1860. Form of affirmation in lieu of oath, April 8, 1859.

Alliance, Treaties of. Leipsic, April 9, 1631; Vienna, May 27, 1657; the Triple, Jan. 28, 1668; Warsaw, Mar. 31, 1683; the Grand, May 12, 1689; The Hague, Jan. 4, 1717; the Quadruple, Aug. 2, 1718; Vienna, Mar. 16, 1731; Versailles, May 1, 1756; Germanic, July 23, 1785; Paris, May 16, 1795; St. Petersburg,

April 8, 1805; Austrian, Mar. 14, 1812; Sweden, Mar. 24, 1812; Töplitz, Sept. 9, 1813; Holy, Sept. 26, 1815; Constantinople (England, France, and Turkey), Mar. 12, 1854; Turin (Sardinia and Western Powers), Jan. 26, 1855; Sweden with Western Powers, Dec. 19, 1855; Prussia and Italy, June 1866; Triple, Mar. 13, 1887; England and Japan, Jan. 30, 1902; renewed, Aug. 12, 1905.

All Saints' Day. Nov. 1 of each year. Festival instit. probably by Boniface IV. 607. Estab. by Pope Gregory IV. 830.

" **All the Talents** " Ministry, 1806. *See* Administrations.

Alma, Battle of. *See* Battles.

Almanacs. Earliest mentioned 1150, when Solomon Jarchus published one. Purbach published an A. from 1457, and his pupil Regiomontanus printed one in 1475-1506. A. of Nostrodamus 1556. Stamp Duty (England) on A. 1710; abolished 1834. [Refer art. in *Chambers's Encyclopædia.*]

Almeida (Portugal). Taken by Spain 1762, but surrendered shortly afterwards. Captured from British by Soult and the French, Aug. 17, 1810; recovered by Wellington, May 11, 1811.

Alnwick (Northumberland, England). Besieged by Scottish troops, Nov. 13, 1093; taken 1136; burnt by John (England) 1215; by Scots 1448. [Refer Lewis, *Topographical Dicty. of England.*]

Alps. Crossed by Hannibal 217 B.C.; by Romans 154 B.C.; by Napoleon, May 1800. Mont Cenis tunnel through A. commenced 1857; completed Dec. 25, 1870. St. Gothard tunnel commenced 1872; completed Feb. 29, 1880. Simplon tunnel completed Feb. 24, 1905. First flight by aeronaut over A. Sept. 1910.

Alsace-Lorraine. Ceded by France to Germany, May 10, 1871. *See also* France and Germany.

Alsatia. A name given to the district round Whitefriars, London. Certain privileges were claimed by the owners of this place, and certain criminals obtained sanctuary by going to Alsatia. Abolished in 1697. [Refer Scott, *Fortunes of Nigel* (and notes).]

Alt-Ranstadt, Peace of, between Charles XII. of Sweden and the King of Poland, signed Sept. 24, 1706 [refer Voltaire, *Charles XII.*]. Another between Louis XIV. and Charles VI. Mar. 17, 1714.

Alumbagh (India). Captured from mutineers, Sept. 23, 1857.

Aluminium. Metal discovered by Sir H. Davy 1808. The first bar of this metal was made by M. St. Clair Deville 1855.

Amadis of Gaul. Spanish or Portuguese romance, probably written 1342; enlarged 1485; first printed (Spanish) 1519; (French) 1540.

Amboise (France). Huguenot conspiracy against Francis II. and Catherine suppressed at, Jan. 1560. Pacification of A. Mar. 19, 1563.

Ambrose, St. *b.* Treves 340; *d.* Milan 397.

Ambrosian Library, Milan. Fd. by Cardinal Borromeo 1602; opened 1609.

America. Named in honour of Amerigo Vespucci, a Florentine, who visited land in 1499. Norse colonies estab. in 10th and 11th centuries in N. America. Columbus first discovered land at, Oct. 1492. Second expedition to, by Columbus, sailed Sept. 1493. Cabot discovered Labrador 1497. Third expedition of Columbus sailed May 1498. Fourth expedition sailed May 1502. Spaniards discovered Brazil in 1500. Jamestown, first successful English settlement in A., fd. 1607. Settlement in New England 1614; New Plymouth by English Nonconformists 1620. American War of Independence 1776-83. *See also* United States, etc., etc.

American Academies. A. of Science, Boston, 1780; Connecticut A. of Arts and Sciences 1799; Philadelphia A. of Natural Sciences 1812; New York A. of Science, 1818. *See* Academies.

American Literature. The first book published in British America was the *Bay Psalm Book*, printed at Cambridge, New England, in 1640 (*see* Printing). The following are the principal American authors with their dates:—

Abbott, Jacob, 1803-1879.
Abbott, John Stevens Cabot, 1805-1877.
Alcott, Louisa M., 1832-1888.
Allston, Washington, 1779-1843.
Bancroft, Geo., 1800-1891.
Beecher, Henry Ward, 1813-1887.
Bird, Robert Montgomery, 1805-1854.
Boker, George Henry, 1823-1890.
Bradstreet, Anne, 1612-1672.
Browne, Charles Farrar (" Artemus Ward "), 1834-1867.
Bryant, William Cullen, 1794-1878.
Catlin, George, 1796-1872.
Child, Francis J., 1825-1896.
Clemens, Samuel Langhorne (" Mark Twain "), 1835-1910.
Cooper, James Fenimore, 1789-1851.
Crawford, F. Marion, 1854-1909.
Cummins, Maria Susanne, 1827-1866.
Curtis, George W., 1824-1892.
Dana, Richard Henry, senr., 1787-1879.
Dana, Richard Henry, junr., 1815-1882.
Edwards, Jonathan, 1703-1758.
Eggleston, Edward, 1837-1902.
Emerson, Ralph Waldo, 1803-1882.
Field, Eugene, 1850-1895.
Fiske, John, 1842-1901.
Franklin, Benjamin, 1706-1790.
Frenau, Philip, 1752-1832.
Fuller, Sarah Margaret, 1810-1850.
Gilder, Richard Watson, 1844-1909.
Greeley, Horace, 1811-1872.
Harland, Henry, 1861-1905.

AMERICAN LITERATURE (*continued*)—
  Harris, Joel Chandler, 1848-1908.
  Harte, Francis Bret, 1839-1902.
  Hawthorne, Nathaniel, 1804-1864.
  Hay, John, 1838-1906.
  Holmes, Oliver Wendell, 1809-1894.
  Irving, Washington, 1783-1859.
  Judd, Sylvester, 1813-1853.
  Lanier, Sidney, 1842-1881.
  Leland, Charles Godfrey, 1824-1903.
  Locke, David Ross (Petroleum V. Nasby), 1833-1888.
  Longfellow, Henry Wadsworth, 1807-1882.
  Lowell, James Russell, 1819-1891.
  Mather, Cotton, 1663-1728.
  Melville, Herman, 1819-1891.
  Motley, John Lothorp, 1814-1877.
  Neal, John, 1793-1876.
  Norton, Charles Eliot, 1827-1909.
  Parker, Theodore, 1810-1860.
  Parkman, Francis, 1823-1893.
  Poe, Edgar Allan, 1809-1849.
  Prescott, William Hickling, 1796-1859.
  Read, Thomas Buchanan, 1822-1872.
  Shaw, Henry Wheeler (" Josh Billings "), 1818-1885.
  Sigourney, Mrs. Lydia (Huntley), 1791-1865.
  Simms, William Gilmore, 1806-1870.
  Stedman, Edmund Clarence, 1833-1908.
  Stockton, Francis R., 1834-1902.
  Stowe, Mrs. Harriet Beecher, 1811-1896.
  Taylor, Bayard, 1825-1878.
  Thoreau, Henry D., 1817-1862.
  Ticknor, George, 1791-1871.
  Tuckerman, Henry Theodore, 1813-1871.
  Twain, Mark. *See* Clemens.
  Underwood, Francis Henry, 1825-1894.
  Wallace, Lewis, 1827-1905.
  Ward, Artemus. *See* Browne.
  Warner, Susan, 1819-1885.
  Webster, Noah, 1758-1843.
  Wetherell, Elizabeth. *See* Warner.
  White, Richard Grant, 1822-1885.
  Whitman, Walt, 1819-1892.
  Whitney, William Dwight, 1827-1894.
  Whittier, John Greenleaf, 1807-1892.
  Willis, Nathaniel Parker, 1806-1867.
  Winthrop, Theodore, 1828-1861.
  Wise, John, 1652-1725.
  Woolman, John, 1720-1772.
[Refer Cousin, *Short Biog. Dicty. of English Literature*, and W. P. Trent, *American Literature* (Short Histories of the Literatures of the World), etc., etc.] *See* Academies.

American Republics. Chili declared its independence 1810; Colombia, Paraguay, Venezuela, 1811; Argentine 1816; Peru, Mexico, Central American States of Guatemala, San Salvador, Honduras, Nicaragua, and Costa Rica, 1821; Bolivia 1824; Uruguay 1825; Ecuador 1831; Brazil 1889.

American Telegraph. The first line was constructed between Washington and Baltimore 1844.

Amiens (France). Cathedral built 1220-88 [refer Ruskin, *Bible of Amiens*]. Taken by Spanish, Mar. 11, 1597; retaken by French, Sept. 25, 1597. Peace treaty signed Mar. 25, 1802, between England, France, Spain, and Holland. War again declared 1803. Germans entered A. Nov. 28, 1870, during Franco-Prussian War.

Amiens, Mise of. The award pronounced by Louis XI. of France, Jan. 23, 1264, in the dispute between Henry III. of England and his barons. [Refer Prothero, *Simon de Montfort.*] *See also* Oxford, the Provisions of.

Amoy (China). Trading with A. permitted 1676. The fort destroyed by English, July 1840. Town captured, Aug. 26, 1841. Port opened by treaty for trade, Aug. 26, 1842. *See* China.

Amsterdam (Holland). Fd. 1204; surrendered to King of Prussia 1787; to French, Jan. 18, 1795. Dutch government res. Dec. 1814. William Frederick, Prince of Nassau and Orange, declared sovereign prince of Holland at A. May 1815.

Anabaptists. Thomas Münzer said to be the founder of; started to preach about 1520. A mob of A. led by John Matthias attacked Münster 1532. Several laws against them from 1525-34. [Refer Bax, *Rise and Fall of the A.*] *See also* Baptists.

Anæsthetics. Sir Humphry Davy first used protoxide of nitrogen (laughing-gas) as an A. 1800. Ether first used by Morton, a dentist, 1846. Chloroform first used by Sir J. Y. Simpson 1847. Dr. Lauder Brunton's experiments at Hyderabad 1889-90. *See also* Chloroform, Ether, etc.

Anarchism. Phase of revolutionary socialism, demanding complete liberty for all men; fathered by Proudhon 1809-65. Notable outbreaks Chicago 1886; Spain, France 1892; Barcelona, Vaillant, 1893; Paris, Greenwich, London, 1894. President Carnot assassinated by anarchists 1894; Empress of Austria 1898. Agitations in Italy 1903; in Russia 1904-5.

Anatomical Society of Great Britain. Fd. 1887.

Ancient Buildings, Society for Protection of. Estab. 1877.

Ancient Lights. Law passed Aug 1, 1832.

Ancona (Italy). Built by Trajan 107. Besieged (1) by Frederick Barbarossa 1167, (2) by Christian, Archbishop of Mainz, 1173 [refer Gibbon, *Rome*]. Annexed to papal states 1532. Captured by French 1797; by Austrians 1799; by French 1801. Res. to papal states 1802. Occupied by French 1832; evacuated 1838. Bombarded by Austrians, June 18, 1849. A. (with other towns) rebelled against Papacy, Sept. 1860, and has been since part of Italian kingdom. [Refer Sismondi, *Hist. of Italian Republics*, ed. Boulter.]

Andrew, St., or **The Thistle, Order of.** Fd. by James V. of Scotland 1540; discontinued 1542; renewed by James II. of Great Britain 1687, when eight knights received the order. Number increased to twelve by Queen Anne 1703; to sixteen by George IV. 1827. Chapel, St. Giles's Cathedral, Edinburgh, gifted 1910. [Refer art. in *Encyc. Brit.*]

Andrews, St. (Scotland). Royal burgh after 1140. Cathedral commenced in 1162; consecrated 1318; destroyed by a mob 1559. University fd. 1411. Robert Bruce held his first parliament at 1309. [Refer Lewis, *Topographical Dicty. of Scotland.*]

Andrussov, Peace of, between Russia and Poland, Jan. 30, 1667.

Angers (France). Taken from Romans A.D. 464; fortified *circa* 859-60. Castle completed by Louis IX. Town burnt by King John of England 1206; taken by Huguenots 1585; attacked by Vendéan army 1793. Church of St. Serge built 1050.

Anglesey (Wales). Conquered by Suetonius Paulinus A.D. 61; by Agricola 78; by Egbert, King of West Saxons, in 9th century, when it was named Anglesey, *i.e.* " the Englishman's Isle." Finally conquered by Edward I. 1284. [Refer Lewis, *Topographical Dicty. of Wales.*]

Angoulême (France). Became English possession by marriage of Henry II. with Eleanor of Aquitaine, 1152; annexed to France 1303; res. to England 1360; reconquered by French 1370. [Refer Low and Pulling, *Dicty. of Eng. Hist.*]

Aniline. Product of dry distillation of indigo; source of many dyes. Discovered in 1826 by Unverdorben. [Refer arts. on Aniline and Dyeing in *Chambers's Encyclopædia.*]

Anjou (France). Captured by Henry II. of England 1156; by Philip II. of France from King John 1205; retaken by Edward III. and afterwards given up 1360. United to French Crown 1481. Battle of A. or Beaugé, English defeated by French, Mar. 22, 1421.

Annapolis (Nova Scotia). Settled by French 1604; taken by English 1614 and 1710. Ceded to England by France 1713.

Annates, or **First Fruits.** First year's profits of a living claimed by the bishop. The custom was suppressed in France by edict of Charles VI. in 1406, 1417, 1418, and by Louis XI. in 1463 and 1464. Prohibited in England by Henry IV. Parliament granted them to the Crown in 1534, but in 1703 Queen Anne applied them to the augmentation of poor livings. *See also* Queen Anne's Bounty.

Anne's (Queen) Bounty Act. *See* Queen Anne's Bounty.

Annual Register. A yearly record of public events first published in London 1759. Original title: *The Annual Register, | or a view of the | History, | Politics | and | Literature | for the Year* 1758. For 30 years Edmund Burke (1729-97) wrote the survey of events.

Annunciation, Order of the. An order of knighthood fd. in 1360 by Amadeus, Duke of Savoy. Is now the highest Italian order of knighthood.

Annunciation, The Feast of the, is held on March 25 of each year, and was instit. in the 7th century. In England also known as Lady Day (*q.v.*).

Antarctic Regions. Land discovered in by Capt. Biscoe, Feb. 1831; by Capt. D'Urville 1838. Principal expeditions to: C. E. Borchgrevink lands at Cape Adair, Feb. 23, 1895; 2nd expedition, equipped by Sir Geo. Newnes, reached Cape Adair, Feb. 17, 1899; De Gerlache expedition, Aug. 16, 1897—Mar. 28, 1899; German expedition, under Capt. H. Ruser, Aug. 11, 1901; British expedition, under Capt. Scott, Dec. 24, 1901—Sept. 10, 1904; Dr. Bruce's Scottish expedition, Jan. 1903—July 1904; Dr. Jean Charcot, French expedition 1904-5 and 1908-10; Lieut. Shackleton's (now Sir Ernest) expedition (*Discovery*) 1907-9; Capt. Scott, British expedition 1910.

Anti-Corn Law League. Formed at Manchester, Sept. 18, 1838; deputies assembled London, Feb. 8, 1842; dissolved July 2, 1846. *See* Corn Laws.

Anti-Federalist. Word came into use about 1788, and referred to those who opposed the adoption of the United States Constitution. [Refer Harper, *Cyclopædia U.S. History*.]

Antigua (Leeward Islands). Discovered by Columbus 1493. English settlement fd. 1632. Formally ceded to England by Treaty of Breda 1666. Became part of federation of Leeward Is. 1871. [Refer Martin, *Hist. of British Colonies*.]

Anti-Popes:—

Felix II., 355.	Benedict IX., 1033.
Ursinus, 367.	Sylvester III., Gregory VI. 1045.
Eulalius, 418.	Clement II., 1046.
Laurentius, 498.	Benedict X., 1058.
Dioscorus, 530.	Honorius II., 1061.
Theodorus and Pascal, 686.	Clement III., 1080.
Theophylactus, 757.	Gregory VIII., 1118.
Constantine, 767.	Cœlestine II., 1121.
Philip, 768.	Anacletus II., 1130.
Zinzinnus, 824.	Victor IV., 1138, 1159.
Anastasius, 855.	Paschal III., 1164.
Sergius, 891.	Calixtus III., 1168.
Boniface VI., 896.	Innocent III., 1178.
Leo VIII., 963.	Clement VII., 1378.
Benedict V. 964.	Benedict XIII. 1394.
Boniface VII., 974, 984.	Gregory XII., 1406.
John XVI., 997.	Clement VIII., 1424.
Gregory, 1012.	Felix V., 1439.

See also Popes.

Antiquaries' Society. Fd. 1572; dissolved by James I. 1617; reconstituted, Nov. 5, 1707. Charter granted, Nov. 2, 1751.

Anti-Slavery Association. *See* Slave Trade.

Antwerp (N.W. Belgium). Republic in 11th century. Citadel commenced 1567; completed 1568; burnt by Spaniards, Nov. 4, 1576. Besieged by Parma, 1584; Marlborough captured, June 6, 1706; Marshal Saxe captured, May 9, 1746; captured by French, Nov. 29, 1792. 1814-30 part of Netherland kingdom. Dec. 4, 1832, bombarded by French. [Refer Motley, *Dutch Republic*.]

Apollo Belvedere. Statue brought from ruins of Antium 1503; placed in Vatican at Rome by Julius II. 1511. The French during their occupation of Rome transported it to France 1797, but it was later restored to its former position. For a description of this statue refer Smith, *Classical Dicty.*, new ed. (Everyman's Lib.).

Apostles' Creed. Not composed by the Apostles; has been attributed to many. Earliest mention is by Rufinus, who *d.* about A.D. 410.

Apothecaries. First A. in England, John Falcourt of Lucca, 1362. Licensed by Bishop of London 1511. Society chartered 1606 (with Grocers); separately 1617. [Refer Barrett, *Hist. of the Apothecaries of London*.]

Appeal, Criminal. *See* Criminal Laws.

Appellants or **Lords Appellant.** The nobles who protested against certain ministers of Richard II. in 1387. They caused the death of two of these ministers. In 1388 the Lords Appellant convened the Merciless Parliament.

Appian Way (Rome). A famous roadway formed by Appius Claudius Cæcus about 313 B.C. Excavations were instit. by the papal court 1850-3, and part of the road was reopened.

Apprentices, Statute of. Passed by English Parliament 1563, by which no person was allowed to work at a trade unless he had previously served seven years' apprenticeship in that trade. Repealed 1814. [Refer art. in Low and Pulling, *Dicty. of Eng. History*.]

Aquitaine (S.E. France). Conquered by Franks A.D. 507; separate state 700; became part of English Crown by marriage of Henry II. and Eleanor of Aquitaine 1152; province finally lost under Henry VI.

Arabia (W. Asia). Arabs supposed to have descended from Ishmael, *b.* 1910 B.C. Portion of, becomes Roman province A.D. 105; abandoned by Hadrian A.D. 117. Mahommed *b.* at Mecca A.D. 567 or 569; captured Mecca 630; *d.* leaving A. practically unified 632. Fall of caliphate of Bagdad 1258. Conquered by Ottomans 1518-39. [Refer Doughty, *Arabia Deserta*.]

Aragon (Spain). Colonised by Carthaginians 300 B.C. First king, Ramiro I. A.D. 1035. United to Castile 1479. [Refer Irving, *Conquest of Granada*.]

Arbitration, Courts of. First estab. in Denmark 1795; estab. in France by Napoleon I. 1806. A. was recognised in England 1698; extended, Aug. 14, 1833; further extended, Aug. 12, 1854. For international A. *see* under Hague, Peace, etc.

Arc de Triomphe de l'Etoile (Paris). Begun 1806, completed 1836. The German army marched under it on entering Paris 1871.

Archæological Association and Institute (London). Estab. Dec. 1843.

Archangel (W. Russia). Town fd. 1584;½ blockaded by English fleet 1854.

Archbishop. First estab. in East A.D. 320; in Rome A.D. 420. *See* Canterbury and York, and under headings of various archbishops' sees.

Arches, Court of. Ecclesiastical Courts fd. 1085. The old court removed from St. Mary le Bow, Cheapside, to Doctors' Commons 1567; to Lambeth Palace 1876.

Architectural Society. London A.S. estab. 1806; A.S. 1831; Institute of British Architects 1834; incorp. Royal Charter, Jan. 11, 1837.

Arcot (India). Defence of by Gen. Clive 1751.

Arctic Regions, principal expeditions to:—

Date	Explorer	Date	Explorer
1498 } 1517 }	Sebastian Cabot.	1825-27	Franklin.
		1826-28	Buchan.
1527	Robert Thorne.	1829-33	John Ross.
1553	Sir Hugh Willoughby.	1833-35	Back.
1576	Frobisher.	1836-37	Back.
1580	Pet and Jackman.	1836-39	Dean and Simpson
1584 } 1595 }	William Barentsz.	1845-46	Franklin.
		1846-47	Rae.
1585 } 1586 } 1587 }	John Davis.	1848-49 {	John Ross. Richardson.
1602	George Waymouth.	1848-52	Moore.
1607-10	Hudson.	1849-50 {	Hooper. Saunders.
1615	Bylot.	1849-51	Pullen.
1616	Bylot and Baffin.		John Ross.
1631	James.	1850-51 {	Penny.
1676	Capt. Wood.		De Haven and Kane.
1728 } 1729 } 1741 }	Behring.	1850-54	M'Clure.
		1850-55	Collinson.
		1851-52	Kennedy.
1773	Phipps and Lutwidge (Horatio Nelson in this expedition.)	1851-54	Rae.
		1852-54 {	Maguire. Belcher. Kellett. Pullen.
1776	Cooke and Clerke.		
1818	John Ross.	1853-55	Kane.
1818	Buchan and Franklin.	1857-59	M'Clintock.
1819-21	Franklin.	1859-60	Hayes.
1819-20	Parry.	1870-72	Hall.
1824	Lyon.	1871-72	Merriman.
1824-25	Parry.		

ARCTIC REGIONS (*continued*)—

Date	Explorer	Date	Explorer
1872-73	Green.	1895	Jackson.
1875-76	Nares and Stephenson.	1897	Andrée.
1879	Gordon-Bennett.	1899	Wellman.
1880	Leigh Smith.	1902	{ Peary.
1887	Col. Gilder.		{ Sverdrup.
1893-96	Dr. Nansen.	1909	Peary (disputed discovery
1893	Peary.		of North Pole April 6th).

Argentine Republic (S. America). The La Plata river visited by Spaniards 1516. Buenos Ayres (*q.v.*) fd. 1535. Formerly part of the viceroyalty of Peru; provisional government formed 1810; joined insurrection 1811, and became independent 1816; independence acknowledged by Spain 1842 [refer Koebel, *Modern Argentina*]. Constitution 1853, with modifications 1862.

Argon. A gaseous vapour of the atmosphere; discovery announced by Lord Rayleigh and Prof. Ramsay 1894.

Arianism. A religious opinion deemed heresy by the Orthodox Church, propounded by Arius about A.D. 318. The Synod of Bithynia (323) upheld him, and St. Athanasius, his opponent, was banished. The Council of Nice (325) condemned Arius and his doctrines. Arius *d.* A.D. 337, and his opinions were afterwards condemned by numerous councils. [Refer Gibbon, *Rome*.]

Arizona (U.S.A.). Explored by Spaniards 1570; passed to U.S. in 1848; territory organised 1863; admitted to the Union as a state 1910. [Refer Harper, *Encyclopædia of U.S. History*.]

Arkansas (U.S.A.). First settled by French 1685. Territory purchased from French by U.S. in 1803; organised as a territory 1819. Admitted to the Union as a state 1836. [Refer Harper, *Encyclopædia of U.S. History*.]

Armada, Spanish. Quitted Lisbon May 30, 1588; arrived off Lizard, July 19; Howard met A. July 21, and kept up running fight until July 25; A. anchored in Calais roads, July 27; met there by Howard and pursued until Aug. 22. [Refer Low and Pulling, *Dicty. of English History*.]

Armed Neutrality. A confederacy of the northern powers against England, commenced by Russia 1780; its objects defeated 1781; renewed, Dec. 16, 1800; dissolved after Nelson's victory at Copenhagen, Dec. 16, 1801. [Refer Alison, *History of Europe*.]

Armenia (Asia Minor). Subject in turns to Assyrian, Median, and Persian empires; Greeks and Romans in turns in power in later centuries. Struggle between Greeks and Mussulmans 7th and following centuries; reigning dynasty overthrown by the Mongols 1373, when Armenia finally lost its independence. Country now divided into Turkish, Russian, and Persian Armenia. Massacres 1895-7. [Refer F. B. Lynch, *Armenia*, 2 vols.]

Army, American. *See* United States.

Army, British. First five infantry regiments estab. 1633-80; dragoons estab. by James II. 1685-8; standing armies declared illegal 1679; first mutiny, Oct. 1697; A. Service Acts passed 1847 and 1855; A. Enlistment Act, June 20, 1867; flogging abolished in time of peace, Mar. 1868; A. Service Corps estab. Nov. 12, 1869; A. Regulation Bill, July 1871; new A. scheme proposed by Mr. Haldane, Sept. 12, 1906. *See* Volunteers, etc.

Army Plot. An attempt in 1641 to use the English army to coerce parliament. Charles I. was a party, and Percy Wilmot, Commissary-General, the principal instigator. [Refer Low and Pulling, *Dicty. Eng. Hist.*]

Arnhem (Holland). Taken by Spaniards 1585. Sir Philip Sidney *d.* at 1586. Fortified by Cochran 1702. Captured by French 1795; retaken by Prussians, Nov. 13, 1813.

Arras, Treaties of. Armagnacs and Burgundians, 1414; France and Burgundy, Sept. 21, 1435; Louis XI. and Maximilian 1482. Catholic union between Hainault, Douai, and Artois signed at A. Jan. 5, 1579.

Arrest, Freedom from. A privilege enjoyed by members of parliament from very early times, confirmed by Edward I. 1290. Recognised by Act of Parliament 1433. *See also* Parliament.

Arthur, King of Britain. Supposed to have lived about the 6th century A.D. Sir Thomas Malory's history of Arthur (*Morte d'Arthur*) was printed by Caxton in 1485. [Refer to map of the Arthurian regions in *A Literary and Historical Atlas of Europe* (Everyman's Lib. 1910).]

Articles of Religion. *See* Thirty-nine Articles.

Arts, Society of (London). Estab. Mar. 29, 1754; incorporated 1847. Scottish ditto estab. 1821; incorporated 1841.

Ashantee Wars (W. Africa). Great Britain and Ashantees, 1863-4 and 1873-4; treaty of peace between Ashantees and Great Britain signed, Feb. 13, 1874; king protests against British Protectorate, April 1895; ultimatum sent, Oct. 1895; British troops arrive, Dec. 1895; relief of Coomassie, July 15, 1900. [Refer Low and Pulling, *Dicty. of Eng. Hist.*]

Ashburton Treaty. Concluded between Great Britain and America 1846, settling frontiers between Canada and U.S.A.

Ashmolean Library. *See* Libraries.

Ash Wednesday. First day of Lent. Its solemn observation was instituted by Pope Gregory the Great (590-604), and confirmed by Pope Celestine III. 1191.

Assassination Plot against William III. of England discovered by Prendergast, Feb. 15, 1696. [Refer Macaulay, *History of England.*]

Assiento, The, or **Contract.** Orig. between France and Spain in 1702 for supplying negro slaves to the Spanish colonies. The right was surrendered to Great Britain by Spain 1713. It was lost twice, and finally res. in 1748 for the remaining period of four years. Refer art. in Low and Pulling, *Dicty. of Eng. Hist.*]

Assize Courts. Appointed and regulated 1215; confirmed 1225 and 1284.

Assize of Clarendon. A measure of judicial reform instit. by Henry II. of England in 1166. It gave legislative recognition to the jury system in criminal trials (*see* Jury). [Refer art. in Low and Pulling, *Dicty. of Eng. Hist.*]

Astronomical Association, British. First meeting, Oct. 24, 1890.

Astronomical Society, Royal. Fd. 1820; incorp. 1831.

Astronomy, principal discoveries, etc., in science of. Copernicus (founder of present system), *b.* 1473, *d.* 1543; Kepler discovered planetary motions 1609, 1618; Galileo discovered Jupiter's moons, sun spots, 1610; aberration of light of fixed stars by Horrebow 1652; Newton's discoveries 1666, etc.; Halley's observations 1676, etc.; Herschel's observations 1781, etc.; Lord Rosse completes famous telescope 1845; Prof. Perrine discovered new satellites of Jupiter 1904-5, 1908. [Refer Grant, *History of Physical Astronomy.*]

Athanasian Creed. Written about A.D. 813-50; *not* the work of St. Athanasius (*circa* 326-73). Great meeting of laity at St. James's Hall in defence of the A. C. Jan. 31, 1873. Lower House of the Convocation of Canterbury pass resolution for retention of A. C. in Prayer Book, without "damnatory clauses," July 1905. New translation of A. C. issued, suggested by Lambeth Conference (1908), Nov. 10, 1909. [Refer Lumby, *History of the Creeds*, 1874, etc.]

Athenæum Club (London). Fd. 1823.

Athens (Greece). Taken by Xerxes 480 B.C.; burnt by Mardonius 479; rebuilt 478 B.C.; taken by Lysander 404 B.C.; subjugated by Romans 144 B.C.; captured by Sulla 87 B.C. [refer Smith, *Classical Dicty.* (Everyman's Lib.)]; by Venetians A.D. 1466, and res. to Turks 1479; retaken 1687; besieged and taken by Greeks 1822; retaken by Turks, May 6, 1827; made capital of modern Greece 1833; occupied by French and English 1854-6. *See also* Greece.

Atlantic Cable. Started to be laid, Aug. 1857; completed, Aug. 1858. First message despatched, Aug. 5, 1858. New Atlantic cable completed, Sept. 10, 1874.

Attainder, Bill of. A legislative act of the two Houses of Parliament, orig. aimed at persons flying from justice. First recorded employment of the bill was in 1321 against the Despenser family. The most famous act was the attainder of Lord Strafford in 1641, which is the first time the parliament exercised its full rights in opposition to the king (Charles I.) in this matter. The last example of a Bill of Attainder being issued was in 1697, when Sir John Fenwick was attainted and executed for his participation in the Assassination Plot (*q.v.*). [Refer art. in Low and Pulling, *Dicty. of Eng. Hist.*]

Atterbury's Plot. A Jacobite plot, concocted by five nobles in 1721, of whom Francis A., Bishop of Rochester (1662-1732), was the ringleader. The plot was frustrated, and A. himself was banished. Refer art. on Atterbury in *Ency. Brit.*]

Attorney-General. Office created 1278. William de Giselham was the first to hold office. Since 1673 the A.-G. has continued to sit in the House of Commons. [Refer art. in *Chambers's Encyclopædia*.]

Augsburg, Confession of. Drawn up by Melanchthon and Luther and presented to Charles V. at Diet of A. June 25, 1530 (*see* Diets). Religious Peace of A. 1555 [refer Kostlin, *Life of Martin Luther*, etc., etc.]. Treaty of, between Holland and other European powers against France, July 9, 1686.

Australasia. Australia and New Britain (N. Pomerania). N. Caledonia discovered by Cook 1774; colonised by French 1853; French penal settlement 1884. N. Guinea discovered by Portuguese 1511-30; British N. Guinea (Papua) colonised 1888. N. Hebrides discovered by Quiros 1606; Anglo-French Convention 1906. N. Ireland, German protectorate, 1884. New Zealand discovered by Tasman 1612; circumnavigated by Cook 1769; British colony 1840. Tasmania (Van Dieman's Land) discovered by Tasman 1642; visited by Furneaux 1773; by Cook 1777. *See* New Zealand, Tasmania, etc.

Australia. First discovered by Dutch 1602. Explored by Capt. Dampier 1686; by Capt. Cook 1770; Bass and Flinders 1798. Colonised by English convicts 1788. Divided into provinces 1829, 1834, 1850, 1859. Australian Colonies Act passed 1850, granted the power to various provinces to elect their own constitution. South Australian Constitution, Oct. 27, 1856. Victoria Parliament opened at Melbourne, Jan. 17, 1867. Commonwealth Bill of Australia Constitution, July 9, 1900. First governor-general appointed, July 14, 1900; installed at Sydney, Jan. 1, 1901. [Refer Rusden, *Hist. of Australia*.]

Austria. Orig. Noricum and part of Pannonia. Made a Roman province *circa* 33 B.C.; Barbarians driven from and present country formed by Charlemagne 791-6; created a duchy 1156; Carinthia annexed to 1337; created arch-duchy, Jan. 6, 1453; Bohemia and Silesia united to 1529; Hungary annexed to 1570; Austro-Prussian War 1866. Emperor Franz Joseph celebrated Jubilee 1910. [Refer Coxe, *Hist. of the House of Austria*.]

Austrian Succession, War of the (1741-8). Caused by the death of the Emperor Charles VI. of Germany without male issue. In 1742 England joined in the war. It was ended by the Peace of Aix-la-Chapelle, Oct. 1748. [Refer Ranke, *Hist. of Prussia*.]

Authors. *See* under American, English, French, Spanish Literatures, etc.

Aviation. Borelli's artificial wings 1670; Sir Geo. Caley's machine 1796; Henson's aerostat 1843; Wenham's aeroplane 1866; Dr. Pettigrew's elastic screws demonstrated 1867; Moy's aerial steamer, 1874; Langley's steam-driven model 1893; Sir H. Maxim's experiments 1889-90, 1893-94; Lilienthal killed on gliding machine 1896; W. and O. Wright's experiments 1900; S. Dumont's aeroplane 1906; Farman biplane 1907; Blériot flew across Channel, July 25, 1909; Paulhan's altitude record, Jan. 1910; Beaumont's long distance record completed, July 26, 1911.

Avignon. Popes resided at 1309-77. *See* Papacy.

Avoirdupois Weight. First statute directing use of 1532. *See* Weights and Measures.

Aylesbury Election Case, 1704. Brought about a dispute between Lords and Commons, caused through an action brought by Matthew Ashby against the returning officer of Aylesbury for disallowing his (Ashby's) vote. The House of Lords reversed the Queen's Bench verdict, which was originally against Ashby. [Refer art. in Low and Pulling, *Dicty. of Eng. Hist.*]

Azov (Russia). Fd. 12th century; taken by Tamerlane 1395; by Russians 1690, and res. to Turks 1711; fortifications demolished 1739; ceded to Russia 1769.

B

Babington's Conspiracy. Called after Anthony B. A plot to assassinate Queen Elizabeth. Leaders executed Sept. 1586. [Refer Lingard, *Hist. of England.*]

Babylon. Was supposed to have been built *circa* 2230 B.C.; became seat of Chaldæan government 1700 B.C.; captured by Cyrus, King of Persia, 538 B.C.; by Alexander 331 B.C. [Refer Herodotus, and Smith, *Classical Dicty.* (Everyman's Lib.).]

Badajoz (Spain). Surrendered to French under Soult, Mar. 11, 1811; taken by Wellington, April 6, 1812. [Refer Napier, *Peninsular War.*]

Baffin's Bay (Canada). Discovered by William Baffin 1616.

Bagdad. Seat of Saracen Empire 762; taken by Tartars 1258. Part of Turkish Empire since 1638.

Bahamas (West Indies). Discovered by Columbus 1492. New Providence settled by English 1629; English expelled by Spaniards 1641; English take possession again 1666; expelled by French and Spaniards 1703; re-colonised by English 1718; reduced by Spain 1781; res. 1783 by treaty. [Refer Martin, *Hist. of Brit. Colonies.*]

Bail, Laws regarding. Defined and regulated 1275, 1299, 1483-4, 1487, 1554, 1678, 1692, 1827, 1838, 1851, 1852, 1854, 1898.

Bailey, Old (Courts of Justice, London). Built 1773; destroyed 1780; rebuilt and enlarged 1809; entirely rebuilt 1909.

Balaklava. *See* Battles.

Balance of Power. Principle first laid down after Italian invasion of Charles VIII. of France 1494; recognised by Treaty of Munster 1648. [Refer F. E. Smith, *International Law.*]

Balearic Islands (Mediterranean). Conquered by Romans 123 B.C.; by Vandals A.D. 426; by Moors about 1005, and in their possession until 1286, when they were annexed by Spain. *See* Majorca and Minorca

Balkans. Passage of accomplished by Russians, July 26, 1829, and July 13, 1877. Became frontier line of Turkish dominions by Treaty of Berlin, July 13, 1878.

Balloons. Principal experiments, etc., with: Joseph Montgolfier makes first fire balloon 1782. Brothers Montgolfier successfully make an ascent in a fire balloon 1783. First ascent in balloon filled with hydrogen at Paris by the brothers Charles, Aug. 1783. First ascent in England by Vincent Lunardi, Sept. 1784. Channel crossed by Blanchard and Jefferies, Jan. 7, 1785. Nassau balloon left London and descended at Nassau 1836. Nadar's famous balloon ascended with 14 persons, Oct. 4, 1863 (the first balloon with steering apparatus). Glaisher and Coxwell rose to a height of seven miles in a balloon, Sept. 5, 1862. Godard's Montgolfier balloon ascended, July 28 and Aug. 3, 1864. Coxwell's ascent from Belfast, July 3, 1865. Col. Burnaby crossed English Channel from Dover to Dieppe, Mar. 23, 1882. Simmons' journey from Maldon (England) to Arras, France, June 10, 1882. Mr. Percival Spencer's voyages across English Channel, Dec. 20, 1898; July 29 and Sept. 15, 1899. Giffard's experiments with dirigible 1852. Zeppelin 1900, 1908. M. Santos Dumont's experiments with steerable balloon, July-Oct. 1901; Feb. 1902. *See also* Aviation.

Ballot-Box. First used in England at election of London aldermen 1526. Bill authorising parliamentary voting by ballot thrown out by Lords 1710; passed July 18, 1872. First parliamentary election in England by ballot at Pontefract, Aug. 15, 1872.

Balmoral Castle. Purchased by Prince Albert in 1852; present building commenced 1853.

Baltic Sea. Whole surface frozen over 1658, 1809. Holstein Canal, connecting river Eider with Baltic, opened 1785; B. and North Sea Canal for large vessels 1887-95.

Baltic and Black Sea Canal. Proposed Nov. 1897; begun 1898; unfinished; estimated cost of whole, £20,000,000.

Baltic Expeditions. (1) Under Admirals Parker and Nelson 1801. (2) Under Admiral Gambier and Lord Cathcart 1854. (3) Under Admiral Napier, Mar. 11, 1854. (4) Under Rear-Admiral Dundas, April 4, 1855.

Baltimore (U.S.A.). Fd. 1729. Named after Lord Baltimore. Incorp. 1796. *See also* Maryland.

Bampton Lectures. Begun 1780. Called after founder, the Rev. John Bampton, who left £120 per annum for the purpose.

Ban or **Banning.** An edict against certain offenders during Henry III.'s reign proclaimed in Westminster Hall, May 3, 1253. The Dean of St. Paul's placed a ban on all those who searched for gold in the Church of St. Martin's-in-the-Fields 1299.

Banbury (England). Castle erected at by Alexander, Bishop of Lincoln, 1135. Battle of (Wars of Roses) 1469. Surrendered to Charles I. Oct. 1642; besieged 1643, 1644, and in 1646, when it surrendered to parliamentary forces. [Refer Lewis, *Topographical Dicty. of England*.]

Banda Oriental. *See* Uruguay.

Bangor. Cathedral fd., St. Deiniol; rebuilt 1496-1532. N. Wales University College opened at, Oct. 18, 1884.

Bank. Banks highly organised in Greece and Rome. In A.D. 808 Lombard Jews estab. a B. in Italy; B. of Venice estab. 1171; B. of Amsterdam 1609; B. of Barcelona (earliest existing B.) estab. about 1401; first B. estab. in England by Francis Child about 1663; B. of Stockholm 1668, the first B. to issue notes. [Refer W. G. Summer, *History of Banking*, 1896.]

Bank of England. Fd. by Wm. Paterson and Michael Godfrey. Incorp. by charter, July 27, 1694. Special privileges: monopoly conferred 1708; restricted 1826, 1833. Suspended payment 1797; payments resumed 1819. Under Bank Charter is remodelled, July 19, 1844; Bank Charter suspended: Oct. 25, 1847; Nov. 12, 1857; May 11, 1866. Important changes in management, June 16, 1892. [Refer A. Andréadis, *History of Bank of England*, 1909.]

Bank of Ireland. Estab. June 1, 1783. Irish Banking Act passed, July 21, 1845.

Bank of Scotland. Set up at Edinburgh by Act of Scottish Parliament 1695; chartered, July 8, 1727. [Refer Ken, *History of Banking in Scotland.*]

Bank Holidays Act. Intro. by Sir John Lubbock; passed May 25, 1871.

Bankruptcy (Great Britain). Court of, estab. by Act of Parliament 1831. Important changes in laws regarding B. made 1861, 1870, 1885, 1887, 1890.

Bankruptcy Acts (U.S.A.). Bill passed by Congress, Aug. 19, 1841; repealed Mar. 3, 1843. Uniform System of B. Bill intro. by E. B. Taylor, Dec. 20, 1889; passed July 24, 1890.

Banks, American. Congress estab. first B. at Philadelphia, Jan. 7, 1782, known as B. of N. America; second B. estab. at Boston 1784; B. of U.S. estab. Philadelphia, Dec. 20, 1790; B. of New York estab. 1790; first National B. of Portland estab. July 1865.

Bannockburn. *See* Battles.

Baptists (for earlier history of, *see* Anabaptists). First church fd. in London 1607-8; Confession of Faith published 1689; large settlement of B. on Rhode Island 1635; B. Missionary Soc. fd. 1792. First B. World Congress, London, July 11-18, 1905. The first B. church in America is said to have been fd. at Tiverton, Rhode Island, in 1607. [Refer Schaff-Herzog, *Encyclo. of Religious Knowledge*, vol. i.]

Barbadoes (West Indies). Discovered by Portuguese about 1600; possessed by English 1605; Jamestown fd. at, by Sir William Courteen 1625; taken by Parliamentarians during Civil War 1652; bishopric estab. 1824. [Refer Martin, *Hist. of British Colonies.*]

Barcelona (N.E. Spain). Supposed to have been built by Hamilcar Barca, 3rd century B.C. Conquered by Charlemagne 9th century A.D.; incorp. with Aragon 1164. Treaty of B. between France and Spain 1493. Besieged by French 1694. Taken by English 1706; by French and English 1714; by Napoleon 1808. Res. to Spain by Treaty of Paris 1814. Execution of Ferrer for conspiracy at, Oct. 13, 1909. *See also* Spain.

Barebones Parliament. Met July 4, 1653; dissolved Dec. 13, 1653. Named after a certain Praise-God Barebones, who took a prominent part in the debates. [Refer Ranke, *Hist. of England.*]

Barfleur (France). William the Conqueror set out from B. to invade England 1066. William of Normandy, son of Henry I. of England, wrecked near B. Nov. 28, 1120; destroyed by English 1346. French navy destroyed near B. by Admiral Russell, May 19, 1692.

Barometer. First made by Torricelli, a Florentine, about 1643. Pascal's experiments 1646. Aneroid B. on principle of vacuum vase discovered by Conté 1798. It was put to practical use by Vidi, who patented the Aneroid B. in England 1844. Vidi *d.* 1866. [Refer art. in *Chambers's Encyclopædia*.]

Baronet. Order of knighthood instit. by James I. of England, May 22, 1611, to replenish his exchequer. The first B. was Sir Nicholas Bacon of Redgrave.

Barons' War. Caused by disputes between Henry III. of England and the barons; broke out May 14, 1264, at Lewes: barons victorious; b. of Evesham Aug. 4, 1265: De Montfort killed and barons defeated. [Refer Blaauw, *History of Barons' War*, 1871 ed.]

Barrier Treaty, ceding Low Countries to Emperor Charles IV. of Austria, signed Nov. 15, 1715; annulled by Treaty of Fontainebleau (*q.v.*). [Refer McCarthy, *Reign of Queen Anne.*]

Barrow-in-Furness (Lancs. England). Docks opened at, Sept. 19, 1867.

Bartholomew, St. Festival of, Aug. 24. Old fair held on festival 1133-1855. Hospital of St. B. (London) fd. 1123; incorp. 1546; rebuilt 1729. Medical College fd. 1843. Massacre of St. B. Aug. 24, 1572.

Basel, or **Basle** (Switzerland). University fd. at 1460; 18th General Church Council at, Dec. 1431—May 1443.

Bassein, Treaty of, concluded between Great Britain and Bajee Ras, the Peishwa, Dec. 31, 1802. [Refer Mill, *Hist. of India.*]

Bastille (Paris). Built 1369-83; stormed and destroyed, July 14-15, 1789. [Refer to Carlyle, *French Revolution*, etc.]

Basutoland (S. Africa). Annexed by Great Britain 1868. Annexed to Cape Colony 1871.

Bath (England). Saxon King Edgar crowned at A.D. 973. Abbey commenced 1405; completed 1609. Pump-room opened 1704. Remains of Roman baths first discovered 1877.

Bath, Order of the. Formally constituted, Oct. 11, 1399, until Charles II.'s reign, when it fell into disuse; revived May 18, 1725. Remodelled by Prince Regent 1815. [Refer Low and Pulling, *Dicty. of Eng. Hist.*]

Bath Administration. Earl of Bath First Lord, Feb. 10-12, 1746.

Battle, Trial by. Last waged in Court of Common Pleas, Westminster, 1571; in Court of Chivalry 1631; in Court of Durham 1638. Trial by battle was not expunged from our code until 1819. In the preceding year 'a murderer escaped the penalty of his crime by challenging the brother of his victim to single combat, and was discharged because his challenge was declined. [Refer Gibbon, *Rome*.]

Battle Abbey (Sussex, England). Built by William the Conqueror 1067, on site of b. of Hastings.

Battles (arranged alphabetically):—

ON LAND.

Abancay, July 12, 1537.
Aboukir, July 25, 1798.
Achalzie, Aug. 24, 1828.
Acs, July 2, 1849.
Adowa, March 1, 1896.
Adrianople, (1) July 3, 323.
　(2) Aug. 9, 378.
　(3) Aug. 20, 1829.
Aghrim, July 12, 1691.
Agincourt, Oct. 25, 1415.
Agnadel, May 14, 1509.
Aiznadin, July 13, 633.
Albans, St., (1) May 23, 1455.
　(2) Feb. 17, 1461.
Albany, Aug. 16, 1777.
Albuera, May 16, 1811.
Albufera, Jan. 4, 1812.
Alexandria, (1) Mar. 21, 1801.
　(2) Sept. 23, 1807.
Alford, July 2, 1645.
Aliwal, Jan. 28, 1846.
Allen Moor, 1645.
Alma, Sept. 20, 1854.
Almanza, April 25, 1707.
Almenara, July 28, 1710.
Altivia, June 25, 1838.
Angora, July 28, 1402.
Anjou, Mar. 22, 1421.
Anneau, Nov. 24, 1587.
Antietam, Sept. 16, 1862.
Antioch, June 28, 1098.
Antoine, July 2, 1652.
*Arbela, Oct. 1, 331 B.C.
Arcis-sur-Aube, Mar. 20, 1814.
Arcole, Nov. 14-17, 1796.
Argentaria, 373.
Argaum, Nov. 29, 1803.
Arklow, June 10, 1798.
Arques, Sept. 13-28, 1589.
Ashdown, 1016
Aspern, May 22-23, 1809.
Assaye, Sept. 23, 1803.

Asunden (Lake), Jan. 1520.
Atbara, The, April 8, 1898.
Atherton Moor, June 30, 1643.
Auerstädt, Oct. 14, 1806.
Augsburg, Aug. 29, 1795.
Austerlitz, Dec. 2, 1805.
Ayachucho, Dec. 9, 1824.
Aylesford, 455.
Balaklava, Oct. 26, 1854.
Bannockburn, June 25, 1314.
Bapaume, Jan. 3, 1871.
Barbout, Sept. 28, 1829.
Barnet, April 14, 1471.
Barrosa, Mar. 6, 1811.
Battlefield, July 23, 1403.
Bautzen, May 20-21, 1813.
Baylen, July 20, 1808.
Beaugé. *See* Anjou.
Belfort, Jan. 15-17, 1871.
Belgrade, Sept. 4, 1456.
Belmont, Nov. 23, 1899.
Bergen, (1) April 13, 1759.
　(2) Sept. 19, 1799.
　(3) Oct. 2, 1799.
Beresina, Nov. 26-28, 1812.
Bethel, Great, May 10, 1861.
Bitonto, May 27, 1734.
*Blenheim, Aug. 13, 1704.
Bloreheath, Sept. 23, 1459.
Blumenau, July 22, 1866.
Borodino, Sept. 7, 1812.
Borrisow, Nov. 27, 1812.
Bosworth Field, Aug. 22, 1485.
Bothwell Bridge, July 22, 1679.
Boxtel, Sept. 17, 1794.
Boyne, July 1, 1690.
Brailow, June 19, 1773.
Brandywine, Sept. 11, 1777.
Brechin, May 18, 1452.
Brentford, Nov. 12, 1642.
Breslau, Nov. 22, 1757.

C

BATTLES (*continued*)—

Briars Creek, (1) Mar. 1779.
  (2) May 3, 1779.
Brienne, Feb. 1-2, 1814.
Bruanburg, 938.
Bull's Run, (1) July 21, 1861.
  (2) Aug. 28-29, 1862.
Bunker's Hill, June 17, 1775.
Burlington Heights, June 6, 1813.
Busaco, Sept. 27, 1810.
Camden (U.S.A.), (1) Aug. 16, 1780.
  (2) April 25, 1781.
Cannæ, Aug. 2, 216 B.C.
Cassano, (1) Aug. 16, 1705.
  (2) April 27-29, 1799.
Castelbar, Aug. 7, 1798.
Castella, April 13, 1813.
Castelnuovo, Nov. 21, 1796.
Castiglione, Aug. 3, 1796.
Castillon, July 7, 1453.
Cateau, Mar. 28, 1798.
Cawnpore, (1) July 16, 1857.
  (2) Nov. 27, 1857.
  (3) Dec. 3, 1857.
Cedar Mountain, Aug. 9, 1862.
Cerignola, April 28, 1503.
Cerisoles, April 14, 1544.
Chæronea, Aug. 7, 338 B.C.
Chalgrove, June 18, 1643.
*Chalons, A.D. 451.
Chancellorsville, (1) May 1-3, 1863.
  (2) May 5-6, 1864.
Châteaudun, Oct. 18, 1870.
Chattanooga, Nov. 25, 1863.
Chicahominy, June 25—July 1, 1862.
Chicamauga, Sept. 19-20, 1863.
Chillianwallah, Jan. 13, 1849.
Chippewa, (1) July 5, 1814.
  (2) July 25, 1814.
Citate, Jan. 6, 1854.
Clifton Moor, Dec. 18, 1745.
Clontarf, April 23, 1014.
Coal Harbour, June 1, 1864.
Colenso, Dec. 15, 1899.
Corinth, Oct. 4, 1862.
Corunna, Jan. 16, 1809.
Coutras, Oct. 1587.

Cozitat, Jan. 6, 1854.
Craon, Mar. 7, 1814.
Crecy or Cressy, Aug. 26, 1346.
Cropedy Bridge, June 29, 1644.
Culloden, April 16, 1746.
Cunnersdorf, Aug. 12, 1759.
Custozza, June 24, 1866.
Czaslau, May 17, 1742.
Danewirke, April 23, 1848.
Delhi, May 30, 31, June 8, July 4, 9, 18, 23, 1857.
Denis, St., Nov. 10, 1567.
Dennewitz, Sept. 6, 1813.
Dettingen, June 27, 1743.
Devizes, June 13, 1643.
Donington, Mar. 21, 1645.
Douro, May 12, 1809.
Dresden, Aug. 26, 1813.
Druex, Dec. 19, 1562.
Drumclog, June 1, 1659.
Dunbar, (1) April 27, 1296.
  (2) Sept. 3, 1650.
Dunes, June 17, 1658.
Dungan Hill, July 10, 1647.
Dunkirk, June 14, 1658.
Eckmuhl, April 22, 1809.
Edgehill, Oct. 23, 1642.
Elandslaagte, Oct. 21, 1899.
Elchingen, Oct. 14, 1805.
Enghein, Aug. 3, 1692.
Espirres, May 22, 1794.
Essling, May 21-22, 1809.
Euslin, Nov. 25, 1899.
Eutaw, Sept. 8, 1781.
Evesham, Aug. 4, 1265.
Eylau, Feb. 8, 1807.
Fair Oaks, May 31, 1862.
Falkirk, (1) July 22, 1298.
  (2) Jan. 17, 1746.
Famars, May 23, 1793.
Ferozeshah, Dec. 21, 1845.
Fleurus, (1) June 30, 1690.
  (2) June 26, 1794.
Flodden Field, Sept. 9, 1513.
Fontenoy, May 11, 1745.
Fornovo, July 6, 1495.
Fortenay, June 25, 841.
Fredericksburg, (1) Dec. 13, 1862.
  (2) May 3-4, 1863.

BATTLES (*continued*)—

Friedland, June 14, 1807.
Fuentes d'Oñoro, May 3-5, 1811
Gaugamela, Oct. 1, 331 B.C.
Germantown, Oct. 4, 1777.
Gettysburg, July 1-3, 1863.
Gitschin, June 29, 1866.
Glencoe (S. Africa), Oct. 20 1899.
Goojerat, Feb. 21, 1849.
Gorey, Jan. 4, 1798.
Grachow, Feb. 20, 1831.
Grandella, Feb. 27, 1266.
Granson, Mar. 2, 1476.
Guinegate, Aug. 16, 1513.
Halidon Hill, July 13, 1333.
Hanau, Oct. 30, 1813.
Harlaw, July 24, 1411.
Hasbain, Sept. 23, 1408.
Hastings, Oct. 14, 1066.
Herrara, Aug. 24, 1837.
Hexham, May 15, 1464.
Hohenlinden, Dec. 3, 1800.
Homildon, Sept. 14, 1462.
Idstedt, July 25, 1850.
Ingogo, Feb. 8, 1881.
Ingour, Nov. 6, 1855.
Inkermann, Nov. 5, 1854.
Ipsus, 301 B.C.
Ivry, Mar. 14, 1590.
Janvilliers, Feb. 14, 1814.
Jarnac, Mar. 13, 1569.
Jena, Oct. 14, 1806.
Jenappes, Nov. 6, 1792.
Kalitsch, Feb. 13, 1813.
Katzbach, Aug. 26, 1813.
Khart, July 19, 1829.
Killiecrankie, July 17, 1689.
Kilsyth, Aug. 15, 1645.
Kissingen, July 10, 1866.
Koniah, Dec. 21, 1821.
Koniggratz, July 3, 1866.
Krasnoi, Nov. 17, 1812.
Kunnersdorf, Aug. 12, 1759.
Kurekdere, Aug. 6, 1854.
La Bicocca, April 29, 1522.
Laffeldt, July 2, 1747.
La Hague, May 19, 1692.
Landen, July 29, 1693.
Langensalza, June 27, 1866.
Langs Nek, Jan. 28, 1881.

Langside (Glasgow), May 13, 1568.
Lansdown, July 5, 1643.
Laon, Mar. 9, 1814.
Leipsic, Oct. 16-18, 1813
Lens, Aug. 20, 1648.
Leuctra, 371 B.C.
Leuthen, Dec. 5, 1757.
Lewes, May 13, 1264.
Lexington, (1) April 19, 1775.
   (2) Sept. 20, 1861.
Libenau, June 25, 1866.
Ligny, June 16, 1815.
Lincelles, Aug. 18, 1793.
Lincoln, (1) Feb. 2, 1141.
   (2) May 20, 1217.
Linlithgow Bridge, 1525.
Lioppo, May 16, 1860.
Lipstadt, Nov. 6, 1632.
Lodi, May 10, 1796.
Lonato, Aug. 3, 1796.
Lutterberg, Oct. 7, 1758.
Lutzen, (1) Nov. 6, 1632.
   (2) May 2, 1813.
Magenta, June 4, 1859.
Magersfontein, Dec. 10-11, 1899.
Magnano, April 5, 1799.
Maharagpore, Dec. 29, 1843.
Maida, July 6, 1806.
Majuba, Feb. 27, 1881.
Malavelly, Mar. 27, 1799.
Malplaquet, Sept. 11, 1709.
Mantinea, (1) June 418 B.C.
   (2) 362.
   (3) 207.
*Marathon, Sept. 28, 490 B.C.
Marengo, June 14, 1800.
Margus, (1) 285.
   (2) 505.
Marignano, (1) Sept. 13-14, 1515.
   (2) Feb. 23, 1525.
   (3) June 8, 1859.
Marston Moor, July 2, 1644.
Matarmoras, May 8, 1846.
Meeanee, Feb. 17, 1843.
Melazzo, June 20, 1860.
*Metaurus, 207 B.C.
Metz, Aug. 31, 1870.
Millesimo, April 13, 1796.
Milliduse, July 2, 1829.

BATTLES (*continued*)—

Mincio, (1) May 29, 1796.
  (2) Feb. 8, 1814.
Minden, Aug. 1, 1759
Mockern, (1) April 13, 1813.
  (2) Oct. 16, 1813.
Modder River, Nov. 28, 1899.
Mœskirch, May 3, 1800.
Mohatz, (1) Aug. 10, 1526.
  (2) 1687.
Mohilow, July 23, 1812.
Molwitz, April 10, 1741.
Montebello, (1) June 9, 1800.
  (2) May 21, 1859.
Montenotte, April 12, 1796.
Moodkee, Dec. 18, 1845.
Mooltan, Nov. 7, 1848.
Morat, April 2, 1476.
Morgarten, Nov. 15, 1315.
Mortimer's Cross, Feb. 2, 1461.
Moskwa, Sept. 7, 1812.
Mount Tabor, April 16, 1799.
Munchengrätz, June 28, 1866.
Muret, Sept. 12, 1213.
Murfreesborough, (1) Dec. 31, 1862.
  (2) Jan. 2, 1863.
Naas, May 24, 1798.
Nachod, June 26, 1866.
Najpara, April 3, 1367.
Nantwich, Jan. 25, 1644.
Narva, Nov. 30, 1700.
Naseby, June 14, 1645.
Neerwinden, Mar. 18, 1793.
Neubrunn, June 25, 1866.
Nevills Cross, Oct. 12, 1746.
Newburn, Aug. 27, 1640.
Newbury, (1) Sept. 20, 1643.
  (2) Oct. 27, 1644.
Newton, Aug. 1, 1689.
Nicholson's Nek, Oct. 30, 1899.
Nisbet, May 7, 1402.
Nive, Dec. 9-13, 1813.
Niville, Nov. 10, 1813.
Nordlingen, (1) Aug. 27, 1634.
  (2) Aug. 7, 1645.
Northallerton, Aug. 22, 1138.
Northampton, July 10, 1460.
Novara, Mar. 23, 1849.
Novi, (1) Aug. 16, 1799.
  (2) Jan. 8, 1800.

Obidos, Aug. 17, 1808.
Oltenitza, Nov. 4, 1853.
Omdurman, Sept. 5, 1898.
*Orleans, (1) April 29, 1429.
  (2) Oct. 11, 1870.
Orthez, Feb. 27, 1814.
Ostrolenka, May 26, 1831.
Otterbourne, Aug. 15, 1388.
Oudenarde, July 11, 1708.
Oulart, May 27, 1798.
Ourique, July 25, 1139.
Paardeberg, Feb. 18, 1900.
Palestro, May 31, 1859.
Parma, June 29, 1734.
Patiay, June 18, 1429.
Pavia, Sept. 24, 1525.
Pfaffendorf, Aug. 15, 1760.
Pharsalus, June 6, 48 B.C.
Philliphaugh, Sept. 13, 1645.
Piacenza, June 16, 1746.
Pinkie, Sept. 10, 1547.
Pirmaseus, Sept. 14, 1793.
Plassey, June 25, 1757.
Plevna, July, Sept., and Dec. 1877.
Podoll, June 26-27, 1866.
Poitiers, Sept. 19, 1356.
Polotzk, July 30-31, 1812.
Port Arthur, Nov. 21, 1894.
Porto Novo, July 1, 1781.
Prague, (1) May 5, 1757.
  (2) Oct. 10, 1794.
  (3) Feb. 24-25, 1831.
  (4) Mar. 31, 1831.
Preston, (1) Aug. 17, 1648.
  (2) Nov. 12, 13, 1715.
Prestonpans, Sept. 21, 1745.
*Pultowa, July 8, 1709.
Pultusk, Dec. 26, 1806.
Pyramids, The, July 21, 1798.
Pyrenees, The, July 28, 1813.
Quatre Bras, June 16, 1815.
Ramillies, May 23, 1706.
Rathmines, Aug. 2, 1649.
Raucoux, Oct. 11, 1746.
Ravenna, April 11, 1512.
Redhina, Mar. 12, 1812.
Rheinfeld, Mar. 3, 1638.
Rietfontein, Oct. 24, 1899.
Rio Secco, July 13, 1808.

BATTLES (*continued*)—

Rivoli, Jan. 14, 1797.
Rocroi, May 19, 1643.
Rolica, Aug. 9, 1808.
Rorke's Drift, Jan. 22, 1879.
Rosbach, (1) Nov. 17, 1352.
   (2) Nov. 5, 1757.
Rosebecque, Nov. 28, 1382.
Ross, June 4, 1798.
Roveredo, Sept. 4, 1796.
Ruremonde, Oct. 5, 1794.
Ruti, Mar. 7, 1821.
Saarbrück, Aug. 20, 1870.
Sadowa, July 3, 1866.
Saguntum, Oct. 25, 1811.
St. Dizier, Jan. 27, 1814.
St. Quentin, (1) Aug. 10, 1557.
   (2) Jan. 19, 1871.
Saintes, July 22, 1242.
Salamanca, July 22, 1812.
Sampach, July 9, 1386.
Santa Lucia, May 6, 1848.
Saragossa, Aug. 9, 1710.
*Saratoga, Oct. 17, 1777.
Secessionville, June 16, 1862.
Sedan, Aug. 31, Sept. 1, 1870.
Sedgemoor, July 6, 1685.
Seminara, April 21, 1503.
Selby, April 11, 1644.
Semincas, 938.
Seneffe, Aug. 11, 1674.
Seringapatam, (1) May 15, 1791.
   (2) Feb. 6, 1792.
Sesia, The, Jan. 1524.
Sheriffmuir, Nov. 13, 1715.
Shrewsbury, July 21, 1403.
Siedlitz, April 10, 1831.
Skalitz, June 28, 1866.
Smolensko, Aug. 17, 1812.
Smoliantzy, Nov. 14, 1812.
Sobraon, Feb. 10, 1846.
Solferino, June 24, 1859.
Solway Moss, Nov. 25, 1542.
Soor, June 28, 1866.
Soravren, July 28, 1813.
Spion Kop, Jan. 25, 1900.
Spurs, The. *See* Guinegate.
Standard, The, Aug. 22, 1138.
Steinkirk, July 24, 1692.
Stoke, June 16, 1487.

Strasburg, Aug. 16, 1870.
Suakin, Dec. 20, 1888.
*Syracuse, 413 B.C.
Szegedin, Aug. 4, 1849.
Talavera, July 27-28, 1809.
Tara, May 26, 1798.
Tarbes, Mar. 21, 1814.
Tchernaya, Aug. 16, 1855.
Teb, Feb. 29, 1884.
Tel-el-Kebir, Sept. 13, 1882.
Tenchebrai, Sept. 27, 1106.
Teutoburg (victory of Arminius), A.D. 9.
Tewkesbury, May 4, 1471.
Thabor, April 1799.
Toplitz, Aug. 30, 1813.
Torgau, Nov. 11, 1760.
Toulouse, April 10, 1814.
Tournay, May 8, 1793.
*Tours, Oct. 10, 732.
Towton, Mar. 29, 1461.
Trebbia, June 20, 1799.
Truellas, Sept. 22, 1793.
Tudela, Nov. 23, 1808.
Uctes, Jan. 13, 1809.
Valeggio, July 25, 1848.
*Valmy, Sept. 20, 1792.
Valteline, Aug. 19, 1812.
Valtezza, May 27, 1821.
Vauchamps, Feb. 13, 1814.
Villa Franca, April 10, 1812.
Vimiera, Aug. 21, 1808.
Vinegar Hill, June 21, 1798.
Vittoria, June 21, 1813.
Volturno, Oct. 1, 1860.
Wagram, July 6, 1809.
Waitzen, July 16, 1849.
Wakefield, Dec. 30, 1460.
Walcheren, Aug. 15, 1809.
*Waterloo, June 18, 1815.
Wavre, June 18, 1815.
Wawz, Mar. 31, 1831.
White Oak Swamp, June 30, 1862.
White Oaks, June 26, 1862.
White Plains, Nov. 30, 1796.
Wilderness, May 5-6, 1864.
Williamsburg, May 11, 1862.
Wilna, June 18, 1831.
Witepsk, Nov. 14, 1812.

BATTLES (*continued*)—

Worcester, (1) Sept. 23, 1642.
   (2) Sept. 3, 1651.
Worth, Aug. 6, 1870.
Wurtzburg, Sept. 3, 1796.
Würtzchen, May 20, 1813.
Ximena, Sept. 10, 1811.
Yermuk, Nov. A.D. 636.

Zelichow, April 6, 1831.
Zenta, Sept. 11, 1697.
Zorndorf, Aug. 25-26, 1758.
Zullichau, June 4, 1799.
Zurich, Sept. 24, 1799.

See also Sieges.

NAVAL BATTLES.

Acre, Nov. 2, 1840.
Actium, Sept. 2, 31 B.C.
Aix Roads, April 11-12, 1809.
Alexandria bombarded, July 11-13, 1882.
Algeciras Bay, July 6 and 12, 1801.
Algiers bombarded, Aug. 27, 1816.
*Armada, July 21-28, 1588.
Beachy Head, June 30, 1690.
Bellair, Aug. 30, 1814.
Brest, Oct. 14, 1747.
Camperdown, Oct. 11, 1797.
Carthagena, Aug. 19, 1702.
Copenhagen, (1) April 2, 1801.
   (2) Sept. 5, 1807.
Cuba blockaded, April 22, 1898 *et seq.*
Dogger Bank, Aug. 5, 1781.
Dominica, April 12, 1782.
Dover (off), (1) May 19, 1652.
   (2) June 2-3, 1653.
Finisterre, Cape of, May 3, 1747.
Gibraltar, Bay of, Sept. 13, 1782.
Guadaloupe, April 12, 1782.
Hampton Roads, Mar. 8-9, 1862.
Hango, July 27, 1714.
Harwich, June 3, 1665.
Howe's victory, June 1, 1794.
Lagos, Aug. 18, 1759.
La Hogue, (1) Feb. 18, 1652.
   (2) May 23, 1692.

Lake Champlain, Sept. 11, 1814.
Lepanto, Oct. 7, 1571.
Lissa, July 20, 1866.
Malaga, Aug. 13, 1704.
Manila, blockade and battle, May 1898.
Milford Haven, 1485.
Navarino, Oct. 20, 1827.
Negapatam, July 3, 1782.
Nile, The, Aug. 1, 1798.
Passaro, Aug. 11, 1718.
Portland (off), Feb. 18-20, 1653.
Puerto Rico bombardment, June 18, 1898.
Rosas Bay, Nov. 1, 1809.
Salamis, 480 B.C.
Samos, Aug. 17, 1824.
Santiago Forts bombarded, May 1898.
Sebastopol bombarded, Oct. 17, 1854.
Sinope, Nov. 30, 1853.
Sluys, June 24, 1340.
Solebay, May 28, 1672.
St. Vincent, Cape of, (1) June 16, 1693.
   (2) Jan. 16, 1780.
   (3) Feb. 14, 1797.
Tchesmé, July 7-9, 1770.
Trafalgar, Oct. 21, 1805.
Trantenan, June 27, 1866.
Tsu Shima, May 27, 28, 1905.
Ushant, July 27, 1778.

* Described by Creasy in his *The Fifteen Decisive Battles of the World*. Maps and plans of these 15 and other important battles are to be found in *A Literary and Historical Atlas of Europe* (Everyman's Lib.). *See also* Sieges.

Bavaria (S. Germany). Celtic Gauls conquered by Franks 660. Governed by French until Charlemagne deposed Tasilon II. Became part of German Empire 1870. Expelled Jesuits 1873.

Bayonet. Supposed to have been invented at Bayonne about 1647, but was in use before; used at b. of Killiecrankie 1689.

Bayonne (France). Meeting-place of Catherine de Medici and the Spanish Duke of Alva to arrange plans for massacre of Huguenots 1565. Charles IV. of Spain abdicated at B. in favour of Napoleon. Invested by British 1814. Convention of B. signed May 10, 1808. [Refer art. in *Encyclopædia Britannica*.]

Beaconsfield Administration. *See* Disraeli.

Beauvais (France). Besieged unsuccessfully by Charles of Burgundy 1472, owing to valour of Jeanne Lainé, surnamed La Hachette. Monument erected to latter at B. 1850. [Refer Michelet, *Hist. of France.*]

Bedford (England). Burned by Danes A.D. 1010; school fd. 1561: Bunyan imprisoned 1660-72. [Refer Lewis, *Topographical Dicty. of England.*]

" **Beggars, The.**" *See* Gueux.

Behring's Strait (N.E. Asia). Discovered by Behring 1728. Explored by Capt. Cook 1778. Closed to foreign fisheries by Russia 1821.

Belfast (Ireland). Castle destroyed about 1178. B. destroyed by Edward Bruce 1316; by Earl of Kildare 1503. Castle repaired 1552. B. granted by James I. to Sir Arthur Chichester 1613. Taken by Gen. Monk 1648; by Lord Montgomery 1649. Castle accidentally burnt 1708. [Refer Benn, *History of Belfast.*]

Belgium. Conquered by Julius Cæsar 51 B.C. Revolution commenced Aug. 25, 1830; independence acknowledged, Dec. 26, 1830. Treaty between Holland and Belgium regarding latter's independence signed at London, April 19, 1839; commercial treaty with Great Britain, Aug. 22, 1862. 1st king, Leopold I. *b.* 1790; *d.* 1865. 2nd king, Leopold II. *b.* 1835; *d.* 1909. 3rd king, Albert. [Refer Smythe, *Story of Belgium.*]

Belgrade (Servia). Seized by Hungarians from Greece 1072; besieged by Turks unsuccessfully 1456; captured by Turks 1521; imperial forces 1688; Turks 1690; Prince Eugene 1717; res. to Turks 1739; captured by Austrians 1789; res. to Turks 1791; surrendered to Servia 1867; independence of Servia declared at B., Aug. 22, 1878; king and queen murdered by army, June 10, 1903. *See* Servia.

Belle Alliance (Belgium). Here Wellington and Blucher met after b. of Waterloo, June 18, 1815.

Bell Rock Lighthouse (German Ocean). Built by Robert Stevenson 1807-11. The rock itself is famous by reason of Southey's ballad *The Inchcape Rock.*

Bells. Intro. into the church by Paulinus of Nola in Campania A.D. 410. In the capitulation of Jerusalem in A.D. 637 the twelfth article stipulated that the Christians " *shall not ring, but only toll their bells.*" First mentioned as used in churches in England by the Venerable Bede, who *d.* 735. [Refer Gibbon, *Rome*, ch. li.] *See also* Curfew Bell.

Beloochistan (Asia). Taken by British 1839, 1840, and 1841 successively.

Benedictines. Monastic order fd. by St. Benedict 529. Intro. into England 596. Expelled from France 1880. The order commissioned by Pope Pius X. to undertake the revision of the Vulgate, May 1907.

Benefit of Clergy. By which the clergy in England were exempt from trial by the civil court. Ben Jonson escaped gallows by, 1598. Totally abolished by acts passed 1779 and 1827. [Refer art. in *Chambers's Encyclopædia*.]

Benevento (*Beneventum*, Italy). Possessed by Romans about 274 B.C.; conquered by Lombards and formed into a duchy 571. Charles of Anjou defeated Manfred of Sicily at B. Feb. 26, 1266. Seized by King of Naples, but res. 1773; taken by French 1798; res. to pope 1815; annexed to Italy 1866.

Benevolences. Forced loans levied by sovereigns of England declared illegal by Bill of Rights (*q.v.*) 1689.

Bengal (India). Independent 1340; annexed to Mogul Empire 1529. Made chief presidency of British India, June 16, 1773. Warren Hastings governor of 1772.

Berlin (N. Germany). Seized by Russians and Austrians, Oct. 1760; entered by French after b. of Jena 1806. B. decree issued by Napoleon, Nov. 20, 1806. Capital of German Empire from 1871. B. Congress, July 13, 1878—May 1880; B. Conference, June 16—July 1, 1880. *See* Germany.

Bermudas or **Sommers' Islands** (Atlantic Ocean). Discovered by Juan Bermudes 1522; inhabited 1609 by landing of Sir Geo. Sommers.

Berne (Switzerland). Principal canton of S.; joined Swiss League 1352. The town of B. resisted Rudolph of Hapsburg 1288; surrendered to French, April 12, 1798; made capital of Switzerland 1848. International Geographical Congress, Aug. 1891. For Copyright Conventions *see* Copyright.

Berwick-on-Tweed (Northumberland, England). Given up to England by Scotland 1176; seized by Robert Bruce 1318; surrendered to English 1333. Independent of England and Scotland 1551. Surrendered to Cromwell 1648; to Gen. Monk 1659. [Refer Lewis, *Topographical Dicty. of England*.]

Betting Act. Passed June 8, 1874.

Betting-Houses (Great Britain). Suppressed 1853.

Beyrout (Syria). Destroyed by earthquake 566. Seized by Ibrahim Pasha 1832; Egyptian army totally defeated at, Oct. 1840; terrible massacre at, May 1860.

Bible, Books of. Showing approximately the different periods with which they deal:—

Old Testament.

Genesis	. B.C. 4004–1635		Ecclesiastes	.	B.C. 977
Exodus	1706–1490		Song of Solomon		1014
Leviticus	1490		Isaiah	.	760–698
Numbers	1490–1451		Jeremiah		629–588
Deuteronomy	1451		Lamentations	.	588
Joshua	1451–1420		Ezekiel	.	595–574
Judges	1425–1120		Daniel	.	607–534
Ruth	1322–1312		Hosea	.	785–725
1 Samuel	1171–1056		Joel	.	800
2 Samuel	1056–1017		Amos	.	787
1 Kings	1015–897		Obadiah	.	587
2 Kings	896–562		Jonah	.	862
1 Chronicles	4004–1015		Micah	.	750–710
2 Chronicles	1015–536		Nahum	.	713
Ezra	536–456		Habakkuk	.	626
Nehemiah	446–434		Zephaniah	.	630
Esther	521–495		Haggai	.	520
Job	1520		Zechariah	.	520–518
Psalms	1063–1015		Malachi	.	397
Proverbs	1000–700				

New Testament.

Matthew	. B.C. 5–A.D. 33		1 Timothy	.	A.D. 65
Mark	. A.D. 26–A.D. 33		2 Timothy	.	66
Luke	. B.C. 2–A.D. 33		Titus	.	65
John	. A.D. 30–A.D. 33		Philemon	.	64
Acts	33–65		Hebrews	.	64
Romans	60		James	.	60
1 Corinthians	59		1 Peter	.	60
2 Corinthians	60		2 Peter	.	66
Galatians	58		1 John	.	90
Ephesians	64		2 John	.	90
Philippians	64		3 John	.	90
Colossians	64		Jude	.	66
1 Thessalonians	54		Revelation	.	96
2 Thessalonians	54				

Bible, Translations of. The first translation of the O.T. called the Septuagint (in Greek) about 286 B.C. Origen's translation commenced A.D. 231. First Latin translation (the Vulgate) revised by St. Jerome A.D. 384. Psalms translated into Saxon A.D. 706. Cædmon's metrical paraphrase of a portion of the B. A.D. 680.

Divided into chapters by Lanfranc in 11th century; into verses by Stephens 1551. English versions—MS. paraphrase of the whole B. 1290; Wickliffe's version 1356-84; first part printed *Seven Penitential Psalms* 1505; Tyndale's (N.T. printed) 1526; Coverdale's (first complete English B. printed) 1535; Cranmer's B. first authorised 1539; authorised version published 1611 (*see* Hampton Court Conference); revised version 1881. First Latin B. printed with movable metal type (known as Gutenberg B.) 1450-5; first German B. printed Strassburg 1466; first English B. published in America at Philadelphia 1782. [Refer to Miss Stone's *Reformation and Renaissance* for valuable information on pre-Reformation Bibles.]

Bible Society, British and Foreign. Begun 1803; organised 1804. George Borrow agent for 1833-41 [refer Borrow, *Bible in Spain*]. American B.S. organised New York, May 8, 1815; American and Foreign B.S., May 1837. A bull from the pope against Bible Societies was issued June 1816. [Refer Canton, *Story of the British and Foreign B.S.*]

Bilbao (Spain). Fd. about 1300; taken by French, July 1795, and in 1808; bombarded by Carlists, but relieved 1874.

Billiards. "Let it alone, let us to billiards" (Shakespeare, *Antony and Cleopatra*, Act. II. scene v.), shows that the game was known in England in Shakespeare's time. The game has been ascribed to Henrique Devique 1571.

Billingsgate (E. London). Opened in 1588 as a landing-place for provisions; as a free market 1699; extended 1848; rebuilt 1852, 1876. [Refer Taylor, *Historical Guide to London.*]

Bill of Attainder. *See* Attainder.

Bill of Rights. *See* Rights.

Birkenhead (England). Dock opened, Aug. 1847.

Birmingham (England). Appears in Domesday Book as *Bermingeham*. Taken by Royalists 1643. Canal opened 1767; Town Hall built 1833; incorp. 1838; Chartist riot at, July 15, 1839. John Bright elected M.P. of B. 1857, 1859, 1873, etc. [Refer Dent, *Old and New Birmingham.*]

Birmingham Musical Festival. Instit. 1768, and held every three years since.

Bishops (England). See of London supposed to have been fd. A.D. 179. Order abolished by parliament 1646; res. 1661. Trial of the seven bishops 1688. *See* under various bishops' sees.

Bishops (Scotland). Replaced by "Superintendents" 1561; res. 1573; abolished 1638; res. 1661; expelled by Scottish Convention, April 1689. Bishops of Scotch Episcopal Church not recognised by state.

Bishops (U.S.A.) The first bishop consecrated for the U.S.A. was Samuel Seabury, who was made Bishop of Connecticut in Nov. 1784. First Bishop of New York consecrated in London on Feb. 4, 1787.

Black Death. Supposed to have originated in China; raged there 1340-8; ravaged Europe 1340-9, 1361-2, and 1369 [refer descriptions in Boccaccio, *Decameron*]; a plague called the B. D. ravaged Dublin 1866.

Blackfriars Bridge (London). Old bridge 1770-1864; new bridge opened, Nov. 6, 1869; enlarged 1909.

Black Friday. Overend, Gurney, and Co., the great bankers, stopped payment on a Friday in May 1866, which caused a great commercial panic; partners committed for trial as conspirators to defraud, but acquitted, Dec. 1869.

Blackheath (England). Wat Tyler assembles on, June 12, 1381; Jack Cade, June 1, 1450. Cornish rebels defeated at, June 22, 1497.

Black Hole of Calcutta. Suraja Dowlah, nawab of Bengal, imprisoned 146 English people in, on June 19, 1756.

Black Letter. *See* Printing.

Black Monday. On April 14, 1360, hailstones killed horses and men of Edward III.'s army before Paris. The day known as Black Monday. The same name is also given to the day when a number of English were slaughtered near Dublin 1209.

Black Prince. Eldest son of Edward III.; *b.* June 15, 1330; at b. of Poitiers 1356; *d.* June 8, 1376.

Black Rod. Office instit. 1349.

Black or Euxine Sea. Turks exclude all foreign ships from 1453. Russians obtain right to trade in 1774; Austria 1784; France and Britain 1802. B. S. Conference 1871. Territory recognised as Russian, Aug. 4, 1896.

Black Watch Regiment. Formed for protection of Highlands about 1668; incorp. as the 42nd Regiment 1739.

Bleaching. Invented by Dutch; first bleach-field in Scotland estab. at Salton, about 1730; intro. into England 1768; Berthollet's discoveries with chlorine about 1785; Tennant's patent 1798; Mather's improvements 1885.

Blenheim. *See* Battles.

Blois (France). Sold to Louis Duke of Orleans 1391; States-general held at 1576 and 1588; Henry of Guise assassinated at, Dec. 23, 1588.

Blood, Circulation of the. Principal discoveries regarding, due to William Harvey between 1619 and 1628. [Refer Harvey, *Circulation of the Blood* (Everyman Lib.).]

Blood's (Colonel) Conspiracy. Attempt to steal Crown jewels, May 9, 1671. Colonel Thomas B. *b.* 1618, *d.* 1680. [Refer Seccombe, *Lives of Twelve Bad Men*.]

" **Bloody Assizes.**" This title has been fixed to the trials by Judge Jeffreys in Aug. 1685, after Monmouth's rebellion (*q.v.*). Jeffreys is known as " Bloody Jeffreys."

Blue-Books. Reports of parliamentary debates, etc., so called from their blue paper wrappers. These reports first printed in 1681. [Refer art. in *Chambers's Encyclopædia*.]

Bodleian Library (Oxford). Fd. 1598; opened 1602. [Refer Macray, *Annals of the Bodleian Library*.] *See* Libraries.

Boers. Emigrated from Cape Colony 1835-7; fd. Orange Free State 1836; Transvaal Republic 1848. *See* South African War, Cape of Good Hope, Transvaal War, etc.

Bohemia (Europe). Became a dukedom A.D. 891; kingdom A.D. 1198; part of Austria 1648. *See* Prague.

Bokhara (Asia). Conquered by Arabs in 8th century, under whom it flourished until 1220. Seized by Usbeks 1505; British envoys murdered at 1842; war with Russia 1866-8; treaty with Russia 1873.

Bologna (Italy). Roman colony 189 B.C. University fd. A.D. 1116. Pope Julius II. took and entered, Nov. 11, 1506 [refer Matarazzo, *Chronicles of Perugia*, Eng. trans.]. Taken by French 1796; by Austrians 1799; by French 1800; res. to pope 1815; taken by Austrians, May 16, 1849, who evacuated, June 12, 1859, and papal legate leaves. Became part of kingdom of Italy 1860. [Refer Sismondi, *History of the Italian Republic*, Eng. trans., ed. Boulter.]

Bombay (India). Acquired by Portuguese 1530; given to Charles II. of England as marriage portion of Catherine of Portugal 1662; granted to East India Company 1668. Visited by Prince of Wales (Edward VII.), Nov. 8, 1875. *See* India.

Bonaparte. *See* France and Napoleon, etc.

Bonn (Germany). Academy at, fd. 1777; made a university 1784; abolished 1802; res. and enlarged 1818. Prince Albert (Prince Consort) educated at, from 1837.

Books. *See* Printing, Copyright, etc.

Bordeaux (France). Taken by Goths A.D. 412; by Cloris 508; became part of England 1151; surrendered to France, Oct. 14, 1453; entered by British troops, Feb. 27, 1814.

Borneo (Indian Ocean). Largest island except Australia. Visited by Dutch in 17th century. Settled by Sir James Brooke 1841. British North Borneo Co. fd. 1881. Made a British protectorate 1895.

Bosnia (Turkey). Incorp. with Turkey 1463; rebellion against Turkish rule 1849-51. *See* Turkey.

Boston (Massachusetts, U.S.A.). Fd. about 1627. Tea chests destroyed in B. Harbour, Dec. 1773. First American newspaper,

Boston News Letter, April 1704 (*see* Newspapers). Harbour closed, Mar. 25, 1774; B. besieged by Americans 1775; evacuated by British 1776. Great fires at, Nov. 1872, Nov. 1889, and May 17, 1894. [Refer Harper, *Encyclopædia U.S. History*.]

Botanic Gardens (Kew). Estab. 1760; enlarged 1841-65.

Botanic Society's Gardens, Royal (Regent's Park). Estab. 1839.

Botany Bay (Australia). Discovered April 28, 1770, by Capt. Cook. Penal colony estab. at 1787.

Bothwell Bridge (Lanark, Scotland). Earl of Monmouth routed Scottish Covenanters, June 22, 1679.

Boulogne (France). Part of Burgundy 1435; of France 1447. Treaty between Henry VIII. (of England) and Francis I. at B. Oct. 28, 1532. Besieged by English 1492; taken by English, Sept. 14, 1544; res. 1550.

Bourbon, House of. First Duke of B. 1327. From this house sprang royal families of France and Spain—King Alfonso XIII. now only reigning monarch of this house, formally enthroned May 17, 1902.

Boyne (E. Ireland). River near which James II. of England was defeated by William III., July 1, 1690.

Brabant (Holland and Belgium). United to Netherlands 1814; South B. given to Belgium 1830. [Refer Motley, *Dutch Republic*.]

Brazil (S. America). Discovered by Portuguese 1500; settled there 1531. First governor appointed 1549. Conquered by Spain 1578; by the Dutch 1630; recovered by Portuguese 1654. Made a kingdom 1815; declared an independent empire 1822. War with Uruguay 1865. Emperor banished and republic declared 1889, and recognised by Great Britain and the U.S.A. 1890. New constitution formed June 1890. Civil war 1893-4. Permanent arbitration treaty with Great Britain signed June 18, 1909. [Refer Southey, *History of Brazil*.]

Breda (Central Holland). Captured from Spaniards by Prince Maurice of Nassau, 1590; retaken by Spaniards 1625; by Dutch, Oct. 1637. Compromise of B. 1566. Taken by French 1793; French expelled 1813. [Refer Motley, *Dutch Republic*.]

Brehon's Laws. Ancient law of Ireland. Penalties against submitting to 1366. Lord Eglinton's Commission for translating and publishing the B. L. 1852; first vol. published 1865; whole work completed 1901.

Bremen (Germany). Held by Sweden 1648-1712, when it was taken by Denmark; sold to Hanover 1731; taken by French 1757; res. 1758; annexed by Napoleon 1810; independence res. 1813.

Breslau (Silesia). Conquered by Frederick of Prussia, Jan. 1741.

Brest (W. France). Given to English 1370; returned 1390; captured by English 1391; ransomed 1395. British forces (under Lord Berkeley) defeated, June 8, 1694; Admiral Hawke's victory over French fleet, Oct. 14, 1747; Admiral Howe's victory, June 1, 1794.

Bretagne. *See* Britanny.

Brethren of the Common Lot or **Life.** The name given to a brotherhood fd. in the Low Countries by Gerard Groot of Deventer about 1380, for the education of youth. Erasmus was at one of their schools in Hertogenbosch about 1483. [Refer Lindsay, *History of the Reformation*, etc.]

Bretigny, Peace of, between England and France, May 8, 136c.

Bridewell (London). Palace of King John 1210; presented by Edward VI. for a workhouse 1553. New B. Prison erected 1829; pulled down 1864.

Bridgewater Canal. Begun 1759; opened July 17, 1761.

Brighton (England). Visit of Prince of Wales (afterwards George IV.) 1783. Pavilion fd. by Prince of Wales 1784.

Bristol (Glouc. Eng.). Built by Brennus 380 B.C. Taken by Earl of Gloucester from King Stephen A.D. 1138. St. Mary's Church built 1292. Attacked by Cromwell 1655. Attempt to fire shipping in harbour 1777. Cathedral fd. 1148; reopened after repairs and restoration 1861. [Refer Lewis, *Topographical Dicty. of England.*]

Britain. Invaded by Julius Cæsar 55 B.C. Romans massacred by Boadicea A.D. 61; she was defeated in same year. Agricola's invasion A.D. 78-84; invasion of Picts and Scots 360; Romans quit B. 436; Saxon invasion 495; St. Augustine lands 597. *See* England, Great Britain, etc.

Britanny, or **Bretagne** (France). Ceded to England 1159; descended to Henry II.'s son 1171-86; succession disputed 1343. B. united to monarchy 1532. Held by Spaniards 1591; recovered by Henry IV. 1594.

British Association. Estab. 1831. Kew Observatory presented to, by Queen Victoria 1842.

British Columbia (W. Canada). Discovered by Perez, 1774; visited by Cook 1778. Made a British colony, Aug. 1858. Vancouver Island incor. with 1866. Annexed to Canada 1871. [Refer Martin, *British Colonies.*]

British Museum. Grant made by parliament, April 5, 1753. Old Royal Library presented to 1757. Building opened, Jan. 15, 1759. New buildings erected 1823-47. Elgin Marbles presented 1816; Grenville Library 1847. Reading-room opened, May 18, 1857. Natural history collection removed to S. Kensington 1880. Foundation stone of extension laid by Edward VII. June 27, 1907. *See also* Libraries.

Broad-Bottom Administration. Formed out of a coalition of parties, Nov. 24, 1744; dissolved by death of Mr. Pelham, Mar. 6, 1754.

Brooklyn (New York). Settled by Dutch 1636; incorp. 1834. Bridge from B. to New York city opened, May 24, 1883.

Browning Society, for the study of the works of Robert Browning. Fd. by Dr. Furnivall, Oct. 28, 1881. B. Settlement fd. Walworth 1895.

Brownists. Religious sect fd. by Robert Browne (1550-1633) about 1580. [Refer McClintock and Strong, *Dicty. of Eccles. Bibl. Lit.*]

Bruce's Travels, to discover source of the Nile, by James B. Set out, June 1768; reached Gondar 1770; obtained sight of the Nile sources, Nov. 14, 1770; returned to England 1773. B. *d.* 1794.

Bruges (N.W. Belgium). Capital of Flanders in 7th century. In mediæval times a great market and commercial centre; given to France 1794, to Holland 1814, Belgium 1830.

Brunswick (N. Germany). Included by Napoleon in the kingdom of Westphalia 1806; res. 1815. Joined North German Confederation, Aug. 18, 1866. Charles William Ferdinand, Duke of B., great general, mortally wounded at b. of Auerstadt, Oct. 14, 1806.

Brussels (Belgium). Mentioned in 8th century as *Bruchsella.* Cathedral completed 1273. Capital of Low Countries 1507. Alva's rule 1567. Union of B. 1578. Bombarded by Villeroi, Aug. 1695. Taken by French 1701; by Duke of Marlborough 1706; by Saxe 1746; by Dumouriez 1792. Capital of Belgium 1831. University fd. 1834.

Buccaneers. Name first applied in 16th century to associations of piratical adventurers, chiefly of French and English nationality. In 1630 they captured the island of Tortuga and used it as a stronghold. In 1655 they captured Jamaica. Their principal attacks were on the Spaniards, and in 1685 they defied the Spanish fleet in the Bay of Panama. Their last great achievement was the capture of Cartagena 1697. [Refer Esquemeling, *Buccaneers of America.*]

Buckingham Palace. Built 1703. Property of Queen Charlotte 1761. New building occupied by Queen Victoria, July 13, 1837.

Budget. Sir R. Peel's B. (Income Tax) 1842; Sir R. Peel's B. (Free Trade) 1846; Mr. Gladstone's B. (French Treaty) 1860. Mr. Asquith's budgets, with estimated expenditure £140,757,000, intro. April 18, 1907, and £152,869,000, May 7, 1908. Mr. Lloyd George estimated expenditure £162,102,000 in B. intro. April 29, 1909; £198,930,000 in B. intro. June 30, 1910, thrown out by House of Lords, re-intro. with expenditure £199,482,000 June 15, 1911. Increase of nearly £60,000,000 expenditure since 1907. *See* Parliament.

Budget Protest League. Formed by certain members of the opposition in the House of Commons to protest against Finance Bill, June 17, 1909. A *Budget League* opposing this formed by certain members of the government, June 23, 1909. [Refer *Annual Register*, 1909.]

Buenos Ayres (America). Fd. 1535; rebuilt 1585. Taken by British, June 27, 1806; retaken by Spanish, Aug. 12; by British, Oct. 29. Constitution voted, May 23, 1853; independent state 1853; reunited to Argentine, Nov. 1859. Jesuits' college burnt by mob, Feb. 28, 1875. Population nearly 1,000,000 in 1911. [Refer Prescott, *Conquest of Mexico*, etc.

Buffalo (New York). Fd. 1801; incorp. 1832; burned by British forces 1813. President McKinley fatally wounded by anarchist at, Sept. 5, 1901.

Bulgaria (S. Europe). Part of Balkan Peninsula. Kingdom estab. about A.D. 680. Acknowledged authority of Byzantine emperors 1018. Kingdom re-estab. 1186. Insurrection suppressed 1876. Made an autonomous principality tributary to Turkey 1878; first parliament met, Feb. 22, 1879. Seat of Russo-Turkish War 1877-8. War with Servia, Nov. 14, 1884; peace signed 1886. Conspiracy of Major Panitza discovered 1890. Declared itself free from Turkish suzerainty 1909. [Refer Fraser, *Pictures from the Balkans*.]

Bull-Baiting. Bill to abolish in England 1835.

Bull-Fighting. Intro. into Spain about 1260. Prohibited in France 1894.

Bunhill Fields (London, E.C.). Used by Dissenters. Burying ground, first used 1665; John Bunyan buried there 1688; George Fox 1690; De Foe 1731; Susannah Wesley 1742; Isaac Watts 1748; William Blake 1828; Thomas Stothard, R.A., 1834.

Bunker's Hill. *See* Battles.

Burgos (Spain). Burial-place of the Cid, 1099. Entered by the Duke of Wellington, Sept. 19, 1812; besieged same year; bombarded by French, June 12, 1813.

Burgundy (France). Conquered by Franks A.D. 434; dukedom 877; given to Maximilian 1493; res. to France 1678.

Burlingame Treaty, between U.S.A. and China. Negotiated at Washington, July 28, 1868; officially recognised, Dec. 1, 1868. Authorised mutual immigration, " *The inalienable right of man to change his habitation;*" called after Mr. Anson B. (1820-1870), who was responsible for the treaty. [Refer Harper, *Encyclopædia of U.S. History*.]

Burlington House (Piccadilly). Built for Lord B. 1664; rebuilt 1731; bought by government, July 1854. Royal, Linnæan, and Chemical Societies' quarters at 1857. Royal Academy first opened at, May 3, 1869.

Burmah (India). Fd. about 1066; seat of government of B. fd. at Ava A.D. 1364; war with Great Britain 1824-6; rebellion against king suppressed by British aid 1866; Sir Douglas Forsyth's mission to 1875; British war against 1885. British B. constituted 1862; numerous rebellions since; Gen. Roberts' campaign 1886-7. United to British India 1886; Gen. Wolseley's expedition 1889. [Refer Phayre, *History of Burmah.*]

Bury St. Edmunds (England). Named after St. Edmund, King of East Anglia, who was buried there A.D. 870. Magna Charta prepared at, Nov. 20, 1214. Desolated by plague 1636.

Bute Administration. From Earl of B., First Lord, May 12, 1762—April 8, 1763. [Refer *Letters of Junius*, etc.]

Byzantine Empire. *See* East, Empire of the.

C

Cabal. The cabinet formed by Charles II. after the fall of the Earl of Clarendon was called the " Cabal " 1667-73. [Refer Harris, *Life of Charles II.*, 2 vols. 1766.]

Cabinets. *See* Administrations.

Cable. Hempen cables employed by British navy prior to 1811, when iron cables were introduced. First successful submarine cable between S. Foreland and Sangatte 1851; first Atlantic cable estab. July 29—Aug. 16, 1857.

Cabriolets (shortened to Cabs). Intro. into London 1823.

Cabul. *See* Afghan War.

Cade's Insurrection. Mob led by Jack C. May 1450; entered London June 27. C. killed July 11. *See* Shakespeare.

Cadiz (Spain). A large number of the Spanish Armada vessels were burned in C. Harbour by Drake 1587. Taken by Earl of Essex, Sept. 15, 1596; bombarded by English, July 1797; blockaded by Lord St. Vincent 1797-9; besieged by French, July 1812; taken by French, Oct. 1823, and held by them till 1828. [Refer art. on Spain.]

Cadmium. Metal discovered by Stromeyer and Hermann 1817.

Cædmon. *See* English Literature.

Caen (France). Old capital of the Norman dominion, and burial-place of William the Conqueror and his queen. Taken by English 1346, 1417; retaken by French, July 1, 1450.

Caere (W. Italy). Invaded by Gauls 390 B.C. Treaty with Rome 390; incorporated with Roman state 353.

Caesium. An alkaline metal discovered by Bunsen and Kirchhoff 1860.

Ça ira! The opening words of a song made famous by the French Revolution. First heard Oct. 5, 1789. [Refer Carlyle, *French Revolution.*]

Cairo (Egypt). Captured by Turks 1517. Great earthquake at, June 1754. Taken by Napoleon I. July 23, 1798; recaptured with British help, June 27, 1801. *See* Egypt.

Calabria (Italy). The name by which the S.E. peninsula of Italy, the Messapia of the Greeks, was known to the Romans; conquered by them 266 B.C [refer *Atlas of Classical Geog.* (Everyman's Lib.)]; subdued by Odoacer A.D. 476; part of the Ostrogothic kingdom of Theodoric 493; recovered for empire by Belisarius 536. After 873 Calabria constituted part of the S.W. peninsula. Invaded by Otho I. 968, who defeated Greeks 969; invaded by Peter of Aragon 1283; invaded by Sicilians 1296. Part of kingdom of Naples 1597. [Refer Ross and Cooper, *The Highlands of Calabria.*]

Calais (France). The last French possession to be captured from the English; taken by Edward III. Aug. 4, 1347; finally taken from the English by the Duke of Guise, Jan. 7, 1558; taken by Spaniards, April 1596; res. 1598.

Calcutta (India). English factory estab. at 1690. Confinement of prisoners in Black Hole, Jan. 18, 1756, after capture of town by Dowlah; retaken Jan. 1, 1757; made centre of British India 1773. [Refer Macaulay, *Essay on Lord Clive*.]

Caledonian Canal (Scotland). Commenced May 1, 1803; opened Nov. 1822.

Calendar. Romulus said to have divided the year into 10 months, including in all 304 days; Numa added two months; Decemvirs added a day in 452 B.C.; Cæsar fixed mean length of year at 365¼ days, with 366 days every fourth year, in 46 B.C.; reformed by Julius Cæsar by introduction of ninety days into the year and leap years for the future 46 B.C.; correction suggested by Roger Bacon 1267; adopted by Pope Gregory XIII. 1582 (known as Gregorian system); rejected by Joseph Scaliger and Protestants 1583; new style introduced into England 1752. At the time of the French Revolution a new C. was intro. into France 1793; it ceased Jan. 1, 1806. [Refer Plunkett, *Ancient Calendars and Constellations*.]

California (U.S.A.). Discovered by Spaniards 1534; visited by Drake 1578; subject to Mexico 1823; occupied by U.S. army 1846; ceded to U.S. 1848; admitted to Union as a state 1850. *See also* San Francisco. [Refer Harper, *Encyclopædia of U.S. History*.]

Calmar, Union of. United Sweden, Denmark, and Norway under one crown, June 1397; dissolved 1523.

Calotype. A method of photography discovered by Dr. Fox Talbot 1840. *See* Photography.

Calvinists. A religious sect named after John Calvin (*b.* Noyon, July 10, 1509); separated from Lutherans 1561. Calvin *d.* May 27, 1564. *See* Edict of Nantes.

Cambrai (France). Church Councils at 1064, 1303, 1383, 1565. Captured by the Emperor Charles V. 1544; by French 1667; French defeated by British under Duke of York, April 24, 1794; taken by Austrians, Sept. 10, 1798; by British under Sir Charles Colville 1815. League of C. Dec. 10, 1508; Paix des Dames Treaty 1529.

Cambridge (England). Orig. ancient Roman *Camboricum*. Taken by barons 1215. Residence of Henry II., who repaired castle 1265. Castle possessed by Cromwell 1643. Fitzwilliam Museum fd. at 1816. [Refer the Dean of Ely, *Cambridge and its Story*.]

Cambridge (Massachusetts, U.S.A.). Harvard College (*q.v.*), the foremost American university, was fd. here, Oct. 28, 1636. One of the earliest, if not the earliest, printing presses was set up at C., which published the *Bay Psalm Book*, the first book printed in British America, in 1640. [Refer Tring, *American Literature*, etc.]

Cambridge University. Supposed fd. by Sigebert, King of East Anglia, A.D. 631; res. by Edward the Elder 915; first charter granted 1231. Records of University burnt by Wat Tyler 1381. Refused to admit Francis, a Benedictine monk recommended by James II. Feb. 9, 1687; Vice-Chancellor deprived of his office in consequence, May 27, 1687; reinstated 1688. The following are the principal colleges and halls with the dates of their foundation and their founders:—

Ayerst Hall, opened April 21, 1884, by Vice-Chancellor; closed Michaelmas 1896.

Caius (Gonville and Caius College), fd. by Edmund Gonville 1348. John Caius, M.D., in 1558 obtained royal charter.

Cavendish College, fd. 1876 by County College Association; closed Dec. 1891.

Christ's College, fd. 1505 by Lady Margaret, Countess of Richmond and Derby, mother of King Henry VII.

Clare College, fd. 1326 by Lady Elizabeth, sister of Gilbert, Earl of Clare.

Corpus Christi, fd. 1352; owes foundation to two early societies which existed in Cambridge in 14th century, called the Guilds of Corpus Christi and of the Blessed Virgin Mary.

Downing College, fd. Sept. 22, 1800, by Sir George Downing, Bt.; received charter, Sept. 22, 1800.

Emmanuel College, fd. 1584 by Sir Walter Mildmay, Chancellor of the Exchequer.

Jesus College, fd. 1496 by John Alcock, Bishop of Ely.

King's College, fd. 1441 by Henry VI.

Magdalene College, fd. 1519 by Thomas, Baron Audley, of Walden.

Pembroke College, fd. 1347 under name of Valence-Mary, who was in reality Mary de St. Paul, widow of Aymer de Valence, Earl of Pembroke. Henry VI. was a liberal benefactor, and is known as second founder.

Queens' College, fd. 1448 by Queen Margaret of Anjou, wife of Henry VI.; re-fd. in 1465 by Elizabeth Woodville, wife of Edward IV.

St. Catharine's College, fd. 1473 by Robert Wodelarke, D.D., Chancellor of the University.

College of St. John the Evangelist (St. John's College), fd. 1511 by Lady Margaret (founder of Christ's College, q.v.).

St. Peter's College (or Peterhouse), fd. 1284 by Hugh de Balsham, Bishop of Ely.

Selwyn College, fd. 1882, built by public subscription in memory of George Augustus Selwyn, Bishop of Lichfield.

Sidney Sussex College, fd. 1596 under will of Lady Frances Sidney, Dowager Countess of Sussex.

Trinity College, fd. 1546 by Henry VIII., who combined three other smaller colleges into one, and added to revenues.

Trinity Hall, fd. 1350 by William Bateman, Bishop of Norwich.

[Refer *Cambridge University Calendar* for histories of various colleges, *College Histories*, 1898, etc., 16 vols., etc., etc.]

Cameroons (W. Africa). Colonised by Germans 1884.

Camiciata, The, or **Mock Assault**. Made on Rome by the Duke of Alva, Aug. 26, 1557, for political purposes. [Refer Motley, *Dutch Republic*.]

Camisards. Cevenne Huguenots, who made themselves felt after the revocation of the Edict of Nantes 1685. Great massacres of C. in 1703 by Marshal Montrevel. [Refer Bray, *Revolt of the Protestants of the Cevennes*.]

Campbell's Acts, named after the Lord Chancellor, John C. (1779-1861), were three in number: (1) Act against libel and slander (1843). (2) Act compelling railways to compensate passengers suffering through culpable accidents. (3) Act against obscene books, pamphlets, pictures, etc.

Canada (N. America). Discovered by John and Sebastian Cabot 1497. The St. Lawrence discovered by Jacques Cartier 1535, and from hearing the Indians make frequent use of the word *Kanata*, a village, carried away the impression that the name applied to the whole country [refer Isaac Taylor]. Quebec fd. by Champlain 1608. C. explored by La Salle 1676, 1687. C. given up to England by France 1763 after war of 1759-60 (*see* Quebec), in which Gen. Wolfe distinguished himself. C. divided into two provinces 1791; reunited 1840; again separated on establishment of the Confederation 1867. Act for union of C., Nova Scotia, and New Brunswick, under title of Dominion of C., passed in English House of Commons, Mar. 29, 1867. Territories of Hudson Bay (Manitoba), added 1869; of British Columbia 1871; of Prince Edward Island 1873. Canadian Pacific Railway opened, Nov. 8, 1885. The following are the governor-generals since the Union:—

Lord Monck 1867-8	Lord Stanley of Preston 1888-93
Lord Lisgar 1868-72	Earl of Aberdeen 1893-8
Lord Dufferin 1872-8	Earl of Minto 1898-1904
Marquis of Lorne 1878-83	Earl Grey 1904-1911
Lord Lansdowne 1883-8	Duke of Connaught 1911

[Refer Smith, *Canada and the Canadian Question*.]

Canals. For the principal ones in Great Britain and Ireland, *see* under various headings. The following are the most noted canals outside Great Britain, with the dates of their openings:—

American Erie 1817	Cattegat and Baltic 1806
Amsterdam 1825	Du Midi (Languedoc) 1681
Amsterdam and North Sea 1876	Ganges 1854
Baltic and North Sea, April 1891	Kiel 1785
Bordeaux and Narbonne 1884	Orleans 1675
Bourbon 1790	Seine et Loire 1791
Burgundy 1775	

See also under Suez and Panama, etc.

Canary or **Fortunate Islands** (N.W. Africa). Granted by Pope Clement VI. to Louis Count of Clermont 1346; fitted out a fleet but abandoned the enterprise 1348; since 1495 under Spanish rule.

Candahar. *See* Kandahar.

Candia. *See* Crete.

Candlemas (orig. Candle Mass). From a very early, indeed unknown date in the Christian history, the 2nd of February has been held as the festival of the Purification of the Virgin [Chambers, *Book of Days*]. In 1539 Henry VIII. by a proclamation ordered the Ceremony of the Candles on this day. Forbidden in the English Church by order of Council 1548. [Refer Brand, *Popular Antiquities*.]

Cannon. Erroneously said to have been early known in Hindostan and to the Chinese [refer Gibbon, *Rome*]. It is certain that it was used by Edward III. in his campaign against the Scots 1327; also at the siege of Calais by the English 1347; and by the Turks in the sieges of Constantinople in 1394 and 1453 [refer Gibbon, *Rome*]. First war cannon cast in England at Uckfield 1453.

Canon. The office of C. appears to have been intro. into the Church in the 8th century, and arose from the desire to impose something like a monastic rule on the cathedral clergy.

Canonisation " was not known before the 10th century, but some hold that the first C. was celebrated by Leo III. A.D. 804 " [Eadie, *Ecclesiastical Dicty*.]. In consequence of the number of saints during the Dark Ages, the canonising of any deceased Christian was prohibited in the 9th century without the bishop's consent. John XV. was the first pope who exercised the assumed right, and in A.D. 995 made Udalric, Bishop of Augsburg, a saint. The worship of " canonised saints " was enjoined by the Council of Trent (1545-63). [Refer McClintock and Strong, *Encyclopædia of Biblical and Eccles. Literature*, 1868.]

Canon Law. Commenced by Gratian, a Benedictine monk of Bologna, A.D. 1127; intro. into England 1140; completed by Gratian 1151. [Refer McClintock and Strong, *Encyclopædia of Biblical and Eccles. Lit.*]

Canossa (Modena). Pope Gregory VII. (Hildebrand) forced Henry IV. of Germany to submit to humiliating penance here 1077. Castle destroyed by inhabitants of Reggio 1255. [Refer Stephen, *Essays in Ecclesiastical Biography*.]

Canterbury (England). Occupies the site of the Roman *Durovernum*, afterwards known as *Cantwarabyrig*. St. Augustine arrived from Rome at C. A.D. 596. Castle taken by Louis of France 1215. Kentish rebels under Wat Tyler left C. for London 1381. Cathedral fd. by Augustine 602; pillaged by Roric 851; entirely rebuilt by Archbishop Lanfranc 1070; choir rebuilt on larger scale by Archbishop Anselm and res. 1172. Thomas à Becket murdered in C. 1170; shrine to him erected 1175, which was demolished and robbed of its valuable gifts by Henry VIII. 1538. St. Martin's Church, frequented by Queen Bertha before the landing of Augustine, said to be the oldest Saxon church in England. Chequers Inn for pilgrims, mentioned by Chaucer, built 1400; mostly burnt down 1865. [Refer Dean Stanley, *Memorials of Canterbury*.]

Canterbury, Archbishops of. The following is a list since the foundation of the see:—

Augustine 597-605
Laurentius 605-619
Mellitus 619-624
Justus 624-627
Honorius 627-653
Deusdedit 655-664
Theodore 668-690
Berhtuald 693-731
Taetwine 731-734
Nothelm 734-740
Cuthbert 740-758
Breogwine 759-762
Jaenberht 763-790
Æthelheard 790-803
Wulfred 803-829
Fleogild 829-830
Ceolnoth 830-870
Æthelred 870-889
Plegemund 891-923
Æthelm 923-925
Wulfelm 928-941
Odo 941-958
Ælsine 958-959
Dunstan 959-988
Æthelgar 988-989
Sigeric 990-995
Ælfric 995-1006
Ælfeah or Alphege 1006-1012
Lyfing 1013-1020
Æthelnoth 1020-1038
Eadsige 1038-1050
Robert of Jumiège 1050-1052
Stigand 1052-1070
Lanfranc 1070-1089
Anselm 1093-1109
Ralph de Turbine 1114-1122
William de Curbellio 1123-1136
Theobald 1139-1161
Thomas Becket 1162-1170
Richard 1174-1184
Baldwin 1185-1190
Reginald Fitz-Joceline 1191
Hubert Walter 1193-1205
Stephen Langton 1207-1228
Richard Wethershed 1229-1231
Edmund de Abbendon 1233-1240
Boniface of Savoy 1240-1270
Robert Kilwardby 1273-1278
John Peckham 1279-1292
Robert Winchelsey 1293-1313

Walter Reynolds 1313-1327
Simon de Meopham 1327-1333
John Stratford 1333-1348
John de Ufford 1348-1349
Thomas Bradwardin 1349
Simon Islip 1349-1366
Simon Langham 1366-1368
William Wittlesey 1368-1374
Simon Sudbury 1375-1381
William Courtenay 1381-1396
Thomas Arundel 1396-1414
Henry Chicheley 1414-1443
John Stafford 1443-1452
John Kemp 1452-1454
Thomas Bourchier 1454-1486
John Morton 1486-1500
Henry Deane 1501-1503
William Warham 1503-1532
Thomas Cranmer 1533-1556
Reginald Pole 1556-1558
Matthew Parker 1559-1575
Edmund Grindal 1575-1583
John Whitgift 1583-1604
Richard Bancroft 1604-1610
George Abbot 1611-1633
William Laud 1633-1645
William Juxon 1660-1663
Gilbert Sheldon 1663-1677
William Sancroft 1678-1691
John Tillotson 1691-1694
Thomas Tenison 1694-1715
William Wake 1716-1737
John Potter 1737-1747
Thomas Herring 1747-1757
Matthew Hutton 1757-1758
Thomas Secker 1758-1768
Frederick Cornwallis 1768-1783
John Moore 1783-1805
Charles Manners Sutton 1805-1828
William Howley 1828-1848
John Bird Sumner 1848-1862
Charles Thomas Longley 1862-1868
Archibald Campbell Tait, 1868-1882
Edward White Benson 1882-1896
Frederick Temple 1896-1902
Randall Thomas Davidson 1903

[Refer W. F. Hook, *Lives of Archbishops of Canterbury to* 1663; J. M. Fuller, *Throne of Canterbury*.]

"**Canterbury Christmas.**" On Wednesday, Dec. 22, 1647, the crier of Canterbury proclaimed by decree of Parliament that the festivities of Christmas and other superstitious revivals should be put down, which command was strenuously resisted. [Refer Brand, *Popular Antiquities.*]

"**Canterbury Tales,**" by Geoffrey Chaucer (1300?-1400); first printed by Caxton 1475-6.

Canton (China). King of Portugal obtained right to trade with 1517. First visited by English 1634; besieged and taken by Sir Hugh Gough, May 31, 1841; Convention of C. July 1841.

Cape Coast Castle (E. Africa). Principal British fort on Gold Coast. Early settlement of Portuguese 1610; taken from them by Dutch 1643; ceded to England by Peace of Breda 1667. *See* Gold Coast.

Cape Colony (S. Africa). Cape of Good Hope discovered by Bartholomew de Diaz 1487. Cape Town fd. by Dutch 1650. Colony at Cape Town captured by English, Sept. 16, 1795; res. 1802; retaken Jan. 9, 1806. War with Kaffirs 1811-12, 1819. Finally ceded to English by King of Netherlands, Aug. 13, 1814. Arrival of over 5000 British emigrants 1820. Kaffirs raided English settlements, Oct. 1834. Third Kaffir War 1835; fourth Kaffir War 1846; fifth Kaffir War 1850-3. Boers in large numbers crossed Orange River and left colony 1835. Legislative Council estab. 1837. Natal annexed to Cape Colony, Aug. 2, 1843. Government proclaimed its authority over Orange River sovereignty, Feb. 3, 1848. Orange River territory annexed to Cape Colony, Mar. 1851. Representative Government estab. July 1, 1853. Orange River territory formed into a free state, Mar. 1854. Discovery of diamonds 1867-70. Transvaal Republic annexed for protection, April 12, 1877. Transvaal independent as S. African Republic 1880 (*see* Transvaal). Houses of Parliament opened 1885. Arrival of Lords Roberts and Kitchener during S. African War (*q.v.*), Jan. 10, 1900. Annexation of Orange Free State, May 28, 1900; of Transvaal, Sept. 3, 1900. *See also* Transvaal, Orange Free State, South African War, etc., etc. [Refer Theal, *South Africa.*]

"**Caps and Hats.**" On the assembly of the Swedish Diet, May 30, 1738, the house divided itself into two parties—the *Hats*, who opposed, and the *Caps*, who favoured the alliance with Russia. The former gained their point, allied with France, and war was declared, Aug. 1741; parties suppressed 1772.

Capua (Italy). Made a Roman colony 59 B.C. Captured by Vandals A.D. 456; destroyed by Saracens 840; rebuilt 9th century. Councils at 391, 1087, 1118. Captured by Cæsar Borgia, July 24, 1501; occupied by French, Jan. 23, 1799; surrendered to British, July 28, 1799; capitulated to Sardinian forces, Nov. 1860.

Capuchins. Offshoot of Franciscans, fd. by Matteo di Bassi, about 1520; sanctioned by Pope Clement VII. 1528.

Cardiff (S. Wales). Of very early origin. Besieged by Owen Glendower 1404. Oldest charter extant dated Oct. 14, 1338. University of South Wales and Monmouthshire estab. at, 1883.

Cardinals (*see also* Conclave). Term first applied to chief priest of a parish. Pope Stephen IV. about A.D. 770 seems to have been the first to select seven bishops out of the Roman see and gave them the title of cardinal. At a council in Rome in A.D. 853, Pope Leo IV. calls them *presbyteros sui cardinis.* The Council of Rome, under Pope Nicholas II. 1059, granted the College of Cardinals the principal voice in the election of a pope. The number in the College of Cardinals was finally fixed at seventy in 1586. [Refer McClintock and Strong, *Encyclopædia of Biblical and Eccles. Lit.*]

Cards, or the Books of the Four Kings, seem to have evolved from chess (*q.v.*). Known in ancient times as *Chartmanga* or the Four Rajas. Edward I. of England learned to play in the Holy Land 1278. Known to Venetians in 1441, when the government prevented the importation of foreign cards. Intro. into France 1493. [Refer Brand, *Popular Antiquities.*]

Carlisle (England). *Luguvallum* of Roman Britain. Wall built by Hadrian A.D. 121; fortified by William Rufus 1092; Charles II. entered, Aug. 6, 1651; surrendered to young Pretender, Nov. 15, 1745; submitted to Duke (" Butcher ") of Cumberland, Nov. 15, 1745. [Refer Lewis, *Topographical Dicty. of Scotland.*]

Carlisle Administration. *See* Halifax.

Carlsbad (Bohemia). Medicinal hot springs discovered by Emperor Charles IV. 1358; baths fd. 1364. Congress of powers 1819 to repress liberal press, etc.

Carmelite Order. Monastic order of " St. Mary of Mount Carmel " fd. by Berthold, Count of Limoges, about 1156 on Mt. Carmel; received its first rule from Albert, Patriarch of Jerusalem, 1209; sanctioned by Pope Honorius III. 1224. First general chapter held in England 1245. [Refer McClintock and Strong.]

Carnarvon or **Caernarvon** (Wales). The first Prince of Wales (afterwards Edward II.) *b.* at, April 25, 1284. Castle commenced by Edward I. in 1283. Prince of Wales invested at, July 13, 1911.

Carrickfergus (Ireland). William of Orange (William III.) landed at, June 11, 1690.

Carthusian Order. Monastic order fd. by St. Bruno A.D. 1086; recognised by Pope 1170. In England the Carthusians settled in 1180, and had a famous monastery in London, since called from the Carthusians who settled there the " Charter-House." [Refer McClintock and Strong, *op. cit.*]

Cassel or **Cashel** (Germany). Known as *Chassala* in 10th century. Fortified 1526. Refuge for French Protestants after 1685. Taken by French 1760; besieged by Count Lippe 1761, and by Prince Ferdinand, who took it Nov. 1, 1762; fortifications destroyed 1767; occupied by French 1806. Capital of Kingdom of Westphalia 1807-13.

Castile or **Castille** (Spain). First count, Roderic A.D. 791; subject to King of Leon 1028; a kingdom in 1039; Ferdinand and Isabella sovereigns of 1474; annexed to Spanish Crown 1504. [Refer Calvert, *Spain*, 2 vols.]

Cateau Cambresis, Peace of. Concluded between Henry II. of France and Philip II. of Spain, April 2 and 3, 1559.

Catholic Apostolic Church. Known as " Irvingites " from its association with Rev. Edward Irving (1792-1834). Its followers, however, repudiate the name " Irvingites." Their chief ministers, known as apostles, separated July 14, 1835; their liturgy was framed in 1842. [Refer art. in *Ency. Brit.*]

Catholic Association, Irish. Organised 1824; act for its suppression 1825, but it continued until Feb. 12, 1829, when it was voluntarily dissolved. [Refer McCarthy, *History of our own Times.*]

Catholic League in France. Organised against Huguenots (*q.v.*) by the Duke of Guise; Henry III. joined 1576, and renewed civil war. [Refer Cambridge Modern History, *Wars of Religion.*]

Catholics. *See* Roman Catholics in Great Britain and Old Catholics.

Cato Street Conspiracy. So called from the place (now Homer St., Edgware Road, London) where the conspirators met to arrange their plans; formed by Arthur Thistlewood, Sat. Feb. 19, 1820, to murder Lord Castlereagh and other ministers. Thistlewood executed with four accomplices, May 1, 1820. [Refer *Annual Register* (vol. 62), 1820, 2 parts, for description of trials of conspirators.]

Cawnpore (India). Formally possessed by Great Britain 1801. Besieged by Nana Sahib 1857; massacre of women and children by mutineers, July 1857.

Caxton, William (?1421-91). *See* Printing.

Celibacy of the Clergy. Spanish synod of Elvira first council to enjoin it on clergy A.D. 305; condemned by Vigilantius, a presbyter of Barcelona, A.D. 406; strictly enjoined by First Lateran Council 649. [Refer McClintock and Strong, *op. cit.*]

Census. A Census Bill was intro. into parliament 1753, but was rejected on the plea that a census of the people was dangerous to the liberties of free-born Englishmen. The first census taken in Great Britain was in 1801. Act passed Aug. 18, 1890. In the U.S.A. the first census was taken in 1790. Census taken in United Kingdom, showing return of 45,216,665 inhabitants, an increase of over 3¾ millions during last 10 years, April 2, 1911.

Ceylon (India). Portuguese settled at 1517; captured by Dutch 1656; taken by English 1795; ceded to Great Britain by Peace of Amiens, Mar. 27, 1802; war with native chiefs, Jan. 1815—Mar. 2, 1815. [Refer Martin, *British Colonies.*]

Chalgrove Field. *See* Battles.

Challenger Expedition. A British scientific exploration under Sir George Nares, so called from the name of the ship *Challenger*, which left England on Dec. 7, 1872, and returned May 24, 1876.

Chambers of Commerce. The oldest in Great Britain is the one at Glasgow, instit. Jan. 1, 1783; royal charter granted at same time. Manchester Chamber of Commerce instit. 1820; London 1882. New York Chamber instit. 1768; incorp. 1770.

"Chambers of Reunion." Estab. by Louis XIV. of France for the purpose of asserting claims, through old feudal titles, to territories on German frontier 1679.

"Chambre Ardente, La." First instit. by Francis I. in 1535; revived by Henry II. and created for the trial of heretics, Oct. 1547. [Refer Baird, *History of the Rise of the Huguenots*.]

Champagne (France). Annexed to Crown of Navarre by Theobald 1234; ceded by Joanna II. to Philip V. of France 1318; invaded by Emperor Charles II. 1523; entered by Prussians under Duke of Brunswick 1792.

Champ de Mars. First grand federation of the, July 14, 1790; the second, July 14, 1791, at which a petition was signed praying for the abdication of Louis XVI. [Refer Carlyle, *French Revolution*, etc.] *See* Paris.

Chancellor. Orig. the *Cancellarius*, or door-keeper, who admitted suitors into the presence of the sovereign; first made an imperial minister by Carinus, Consul of Rome, 284. C. of England, Lord High, Edward the Elder appointed his nephew Thurketyl the first in England; he resigned the office 948. The following are the most notable:—

Cardinal Wolsey 1515.
Sir Thomas More 1529.
Stephen Gardiner, Bp. of Winchester, 1553.
Sir Francis Bacon (*q.v.*) 1617.
Hyde, Earl of Clarendon, 1660.
Antony Ashley, Earl of Shaftesbury, 1672.
George, Lord Jeffreys, 1685.
Philip Yorke, Lord Hardwicke, 1737.
Edward, Lord Thurlow, 1778, 1783.
John Scott, Lord Eldon, 1801, 1807.
Thomas, Lord Erskine, 1806.
John Singleton Copley, Lord Lyndhurst, 1827, 1834, 1841.
Henry, Lord Brougham and Vaux, 1830.
Robert Monsey Rolfe, Lord Cranworth, 1852, 1865.
Frederic Thesiger, Lord Chelmsford, 1858, 1866.
John, Lord Campbell (*see* Campbell's Acts), 1859.
Richard Bethell, Lord Westbury, 1861.
Hugh Cairns, Lord Cairns, 1868, 1874.
William Page Wood, Lord Hatherley, 1868.
Roundell Palmer, Lord Selbourne, 1872, 1880.
Sir Hardinge Gifford, Lord Halsbury, 1885, 1886, 1895, 1902.
Sir Farrer Herschel, Lord Herschel, 1886, 1892.
Robert Threshie Reid, Lord Loreburn, 1906, 1910.

[Refer Lord Campbell, *Lives of the Chancellors*.]

Chancellor of the Exchequer. *See* Exchequer.

Chancellor of Ireland, Lord High. Earliest nomination that of Stephen Ridel during Richard I.'s reign 1189.

Chancellor of Scotland, Lord High. Office abolished in 1708 at the Union, a Keeper of the Great Seal being appointed, occupying a similar position.

Chancery, Court of. Supposed to have originated with Alfred the Great (A.D. 871-901). Its abolition was voted by Barebones Parliament (*q.v.*) 1653; remodelled 1852, 1853, 1855, 1858, 1867; merged in newly-formed High Court of Judicature, Nov. 1, 1875. [Refer art. in *Encyclopædia Britannica*.]

Channel Islands. *See* Jersey, Guernsey, etc.

Chapters, The Three. A title given to three doctrinal treatises finally condemned by Fifth Council of Constantinople A.D. 553. [Refer McClintock and Strong. *op. cit.*]

Charlemagne or **Charles I.**, or the great son of Pepin and Bertha; *b.* probably April 2, A.D. 742, *d.* Jan. 28, 814. Crowned Emperor of the West by Romans 800. [Refer H. W. C. Davis, *Charles I., Emperor of the West* (Heroes of the Nations Series), etc., etc.]

Charter, The Great. *See* Magna Charta.

Charterhouse. Corruption of *Chartreuse*. " Carthusian " (*q.v.*) monastery fd. 1371, but when monasteries were dissolved by Henry VIII. it was made a place of deposit for the king's nets and pavilions, until it was granted to the Duke of Norfolk 1539. Purchased by Thomas Sutton, who fd. a school and hospital 1611. School transferred to Godalming, Surrey, 1872. [Refer E. P. E. Wilmot, *Charterhouse Old and New*, 1895.]

Charters of corporate towns, granted by Henry I., give security to industry and promote manufactures 1132; remodelled by Charles II. 1682; the new charter resisted at Nottingham, accepted by Plymouth and other corporations 1684. Ancient charters res. 1698; revised by Royal Commission 1833; altered by Municipal Reform Act 1835.

Chartism. A movement in Great Britain for extension of political power to the working classes, caused by passing of Reform Bill 1832. In 1838 was drawn up by certain representatives of the people the " People's Charter," and riots known as Chartist riots were enacted all over the country. In 1848 the movement came to a head, and was suppressed. [Refer R. G. Gammage, *History of Chartist Movement*, etc., etc.]

Chartres (France). Henry I. of England interviewed Pope Innocent II. at 1131; taken by Count of Dunois 1432; besieged by Duke of Condé 1568. Cathedral, a fire is recorded in the building as early as A.D. 753; extensive rebuilding 1020-8. Towers built 1145-50. [Refer Massé, *The City of Chartres, its Cathedral and Churches*.]

Chasuble. Vestment worn in Church service; restricted to priests only by Council of Toledo A.D. 633; enjoined as the celebrant's robe at Holy Communion by Prayer Book of 1549; prohibited 1552; legalised again 1559. Its use dropped into neglect, but was again revived in 1851. [Refer art. in *Chambers's Encyclopædia*.]

Chatham (England). Dockyard built by Queen Elizabeth 1588; removed to its present position 1662. Surprised by Dutch under De Ruyter 1667. New docks opened, June 21, 1871; additional docks completed 1883; fortifications enlarged 1888.

Chatham Administration. William Pitt, Earl of Chatham, First Minister; succeeded the first Rockingham Administration, Aug. 1766; terminated 1767.

Chatham Chest. Estab. by Queen Elizabeth and her two chief admirals for the relief of aged or wounded seamen; it was removed from Chatham to Greenwich 1803.

Chaucer, Geoffrey. *See* "Canterbury Tales."

Chelsea Hospital or **College** (London) for old disabled soldiers of British army. Foundation stone laid 1682; building by Christopher Wren opened 1692. [Refer *Early History of the Royal Hosp. at Chelsea*, 1872 (official publication).]

Cheltenham (Gloucestershire, England). A priory of Benedictine monks was fd. about 790. Edward the Confessor became lord of the manor and granted a charter in 1041. The Grammar School and almshouses were fd. in 1578 by Richard Pate. Proceedings were taken in parliament against the tobacco plantation owners in 1565. The plantations (which were the first of their kind) were commenced in 1565. In 1658 troops were sent from Gloucester to destroy the plantations. The Cheltenham Waters were first discovered in 1716, and many wells were sunk, and the town estab. as an inland watering-place. Pump-rooms were opened at Montpellier and Pittville in 1809 and 1830 respectively. George III. visited Cheltenham, July 1788, to take the waters. The Cheltenham College was estab. in 1841, followed by the Ladies' College in 1853. The town was incorp. in 1876.

Chemistry. In earlier times known as alchemy; supposed to have been inaugurated in Egypt. Diocletian ordered the destruction of all the works of the alchemists, which were mainly devoted to the transmutation of metals, A.D. 297 [refer Gibbon, *Rome*]. A licence for practising alchemy was granted to Richard Carter in London 1476. Chemistry not a science until the 17th century. In 1772 Dr. Priestley published his discoveries, which commenced a new era in the science. [Refer Von Meyer, *History of Chemistry*, Eng. trans. 1906, etc.]

Cherasco, Treaty of, between Louis XIII. of France and Victor Amadeus, Duke of Savoy, April 6, 1631.

Cherbourg (France). Captured by Henry V. of England, Aug. 1417; retaken by French, Aug. 12, 1450; fortifications destroyed by English, Oct. 1758; occupied by Germans, Dec. 8, 1870.

Chesapeake Bay (U.S.A.). Explored by Capt. John Smith 1607, who arrived there with colonists. British incursions in 1779. Count De Grasse with French fleet arrived at, Aug. 30, 1781.

Blockaded by English. Feb. 5, 1812. [Refer Harper, *Encyclopædia of U.S. History.*]

Chess. Origin of the game lost in obscurity; learnt by the Persians from India. Persians' name for it was *shatranj*. In A.D. 950 an Arabic author, Masudi, spoke of the game as having existed before his time. *The Game and Playe of Chesse*, second book printed by Caxton, appeared 1474. The first important writer on modern C. was the Spaniard, Ruy Lopez de Segura 1561. From Spain the game was probably intro. into England through France at a much earlier date. [Refer Professor Duncan Forbes, *History of Chess*, 1860.]

Chester (England). The *Deva* of the Romans, who were expelled A.D. 476; called by Britons *Caerleon*. Destroyed by Danes 894; rebuilt by Edward the Elder 907; taken by parliamentary forces 1645; castle attacked by Fenians 1867. [Refer Windle, *Chester.*]

Chicago (U.S.A.). First settled 1831; incorp. 1837; almost entirely destroyed by fire, Oct. 7-11, 1871; rebuilt 1872-3. [Refer Harper, *Encyclopædia of U.S. History.*]

Chichester (Sussex, England). Built about A.D. 540 by Cissa. Cathedral completed about 1108; rebuilt 1187. City captured by parliamentarians 1643; fortifications destroyed 1648.

Chile or **Chili** (S. America). Peruvians acquired territory from Indians inhabiting Chile 1450. Discovered by Magellan 1520. Peruvian dominion ceased 1533. Spanish invasion, 1535-6, driven back. Detached from Peru 1568. Treaty of Spain and Chile fixing boundary 1722. Chileans declared independence of Spain, Sept. 18, 1810. Constitution estab. May 22, 1833. War declared against Spain, Sept. 29, 1864. Treaty with Peru against Spain, Jan. 14, 1866. War with Bolivia and Peru, Mar. 1, 1879. Peace treaty with Spain confirmed, Sept. 1881. Peace treaty with Bolivia, Jan. 25, 1882; war resumed, July 1882. Peace with Peru, Oct. 20, 1883. Navy revolted against president, Jan. 7, 1891. Treaty ending territorial dispute of twenty years' standing between Chile and Bolivia signed, Oct. 17, 1904. [Refer to works by Sir Clements R. Markham.]

Chimneys. First intro. into England 1200. Tax on C. called "hearth-money" levied 1662; abolished 1688.

China (Eastern Asia). Invaded by Tartars, who were driven back 936 B.C. Great wall commenced 201 B.C. Confucius supposed to have been *b.* 551 B.C. First Roman Catholic missionaries arrived 1292. Death of Francis Xavier at Macao 1552. Korea (*q.v.*) annexed 1592. Unsuccessful British expedition to C. 1596. English occupied Macao 1808. Admiral Maitland arrived at Macao, July 12, 1838. British declare war 1840. Treaty of Nanking signed between England and C. Aug. 29, 1842. Tai-ping Rebellion, Aug. 1850. War with Great Britain allied with France 1857. Treaty with Great Britain signed at Tien-tsin, June 1858. Peace convention, Oct. 24, 1860 (Lord Elgin and Prince Kung). Emperor of C. issued a manifesto accepting war with Japan, and throwing the blame for bloodshed upon that country, Aug. 2, 1894. Massacre of Chinese at Port Arthur by Japanese, Nov. 21, 1894. Peace treaty ratified between Japan and C. May 8, 1895. Boxer riots 1900. [Refer art. in *Chambers's Encyclopædia*.]

Chinese Labour Question. Proposed introduction of Chinese labour into Transvaal, Jan. 1904; petition in favour of, Jan. 25, 1904. First contingent of Chinese labourers arrived, June 22, 1904. Blue-book on the question issued, Dec. 7, 1905. Debate in House of Lords, Mar. 4-10, 1904. Sir H. Campbell-Bannerman's motion for a vote of censure on the government for allowing Chinese labour rejected, Mar. 21, 1904.

Chinon (France). Geoffrey of Anjou imprisoned in castle of C. 1068-96. Henry II. of England died at, July 6, 1189. Arrival of Joan of Arc at to meet Charles II. Feb. 24, 1429.

Chislehurst (England). Residence of the ex-Emperor Napoleon III. of France from Mar. 20, 1871 to Jan. 9, 1874.

Chlorine. Discovered by Scheele 1774; experiments of Gay Lussac and Thénard 1809; apparatus for making C. invented by Smith 1847.

Chloroform. *See* Anæsthetics.

Christ's College. *See* Cambridge University.

Christiania (Norway). Built by Christian IV. of Denmark 1624.

Christian Knowledge, Society for Promoting. Fd. 1698.

Christian Scientists. The theory of Christian Science was " discovered " by Mrs. Mary Eddy Baker in 1866. The Church of Christ Scientist was estab. in Boston, Mass., in 1879. The Massachusetts Metaphysical College fd. at Boston 1881.

Christ's Hospital (London). The *Blue Coat* School. Fd. 1552 on site of the monastery of the Grey Friars. Charter dated June 26, 1553. Mathematical ward added by Charles II. 1673. First stone of New Hall in London laid, April 28, 1825; opened, May 29, 1829. School moved to West Horsham, May 29, 1902. New buildings for the girls' school at Hertford opened, July 23, 1906. [Refer Pearce, *Annals of Christ's Hospital*.]

Church Discipline Act. Passed Aug. 7, 1840. New bill passed, Mar. 13, 1903; May 13, 1903.

Church of England. *See* England, Church of.

Church of North America. *See* North America, Church of.

Church of Scotland. *See* Scotland, Church of.

Cimbri or **Cumbri.** A gathering of Celtic tribes, in concert with the Gothic Teutons, advanced into Illyrium and defeated the consul, Papirius Carbo, 113 B.C.; repulsed by Drusus in Thrace 112 B.C., are refused an allotment of lands to settle on; defeat the consul, Junius Silanus, ravage the country till they were checked in Thrace by Minucius Rufus 109; were victorious over the consul, Aurelius Scaurus, 108; forced their way into Roman Gaul, where they defeated the consul, C. Manlius, and the pro-consul, Cæpio, 105; invaded Spain 104; driven out by the natives 103; defeated the pro-consul, Lutatius

Catulus; forced a passage into Italy, were totally crushed by Marius at Vercellæ, their league dissolved and annihilated, or rather scattered, 102.

Cincinnati (Ohio, U.S.A.). Major Doughty in 1790 built Fort Washington, around which grew the present town. Incorporated as a city 1814. During invasion of Kentucky at the time of the Civil War, an attempt was made by Gen. Kirby Smith to take C. but he was driven back 1862. [Refer Harper, *Encyclo. of U.S. History,* vol ii.]

Cincinnati, Order of. A society formed by Americans during revolutionary war; formed 1783; called after the Roman Cincinnatus; first general meeting held May 1784. [Refer Bancroft, *History of the U.S.A.* vol. vi.]

Cinque Ports (England). Orig. five in number: Dover, Hastings, Hythe, Romney, and Sandwich; Rye and Winchelsea were added later. Fortified by William I. 1067; Henry III. granted privileges to 1216.

Cintra (Portugal). Convention of, concluded between Sir Hew Dalrymple and Marshal Junot, Aug. 22, 1808. The convention caused great unpopularity, and a court of inquiry was held at Chelsea, Nov. 17, 1808. The decision of Sir Hew Dalrymple was upheld. [Refer *Annual Register,* 1808].

Circuits, Judiciary. Estab. by Northampton Council, Jan. 26, 1176; in Scotland 1712; settled by Order in Council, Feb. 5, 1876; modified, June 10, 1884, and again in Dec. 1887.

Civil List. The revenue awarded to the sovereigns of England. Arrears provided for, Mar. 2, 1769; again paid by a vote of the Commons, April 9, 1777. Sir H. Parnell's motion for inquiry into C. L. causes resignation of the Wellington Ministry, Nov. 15, 1830; select committees appointed to inquire into, Feb. 2, 1860; June 25, 1901.

Civil Rights Bill. Intro. into U.S. Senate, Jan. 29, 1866; passed, Mar. 13, 1866; amended 1875. [Refer Harper, *Encyclo. of U.S. History,* vol. ii.]

Civil War in U.S.A. *See* United States.

Civil Wars in Great Britain:—

    King Stephen and Matilda 1138-53.
    King John and Barons 1214-16.
    Henry III. and Barons 1262-8.
    Edward II. and Barons 1321-27.
    Henry IV. and Owen Glendower 1403-5.
    Wars of the Roses (*q.v.*) 1455-71.
    Richard III. and Henry VII. 1485.
    Charles I. and Parliament 1642-6.
    Charles II. and Parliament 1650-1.
    James II. and Duke of Monmouth 1685.
    James II. and William III. 1689-90.
    George I. and Pretender 1715-16.
    George II. and Young Pretender 1745-6.

E

Clarendon, Constitutions of. Drawn up chiefly by Richard de Lucy at a council at Clarendon, near Salisbury, to limit the power of the clergy, Jan. 25, 1164. Abandoned by Henry II. 1174. [Refer Low and Pulling, *Dicty. of Eng. Hist.*]

Clarendon Press (Oxford). Estab. with profits of Clarendon's *History of the Rebellion*, Oct. 1713. New printing offices erected 1825-30.

Clayton-Bulwer Treaty. Negotiated in April 1850 by John Middleton Clayton of the U.S. and Sir Edward Bulwer of Great Britain. A new convention was signed in Feb. 1900 abrogating the former treaty. Secretary Hay appeared for U.S. and Lord Pauncefote for Great Britain. [Refer Harper, *Encyclo. U.S. History*, vol. ii.]

Clearing-House. Bankers' C.-H. for exchange of drafts and bills set up in Lombard Street in 1775; joined by Bank of England, May 1804. Railway C.-H. established Jan. 2, 1842.

Cleves (Germany). War of Succession in 1609; given to Elector of Brandenburg 1666; seized by French 1757; res. to Germany 1763.

Clocks. Chinese claim invention of B.C. 2000; perfect clock set up in palace of Charles V. of France by De Vick 1379; law of pendulum first applied to clockwork by Huygens about 1657; first manufactured in America by Eli Terry, 1800.

Closure. First used in English Parliament by Speaker, Feb. 24, 1885. Power transferred to House, March 19, 1887.

Cloth of Gold, Field of the. An interview between Henry VIII. of England and Francis I. of France, the former refusing to resign his claim as Maximilian's successor, June 1520, held on a plain between Andres and Guisnes; the magnificence of the decorations, etc., occasioned the above title. [Refer Tanner, *The Renaissance and Reformation*.]

Clubs. First heard of in England during Elizabeth's reign. Shakespeare and his friends met at the Mermaid Tavern. Ben Jonson set up a club at the Devil Tavern. The Kit-Cat instituted 1700; Beef Steak 1735; Johnson's Club 1764; Almack's 1765; Athenæum 1824; Reform 1836; Savage 1857. There are now over 500 clubs in London alone.

Coach. First used in England in middle of 16th century. Bill to prevent men from riding in coach as too effeminate, 1601.

Coal seems to have been used for fuel by ancient Britons, but the first proper notice we have is that it was mined in Newcastle 1233; forbidden to be burnt in England 1273. Nobility and gentry of London petition against use of 1306. Not in general use in England until 1625.

Coalition Ministry. *See* Broad-Bottom.

Coalition of European States against France, generally brought about by British influence:—

1. Great Britain, Austria, and Prussia, 1793.
2. Great Britain, Germany, Russia, Naples, Portugal, and Turkey, 1799.
3. Great Britain, Austria, Naples, and Russia, 1805.
4. Great Britain, Prussia, Russia, and Saxony, 1806.
5. Great Britain and Austria, 1809.
6. Prussia and Russia, 1813.

Cobden Club. Instit. in London, July 21, 1866, to spread and develop the principles of Richard Cobden.

Cock-Fighting. Probably intro. into England by the Romans. Prohibited by Edward III. 1365; by Henry VIII. 1569; by Cromwell 1653; and finally in 1849.

Cock Lane Ghost. A sensation which was caused by the fraudulent representations of William Parsons, his wife, and daughter in 1760 and 1761 at Cock Lane, London. Parsons and his wife were convicted and imprisoned, July 10, 1762. [Refer *Annual Register*.]

Cognac, Treaty of, or **Holy League,** between Francis I. and Italian states, May 22, 1526. [Refer Sismondi, *History of the Italian States*.]

Colchester (England). Orig. *Camulodunum*. First charter 1189. Castle surrendered to Fairfax during Civil War 1648.

Cologne (E. Germany). Originally known as *Col. Agrippina*. Fd. by Empress Agrippina A.D. 50. Diet of C. held by Charlemagne 782. Cathedral fd. by Archbishop Conrad von Hochstade 1248.

Colombia (S. America). Explored by Columbus 1502. Republic formed by uniting New Granada with Venezuela, Dec. 17, 1819. Independence recognised by Great Britain 1825. United States of C. formed 1861; Republic of C. formed 1886. [Refer Petre, *The Republic of Colombia*.]

Colonies (Great Britain). Act passed for their protection 1862; Colonial Naval Defence Act 1865. Colonial Defences Commission, Sept. 1879. Colonial conferences, May 4, 1887; Aug. 1902. The following are the chief colonies, with the dates of their acquisition:—

Aden, 1839	Bengal, 1652
African Forts, 1618	Berbera, 1884
Anguilla, 1666	Berbice, 1803
Antigua, 1632	Bermudas, 1609
Ascension, 1815	Bombay, 1662
Australia, South, 1834	Brit. Burmah, 1862
Australia, West, 1829	Brit. Columbia, 1858
Bahama Islands, 1629	Brunei, 1888
Barbadoes, 1605	Canada, 1760
Basutoland, 1871	Cape Breton, 1763
Bechuanaland, 1885	Cape Coast Castle, 1667

COLONIES—Great Britain (*continued*)—

Cape of Good Hope, 1806
Ceylon, 1815
Cyprus, 1878
Demerara and Essequibo, 1803
Dominica, 1763
Elmina and Dutch Guinea, 1872
Falkland Islands, 1833
Fiji, 1874
Gambia, 1631
Gibraltar, 1704
Gold Coast, 1618
Gozo, 1800
Grenada, 1763
Griqualand, 1871
Guiana, 1803
Heligoland, 1807
Honduras, 1670
Hong-Kong, 1841
Jamaica, 1655
Keeling Islands, 1857
Kermadec Islands, 1886
Labuan, 1846
Lagos, 1861
Leeward Isles, 1763
Madras, 1639
Malacca, 1652
Malta, 1800
Mashonaland, 1890
Matabeleland, 1890
Mauritius, 1810
Montserrat, 1632
Natal, 1823
Nevis, 1628

New Brunswick, 1713
Newfoundland, 1500
New Guinea, 1884
New South Wales, 1787
New Zealand, 1840
Niger districts, 1885
Norfolk Islands, 1787
North Borneo, 1840
Nova Scotia, 1622
Orange Free State, 1901
Pegu, 1852
Port Philip, 1841
Prince Edward Island, 1745
Prince of Wales Island, 1786
Queensland, 1860
St. Christopher's, 1623
St. Helena, 1600
St. Lucia, 1803
St. Vincent, 1763
Sarawak, 1888
Sierra Leone, 1787
Singapore, 1819
Socotra, 1886
Tasmania, 1803
Tobago, 1763
Tortola, 1666
Transvaal, 1901
Trinidad, 1797
Vancouver Island, 1781
Virgin Isles, 1666
Windward Isles, 1803
Zululand, 1886

Colorado (U.S.A.) Organised as a territory, Feb. 28, 1861. Admitted to Union, July 4, 1876. [Refer Harper, *Encyclo. U.S. History*, vol. ii.]

Columbia, British (W. Canada). Under control of Hudson Bay Co. until 1858, when it was made a Crown colony; joined Canadian Confederation, July 26, 1871. [Refer Begg, *History of British Columbia*.]

Columbia University (New York, U.S.A.). Fd. in 1754 as King's College; reincorporated as Columbia College 1784; the title of University was adopted in 1896. [Refer Matthews, *American Universities*.]

Columbus, Christopher. *b*. probably in 1446 (the date is not quite certain), and *d*. May 20, 1506. [Refer Helps, *Voyages of Columbus*.]

Columbus, Voyages of:—

1. Started from Saltes, an island near Palos, Friday, Aug. 3, 1492, returning to the same place on Mar. 15, 1493, after visiting San Salvador, Cuba, Hayti, etc.
2. Started Sept. 24, 1493, returning early in 1496, after visiting the West Indies, etc.
3. Started from Spain in 1498, visiting the South American mainland, and returning in 1499.
4. Started from Spain in 1502, visiting the Gulf of Mexico, and returning in 1504.

Combat, Trial by. *See* Battle, Trial by.

Commerce, Treaties of. The first made by England was with the Flemings 1272.

Committee of Safety. Formed by officers of the army after retirement of Richard Cromwell, Oct. 29, 1659. C. of Public Safety installed at Paris, April 6, 1793 [refer Carlyle, *French Revolution*]; also during American War of Independence, first fd. at Massachusetts 1774. [Refer Harper, *Encyclo. U.S. History*, vol. ii.]

Common Council of London. *See* London.

"Common Penny, The." A literal translation of *Das gemeine Pfennig*, a tax first levied in the Germanic Empire 1471 to raise money for the wars against the Turks; renewed 1496; again by Maximilian in 1512 for the expenses of the Venetian war. [Refer Ranke, *History of Reformation in Germany*, Eng. trans. Austin.]

Common Pleas, Court of. Of extremely ancient origin. Fixed at Westminster by Magna Charta (*q.v.*) 1215. By an Order in Council the Courts of Exchequer and Common Pleas were abolished and amalgamated with Queen's Bench Division, Dec. 16, 1880.

Common Prayer, Book of. In 1537 Archbishop Cranmer devised and recommended *The Institution of a Christian Man*, which was an adaptation of the Sarum Primer. A new edition appeared in 1538. In 1539 a similar work was published by Hilserg, Bishop of Rochester. The compilers of the Book of Common Prayer followed the later book in 1549; revised 1552, 1553; suppressed by Mary, Oct. 1553; res. and revised, June 1559; again published with the XXXIX. Articles (*q.v.*), less one not confirmed 1563; new editions, Mar. 1604, 1625, etc.; use prohibited 1640-60; res. 1660; revised 1662. [Refer Lathbury, *History of the Book of Common Prayer*.]

Commons, House of. " The English Parliament (*q.v.*) in the 14th century consisted of two estates, the clergy and the lords, and a third body which had more the character of a representation of localities " [A. L. Smith, *Dicty. of English History*, 1910]. In the year 1341 the Lower House began to exert its power; called upon to ratify depositions of Edward II. and Richard II. 1376; decided that taxes could only originate with Commons 1407. The Petition of Right (1628) (*q.v.*), and the Bill of Rights, recognising that members were free from imprisonment except for felony (1689) (*q.v.*), gave the House many new privileges. Grand Committees estab. 1882. [Refer art. in *Dicty. of English History* as cited above, also Hallam, *Constitutional History ;* Jennings, *History of the British Parliament*, gives a list of the speakers from 1260-1884.] *See* Parliament, England, etc.

Commonwealth of Australia. *See* Australasia.

Commonwealth of England. *See* England.

Commune of Paris. After insurrection of July 1789, the city council of Paris was known under this name. Constituted May 21, 1791; suppressed July 17, 1794 [refer Carlyle]; again proclaimed Mar. 28, 1871; suppressed May 28, 1871. [Refer Alison, *History of Europe.*]

Compromise League. The members of this league were composed of certain Dutch and Flemish noblemen, who drew up a request to Philip II. of Spain, requesting the latter to cease his persecution of the Netherlands; request drawn up 1566. The request was refused, which led to much trouble. [Refer Motley, *op. cit.*]

Concordats. Treaties regarding ecclesiastical affairs between the Pope, as representing the Church, and a particular temporal sovereign. The following are the principal C. with their dates:—

Of Worms, between the Emperor Henry V. and Pope Callistus II. 1122.

Of Nuremberg, between Electors of Germany and Pope Eugenius IV. 1447.

Of Vienna, between Emperor Frederick IV. and Pope Nicholas V. 1448.

To annul Pragmatic Sanction of Bourges, between Charles V. of Spain and Pope Clement VII. 1526.

To restore Catholic Church in France, between Ferdinand VI. of Spain and Pope Benedict XIV. 1753.

Between Napoleon Bonaparte and Pope Pius VII. July 15, 1801; adopted by legislative body, April 8, 1802; inaugurated in Church of Notre Dame, Paris, April 18, 1802.

For regulation of Catholics in Prussia, between Frederick William III. and Pope Pius VII. July 16, 1821.

Between the Emperor Francis Joseph and Pope Pius IX.; abolished 1868.

Conclave (*see also* Cardinals). The present system of the Papal C. was instit. in 1179 by Pope Alexander III., who decreed " that no election should be valid with a majority of less than two-thirds of the sacred college." The Council of Lyons 1274 (Pope Gregory X.) decreed that the cardinals should be locked up until the election was completed. Pope Pius X. was chosen by the latest conclave, which met July 31, 1903. [Refer A. R. Pennington, *The Papal Conclaves*, etc., etc.]

Confederate States. *See* United States.

Confederation, Articles of. Signed in U.S. July 9, 1778 (*see* U.S.A.). [Refer Harper, *Encyclo. U.S. History*, vol. ii.]

Confederation of the Rhine. Formed by Napoleon Bonaparte in 1806 after he had destroyed the Holy Roman Empire; dissolved in 1813. The Germanic Confederation was constituted in its place 1815. [Refer Alison, *History of Europe*.]

Conference. *See* Hampton Court, Savoy Copyright, etc.

Confessions of Faith. *See* under various creeds, Thirty-Nine Articles.

Congress. *See* United States.

Congress. The term applied to a conference of European sovereigns or of their representatives to consider matters of international interest. The following are amongst the most important:—

Aix-la-Chapelle, Sept. 29—Nov. 22, 1818.
Berlin, June 13—July 13, 1878.
Cambrai 1722-25.
Carlsbad, Aug. 1819.
Chatillon, Feb. 4—Mar. 18, 1814.
Constantinople, Dec. 23, 1876—Jan. 20, 1877.
Ferentino 1223.
Frankfort, Aug. 16-31, 1863.
Paris, Jan.—April, 1856.
Prague, July 5—Aug. 9, 1813.
Rastadt, Dec. 9, 1797—April 8, 1799.
Reichenbach, June 27, 1790.
Soissons, June 1, 1728; transferred to Fontainebleau, Dec. 18, 1728. Terminated by Treaty of Seville, Sept. 28, 1729.
Troppau, Oct. 1820 ; continued at Laybach 1821.
Verona, Aug. 1822.
Vienna, Nov. 1, 1814—June 9, 1815.
See also Alliance, Treaties, etc.

Connecticut (U.S.A.). Granted to Lords Say and Brook 1631. One of the first thirteen United States of America 1774. [Refer Harper, *Encyclo. U.S. History*, vol. ii. etc.]

Conscience, Liberty of. *See* Liberty of Conscience.

Conscription. Jourdan's law of C. was passed in France, Sept. 5, 1798; the Austrian law in 1868; the Russian 1870; the German 1871; Italian 1873. In Canada a law was passed, 1868, by which all males (except in certain professions) were liable to serve in the militia.

Conscription (U.S.A.). James Monroe, Secretary for War, in Oct. 1814 proposed conscription; bill intro. into Congress, Oct. 27, 1814 (*see* Hartford Convention). [Refer Harper, *Encyclo. U.S. History*, vol. ii.]

Conservative. The word was said to have been invented by J. W. Croker, a Tory, in 1830. Macaulay, writing in the *Edinburgh Review*, July 1832, says, " We see that, if M. Dumont had died in 1799, he would have died, to use the new cant word, a decided ' Conservative.' "

Consols. Part of the British National Debt (*q.v.*). Word originated in Consolidated Annuities Act of 1757.

Constance. *See* Councils.

Constantinople. Built on site of ancient Byzantium by Emperor Constantine the Great, and solemnly consecrated A.D. 330; rebuilt by Justinian A.D. 532; capital of Eastern Empire until May 29, 1453, when it was captured by the Turks. [Refer Gibbon, *Rome,* etc.] *See* Turkey, Councils.

Continental System. The name given to the method devised by Napoleon Bonaparte for cutting off connection between England and the Continent. Begun with Berlin Decrees issued Nov. 21, 1806. England retorted with an Order in Council, Jan. 7, 1807; overthrown 1812-13. [Refer Alison, *History of Europe.*]

Conventicle Act. First passed Elizabeth's reign 1593; revised by Charles II. May 17, 1664; repealed by Act of Toleration 1689 (*q.v.*).

Convention Parliaments. English parliaments convened without royal authority. There are two well known in English history: (1) April 25, 1660, on the restoration of Charles II.; (2) Feb. 13, 1690, on the accession of William III. and Mary.

Convocation. An assembly of bishops and clergy of the Anglican Church, first called by Edward I. 1295; practically suspended 1717–1840; revived, Feb. 4, 1852.

Cook, Capt. James (1728-79). Voyages: (1) Aug. 6, 1768—July 13, 1771, to discover transit of Venus in the Pacific; visited Tahiti, New Zealand, E. Australia, Java, Cape of Good Hope; (2) April 9, 1772—July 31, 1775, visited Antarctic, cruised S. Pacific, visited Tahiti and New Hebrides, discovered New Caledonia; (3) July 12, 1776—Feb. 14, 1779, to discover N.W. passage to India, visited W. coast of America and Sandwich Islands where murdered by natives of Owhyhee. [Refer *Cook's Voyages.*]

Copenhagen (S. Denmark). Built by Waldemar I., King of Denmark, 1157; surrendered to Christian I. of Norway 1479; to Christian III. 1536; besieged by Charles Gustavus, King of Sweden, 1658; destruction of Danish fleet off, by Nelson and Parker, April 2, 1801; besieged and taken by English, Sept. 5, 1807.

Copyright (Great Britain). In 1547 Edward VI. appointed a printer, by royal letters patent, who had the sole right of producing various books. In 1534 Henry VIII. granted rights to the Cambridge University to print and put to sale *omnes et omnimodos libros,* approved by certain heads of the University. In 1637 the Star Chamber issued decrees relating to book licensing. In Jan. 1642 an order was passed that no book could be reprinted without the consent of the author. The Stationers' Company in 1681 and 1694 passed two bye-laws respecting the copyright of books. The first real statute regarding copyright was intro. into the Commons on Jan. 11, 1709. The act came into force on April 10, 1710, and by it booksellers had the sole right of printing old books which they had acquired for a term of 21 years after April 10, 1710, and no longer; new books for 14 years from date of publication. From 1769 till 1774 perpetual copyright was the law of England. Prints and engravings protected 1777. In 1814 an author's book was copyright for 28 years and the remainder of the author's life, if still living. The present law regarding copyright was passed 1842; it states that copyright of books endures for life of author, and 7 years afterwards; if this term expires within 42 years after publication the copyright is extended to 42 years; copy of every book must be deposited in British Museum. Rt. Hon. Sydney Buxton introduced bill to extend period to 50 years, July 26, 1910; second reading April 7, 1911; abolition of registration proposed by committee. In Germany the period is author's life and 30 years, or not less than 10 years, by act of 1901; in Greece, 15 years from publication; Holland, 50 years or life, whichever is longer; Hungary, life and 50 years, by law of 1884; Italy, life or 40 years from publication; Norway in 1893, Portugal, Russia, Sweden, and Denmark, life and 50 years; Switzerland, life and 30 years; Spain, life and 80 years; Turkey, life or 40 years, whichever is longer. [Refer Birrell, *Seven Lectures on Copyright*, 1899, and art. in *Ency. Brit.*]

Copyright (International). International Copyright Laws passed in House of Commons 1838 and 1852; in American Congress 1891. Congress at Berne 1884. Convention at Berne, Sept. 1886; ratified, Sept. 1887. Congresses at Berne, Aug. 22, 1896; Aug. 8, 1901. [Refer Birrell, *op. cit.*]

Copyright (U.S.A.). Dr. David Ramsay of South Carolina petitioned the Congress to grant him protective rights for his two books, April 5, 1789. Bill was passed 1790. In 1831 a general copyright bill was passed granting sole rights for 28 years and power to renew for another 14 years. All former laws repealed by general act of 1870; amended in 1874. Bill passed to grant 28 years after publication, and at expiration of period another 28 years to author or his heirs, came into force July 1909.

Copyright League, American. Formed to bring about International Copyright (*q.v.*) 1883. [Refer Harper, *Encyclopædia U.S. History*, vol. ii.]

Cordeliers. (1) A monastic order fd. about 1223. (2) A party formed during French Revolution 1790; many of its members were executed, Mar. 24, 1794. [Refer Carlyle, *French Revolution*.]

Cordova or **Cordoba** (Spain). Fd. by the Consul Marcellus 152 B.C. Taken by the Goths A.D. 572; conquered by Spain 1236; captured by French 1808; abandoned 1813; plundered by Carlists, 1836.

Corea. *See* Korea.

Corfu (Island N.W. of Greece). Attacked by Bohemond A.D. 1081; by Roger, King of Sicily, 1146; recovered by Venetians 1148; attacked by Turks 1537, 1716; taken from French by Turks and Russians 1799; university suppressed 1864.

Corinth (Greece). Said to have been fd. by Sisyphus about 1350 B.C. Wars with Athens 458; united with Thebes, Athens, and Argos against Sparta 395; destroyed by the Romans 146; rebuilt by Julius Cæsar 46; attacked by Alaric A.D 396; captured by the Franks 1205; by the Turks 1459; held by the Venetians 1699-1715; by the Turks 1715-1822; destroyed by earthquake, Feb. 1858. [Refer Smith, *Classical Dictionary* (Everyman's Lib.).]

Cork (Ireland). Perkin Warbeck landed at, 1492; taken by Cromwell 1649; taken from the partisans of James II. Sept 21, 1690.

Corn Laws. Passed to relieve scarcity in England of corn 1757. Embargo on exportation 1766. Mr. Robinson's act allowing importation when wheat rose to 80s. quarter, 1815, caused riots. Duties regulated by a " sliding scale " act 1828 (*see* Anti-Corn Law League); agitations against it begun 1841. New " sliding scale " intro. 1842; suspended 1847. Corn Importation Bill, June 6, 1846; repealed June 24, 1869. Duty on corn and flour 1902; repealed 1903.

Coronation Oath settled in new form for William and Mary 1689; modified 1706, 1821, 1910.

Coronation Stone removed from Scone in Scotland; placed in Westminster Abbey 1296.

Corporation Acts (Great Britain). Passed Dec. 20 1661; rigorously enforced 1662; repealed 1828. Corporation Reform Act 1835; amended 1869. Corrupt Practices (Municipal Elections) Act passed, Aug. 6, 1872; Aug. 14, 1884.

Corsica (Mediterranean). Independent republic 1735; a kingdom 1736; reduced by the French 1739; ceded to France 1768; under British dominion, June 8, 1794; insurrection at, June 8, 1796; abandoned by British, Aug. 22, 1796; reoccupied by French, Oct. 22, 1796. [Refer Caird, *History of Corsica*.]

Cortes. *See* Spain.

Corunna. *See* Battles.

Corvee, or forced labour. Unsuccessful attempt of Emperor Joseph II. to relieve the peasantry from 1775; abolished in France by the Convention 1792; abolished in Egypt 1889.

Cossacks. First enter Russia 1444; take Azov from the Turks 1637; defeated at Choczim by John Sobiesky 1673; treaty with Charles XII. of Sweden 1707. [Refer Mackenzie Wallace, *Russia*, 1877.]

Costa Rica (Central America). Discovered by Columbus 1493; first settlements in 1502; declared its independence 1821; boundary dispute with Colombia settled 1900. [Refer Calvo, *Republic of Costa Rica*.]

Cotton. Intro. by the followers of Mahomet into Europe; used in Arabia in A.D. 627. C. was manufactured in Spain in 10th century, in Italy in 14th, in England in 17th, Bombay in 19th century.

Cottonian Library. Fd. by Sir R. Bruce Cotton (1570-1631). In 1730 placed in Ashburnham House, Westminster, where partly burnt; removed to British Museum in 1757. [Refer Edwards, *Memoirs of Libraries*.]

Council. From the three councils of King Alfred sprang our cabinet, privy council, and parliament. Alfred's C. instituted about 886.

Councils of the Church. The four general C. recognised by all churches are those of: Nicæa 325; Constantinople 381; Ephesus 431; and Chalcedon 451. The Greek Church recognises three others in addition: Constantinople (2nd) 553; Constantinople (3rd) 680-1; Nicæa (2nd) 787. The Church of Rome in addition to these another eleven: Constantinople (4th) 869-70; Lateran (1st) 1123; Lateran (2nd) 1139; Lateran (3rd) 1179; Lateran (4th) 1215; Lyons (1st) 1245; Lyons (2nd) 1274; Vienne 1311-12; Florence 1439; Lateran (5th) 1512; Trent 1545-63. The French divines substitute for Lyons, Florence, and Lateran (5th) those of Pisa (1409), Constance (1414-18), and Basel (1431-43). [Refer Gieseler, *Compendium of Eccl. History*, etc., etc.]

Counter-Reformation. The upheaval caused by the preachings of the Reformers caused the Roman Church to examine her own condition, and the reaction which occurred is called the Counter-Reformation. The first definite move in the direction of reform was the organisation of a society called the "Oratory of Divine Love" 1513-21. The Franciscans in 1526 reformed their order, and on Sept. 27, 1540, the order of the Jesuits (*q.v.*) was formally fd. On July 21, 1541, a papal bull set up the Holy Office of the Universal Church, the Inquisition as it was known. These and many other influences caused the Counter-Reformation, and the Council of Trent, Dec. 13, 1545—Dec. 3, 1563, confirmed most of the reforms. [Refer Ward, *The Counter-Reformation*; Tanner, *Reformation and Renaissance*, etc., etc.]. *See* Reformation, Jesuits, Inquisition, etc.

County Courts as now known instit. Aug. 26, 1846. Acts regarding amendment 1875, 1887, 1888.

Court. *See* Chancery, Common Pleas, Session, etc.

Court-Martial regulated by Mutiny Act 1690. *See* Army.

Covenant. *See* Solemn League and Covenant.

Covenanters. Supporters of the Solemn League and Covenant (*q.v.*), assisted with money by Richelieu, raised an army in 1639; negotiated with Charles I. 1640; defeated by Graham of Claverhouse at Drumclog, June 1, 1679, and by the Duke of Monmouth at Bothwell Bridge, June 22, 1679.

Coventry (England). Scene of the legend of Lady Godiva about 1052-7. Mary Queen of Scots at 1569; refused admittance to Charles I. Aug. 20, 1642; walls destroyed by Royalists 1662.

Cracow (Austria). Fd. by Krak, King of Poland, A.D. 760; university estab. 1347; capital of Poland 1320-1609; taken by Charles XII. of Sweden 1702 [refer Voltaire, *Charles XII*.]; by Russians 1768; added to Austria 1795; a republic 1815; finally united to Austria 1846.

" Cradle of American Liberty." Name given to Faneuil Hall, Boston (U.S.A.), the meeting-place of the patriots during the troubles with Great Britain before the revolution; erected 1742; burned and rebuilt 1761. [Refer Harper, *Encyclo. U.S. History*, vol. ii.]

Cranmer, Thomas. *See* Bible.

Cressy or **Crecy.** *See* Battles.

Creeds. *See* Apostles', Athanasian, and Nicene.

Cremona (Italy). Fd. by Romans 221 B.C.; acquired by Venetians 1499; part of the Italian Kingdom 1859.

Crespy or **Crespi** (France). Treaty between Francis I. of France and the Emperor Charles V. signed here, Sept. 1544 [refer Miss Tanner, *Renaissance and Reformation*, for the full terms of this treaty, which is an important factor in the history of the Reformation (*q.v.*)].

Crete or **Candia** (Mediterranean island). Greeks expelled from Carthage by Hassan retire to C. A.D. 698; Saracens seize and build town 822; recovered by Greeks 960; sold to Venetians 1205; besieged and finally taken by Turks 1645-69; various attempts to throw off Turkish yoke, especially 1866-9; Turkey accepted the powers' ultimatum in 1898 and withdrew its army; palace of Minos and " Labyrinth " discovered at Knossos 1899; union with Greece 1908.

Cricket. Development of " club ball " of mediæval times; first mentioned under present name 1598; first club formed 1750.

Crimea (Black Sea). Taken by Russia from Turks 1784; war declared against Russia by England and France, March 28, 1854; allied armies landed, 1854; war concluded, April 1856. *See* Alma, Balaklava, Inkermann, Sebastopol, under Battles. [Refer Kinglake, *History of the Invasion of the Crimea*.]

Criminal Laws of England. Committee formed to inquire into their severity, Mar. 2, 1819; bills to mitigate, May 9, 1820; reformed by Peel's acts 1826-8; Criminal Law Amendment Act (relating to females), Aug. 14, 1885; Criminal Aliens Bill, Aug. 1905; Criminal Appeal 1907; Habitual Criminals Act 1909.

Crofters. Small land holders in Scotland. Royal Commission appointed to inquire into condition of, Mar. 22, 1883—April 28, 1884; act for their benefit passed, June 25, 1886; amended 1888.

Cronstadt or **Cronstot** (Russia). Fd. by Peter the Great 1710; C. Canal 1884.

Crown Pieces. The gold crown was first struck by Henry VIII. (1509-47). The first silver crown was struck by Edward VI. (1547-53). The half-crown originated with Edward VI. [Refer Roth, art. on the " English Coinage " in *A Literary and Historical Atlas of Europe* (Everyman's Lib.).]

Crusades. After the capture of Jerusalem by the Turk, Togul Beg, in 1076, the pilgrims to the Holy City were robbed and ill-treated, but it was not until 1095 that Pope Urban II. was roused by the preachings of Peter the Hermit to consider a crusade. In November 1095 the Council of Clermont invoked Western Europe to defend the Holy Land. The following are the eight great C. :—

First. 1096. (a) Led by Walter the Penniless, a Burgundian, (b) by Peter the Hermit, (c) by Godeschal, a German monk. These were disorganised bands and met with failure. The military C. of 1096 divides itself into four sections: (a) That led by Godfrey de Bouillon from the Rhine and N. Germany; (b) by Hugh, Comte de Vermandois, and others from Central France, Normandy, and Britain; (c) by Prince Bohemond of Tarento from Italy; (d) by Raymond, Comte de Toulouse, from Provence, Spain, and Lombardy. Nicæa was captured on June 20, 1097, and in the same year the Sultan Solyman was defeated at Dorylæum. Antioch was taken, June 3, 1098. Jerusalem was taken, July 15, 1099; and Godfrey de Bouillon elected king on July 23, 1099. B. of Ascalon, Aug. 12, 1099. Acre (q.v.) reduced 1104.

Second. By Louis VII. of France and the Emperor Conrad VII. 1146. Damascus attacked 1149. Jerusalem seized by Saladin 1187.

Third. Commenced by siege of Acre (q.v.) 1189. The Emperor Frederick Barbarossa led an army to Cilicia 1190. Arrival of Richard I. of England and Philippe Auguste 1191. Richard won b. of Azotus, and captured Jaffa and Cæsarea 1191. Jerusalem reached 1192. A truce proclaimed.

Fourth. Set in motion by Pope Innocent III. in 1200. Led by Boniface of Montserrat and the Counts of Flanders and Blois. Constantinople besieged 1203-5.

Fifth. To assist John of Brienne, titular King of Jerusalem, against the Sultan Saphadin, the successor of Saladin, 1216. Led by Louis of Hungary, the Duke of Austria, the Earl of Salisbury, etc. Damietta captured by the English 1219. The Emperor Frederick II. obtained a ten years' treaty, including free access to the Holy City, 1228.

Sixth. Christians driven out of Jerusalem 1238, caused two distinct C. together known as the Sixth. (a) French knights led by Thibaud of Champagne and the Comte de Bretagne; (b) arranged at Council of Northampton, led by Richard, Earl of Cornwall, which in 1240 arranged a treaty similar to that of the Fifth C.

Seventh. Proclaimed by the Council of Lyons 1245. Led by Louis IX. (St. Louis) of France. William Longsword of Salisbury and others set out from Cyprus 1248. Louis taken prisoner at the B. of Mansurah 1250.

CRUSADES (*continued*)—

> Eighth. Proclaimed by Pope Clement IV. 1270. Led by Louis IX.
> of France and Prince Edward of England. Louis IX. died
> at Carthage, Aug. 2, 1270. Jerusalem destroyed 1291, and
> Christians driven out.

[Refer De Joinville, *History of the Crusades* (contemporary); Cox,
History of the Crusades, etc.]

Crystal Palace (*see* Hyde Park). It was re-erected at Sydenham,
Aug. 5, 1852; opened by Queen Victoria, June 10, 1854.

Cuba (West Indies). Discovered by Columbus, Oct. 28, 1492; occupied by Spaniards 1511; Havana fortified 1584; insurrections of
slaves 1844 and 1848; Lopez's expedition against 1851; revolt for
expulsion of Spaniards 1868-71; frequent other revolts all suppressed; occupied by U.S. after Spanish-American War 1898-1901,
when it became a republic; Gomez insurrection 1906; Mr. Taft of
U.S.A. proclaimed provisional governor, Sept. 1906; evacuation of
U.S. troops 1908.

Culloden, Battle of (Inverness). Known as B. of Drummossie by
Highlanders. Young Pretender defeated, with loss of 2500 men,
April 16, 1746. Young Pretender escaped, although £30,000 was
offered for his capture.

Curfew Bell. Intro. into England by William the Conqueror
1068.

Customs. Granted to the Crown in 1274. Commissioners appointed 1671; consolidation of C. Feb. 26, 1787. C. Duties Bill
(Sir R. Peel's), June 26, 1846. Custom House, London, fd. 1559;
rebuilt 1718; new (the present) building, May 12, 1817.

Cycle. Four-wheeled velocipede invented in France by Blanchard and Magurier in 1779; pedals applied to a tricycle by a
Dumfriesshire blacksmith, McMillan, 1834; rubber tyres for iron
1868; bicycles made in England by Coventry Sewing Machine Co.
1869; improved by J. K. Starley 1874; Starley's "Rover" with
nearly equal wheels 1885. First C. club in world, Pickwick Bicycle
Club, fd. in London 1870; Cyclists' Touring Club 1878. Cycles
first manufactured in America by A. A. Pope 1878. [Refer art.
Ency. Brit.]

Cyprus (Mediterranean). Seized by Richard I. of England 1192;
conquered by Turks 1570-1; ceded to Great Britain by Anglo-
Turkish Convention, June 4, 1878. [Refer General di Cesnola,
Cyprus, its Ancient Cities, Tombs, and Temples.]

D

Dacia. A Roman province, including Moldavia, Galacia, etc. Conquered by Trajan A.D. 101-7; Aurelian withdrew Roman forces and left D. to the Goths; another province of same name formed S. of Danube 207; added to dominions of Eastern Empire by Gratian A.D. 379. [Refer Gibbon, *Rome*, etc.]

Daghestan or **Daghistan** (Asia). Conquered by Peter the Great 1723; res. to Persia by Empress Anne 1735; re-annexed to Russia 1813.

Dahomey (Africa). Coast blockaded by Great Britain 1876; French expedition to 1892; became a French protectorate 1894.

"Daily Courant." *See* Newspapers.

Dakota, North and **South** (U.S.A.). *See* North Dakota and South Dakota.

Dalmatia (Austria). Subdued by Statilus Taurus 23 B.C. and by Tiberius A.D. 9. The Emperor Diocletian *b.* at Salona in D. 245; *d.* there 313. Occupied by Marcellinus 461; conquered by Coloman, King of Hungary, between 1098 and 1102 [refer Gibbon, *Rome*, etc.]; in Venetians' power 1117-1358; became an independent kingdom 1382; res. to Venice 1573 [refer Sismondi, *Hist. of Italian Republics*]; ceded to Austria 1797; Napoleon made D. part of the kingdom of Italy 1805; finally ceded to Austria 1814. [Refer Jackson, *Dalmatia*, etc.]

Damascus (Syria). Conquered by Tiglathpileser, King of Assyria, 738 B.C.; unsuccessfully besieged by the Christians 1148; conquered by Timour 1401; by Ibrahim Pasha 1832.

Damnatory Clauses. *See* Athanasian Creed.

Danegelt or **Danegild** (Dane Money). A tax levied by Ethelred II. (*the Unready*) to raise a tribute to buy off the Danes A.D. 991. It long survived the purpose for which it was levied; abolished 1052. [Refer Freeman, *Norman Conquest*, vol. iv. etc.]

Danes or **Northmen.** Inhabited Scandinavian kingdoms of Denmark, Norway, and Sweden (*q.v.*). The *Saxon Chronicle* dates their first appearance in England in A.D. 787. In 835 they were defeated at Hengsdown Hill in Cornwall by King Egbert. Between 866 and 871 they made great inroads into England, and gained large territories. Treaty of Wedmore between the D. and Alfred the Great 882; the latter defeated them 897. Canute the Dane landed in England 1015, and in 1016 was acknowledged King of England (*see* England), and until 1042 England was under Danish kings. Defeated by Harold II. at Stamford Bridge, Sept. 25, 1066. Futile attempt to invade England 1074. [Refer Worsaae, *Danes and Norwegians in England and Ireland*.] *See* Denmark.

Dantzic (Germany). Occupied by Teutonic knights 1308; re-conquered by Poland 1455; place of refuge of Charles VIII. when driven from Sweden 1457; incorp. with Poland by Treaty of Thorn 1466; seized by Russians and Saxons, June 29, 1734; ceded to Prussia 1793; surrendered to Napoleon, May 26, 1807; res. to Prussia 1814.

Danube, River (Germany). Navigation set free by Treaty of Paris 1856; navigation regulated by Berlin Treaty, July 13, 1878; treaty restoring rights to Russia 1883; Tron Gates Canal opened 1898; International Commission for regulating navigation 1904.

Danubian Principalities, The. Moldavia and Wallachia formed into independent states by Convention of Paris, Aug. 19, 1858; united under title of Roumania (q.v.), Dec. 23, 1861.

Dardanelles (S.E. Turkey). Passage forced by Sir John Duckworth, Feb. 19, 1807; repassed, Mar. 1, 1807; Treaty of signed in London after conclusion of Syrian War 1841; British and French fleets enter by the Sultan's invitation, Oct. 8, 1853.

Darien Scheme, The. An attempt to colonise the Isthmus of D. (Central America). The scheme was agitated by Paterson, the founder of the Bank of England, in 1694. Parliament voted supplies, and the expedition sailed on July 26, 1698; arrived after many difficulties at D. Oct. 30, 1698; left there June 18, 1699, owing to opposition by the Spaniards, and only a few out of those who started arrived back in Scotland on Nov. 13, 1699. In 1715 the sufferers of the scheme received compensation. [Refer Macaulay, *History of England*.]

Dark Ages. Period lasting from A.D. 500 to about end of the 15th century. [Refer Hallam's *View of the State of Europe during the Middle Ages*.]

Dartford (Kent, England). Wat Tyler's insurrection started here 1381. The first paper mill in England is said to have been erected here in 1590.

Dartmoor Prison (S. Devon). Fd. Mar. 1806 for the reception of French prisoners of war. It fell into disuse after the war, but was reorganised in 1855 as a convict prison.

Dartmouth (Devonshire, England). The rendezvous of the fleet destined for the Holy Land 1190 (*see* Crusades). French pirates repulsed at D. after burning Plymouth 1404; taken after a four weeks' siege by Prince Maurice 1643; retaken by Gen. Fairfax 1646. [Refer Lewis, *Topographical Dicty. of England*, vol. ii.]

Dartmouth College (New Hampshire, U.S.A.). Chartered 1769. [Refer Harper, *Encyclo. U.S. History*, vol. iii.]

Darwinism. Charles Darwin's (1809-82) theory, the origin of plants and animals, set forth in his works, *On the Origin of Species by Means of Natural Selection*, published in 1859, and *The Descent of Man*, 1871, new ed. 1874.

Dauphin. Eldest son of the King of France. The title was granted as a condition when Dauphiné was ceded to the King of France in 1343. The first D. was Charles (afterwards Charles V. of France) in 1349. The last D. was Louis Antoine, Duke of Angoulême, son of Charles X., who assumed the title on Sept. 16, 1824.

Davy Safety Lamp for miners, invented by Sir Humphrey Davy (1779-1829) in 1816.

Day of Dupes, Nov. 11, 1603, on which Marie de Medici and Anne of Austria were outwitted by Cardinal Richelieu. [Refer Guizot, *History of France.*]

Deal (England). Perkin Warbeck attempted to land at, July 3, 1495. [Refer Chapman, *Deal, Past and Present.*]

Debt, National. *See* National Debt.

Decalogue (Ten Commandments). Intro. into Anglican Liturgy 1552.

Deccan (India). Invaded by Mahometans 1294; greater portion of ceded to Great Britain 1818.

Deceased Wife's Sister, Marriage with. The bill making this legal was first intro. into parliament in 1841, and again in 1847, 1853, 1857, 1859, 1866, 1868, 1874. It passed the Commons in 1882, but was thrown out by the Lords, and the same happened in 1883; dropped by both Houses 1884; again dropped by Lords 1885-6, 1893. In 1896 it was carried in the Lords, but went no further. It finally became law in 1907.

" Decet Romanum Pontificum " Bull. A bull of Pope Leo X. 1512, urging the princes of Germany to condemn Martin Luther without being heard. [Refer Ranke, *History of the Reformation in Germany.*]

Declaration of Independence. *See* U.S.A.

Declaration of Indulgence. There are three acts so called : (1) By Charles II. in 1672, by which all acts against the Nonconformists and Roman Catholics were suspended; this was withdrawn and the Test Act (*q.v.*) passed 1673. (2) By James II. in 1687, similar to the above. (3) By James II. in 1688, which was commanded to be read in the churches (*see* Trial of the Seven Bishops). *See also* Nonconformists.

Declaration of (Colonial) Rights (America). Passed by first American Congress which met at Carpenter's Hall, Philadelphia, Sept. 1774.

Declaration of Rights (English). The foundation of the Bill of R. (*q.v.*) declared amongst other things William and Mary King and Queen of England; passed 1689.

Declaration of Rights (Irish). Drawn up by Grattan, a member of the Irish Parliament, demanding legislative independence for Ireland; accepted by Irish Parliament, April 1782, and practically confirmed by the English Parliament in the same year. *See* Ireland.

Declaration of Rights by Virginia (U.S.A.). Drafted by George Mason, and presented on May 27, 1776; adopted on the following June 12. [Refer Harper, *Encyclo. U.S. History*, vol. iii.]

Decretals. Collection of papal decrees or decretal letters; part of Canon Law. First collection made by Dionysius Exiguus about A.D. 550; word generally applied to the compilation of Gratian in 12th century; first official collection 1210. What is known as the *False Decretals* were supposed to have been written between 425 and 450, but had no existence until 835-45.

Defence Act. *See* Conscription.

Defender of the Faith (*Fidei Defensor*). A title conferred on Henry VIII. of England by a bull of Pope Leo X. Oct. 11, 1521, in recognition of the former's tract against Luther entitled, " On the Seven Sacraments, against Martin Luther, the Heresiarch, by the Illustrious Prince Henry VIII." [Refer Lingard, *History of England*.]

De Heretico Comburendo. *See* Lollards.

Delaware (U.S.A.). Takes its name from Lord De la Warr, who entered D. Bay 1610. Declared an independent state 1776. [Refer Harper, *Encyclopædia U.S. Hist.* vol. iii.]

Delegates, Court of (Great Britain). Estab. by Henry VIII. in 1534; abolished 1832. [Refer Benham, *Dicty. of Religion*, etc.]

Delft (Holland). Fd. by Godfrey le Bossu 1074. The famous earthenware first manufactured here about 1310. Diet of D. agreed to throw off allegiance of King of Spain 1575. Estates of Holland and Zeeland assembled in congress at D. and signed a new Act of Union, April 25, 1576. Assembly of United Provinces arranged Constitution, Jan. 13, 1581. William the Silent assassinated at, July 10, 1884. [Refer Motley, *op. cit.*]

Delhi (India). Taken by Timour 1399; by Nadir Shah 1739; possessed by Great Britain 1803. During Indian Mutiny seized by Sepoys, who massacred the British there 1857; recaptured, Sept. 20, 1857. Prince of Wales (Edward VII.) visited D. Jan. 11, 1876. Queen Victoria proclaimed Empress of India, Jan. 1, 1877. [Refer Mill, *History of India*.] *See* India.

Delphin Classics. Collection of Latin authors in 60 volumes, prepared for Louis XIV.'s son by his tutor, the Bishop of Avranches; published 1674-91.

Deluge. Story of, in most mythologies, especially Babylonish. The date of D. predicted by Noah variously given from that of Septuagint 3246 B.C., to that of Hebrew 2288.

Demerara (British Guiana). Surrendered to British 1781; again taken by Gen. White, April 22, 1796; res. to Dutch, Mar. 1802; recaptured by British, Sept. 25, 1803; ceded to Great Britain by Dutch 1814.

Dendermonde (Holland). Famous interview between William the Silent, Counts Horn, Egmont, Hoogstraaten, and Louis, regarding legislative affairs held 1566. [Refer Motley, *op. cit.*]

Denmark (Europe). *See* Danes. Denmark, Norway, and Sweden united by Union of Calmar, July 12, 1397; Sweden independent 1523; Norway annexed to Sweden by Treaty of Kiel (*q.v.*), Jan. 14, 1814; after a disastrous war, Schleswig and Holstein were placed under Prussian and Austrian administration 1864, and finally ceded to Prussia by Treaty of Prague 1866.

Deodand. An expiatory offering. Formerly anything which had been the immediate cause of the death of a human being was forfeited to the Crown to be sold for pious purposes; abolished 1846.

Departments. France first divided into 83, 1790. *See* France.

Deposition, Bulls of (against England). (1) Issued by Pope Paul III. 1535, excommunicating and deposing Henry VIII. (2) By Pope Pius V. in 1569 against Elizabeth.

Deputies, Chamber of. French legislative assembly so named under Louis XVIII. 1814; dissolved by Charles X. 1827, and May 16, 1830; superseded by National Assembly, May 4, 1848; res. by Louis Napoleon, Dec. 2, 1851. After Jan. 1852 it was known as the " Corps Legislatif."

Derby (England). Colony fd. by Alfred the Great 880. Occupied by the Young Pretender 1745. First silk mill erected at 1718. [Refer Lewis, *Topographical Dicty. of England*, etc.]

Derby Administrations (Earl of Derby, First Lord). (1) After resignation of Lord John Russell, Feb. 27, 1852—Dec. 17, 1852, succeeded by Aberdeen Administration (*q.v.*). (2) Feb. 25, 1858—June 11, 1859, succeeded by Palmerston-Russell Administration (*q.v.*). (3) July 6, 1866—Feb. 25, 1868, when the Earl of Derby resigned, and Mr. Benjamin Disraeli (*q.v.*) reconstructed the party. [Refer *Letters of Queen Victoria.*]

Despard's Plot. Headed by Colonel D. to assassinate George III. 1802. The plotters were executed on Feb. 21, 1803. [Refer *Annual Register.*]

Detroit (U.S.A.). First settled by Antoine Cadillac, July 24, 1701. Originally called *La Ville d' Etroit.* Surrendered to English, Nov. 29, 1700; besieged by Pontiac, May 1763; relieved May 1764; surrendered to Gen. Brock, Aug. 16, 1812. [Refer Harper, *Encyclo. U.S. Hist.* vol. iii.]

Deventer (Holland). Captured by Maurice of Saxony from the Spaniards, June 10, 1591.

Devil's Parliament. Summoned by Henry VI. at Coventry 1459.

Devonport. *See* Plymouth.

Diamond. Manilius spoke of it A.D. 16; Pliny said it was known only to kings, A.D. 100, and described six varieties. Mined in India from earliest times till close of 19th century; S. America from middle of 18th century; S. Africa nearly all transferred, 1870. Phosphorescence produced by friction discovered by Robert Boyle 1663; combustibility established experimentally by Florentine Academicians 1694. Koh-i-nor in possession of Nadir Shah 1739, given by East India Co. to Queen Victoria 1850; Cullinan D. found in Premier Mine in Transvaal 1905, and presented by Transvaal Government to Edward VII. 1907.

Diamond Necklace Affair in France. Queen Marie Antoinette, the countess de la Motte, the impostor Cagliostro, and the Cardinal Rohan were implicated 1785; De Rohan's trial, April 14, 1786. The countess was tried, condemned, but escaped; De Rohan was acquitted. [Refer Carlyle, *Essay*.]

Dictionary. A Chinese D. by Hü Shin, containing 10,000 characters, published 150 B.C.; Italian D. of the Accademia della Crusca published 1612; Samuel Johnson's D. in 1755; Noah Webster's 1806; Sir Wm. Smith's *D. of Greek and Roman Antiquities* 1842, *Biography* 1849, *Geography* 1857; Liddell and Scott's 1843; *Dict. of Nat. Biog.*, ed. by Sidney Lee, 1885–1900; Funk's 1893-5; Murray's (unfinished) commenced 1879.

" Dietes or Sayengis of the Philosophres." Translated from the French by Earl Rivers, a friend and patron of Caxton; was the first dated book printed in England; completed on Nov. 18, 1477, by Caxton. [Refer Gordon Duff, *Printers, Stationers, and Bookbinders of Westminster and London from* 1476-1535.] *See* Printing.

Dieppe (France). Bombarded three times by British fleet: (1) July 1694, (2) 1794, (3) Sept. 14, 1803.

Diet. The following are the principal D. with their dates:—
    Augsburg, (*a*) 1530; (*b*) Sept. 26, 1555.
    La Magione, 1502.
    Roncaglia, Nov. 12, 1158.
    Spire or Speyer, (*a*) 1526; (*b*) 1529.
    Worms, (*a*) 1495; (*b*) 1521 (associated with Martin Luther); (*c*) 1547; (*d*) 1578.

" Dieu et mon Droit " (" God and my Right "). The parole of the day at the battle of Gisors, Sept. 20, 1198, at which Richard I. was present. It first appeared on the Great Seal of Henry VI.; discontinued by Queen Anne, but res. by George I.

Dijon (France). Roman *Divio*. Becomes capital of the Duchy of Burgundy 1180; joined to French Crown 1477; capitulated to Germans, Oct. 1870.

Directors Liability Act (Great Britain). Passed Aug. 18, 1890.

Directory, French. The government estab. in France after Robespierre's death in July 1794; abolished 1799. [Refer Carlyle, *French Rev.*]

"Directory for the Public Worship of God." Drawn up by the Westminster Assembly (*q.v.*) in 1644; ratified by the Scottish Parliament, Feb. 6, 1645. [Refer Lee, *Reform of the Church of Scotland.*]

Disraeli Administrations (Benjamin Disraeli, afterwards Earl of Beaconsfield, First Lord of the Treasury). (1) After resignation of the Earl of Derby through ill-health, Feb. 29, 1868—Dec. 2, 1868.

(2) After resignation of Gladstone Administration (*q.v.*), Feb. 21, 1874—Feb. 1880, followed by Gladstone Administration (*q.v.*). [Refer *Life and Letters of Queen Victoria.*]

Dissenters. *See* Nonconformists and Puritans.

Dissolution of Monasteries. *See* Monasteries.

Distinguished Service Medal (India). Instit. Edward VII. 1907.

Distinguished Service Order. Estab. by Queen Victoria, Nov. 9, 1886.

"Divine Comedy." By Dante Allighieri (1265-1321); first printed at Foligno 1472.

Divine Right of Kings. "In the general order of Providence, princes and tyrants are considered as the ministers of heaven, appointed to rule or to chastise the earth" [Gibbon, *Rome,* ch. xx.]. The early Christians recognised the divine right of the Emperor Constantine (A.D. 274-337). The Stuarts in Great Britain claimed recognition of the divine right of kings 1603-1714.

Diving Bell. First used in Europe about 1538.

Divorce (Great Britain). Bill to prevent women marrying their seducers intro. into parliament 1801. D. Court estab. 1857; D. Amendment Act passed, July 21, 1868. Judicature Act 1873 constituted the Probate, D., and Admiralty division of the High Court of Justice with two judges. D. Commission 1910.

Doctors' Commons. College for professors of civil and canon law, estab. by Dr. Hervie 1568. *See* Arches, Court of.

Doggett's Coat and Badge. Thomas Doggett, the actor, awarded prize of coat and badge to winner of annual race on Thames by six watermen, instit. Aug. 1, 1715, in honour of George I.'s accession. Money was left to continue the prize.

Domingo, St. *See* Hayti.

Dominica (W. Indies). Discovered by Columbus 1493. A free island 1660; ceded to Great Britain by Treaty of Paris 1763; in French possession 1778-83; attacked by French, Feb. 2, 1805; finally res. to Great Britain 1814. [Refer Froude, *English in the West Indies.*]

Dominican Republic. *See* Hayti.

Dominicans (monastic order). Fd. by St. Dominic (1170-1221) in 1217, who obtained a bull from Pope Honorius III. First chapter held at Bologna in 1220. In England they were known as Black Friars, and in 1221 thirteen came and set up a house in Oxford by permission of Stephen Langton. [Refer Drane, *History of St. Dominic.*]

Donatists. A sect fd. by Donatus about A.D. 311. Severe laws passed against the sect in 316, and condemned by the Council of Carthage 411. [Refer Neander, *Church History.*]

Doncaster (England). Conference held here which granted pardons to the partakers in the " Pilgrimage of Grace " rebellion (*q.v.*), Dec. 6, 1536. [Refer Lewis, *Topographical Dicty. of England*, vol. ii.]

Dongan Charter. Granted to the city of New York (*q.v.*) by Thomas Dongan, governor of the city, 1686.

Doomsday or **Domesday Book.** Begun by order of William the Conqueror in 1080, and completed in 1086. The book is now in the Public Record Office, who reprinted it in 1783-1810. [Refer Grose, *Antiquities of England and Wales.*]

Dorchester (Dorset, England). Besieged and burnt by the Danes 1003; fortified by parliamentarians 1642-3. The famous *Bloody Assizes* (*q.v.*) held here 1685. [Refer Lewis, *Topographical Dicty. of England*, vol. ii.]

Dorchester (Oxfordshire, England). King Athelstan held a great council here A.D. 938, when he granted a charter to the Abbey of Malmesbury. [Refer Lewis, *Topographical Dicty. of England*, vol. ii.]

Dordrecht or **Dort** (Netherlands). The meeting of the states of Holland after their revolt from Spain held 1572 [refer Motley]. The famous Synod of D., the first general synod of the Protestants, assembled Nov. 13, 1618, and finished May 25, 1619. [Refer Ranke, *History of Reformation in Germany.*]

Douay (France). Taken from Flemings by Philip the Fair 1297; res. 1368. Attempted seizure by Admiral Coligny failed, Jan. 6, 1557 [refer Motley, *op. cit.*]; surrendered to allied armies under Marlborough, June 26, 1710; retaken Sept. 8, 1712; Roman Catholic English College fd. at 1580 [refer Ranke, *Hist. of Popes*]. The D. version of the Old Test. translation published here by command of the pope 1609.

Douglas Rebellion. Headed by William, Earl of Douglas, 1451, as a result of the appointment of Sir William Crichton by James II. of Scotland. Douglas murdered by James II. in Feb. 1452. Rebellion carried on by relatives, but finally suppressed in 1484. [Refer Maxwell, *History of the House of Douglas.*]

Dover (England). Orig. *Dwyr* and *Dubris*. King John resigned his kingdom to the papal legate at, May 13, 1213. The Emperor Charles V. met by Henry VIII. at 1520. Charles II. landed here after his exile, May 26, 1660. Treaty of D. between Charles II. and Louis XIV. 1670. New naval harbour opened 1909. [Refer Lewis, *Topographical Dicty. of England*, vol. ii.]

Draft Riots in New York (*q.v.*) to resist drafting of the citizens into the Union army 1863.

Drama. Comedy intro. by the Greeks about 578 B.C. Theatrical exhibitions first seen in Rome 364 B.C. Mystery Plays, the origin of D. in England, were intro. about 1110 at Dunstable. The first secular play was probably Udal's *Ralph Roister Doister*, written about 1540. The servants of the Earl of Leicester obtained in 1574 a patent for performing plays in any part of England, and in 1576 they built a theatre at Blackfriars, which was the first building of its kind in England. Shakespeare with others received a similar patent May 19, 1603. The theatres were all closed by a parliamentary act on Sept. 2, 1642. In 1737 plays were ordered to be revised and licensed by the Lord Chamberlain. Royal Commissions into. *See* Globe Theatre, Drury Lane Theatre. [Refer Mantzius, *History of Theatrical Art* (Eng. trans.), 5 vols.]

Drama (American). In 1733 there appears a mention of a theatrical performance in New York. A performance of Otway's *Orphans* was enacted in 1750. The *Beaux' Stratagem* was performed by a company of London actors at Annapolis in 1752.

" Drapier's Letters." In 1722 the English Government gave the contract for making the Irish copper coinage to a Mr. William Wood of Wolverhampton. This act aroused the resentment of the Irish, which was fanned into fever heat by the appearance of *Drapier's Letters*, by Dean Swift, in 1723-4. The coinage was withdrawn in 1724.

Dresden (Germany). Orig. of Slavonic origin; destroyed by fire and rebuilt in 1685; besieged by the allied armies unsuccessfully on Aug. 26, 1813; capitulated after Napoleon had left on Nov. 11, 1813; occupied by Prussians 1866.

Dresden, Treaty of. Concluded by Frederick the Great with Maria Theresa, Dec. 25, 1745; celebrated congress held by Napoleon 1812; b. of, Aug. 27, 1813.

Dreyfus Case (France). Captain Dreyfus sentenced for high treason, Dec. 1894. New trial ordered through Emile Zola's exertions. Dreyfus again found guilty 1899, but pardoned. Case reopened and Dreyfus declared innocent, July 1906. [Refer Steevens, *The Dreyfus Case.*]

Drogheda (Ireland). Taken by Oliver Cromwell and the garrison massacred, Sept. 11, 1649; surrendered to William III. in 1690. [Refer Carlyle, *Cromwell's Letters and Speeches*, etc.]

Drunken Parliament (Scotland). Assembled 1661. The whole assembly were said to be intoxicated. [Refer Jennings, *Anecdotal Hist. of British Parliament.*]

Drury Lane Theatre (London). Opened by King's Company under Thomas Killigrew, April 8, 1663; destroyed by fire, Jan. 1672; new erection by Sir Christopher Wren, May 26, 1674. This latter was pulled down and a new building opened on Mar. 12, 1794; destroyed by fire, Feb. 24, 1809. Present building erected, Oct. 10, 1812. [Refer Mantzius, *History of Theatrical Art,* vol. v.]

Dual Alliance between France and Russia signed 1891; extended 1894 and 1897.

Dublin (Ireland). The existence of this city under the name of *Eblana* was first noticed by Ptolemy, who lived A.D. 140. Christ Church fd. by Sitric 1038. Possessed by Crovan, King of Man, 1066. The Earl of Pembroke (" Strongbow ") captured it 1170. Many citizens murdered by Irish of surrounding hills Easter Monday 1209; the day known as " Black Monday." Castle completed 1220. Besieged by Edward Bruce 1315. Visited by Richard II. 1394 and 1399. Bull for the foundation of a university published 1475. Trinity College fd. 1591. Parliament held at D. after lapse of 27 years 1613. Convocation held to estab. XXXIX. Articles of Religion 1614. Besieged by Marquis of Ormond 1649. Oliver Cromwell arrived at, Aug. 1649. Attempt to seize the castle by the notorious Col. Blood and others frustrated 1663. Visit of James II., who held a parliament 1688. [Refer Lewis, *Topographical Dicty. of Ireland,* vol. i.]

Duelling forbidden in England by an act of Oliver Cromwell 1654. Charles II. also issued a proclamation against D. 1679. Anti-duelling association formed in England, May 1843; and three articles of war were issued in 1844 to prevent the practice in the army. [Refer De Vlassi, *History of Duelling in all Countries,* Eng. trans.]

Dulwich College (London). Fd. and endowed by Edward Alleyn 1619. New school buildings opened 1870.

Duma. *See* Russia.

Dunces, Parliament of. Met at Coventry in 1404; also known as Unlearned Parliament, so called because not a single lawyer composed the assembly.

Dundee (Scotland). Taken by English under the Duke of Lancaster 1385. Attacked by Montrose 1645. Besieged by Gen. Monk after b. of Worcester 1651. The town was so greatly reduced in 1669 that contributions were made for its assistance. Visit of Queen Victoria 1844. [Refer Lewis, *Topographical Dictionary of Scotland.*]

Dungannon Convention. Meeting of Irish volunteers under influence of Grattan passed resolution for parliamentary reform for Ireland, Sept. 8, 1785. [Refer Froude, *English in Ireland.*]

Dunkirk (France). Taken by French 1646; recovered by Archduke Leopold 1652; given up to the English 1658; sold to Louis XIV. by Charles II. Oct. 17, 1662; bombarded by English, July 26, 1694. Works ordered to be demolished by Treaty of Utrecht 1713. Duke of York forced to raise siege of, Sept. 1793.

Duquesne, Fort (U.S.A.). Erected by French 1754. Futile attempt to capture by Gen. Braddock 1755; captured by Gen. John Forbes, and renamed Fort Pitt after the English statesman, Nov. 25, 1758. [Refer Harper, *Encyclo. of U.S. History*, vol. iii.]

Durham (England). Called by the Normans *Duresme*. Bishopric fd. A.D. 995. Besieged by Duncan of Scotland A.D. 1040; entered by William the Conqueror 1067. The present cathedral fd. about 1093. Headquarters of Edward III. and his army 1327. B. of Neville's Cross near 1346. Henry VI. visits shrine of St. Cuthbert 1448. [Refer Lewis, *Topographical Dicty. of England*, vol. ii.] *See* Universities.

Dusseldorf (Germany). Taken by Prince Ferdinand of Brunswick 1758; by French, Sept. 6, 1795; res. to Prussia 1814.

Dutch Republic. *See* Holland.

Dynamite. Patented by Nobel in 1867; manufactured in Ayrshire 1872.

E

Early English Text Society. Fd. by F. G. Furnivall; first publications 1864.

East, Empire of the. " The division of the Roman world between the sons of Theodosius, marks the final establishment of the empire of the East, which from the reign of Arcadius (A.D. 395) to the taking of Constantinople by the Turks, subsisted one thousand and fifty-eight years in a state of premature and perpetual decay " [Gibbon]. Arcadius *d.* 408. Constantinople taken by Mahomet II. May 29, 1453, and Constantine XIII., the last emperor, slain. *See* Turkey Constantinople.

East Anglia. First historical king of, Redwald, 599-617. Kingdom came to an end at Norman Conquest 1066. The following are the kings:—

Uffa 571-578	Anna 635-654
Tytillus 578-599	Ethelhere 654-655
Redwald 599-617	Ethelwold 655-664
Eorpwald 617-628	Ealdwulf 664-713
Sigebert 631-634	Alfwold 713-749
Egric 634-635	

[Refer Freeman, *Old English History*, etc.]

Easter Sunday. The first Sunday after the first full moon occurring after March 21. The festival was instit. about A.D. 68. The Andians or *Quartodecimans* kept E. on the same day as the Jewish Passover, and were persecuted by an edict of Theodosius A.D. 385. [Refer Gibbon, *Rome.*]

East India Company. Incorp. by charter 1600; practically abolished by the *Act for the Better Government of India* 1858; finally extinguished 1873. *See* India. [Refer Kaye, *Administration of the East India Company.*]

Ecclesiastical Commission. First appointed by Queen Elizabeth 1584; by James I. in Scotland 1617; abolished by general assembly in Scotland 1637; in England by parliament 1641; revived by James II. 1687; dissolved Oct. 11, 1688; present Commissioners appointed 1835; incorp. 1836. [Refer Elliot, *The State and the Church.*]

Ecclesiastical Courts. *See* Court of Arches.

Ecclesiastical Reservation. At the Diet of Augsburg in Feb. 1555 it was decided that all ecclesiastical possessions which had been secularised before 1552 were to be retained by the Lutherans, but any ecclesiastic who changed his faith afterwards was to forfeit lands and dignities. [Refer Tanner, *Reformation and the Renaissance*, etc.]

Ecclesiastical States. *See* Papacy.

Ecclesiastical Titles Bill. Intro. by Lord John Russell, Feb. 7, 1850; passed by Lords, July 29, 1850; repealed 1871.

Ecuador (S. America). Formerly part of Colombia. War with Spain 1821-4; with Peru 1828-9; civil war 1876.

Ecumenical Councils. *See* Councils.

Eddystone Lighthouse. Built 1696-9; destroyed Nov. 27, 1703; rebuilt 1708; burnt Dec. 4, 1755; rebuilt 1759; burnt 1770; reconstructed 1774; present edifice opened by Duke of Edinburgh, May 18, 1882.

Edict, Perpetual. Prepared by Salviannus Julianus by order of the Emperor Hadrian A.D. 132. [Refer Gregorovius, *The Emperor Hadrian*, Eng. trans.]

Edict of Châteaubriant by Henry II. of France against the Calvinists, June 27, 1551. [Refer Tanner, *Renaissance and the Reformation*.]

Edict of Nantes, for toleration of Protestants in France, proclaimed by Henry IV. April 13, 1598; revoked by Louis XIV. Oct. 22, 1685. [The complete text of the edict is given in Tanner, *The Renaissance and the Reformation*.]

Edict of Restitution. Issued by the Emperor Frederick II. of Germany, commanding several church lands to be surrendered 1629. [Refer *Cambridge Modern History*, vol. iv.]

Edinburgh (Scotland). Orig. *Dun Edin*. Fd. by Edwin, King of Northumbria, A.D. 626; formed part of Saxon kingdom of Northumbria till 936; regained by Scots 956; charter granted by Richard I. 1329; pillaged by Henry VIII. 1544 and 1547; marriage of Mary Queen of Scots and Lord Darnley at, July 27, 1565; murder of Rizzio at 1566; murder of Darnley, Feb. 10, 1567; John Knox died at 1572; assembly of the Convention of States, Dec. 10, 1599; Charles I. crowned King of Scotland at, May 16, 1633; castle surrendered to Cromwell, Dec. 1650; Porteous riots (*q.v.*) 1736; the Young Pretender occupied Holyrood, Sept. 17, 1745; Scottish National Gallery opened, Mar. 21, 1859; Forth Bridge (*q.v.*) opened, Mar. 4, 1890.

"Edinburgh Review." Fd. Oct. 1802.

Edinburgh University. Fd. 1582 by royal charter of James VI.; ratified by Act of (Scottish) Parliament 1621; constitutional changes by Act of British Parliament 1858. [Refer Bower, *History of the University of Edinburgh*.]

Edmunds' Law. An act passed by the U.S. Congress against polygamy 1882. [Refer Harper, *Encyclopædia of U.S. History*.]

Education (England). *See also* Universities and under titles of various schools. Committee of the Privy Council on E. formed 1839. E. Department estab. in two departments: (*a*) For E. of the people, (*b*) for development of science and art, Feb. 25, 1856. Code of regulations published, April 1860. Royal Commission appointed 1858; reported in 1861. New regulations issued, May 1862. Elementary E. Act passed, Aug. 9, 1870; Free E. Act 1891. E. Bill brought in to form E. committee of each county council 1896, but was dropped. " The Board of E. for England and Wales " formed 1899. E. Act (England and Wales) intro. 1902, and was passed finally on Dec. 18, 1902; further bill intro. but withdrawn 1906. Mr. Runciman's bill abandoned 1908. Royal Commission on University E. in London 1909. [Refer art. in Low and Pulling, *Dicty. of Eng. History*, 1910.]

Education (Ireland). *See also* Universities and various colleges. Gladstone's Irish University Bill thrown out by Commons 1873. Intermediate E. Act passed 1878. Kildare Place Society for Promoting the E. of the Poor on the Principle of Secularism fd. Dublin 1811; received grant from parliament 1819; withdrawn and vested in Commissioners of National E. 1833. Compulsory E. Act 1892. [Refer art. in Low and Pulling, *Dicty. of Eng. History*, 1910.]

Education (Scotland). *See also* Universities and various colleges. Act passed compelling all barons and freeholders to send their sons to schools 1496. Act to provide song schools for instruction of youth in music 1579. Act taxing " *plough- or husband-land according to the worth* " for maintenance of schools 1633. Act for providing schools 1696. E. Act passed 1872. Act passed insisting that all parents should have their children properly educated 1901. [Refer art. in Low and Pulling, *Dicty. of Eng. History*, 1910.]

Education (U.S.A.). E. Bill passed 1884. Blair E. Bill, Mar. 1886. Compulsory E. Bill passed, April 4, 1892. National Educational Association appoint a committee to inquire into system of E. 1892. [Refer Harper, *Encyclopædia of U.S. History*.]

Edward VI.'s Prayer Book. *See* Common Prayer, Book of.

Egypt. First dynasty under King Manes variously dated as 5702 B.C. to 2000 B.C. Early history uncertain [refer to works by modern Egyptologists, Flinders Petrie, etc.]. Yielded to Alexander the Great, who founded Alexandria (*q.v.*) 332 B.C. After Alexander's death, Ptolemy Lagus, his general, fd. new kingdom of Egypt 323 B.C. Dynasty of the Ptolemies 323-30 B.C. Conquered by Octavius A.D. 30. Invasion of Queen Candace of Ethiopia repulsed 22. Fatamite Empire fd. by Mohammed al Mahdi A.D. 908. First invasion of the Turks 1163. Saladin became supreme ruler 1174. Added to Ottoman Empire 1517. Invaded by French under Napoleon 1798; expelled by English and Turks 1801. Revolt of Mehemet Pasha 1831, 1839; peace res. and Mehemet made viceroy (or khedive), July 15, 1841. Commercial treaty with Great Britain, April 19, 1861. British expedition to suppress slavery 1869. Col. Gordon continued expedition, Nov. 1874; returns to England 1877. British subjects ordered to leave E. 1882. Bombardment of Alexandria (*q.v.*), July 1882. Arabi Pasha declares a religious war, July 24, 1882; Tel-el-Kebir captured by British, Sept. 13, 1882. Constitution signed 1883. Anglo-Turkish Convention respecting E. signed,

July 15, 1887. France acknowledged English predominance in E. by treaty of 1904. *See* Sudan, Suez Canal, Alexandria. [Refer Rawlinson, *History of Ancient Egypt ;* Lane, *Modern Egyptians*.]

Eight Articles. Drawn up by Cranmer, Ridley, and Latimer 1555.

Eighty Club. Estab. 1880.

"Eikon Basilike." Formerly attributed to Charles I. but now generally considered to be the work of one John Gauden, published 1649. Milton replied to it in his *Iconoclastes*.

Elba, Isle of (Italy). Taken by Nelson, Aug. 9, 1796. In 1814 it was given to Napoleon, who secretly quitted it and landed in France with a small force 1815.

Elections (Great Britain). *See also* Parliament, House of Commons, Ballot, etc. *Grenville Act* provided for E. of a committee for adjudication of E. cases 1770. Act passed limiting poll to fifteen days, and the scrutiny of votes to be closed six days before the return was made 1784. Period reduced in reigns of George IV. and William IV. *See also* Reform Act, Roman Catholics.

Electoral Commission (U.S.A.). Bill for regulation of elections passed Congress, Jan. 29, 1877. Commission assemble, Feb. 1, 1877. [Refer Harper, *Encyclopædia U.S. History*, vol. iii.]

Electors of Germany. "After the death of [the Emperor] Frederick II. (1250), Germany was left a monster with a hundred heads. A crowd of princes and prelates disputed the ruins of the empire." To bring about a settlement, "Seven of the most powerful feudatories were permitted to assume, with a distinguished name and rank, the exclusive privilege of choosing the Roman emperor" [Gibbon, *Roman Empire*, ch. xlix.]. These princes were called E. Privileges confirmed by the Golden Bill 1356. On the dissolution of the empire in 1804 the elective rights ceased. [Refer works quoted under Germany.]

Electricity. The property of rubbed amber attracting or repelling light substances said to have been discovered by Thales of Miletus 600 B.C. The founder of the science generally supposed to be Dr. Gilbert of Colchester (1540-1603), who made various experiments with a magnetic needle. Robert Boyle (1627-91) added to the knowledge of the subject by experiments, which he described in his *Experiments on the Origin of E.* Otto von Guericke (1602-86) obtained light from E. Experiments by the Royal Society 1676, following observations made by Sir Isaac Newton (1642-1727). Francis Hawksbee experimented with mercury 1705, and described his observations in his *Physico-Mechanical Experiments*, 1709. Stephen Gray (1696-1736) discovered *conduction* 1729. Dufay (1699-1739) by experimenting discovered the two kinds of E. which he named *vitreous* and *resinous*. The *Leyden Jar* or *Phial* invented about 1745; improved by Sir William Watson (1715-1807). The Royal Society's experiments concerning velocity of E. 1747. Dr. Benjamin Franklin of Philadelphia (1706-90) presents the theories of *positive* and *negative* E. John Canton (1715-72) demonstrated *electrification by induction.* The Italian Beccaria (1716-81) experimented with atmospherical E. Robert Symmer's *silk stockings* experiments 1759. Sir David Brewster's (1781-1868) experiments with metals and salts of metals. Henry Cavendish's (1731-1810) experiments with gases. Galvani in 1790 and Volta in 1800 experiment with apparatus for producing E.; the Galvanic battery and Voltaic pile are the outcome of their experiments. Magnetic action of electric current discovered by Œrsted of Copenhagen 1820. Ampère's theory of electro-dynamics 1821. Faraday discovered electro-magnetic rotation 1821. Seebeck discovered thermo-electricity 1822. Ohm's law 1827. Wilhelm Weber invented the electro-dynamometer 1832. Induction of electric currents by Faraday 1831. Law of Lenz 1835. Daniell's battery 1836. Grove's battery 1836. Bunsen's battery 1842. Sir William Thompson invented many valuable instruments for experimenting with and measuring E. 1851, *et seq.* *See* Electric Light, etc.

Electric Light Arc. W. E. Staite patented lamp 1847. The first really successful one was Serrin's, patented 1857. The South Foreland Lighthouse lighted by an E. lamp 1857. Jablochkoff candle invented 1876; adopted in lighting streets, etc. 1878-9. Incandescent Edison and Swan make first incandescent lamp 1879. [Refer art. in *Chambers's Encyclopædia.*]

Electric Lighting Act (Great Britain). Passed Aug. 18, 1882; amended 1888. Board of Trade regulations regarding E. L. issued, May 18, 1889.

Electric Railway. First experiment in electric traction made by Robert Davidson 1837. Werner Siemens at the Berlin Exhibition demonstrated traction with a dynamo-electric machine 1879. A permanent E. R. erected near Berlin 1881. Electric tramcars from Kew to Hammersmith 1882. City and South London Railway opened 1890. First permanent elevated E. R. in U.S.A. at Chicago 1895. [Refer art. in *Chambers's Encyclopædia.*]

Electric Telegraph. *See* Telegraphy.

Eleven Articles. Drawn up by the bishops in Queen Elizabeth's reign 1560.

Elgin Marbles. *See* British Museum.

Ely (Cambridgeshire, England). Abbey fd. by St. Ethelreda A.D. 673; re-fd. by Ethelwold, Bishop of Winchester, 970; cathedral fd. 1083. Court of Refuge by Hereward at 1066; taken by William the Conqueror 1071. Barons' stronghold taken by Prince Edward 1267.

Elzevir Press. Fd. at Leiden, 1580, by Louis E. (1540-1617). He produced many editions of the classics. His five sons and grandsons carried on the work; the house justly renowned for beautiful work. Last representatives grandson Abraham, university printer at Leiden 1681-1712, and great-grandson Peter, bookseller at Utrecht 1667-1675.

Emancipation. *See* Slavery, Roman Catholics.

Eminence. Title conferred on the cardinals by Pope Urban VIII. Jan. 10, 1631.

Emmett's Insurrection. Headed by Robert E. July 23, 1803. E. arrested and executed, Sept. 19, 1803. [Refer Madden, *Lives of the United Irishmen.*]

Employers Liability Act. Passed for seven years, Sept. 7, 1880. New act, Dec. 24, 1888.

"Encyclopédie," The. Appeared at Paris between 1751 and 1772; compiled by D'Alembert and Diderot. It contained opinions of the most advanced and revolutionary kind, and caused a great upheaval amongst the Conservative party in France.

Enforcing Act (U.S.A.). Passed Congress, Jan. 9, 1809, for preserving strict neutrality between England and France.

Engagement, The. Name given to an agreement between Charles I. of England and the Scotch Commissioners in the Isle of Wight 1647.

England, Church of. Christianity was intro. into Britain long before the arrival of Augustine. Three British bishops were present at the Council of Arles 314. The names of Ninian, St. Patrick, Pelagius, and St. Columba are associated with the early Church in these isles. St. Augustine landed and fd. first church at Canterbury 597; Sees of London and Rochester fd. 604; Church of Northumbria fd. by Paulinus 627, of East Anglia by Felix 631, of Wessex by Birinus 634; Conference at Whitby 664; Synod of Hertford 673; death of the Venerable Bede 735; Councils of Cloveshoo 747, 803; Council of Chelsea 787; Council of St. Paul's 1075; Council of Winchester (enforced clerical celibacy) 1076; separation of ecclesiastical and temporal courts 1086; Council of Rockingham 1095; Council at Westminster 1102; Council at London 1107; See of Ely fd. 1109; Legatine Council at Westminster 1125; murder of Becket 1170; England became subject to the pope 1213; Legatine Council at London 1237; organisation of the Convocations of the Clergy 1283; fealty to the pope repudiated 1366; Wyclif condemned 1382; Lollard Act passed 1414; Tyndale's New Test. intro. 1526; scriptural prerogative of the papacy denied by Convocation 1534; Henry VIII. declared sovereign to be head of the Church 1534; visitation of the monasteries 1535; act finally repudiating papal authority 1536; Ten Articles published 1536; authorisation of the Great Bible by the king 1538; Act of the Six Articles 1539; Litany published in English 1544; First Prayer Book of Edward VI. (*see* Common Prayer) 1549; act permitting clerical marriage 1549; Forty-two Articles published 1553; repeal of anti-papal statutes and reconciliation to the papacy 1554; again abolished under Elizabeth 1559; Prayer Book revised 1559; Thirty-nine Articles published 1563; Lambeth Articles drawn up (*q.v.*) 1595; Hampton Court Conference (*q.v.*) 1604; authorised version of the Bible published 1611; Solemn League and Covenant (*q.v.*) 1643; establishment of Presbyterianism 1646; private use of Prayer Book forbidden 1655; restoration of Church and Monarchy 1660; Savoy Conference 1661; order to publish Declaration of Indulgence by James II. 1688; refusal and trial of the seven bishops 1688; establishment of Queen Anne's Bounty 1704; Catholic Relief Act passed 1778; Catholic Emancipation Act 1829; appointment of Ecclesiastical Commission 1835, incorp. 1836; passing of Church Discipline Act 1840; the Oxford Movement 1833-96. *See* Bible, Common Prayer, and under titles of various commissions, convocations, etc. [Refer Wakeman, *Intro. History of Church of England.*]

England, Sovereigns of. The following is a list of the sovereigns of England, with the principal dates in their reigns, up to the Union of the two crowns of England and Scotland. *See* Great Britain, Scotland, Ireland, Britain, etc.

Egbert, " King of the English." 802-839. Victory over Danes at Hengist's Down 836. *See* Danes.

Ethelwulf 839-858.

Ethelbald
Ethelbert } 858 871.
Ethelred I.

Alfred the Great 871-901. Alfred retreated to the Isle of Athelney after defeat by Danes (*q.v.*) 878; b. of Ethandun (Edington), victory over Danes 878; Treaty of Wedmore 879; navy and militia formed by Alfred 896.

Edward the Elder 901-925. Retook London from the Danes 912; became lord of the Welsh 922.

Athelstan 925-940. Defeated Danes at b. of Brunanburh 937.

Edmund 940-946.

Edred 946-955.

Edwy 955-959. Dunstan, Abbot of Glastonbury, banished 956.

Edgar the Peaceable, King of people North of Thames 957-959, King of England 959-975. Recalled Dunstan and made him Archbishop of Canterbury 960.

Edward 975-979.

Ethelred the Unready 979-1016. Invasion of the Danes 980; death of Dunstan 988; Danes won b. of Maldon 991; Danegeld tax (*q.v.*) levied 991; Danes attacked London 994; massacre of the Danes 1002; Ethelred fled to Normandy 1013, but returned.

Edmund Ironside, murdered 1016.

Canute or Cnut 1017-1035. Pilgrimage to Rome 1027-9; conquers Norway 1028; forced Malcolm, King of Scots, to pay him homage 1031.

Harold I. (King North of the Thames) } 1035.
Hardicanute (King South of the Thames)

Harold I. *d.* 1040, and was succeeded by Hardicanute, who reigns over whole country; *d.* 1042.

Edward the Confessor 1042-1066. Death of Earl Godwin 1053.

Harold II. 1066. B. of Stamford Bridge, Sept. 25, 1066; b. of Hastings, Oct. 14, 1066; Harold killed.

Norman Kings :

William I. (the Conqueror) (1066-1087); *m.* Matilda of Flanders 1053. Rebellions in various parts of country 1067-1071;

ENGLAND, SOVEREIGNS OF (*continued*)—

Lanfranc, Archbishop of Canterbury 1070; invasion of Scotland 1072; Barons' rebellion 1074, 1078; Domesday Book instit. 1080.

William II. (Rufus) 1087-1100. Death of Lanfranc 1089.

Henry I. 1100-1135; *m.* Matilda of Scotland 1100, Adela of Louvain 1121. Conquered Normandy 1106; defeated French at Brenneville 1118; the Crown Prince William drowned 1120.

Stephen 1135-1154; *m.* Matilda of Boulogne 1124. Civil war between Stephen and Matilda 1138-1153.

Plantagenet Period :

Henry II. 1154-1189; *m.* Eleanor of Aquitaine 1152. Henry's attack on Toulouse 1159; Constitutions of Clarendon drawn up 1164; murder of Thomas à Becket 1170; juries instit. 1166; invasion of Ireland by the Normans 1171; revolt of the Barons 1173.

Richard I. (the Lion Heart) 1189-1199; *m.* Berengaria of Navarre 1191. Left for Palestine 1189; arrived Acre, June 9, 1191; returned to England, Mar. 13 1194; French war 1194-1199.

John 1199-1216; *m.* Hadwisa of Gloucester 1189 Isabella of Angoulême 1200. Loss of Normandy 1204; John excommunicated by the pope 1209; submission to the pope, May 15, 1213; Magna Charta (*q.v.*) signed, June 19, 1215.

Henry III. 1216-1272; *m.* Eleanor of Provence 1236. House of Commons fd. 1265; Simon de Montfort killed at b. of Evesham 1265.

Edward I. 1272-1307; *m.* Eleanor of Castile 1254, Margaret of France 1299. Statute of Mortmain passed 1279; expulsion of the Jews 1290; defeated Scots at Dunbar 1296; subdued Wallace's rising 1297-1304; incorporated Scotland with England 1305; conquest of Wales 1277; Wales annexed to England 1283, and Edward's son (afterwards Edward II.) proclaimed Prince of Wales 1301.

Edward II. 1307-1327; *m.* Isabella of France 1308. Invasion of Scotland, b. of Bannockburn 1314; truce concluded with Scotland 1323; insurrection of the Barons 1322.

Edward III. 1327-1377; *m.* Philippa of Hainault 1328. Independence of Scotland recognised 1333; commencement of the Hundred Years' War 1328; b. of Creçy 1346; siege of Calais 1346; b. of Poitiers 1356; death of Edward the Black Prince, June 8, 1376.

Richard II. 1377-1399; *m.* Anne of Bohemia 1381, Isabella of France 1395. Wat Tyler's rebellion 1381; John Wyclif 1324-1384; Geoffrey Chaucer 1340-1400; death of John of Gaunt 1399; Lancaster's revolt 1399.

House of Lancaster :

Henry IV. 1399-1413; *m.* Mary Bohun 1380, Joan of Navarre 1403. Glendower's rebellion 1400; persecution of the Lollards commenced 1401; rebellion of the Percies 1403.

Henry V. 1413-1422; *m.* Katherine of France 1420. French war,

Dictionary of Dates

ENGLAND, SOVEREIGNS OF (*continued*)—
    b. of Agincourt, Oct. 25, 1415; new invasion of France 1417;
    Rouen taken 1419; Treaty of Troyes 1420.

Henry VI. 1422-1461 (*d.* 1471); *m.* Margaret of Anjou 1445.
    Siege of Orleans 1428 (Joan of Arc's victory); Cade's rebel-
    lion 1450; Wars of Roses (*q.v.*) commenced by b. of St. Albans,
    May 23, 1455; captured at b. of Northumberland 1460, but
    soon released; fled to Scotland 1461; restored 1470-1471.

House of York :

Edward IV. 1461-1483; *m.* Elizabeth Woodville 1464. Conspiracy
    of the Earl of Warwick (the King-maker) 1469; Warwick
    killed at b. of Barnet 1471; Caxton's printing press set up at
    Westminster 1474 (*see* Printing).

Edward V., April to June 1483. Murdered in the Tower with his
    brother.

Richard III. 1483-1485; *m.* Anne Neville 1473. Henry of Rich-
    mond's rebellion, b. of Bosworth, at which Richard is slain
    1485.

House of Tudor :

Henry VII. 1485-1509; *m.* Elizabeth of York 1486. Court of
    Star Chamber set up 1487; Columbus discovered West Indian
    Islands 1492; Perkin Warbeck's insurrection 1492; Cornish
    rebellion 1497; Cabot reached America 1497; Vasco da
    Gama doubled Cape of Good Hope 1497.

Henry VIII. 1509-1547; *m.* Katherine of Aragon 1509, *d.* 1536;
    Anne Boleyn 1533, executed 1536; Jane Seymour 1536, *d.*
    1537; Anne of Cleves 1540, divorced 1540; Katherine
    Howard 1540, executed 1542; Katherine Parr 1543, survived
    H., dying in 1548. War declared against France 1511-1514;
    b. of Guinegate (*the Spurs*) 1513; war with Scotland, Flodden
    Field 1513; Cardinal Wolsey (1471-1530) made Chancellor
    1515; Field of the Cloth of Gold 1520; Tyndale's translation
    of the Bible 1526 (*see* Bible); fall of Wolsey 1529; Henry
    declared himself supreme head of the Church, and England
    is separated from Rome 1532-1534; Thomas More executed
    1535; Coverdale's translation of the Bible 1536; dissolution
    of the monasteries 1539; Cranmer's *Great Bible* 1539;
    Thomas Cromwell executed, July 28, 1540; war with Scot-
    land, b. of Solway Moss 1542; war with France 1544.

Edward VI. 1547-1553. B. of Pinkie 1547; first Prayer Book of
    Edward VI. 1549, revised 1552.

Mary 1553-1558; *m.* Philip II. of Spain 1554. Execution of Lady
    Jane Grey 1554; Mary's marriage with Philip of Spain, July
    1554; Sir Thomas Wyat's revolt 1554; reunion with Rome
    1554; persecution of the Protestants commenced 1555; war
    with France 1557; Calais lost 1558.

Elizabeth 1558-1603. Prayer Book of Edward VI. again intro.
    1559; Court of High Commission fd. 1583; execution of Mary
    Queen of Scots, Feb. 8, 1587; Spanish Armada 1588; East
    India Company originated 1600; William Shakespeare 1564-
    1616.

ENGLAND, SOVEREIGNS OF (*continued*)—

On the accession of James I. 1603, England and Scotland were united.

[Refer Green, *Short History of the English People ;* Macaulay, *History of England*, etc., etc.]

English History—

Britain invaded by the Romans under Julius Cæsar 55 and 54 B.C.

Cymbeline King of Britain A.D. 4.

Aulus Plautius defeated the Britons 43.

Caractacus is defeated by Ostorius and carried in chains to Rome 50.

Romans defeated by Boadicea 61.

Christianity said to have been taught 64.

Agricola became governor and reforms the government 78.

Scots and Picts invade Britain 360.

Romans quitted Britain 436.

Invasion of Angles and Saxons 449-55.

St. Ethelbert first Christian king 560.

Arrival of St. Augustine and re-establishment of Christianity 597.

Egbert, King of Wessex, virtually King of England 827.

Alfred vanquished the Danes 871-96; he framed a code of laws 890; forms a militia and a navy, surveys and subdivides the country, and promoted learning, 896.

Athelstan's great victory over the Danes and Scots at Brunanburg 937.

Canute the Dane sole monarch 1017.

Saxon dynasty restored under Edward the Confessor 1042.

Harold II. defeated and slain by William of Normandy at the b. of Hastings 1066.

Introduction of the Feudal System *c.* 1070.

Henry I. gained Normandy 1106.

Civil war during the reign of Stephen 1135-54.

Murder of Thomas à Becket 1170.

England divided into six circuits for the administration of justice 1176.

Normandy lost to England 1204.

John signed the Magna Charta 1215.

The Barons' War 1262-8.

Edward I. subdues Wales and united it to England 1283, and was also victorious in Scotland 1296.

Edward II. defeated at the b. of Bannockburn 1314.

Edward III. invaded France; victorious at Creçy 1346, and at Poitiers 1356 (for the Hundred Years' War *see* France).

Insurrection of Wat Tyler 1381.

Death of Wyclif 1385.

Insurrection of the Percies and the Welsh 1402-5.

Wars of the Roses 1455-71.

Edward IV. deposed Henry VI. 1461.

ENGLISH HISTORY (*continued*)—

Printing introduced by Caxton 1471.

Edward V. murdered in the Tower 1483.

Richard III. defeated and slain at Bosworth Field 1485.

Insurrection of Lambert Simnel 1486-7; and of Perkin Warbeck 1492-8.

Court of Star Chamber instituted 1487.

Henry VIII. and Francis I. meet at the " Field of the Cloth of Gold " 1520.

Papal authority abolished 1534.

Visitation of the monasteries 1538.

The Reformation further promoted during the reign of Edward VI.

Authorised Book of Common Prayer 1548.

On the accession of Mary papal authority is restored 1553.

Persecution of Protestants: Ridley, Latimer, and Cranmer burnt 1555-6

Loss of Calais 1558.

The Church of England re-established by Elizabeth 1558.

Execution of Mary Queen of Scots 1587.

The defeat of the Spanish Armada 1588.

On the accession of James I. the two crowns of Scotland and England are united 1603.

The Gunpowder Plot 1605.

The Authorised Version of the Bible 1611.

Hampden's trial respecting " ship money " 1637.

Contest between Charles I. and Parliament.

Impeachment and execution of Strafford 1641.

Charles attempted an " arrest of Five Members " 1642.

Civil War began 1642. *See* under Battles.

Execution of Charles I. 1649.

Oliver Cromwell Protector of the Commonwealth 1653.

War with the Netherlands 1652-7. *See* under Battles.

The monarchy and the Church of England re-established under Charles II. 1660.

The great plague 1665.

The great fire of London 1666.

Secret treaty with France 1620.

Panic created by Oates's " popish plot " 1678.

Duke of Monmouth's rebellion defeated at Sedgemore 1685.

Trial and acquittal of the seven bishops 1688.

Abdication of James II. 1688.

William III. and Mary proclaimed king and queen by the Convention Parliament 1689.

James's unsuccessful attempt to regain his crown and his defeat at the b. of Boyne 1690.

War with France begun, ended by the Treaty of Ryswick 1697.

Campaign in the Netherlands.

Victory of Marlborough at Blenheim 1704.

Union with Scotland 1707.

Treaty of Utrecht 1713.

ENGLISH HISTORY (*continued*)—

Dislike of the Hanoverian succession in Scotland, resulting in Mar's rising 1715-16.

South Sea Bubble 1720.

The Quadruple Alliance 1720.

War with Spain 1739.

The Young Pretender's rising 1745.

War ended by the Treaty of Aix-la-Chapelle 1748.

The Seven Years' War (1756-63). *See* under Battles.

Formation of the East India Company 1600.

Conquest of India began under Colonel (afterwards Lord) Clive 1757.

Victory and death of Wolfe at Quebec 1759.

Beginning of the War of American Independence 1773.

" No Popery " riots 1780.

Separation of America from England 1782.

Treaty of Paris between England, America, France, and Spain 1783.

Proclamation of war between France and England 1793. *See* under Battles.

The Irish Rebellion 1798-9.

Union of Great Britain with Ireland 1801.

Nelson's victory and death at Trafalgar 1805.

Abolition of the slave trade by Act of Parliament 1807.

Wellington's great victory at Waterloo, bringing to an end the great Napoleonic War, 1815.

Great industrial distress, " Manchester Massacre " 1819.

Criminal Law Reform 1823.

Catholic Emancipation Act 1829.

Opening of the first railway, between Liverpool and Manchester 1830.

The Reform Act passed 1832.

Chartist demonstrations in London 1848.

France and England at war with Russia 1854.

The Indian Mutiny 1857-8.

Election of Elementary School Boards 1870.

Afghan War begun 1878.

South African War 1899-1902.

Mr. Chamberlain opened his " fiscal campaign " 1903.

The " Entente Cordiale " between England and France 1905.

Anglo-Japanese agreement 1905.

The " Peoples Budget " thrown out by the House of Lords 1909.

Parliament Bill became law 1911.

English Literature. The following are the principal English writers:—

Acton, J. E. E. D.-A., Lord (historian), 1834-1902.

Addison, Joseph (poet and essayist), 1672-1719.

Ainger, Alfred (biographer and critic), 1837-1904.

Ainsworth, William Harrison (novelist) 1805-82.

Akenside, Mark (poet), 1721-70.

ENGLISH LITERATURE (*continued*)—

Alison, Sir Archibald (historian), 1792-1867.

Allen, C. Grant (scientific writer and novelist), 1848-99.

Andrewes, Lancelot (took part in trans. of authorised version of the Bible), 1555-1626.

Arbuthnot, John (satirist) (originator of the term " John Bull "), 1667-1735.

Arnold, Sir Edwin (poet), 1832-1904.

Arnold, Matthew (poet and critic), 1822-88.

Arnold, Thomas (historian), 1795-1842.

Ascham, Roger (didactic writer), 1515-68.

Atterbury, Francis (controversialist), 1662-1732.

Austen, Jane (novelist), 1775-1817.

Bacon, Francis (philosopher), 1561-1626.

Barclay, Alexander (poet), 1475(?)-1552.

Barnes, William (the Dorsetshire poet), 1801-86.

Barrow, Isaac (divine scholar), 1630-77.

Baxter, Richard (divine scholar), 1615-91.

Beaconsfield, Earl of (Benjamin Disraeli), 1804-81.

Beaumont, Francis (dramatist), 1584-1616.

Bede or Bæda (" the father of English history "), 673-735.

Bentham, Jeremy (political writer), 1748-1832.

Bentley, Richard (theologian, etc.), 1662-1742.

Berkeley, George (philosopher), 1685-1753.

Besant, Sir Walter (novelist), 1836-1901.

Blackie, John Stuart (scholar and man of letters), 1809-95.

Blackmore, Richard D. (novelist), 1825-1900.

Blair, Robert (poet), 1699-1746.

Blake, William (poet and painter), 1757-1827.

Boece or Boethius, Hector (historian), 1465(?)-1536.

Borrow, George (philologist and miscellaneous writer), 1803-81.

Boswell, James (biographer), 1740-95.

Brewster, Sir David (scientific writer), 1781-1868.

Brontë, Anne (novelist), 1820-49.

Brontë, Charlotte (novelist), 1816-55.

Brontë, Emily (novelist), 1818-48.

Brown, Dr. John (physician and essayist), 1810-82.

Browne, Sir Thomas (physician and miscellaneous writer), 1605-82.

Browning, Elizabeth Barrett (poetess), 1806-61.

Browning, Robert (poet), 1812-89.

Bruce, James (traveller), 1730-94. *See* Bruce's Travels.

Buchanan, George (historian), 1506-82.

Buchanan, Robert (poet and novelist), 1841-1901.

Buckle, Henry Thomas (historian), 1821-62.

Bunyan, John (theological romantic writer), 1628-88.

Burke, Edmund (statesman and political philosopher), 1729-97.

Burnet, Gilbert (theologian and historian), 1643-1715.

Burns, Robert (poet), 1759-96.

Burton, Sir Richard Francis (explorer), 1821-90.

Butler, Joseph (theologian), 1692-1752.

Butler, Samuel (satirist), 1612-80.

ENGLISH LITERATURE (*continued*)—

Byron, George Gordon, Lord (poet), 1788-1824.

Cædmon (" the first English poet "), (?)-680.

Camden, William (antiquary), 1551-1623.

Campbell, Thomas (poet), 1777-1844.

Campion, Thomas (poet), 1575(?)-1620(?).

Carew, Thomas (poet), 1594(?)-1639.

Carey, Henry (dramatist and song writer), (?)-1743.

Carlyle, Thomas (historian and essayist), 1795-1881.

Cary, Henry Francis (translator of Dante), 1772-1844.

Caxton, William (printer and translator), 1422-91. *See* Printing.

Chalmers, Thomas (divine writer), 1780-1847.

Chambers, Robert (historian and scientific writer), 1802-71.

Chambers, William (publisher in partnership with the above, his brother), 1800-83.

Chapman, George (dramatist and translator), 1559-1634.

Chatterton, Thomas (poet), 1752-70.

Chaucer, Geoffrey (poet), 1340(?)-1400. *See* "Canterbury Tales."

Chesterfield, Philip Dormer Stanhope, Earl of (statesman and letter writer), 1694-1773.

Cibber, Colley (actor and dramatist), 1671-1757.

Clarendon, Edward Hyde, Earl of, 1608-74. *See* Clarendon Press.

Coleridge, Hartley (poet), 1796-1849.

Coleridge, Samuel Taylor (poet, philosopher, and critic), 1772-1834.

Collins, John Churton (critic), 1848-1908.

Collins, William (poet), 1721-59.

Collins, William Wilkie (novelist), 1824-89.

Congreve, William (dramatist), 1670-1729.

Cotton, Charles (poet and translator), 1630-87.

Coverdale, Miles (translator of the Bible), 1488-1568. *See* Bible.

Cowley, Abraham (poet), 1618-67.

Cowper, William (poet), 1731-1800.

Crabbe, George (poet), 1754-1832.

Craigie, Mrs. Pearl Mary Theresa (Richards) (novelist), 1867-1906.

Crawford, Francis Marion (novelist and historian), 1854-1909.

Creasy, Sir Edward S. (historian), 1812-78.

Creighton, Mandell (Bishop of London) (historian), 1843-1901.

Crowe, Sir Joseph Archer (writer on art), 1825-96.

Cudworth, Ralph (divine writer), 1617-88.

Cunningham, Allan (poet), 1784-1842.

D'Arblay, Frances (Burney) (novelist), 1752-1840.

Darwin, Charles Robert (naturalist), 1809-82. *See* Darwinism.

Dasent, Sir George Webbe (Scandinavian scholar), 1817-96.

Davenant, Sir William (poet and dramatist), 1606-68.

Davy, Sir Humphrey (chemist and man of letters), 1778-1829.

Day, Thomas (miscellaneous writer), 1748-89.

Defoe, Daniel (journalist and novelist), 1661(?)-1731.

De Quincey, Thomas (essayist and miscellaneous writer), 1785-1859.

Dickens, Charles (novelist), 1812-70.

ENGLISH LITERATURE (*continued*)—

D'Israeli, Isaac (miscellaneous writer), 1766-1848.

Dixon, William Hepworth (historian and traveller), 1821-79.

Dodsley, Robert (poet and dramatist), 1703-64.

Donne, John (poet and divine), 1573-1631.

Drayton, Michael (poet), 1563-1631.

Drummond, Henry (theological and scientific writer), 1851-97.

Drummond, William (poet), 1585-1649.

Dryden, John (poet, dramatist, and satirist), 1631-1700.

Dugdale, Sir William (antiquarian), 1605-86.

Du Maurier (novelist and artist), 1834-96.

Dunbar, William (poet), 1465(?)-1530(?).

Duns, Scotus Johannes (schoolman), 1265(?)-1308(?).

Dyce, Alexander (scholar and critic), 1798-1869.

Dyer, Sir Edward (poet), 1545(?)-1607.

Dyer, John (poet), 1700-58.

Earle, John (essayist), 1601(?)-65.

Edgeworth, Maria (novelist), 1767-1849.

Edwards, Jonathan (theologian), 1702(?)-58.

Eliot, George. *See* Evans.

Elyot, Sir Thomas (miscellaneous writer), 1498-1546.

Emerson, R. W. *See* American Literature.

Evans, Mary Ann (" George Eliot ") (novelist), 1819-80.

Evelyn, John (diarist), 1620-1706.

Faraday, Michael (natural philosopher), 1791-1867.

Farrar, Frederick W. (Dean of Canterbury) (theological writer and novelist), 1831-1903.

Fielding, Henry (novelist), 1707-54.

Finlay, George (historian), 1799-1875.

Fiske, John (philologist and historian), 1842-1901.

Fitzgerald, Edward (translator), 1809-83.

Fletcher, John (poet and dramatist), 1579-1625.

Foote, Samuel (dramatist), 1720-1777.

Forster, John (Dickens's biographer), 1812-76.

Foxe, John (martyrologist), 1516-87.

Francis, Sir Philip (reputed author of *The Letters of Junius* (*q.v.*)), 1740-1818.

Freeman, Edward Augustus (historian), 1823-92.

Froude, James Anthony (historian), 1818-94.

Fuller, Thomas (divine and antiquary), 1608-61.

Galt, John (novelist and miscellaneous writer), 1779-1839.

Gardiner, Samuel Rawson (historian), 1829-1902.

Garnett, Richard (biographer and writer on literature), 1835-1906.

Garrick, David (dramatist and actor), 1717-79.

Gaskell, Elizabeth Cleghorn (Stevenson) (novelist), 1810-65.

Gay, John (poet and dramatist), 1685-1732.

Geddes, Alexander (theologian), 1737-1802.

Gibbon, Edward (historian), 1734-94.

" Giraldus Cambrensis " (Gerald de Barri), 1146(?)-1220(?).

Gissing, George (novelist), 1857-1903.

Gladstone, William Ewart (statesman and man of letters), 1809-98.

ENGLISH LITERATURE (*continued*)—

Gleig, George Robert (military writer), 1796-1888.

Godwin, Mrs. Mary (Wollstonecraft) (miscellaneous writer), 1759-97.

Godwin, William (philosopher and novelist), 1756-1836.

Goldsmith, Oliver (poet, dramatist, and essayist), 1728-74.

Gower, John (poet), 1325(?)-1408.

Grant, James (novelist), 1822-87.

Grant, James Augustus (traveller), 1827-92.

Grattan, Thomas Colley (miscellaneous writer), 1792-1864.

Gray, Thomas (poet), 1716-71.

Green, John Richard (historian), 1837-83.

Greene, Robert (poet and dramatist), 1560(?)-92.

Grosseteste, Robert (theologian), (?)-1253.

Grote, George (historian), 1794-1871.

Guest, Lady Charlotte (translator), 1812-95.

Hakluyt, Richard (collector of voyages), 1553(?)-1616.

Hale, Sir Matthew (jurist), 1609-76.

Hales, John (theologian), 1584-1656.

Hallam, Henry (historian), 1777-1859.

Hamilton, Sir William (metaphysician), 1788-1856.

Hare, Augustus John Cuthbert (miscellaneous writer), 1834-1903.

Harland, Henry (novelist), 1861-1905.

Harrington, James (political theorist), 1611-77.

Hawker, Robert Stephen (poet), 1803-75.

Hazlitt, William (essayist and critic), 1778-1830.

Hearn, Lafcadio (journalist and writer on Japan), 1850-1904.

Heber, Reginald (poet), 1783-1826.

Helps, Sir Arthur (essayist and historian), 1813-75.

Hemans, Felicia Dorothea (poetess), 1793-1835.

Henley, William Ernest (poet and critic), 1849-1903.

Herbert of Cherbury, Edward, Lord (philosopher and historian), 1583-1648.

Herbert, George (poet), 1593-1633.

Herrick, Robert (poet), 1591-1674.

Herschel, Sir John F. W. (astronomer), 1792-1871.

Hervey, James (religious writer), 1714-58.

Hervey, John, Lord (writer of memoirs), 1696-1743.

Heywood, John (dramatist), 1497(?)-1580(?).

Heywood, Thomas (dramatist), (?)-1650.

Hobbes, John Oliver. *See* Craigie.

Hobbes, Thomas (philosopher), 1588-1679.

Hoccleve or Occleve, Thomas (poet), 1368(?)-1450(?).

Hogg, James (" the Ettrick Shepherd ") (poet), 1770-1835.

Holinshead or Hollingshead, Raphael or Ralph (historian) (?)-1580(?).

Hone, William (miscellaneous writer), 1780-1842.

Hood, Thomas (poet and comic writer), 1799-1845.

Hook, Theodore Edward (dramatist and novelist), 1788-1841.

Hooker, Richard (theologian), 1554(?)-1600.

ENGLISH LITERATURE (*continued*)—

Howitt, William (1792-1879), Howitt, Mary (1799-1888) (miscellaneous writers).

Hughes, Thomas (novelist), 1822-96.

Hume, David (philosopher and historian), 1711-76.

Hunt, James Henry Leigh (essayist and poet), 1784-1859.

Huxley, Thomas Henry (scientific writer), 1825-95.

Ingelow, Jean (poet), 1820-97.

Irving, Sir Henry (actor), 1838-1905.

James, George Payne R. (novelist), 1799-1860.

Jameson, Mrs. Anna Brownell (writer on art), 1794-1860.

Jebb, Sir Richard Claverhouse (classical scholar), 1841-1905.

Jefferies, Richard (naturalist and novelist), 1848-87.

Jeffrey, Francis (critic and political writer), 1773-1850.

Jerrold, Douglas William (dramatist, etc.), 1803-57.

Jevons, William Stanley (logician), 1835-82.

Johnson, Samuel (Dr.) (moralist, essayist, and lexicographer), 1709-84.

Jonson, Ben (poet and dramatist), 1573-1637.

Jowett, Benjamin (scholar), 1817-93.

Kames, Henry Home, Lord (miscellaneous writer), 1696-1782.

Keats, John (poet), 1795-1821.

Keble, John (poet and divine), 1792-1866.

Kinglake, Alexander William (miscellaneous writer), 1809-91.

Kingsley, Charles (novelist), 1819-75.

Kingsley, Henry (novelist), 1830-76.

Kitto, John (biblical scholar), 1804-54.

Knight, Charles (publisher and writer), 1791-1873.

Knowles, James Sheridan (dramatist), 1784-1862.

Knox, John (reformer and historian), 1505(?)-72.

Kyd, Thomas (dramatist), 1558-95.

Lamb, Charles (essayist and poet), 1775-1834.

Landor, Walter Savage (poet, etc.), 1775-1864.

Lane, Edward William (Arabic scholar), 1801-76.

Langland, William (poet), 1330(?)-1400(?).

Latimer, Hugh (reformer and divine), 1485-1555.

Law, William (divine), 1686-1761.

Layard, Sir Austin Henry (explorer), 1817-94.

Lecky, William Edward Hartpole (historian), 1838-1903

Lee, Nathaniel (dramatist), 1653(?)-92.

Le Fanu, Joseph Sheridan (novelist), 1814-73.

Leighton, Robert (divine), 1611-84.

Lemon, Mark (journalist and humourist), 1809-70.

Leslie, John (historian), 1527-96.

L'Estrange, Sir Roger (journalist and pamphleteer), 1616-1704.

Lever, Charles James (novelist), 1806-72.

Lewes, Geo. Henry (philosopher, etc.), 1817-78.

Leydon, John (poet and Orientalist), 1775-1811.

Liddon, Henry Parker (divine), 1829-90.

Lindsay or Lyndsay, Sir David (poet), 1490-1555.

Lingard, John (historian), 1771-1851.

ENGLISH LITERATURE (*continued*)—

Livingstone, David (missionary explorer) 1813-73. *See* Livingstone's Travels.

Locke, John (philosopher), 1632-1704.

Lockhart, John Gibson (novelist and biographer), 1794-1854.

Lodge, Thomas (poet and dramatist), 1558(?)-1625.

Lovelace, Richard (poet), 1618-58.

Lover, Samuel (song writer and novelist), 1797-1868.

Lyly, John (dramatist, etc.), 1554(?)-1606.

Lytton, Edward George E. Lytton-Bulwer (novelist and statesman), 1803-73.

Macaulay, Thomas Babington, Lord (historian and essayist), 1800-59.

Macdonald, George (poet and novelist), 1824-1905.

Mackintosh, Sir James (philosopher and historian), 1765-1832.

Macleod, Norman (Scottish divine and miscellaneous writer), 1812-72.

Macpherson, James (alleged trans. of the Ossianic poems), 1736(?)-96.

Malory, Sir Thomas (trans. of *Morte d'Arthur*), flourished 1470.

Malthus, Thomas Robert (economist), 1766-1834.

Mandeville, Bernard de (satirist), 1670-1733.

Manning, Henry Edward (Cardinal) (theologian), 1808-92.

Marlowe, Christopher (dramatist), 1564-93.

Marryat, Frederick (novelist), 1792-1848.

Marston, John (dramatist and satirist), 1575(?)-1634.

Martin, Sir Theodore (poet, biographer), 1816-1909.

Martineau, Harriet (novelist and economist), 1802-76.

Martineau, James (Unitarian theologian), 1805-1900.

Marvell, Andrew (poet and satirist), 1621-78.

Massey, Gerald (poet), 1828-1907.

Massinger, Philip (dramatist), 1583-1640.

Masson, David (biographer and historian), 1822-1907.

Max-Müller, Friedrich (philologist), 1823-1900.

Meredith, George (novelist and poet), 1828-1909.

Merivale, Charles (historian), 1808-93.

Middleton, Thomas (dramatist), 1570(?)-1627.

Mill, James (philosopher and historian), 1773-1836.

Mill, John Stuart (philosopher), 1806-73.

Miller, Hugh (geologist), 1802-56.

Milman, Henry Hart (poet and historian), 1791-1868.

Milton, John (poet), 1608-74.

Mitford, Mary Russell (novelist and dramatist), 1787-1855.

Montagu, Lady Mary Wortley (letter writer), 1689-1762.

Montgomery, James (poet), 1771-1854.

Moore, Thomas (poet), 1779-1852.

More, Hannah (miscellaneous and religious writer), 1745-1833.

More, Sir Thomas (historical and political writer), 1478-1535.

Morley, Henry (writer on English literature), 1822-94.

Morris, William (poet, artist, and socialist), 1834-96.

Motley, John Lothrop (historian), 1814-77.

ENGLISH LITERATURE (*continued*)—

Murray, Lindley (grammarian), 1745-1826.

Nairne, Carolina (Oliphant), Baroness, 1766-1845.

Napier, Sir William Francis Patrick (historian and soldier), 1785-1860.

Nash, Thomas (dramatist and miscellaneous writer), 1567-1601.

Newman, John Henry (Cardinal) (theologian and poet), 1801-90.

Newton, Sir Isaac (natural philosopher), 1642-1727.

Newton, John (divine and hymn writer), 1725-1807.

Occam or Ockham, William (schoolman), 1270(?)-1349(?).

Oliphant, Laurence (novelist and miscellaneous writer), 1829-88.

Otway, Thomas (dramatist), 1651 or 1652-85.

Paine, Thomas (political and anti-Christian writer), 1737-1809.

Paley, William (theologian), 1743-1805.

Palgrave, Sir Francis (historian), 1788-1861.

Paris, Matthew (chronicler), *circa* 1195-1259.

Park, Mungo (traveller), 1771-1806.

Pater, Walter Horatio (essayist and critic), 1839-94.

Patmore, Coventry Kersey Dighton (poet), 1823-96.

Pattison, Mark (scholar and biographer), 1813-84.

Payn, James (novelist), 1830-98.

Peacock, Thomas Love (novelist), 1785-1866.

Penn, William (Quaker apologist), 1644-1718.

Pepys, Samuel (diarist), 1633-1703.

Percy, Thomas (antiquary and poet), 1729-1811.

Piozzi, Hester Lynch (Salusbury) (miscellaneous writer), 1741-1821.

Pope, Alexander (poet), 1688-1744.

Porter, Jane (novelist), 1776-1850.

Powell, Frederick York (historian), 1850-1904.

Priestley, Joseph (chemist, theologian, etc.), 1733-1804.

Prior, Matthew (poet), 1664-1721.

Prynne, William (controversial writer), 1600-69.

Purchas, Samuel (compiler of travels), 1575(?)-1626.

Pusey, Edward Bouverie (theologian), 1800-82.

Raleigh, Sir Walter (explorer, historian, etc.), 1552(?)-1618.

Ramsay, Allan (poet), 1686-1758.

Ray, John (naturalist), 1627-1705.

Reade, Charles (novelist), 1814-84.

Reid, Sir Thomas Wemyss (novelist and biographer), 1842-1905.

Richardson, Samuel (novelist), 1689-1761.

Robertson, William (historian), 1721-93.

Rogers, Samuel (poet), 1763-1855.

Roscoe, William (historian), 1753-1831.

Rossetti, Christina Georgina (poetess), 1830-94.

Rossetti, Dante Gabriel (poet), 1828-82.

Ruskin, John (writer on art, economics, etc.), 1819-1900.

Rutherford, Samuel (theologian), 1600(?)-61.

Sackville, Thomas (poet), 1536-1608.

Sandys, George (traveller and translator), 1578-1644.

Savage, Richard (poet), (?) -1743.

ENGLISH LITERATURE (*continued*)—

Scott, Michael (novelist), 1789-1835.

Scott, Sir Walter (novelist and poet), 1771-1832.

Seeley, Sir John Robert (historian and essayist), 1834-95.

Selden, John (jurist and scholar), 1584-1654.

Shaftesbury, Anthony Ashley Cooper, Earl of (philosopher), 1671-1713.

Shakespeare, William (dramatist and poet), 1564-1616. *See* separate article.

Sharp, William ("Fiona Macleod") (novelist and poet), 1856-1905.

Shelley, Percy Bysshe (poet), 1792-1822.

Shenstone, William (poet), 1714-63.

Sheridan, Richard Brinsley (dramatist), 1715-1816.

Shorthouse, Joseph Henry (novelist), 1834-1903.

Sidney or Sydney, Algernon (political writer), 1622-83.

Sidney, Sir Philip (poet), 1554-86.

Skelton, John (poet) 1460(?)-1529.

Skene, William Forbes (historian), 1809-92.

Smart, Christopher (poet), 1722-71.

Smiles, Samuel (biographer and miscellaneous writer), 1812-1904.

Smith, Adam (philosopher and economist), 1723-90.

Smith, Goldwin (historian), 1824-1910.

Smith, Sydney (miscellaneous writer), 1771-1845.

Smith, Sir William (lexicographer), 1813-93.

Smollett, Tobias George (novelist), 1721-71.

Southey, Robert (poet and biographer), 1774-1843.

Southwell, Robert (poet), 1561(?)-95.

Spelman, Sir Henry (historian), 1564(?)-1641.

Spencer. Herbert (philosopher), 1820-1903.

Spenser, Edmund (poet), 1552(?)-99.

Stanley, Arthur Penrhyn (Dean of Westminster) (historian, biographer, and theologian), 1815-81.

Steele, Sir Richard (essayist and dramatist), 1672-1729.

Steevens, George Warrington (journalist, etc.), 1869-1900.

Stephen, Sir James (statesman and historian), 1789-1859.

Stephen, Sir Leslie (biographer and critic), 1832-1904.

Sterling, John (essayist and miscellaneous writer), 1806-44.

Sterne, Laurence (novelist), 1713-68.

Stevenson, Robert Louis (novelist and essayist), 1850-94.

Stewart, Dugald (philosopher), 1753-1828.

Stillingfleet, Edward (theologian), 1635-99.

Stirling-Maxwell, Sir William (historian and writer on art), 1818-78.

Stow, John (historian and antiquary), 1525-1605.

Strickland, Agnes (historical writer), 1796(?)-1874.

Strode, William (poet), 1600-45.

Stubbs, William (Bishop) (historian), 1825-1901.

Suckling, Sir John (poet), 1609-42.

Swift, Jonathan (Dean) (satirist), 1667-1745.

Dictionary of Dates

ENGLISH LITERATURE (*continued*)—

Swinburne, Algernon Charles (poet), 1837-1909.

Symonds, John Addington (historian, etc.), 1840-93.

Taylor, Isaac (philosophical and historical writer), 1787-1865.

Taylor, Isaac (Canon) (miscellaneous writer), 1829-1901.

Taylor, Jeremy (divine,) 1613-67.

Temple, Sir William (essayist), 1628-99.

Tennyson, Alfred, Lord (poet), 1809-92.

Thackeray, William Makepeace (novelist), 1811-63.

Thomson, James (poet), 1700-48.

Tillotson, John (divine), 1630-94.

Tooke, John Horne (philologist), 1736-1812.

Traherne, Thomas (poet and theological writer), 1636(?)-74.

Trollope, Anthony (novelist), 1815-82.

Tupper, Martin Farquhar (versifier), 1810-89.

Tyndale, William (translator of the Bible), 1484(?)-1536.

Tyndall, John (natural philosopher), 1820-93.

Udall, Nicholas (dramatist and scholar), 1505-56.

Ussher, James (divine and scholar), 1581-1656.

Vanbrugh, Sir John (dramatist), 1664-1726.

Waller, Edmund (poet), 1606-87.

Walpole, Horace (miscellaneous writer), 1717-97.

Walton, Izaak (biographer), 1593-1683.

Warburton, William (theologian), 1698-1799.

Warton, Joseph (critic), 1722-1800.

Watson, John (" Ian Maclaren ") (novelist), 1850-1907.

Watts, Isaac (poet and theologian), 1674-1748.

Webster, Augusta (poet), 1840-94.

Webster, John (dramatist), 1580(?)-1625(?).

Wesley, John (theological writer), 1703-91.

Whateley, Richard (theologian), 1787-1863.

White, Gilbert (naturalist), 1720-93.

White, Henry Kirke (poet), 1785-1806.

Whyte-Melville, George John (novelist), 1821-78.

Wiclif or Wyclif, John (theologian), 1320(?)-84.

Wilde, Oscar O'Flahertie Wills (poet and dramatist), 1856-1900

William of Malmesbury (historian), *b.* between 1090-96, *d.* about 1143.

Wilson, John (" Christopher North ") (miscellaneous writer), 1785-1854.

Wither, George (poet), 1588-1667.

Wordsworth, Dorothy (diarist), 1771-1855.

Wordsworth, William (poet), 1770-1850.

Wotton, Sir Henry (poet), 1568-1639.

Wyatt, Sir Thomas (poet), 1503-42.

Wycherley, William (dramatist), 1640(?)-1716.

Yates, Edmund (novelist and dramatist), 1831-94.

Yonge, Charlotte Mary (novelist), 1823-1901.

Young, Arthur (writer on agriculture and travel), 1741-1820.

Young, Edward (poet), 1683-1765.

See Printing, etc. [Refer *Dicty. of Nat. Biog.*, ed. by Sidney Lee.]

Engraving on Metal and Stone. The first metal plate from which impressions on paper were taken seems to have been executed in 1452. It was a *pax* or metal plate used in the Roman Catholic service. Early books containing engravings reproduced from metal plates are the *Kalender*, dated 1465, and the *Monte Santo de Dio*, 1477. The first engraver proper who seems to have done nothing but engrave was Antonio Raimondi (*circa* 1488-1530). Albert Dürer, mentioned below, was an adept at the art. In England the earliest line engravings are those in *The Birth of Mankind*, 1540. The earliest known English engraver was William Rogers, who lived in 1545. The process of mezzotint engraving was invented by Ludwig von Siegen, a German, about 1642. It was intro. into England in 1660 by Prince Rupert, who had seen Von Siegen at work. Aquatint engraving was supposed to have been invented by Saint Non (1730-1804), a Frenchman, and it was first practised in England in 1780. Lithography or engraving on stone was invented by Aloys Senefelder, a German, in 1796. [Refer art. in *Chambers's Encyclopædia*.]

Engraving on Wood. Said to have been invented by the Chinese some centuries before Christ. The modern process, however, seems to date from the 15th century, and the earliest dated example is in a monastery near Memmingen in Germany, which bears the year 1423. The art reached England in 1476, when Caxton published the second edition of the *Game and Playe of Chesse*, containing very rough illustrations. In 1486 Erhard Reuwich published an edition of Breydenbach's *Travels*, containing some engravings which were more than ordinary lines, and showed attempts at shading. A great revolution in the art was brought about by Albert Dürer (1471-1528), whose engravings show careful and accurate draughtsmanship. From Dürer's time the art has developed to its present high standard. [Refer Woodberry, *History of Wood Engraving*.]

Entente Cordiale, between England and France, mainly brought about by the exertions of Edward VII., and the Anglo-French agreement signed April 8, 1904.

Ephesus. The temple of Diana at, one of the Seven Wonders of the World (*q.v.*). Built 552 B.C.; destroyed by Herostratus on the night on which Alexander the Great was *b.* 356 B.C.; res. shortly afterwards [refer Smith, *Classical Dicty.* under Ephesus and Artemis]; finally destroyed by the Goths in their third naval invasion A.D. 262. [Refer Gibbon, *Rome.*]

Epiphany, Feast of. Held every Jan. 6; estab. A.D. 813 to celebrate the manifestation of the Star of Bethlehem.

Episcopal Ordination Act. Passed by Scottish Parliament 1662, ordering that all holders of livings should be ordained.

"Epistolæ Obscurorum Virorum" (*Letters of the Obscure Men*). The work of several Humanists (*q.v.*), at whose head was Ulrich von Hutten. First published 1515; enlarged, Aug. 1516; book ii. 1517.

These letters attacked abuses in Church and State, and were condemned by Leo X. in a bull published Mar. 15, 1517. [Refer W. S. Lilly, *Renaissance Types*, 1901.]

Erastians. A religious sect following the teachings of Erastus (1524-83). Ideas advocated by many divines at the Westminster Assembly, 1643-9 (*q.v.*). [Refer Collier, *Ecclesiastical History*.]

Erie Canal (U.S.A.). First excavation made, July 4, 1817; opened 1825.

Escorial or **Escurial** (palace of the kings of Spain). Begun by Philip II. of Spain; built in the shape of a gridiron, the emblem of the martyrdom of St. Lawrence, to whom it was dedicated. First stone laid, April 23, 1563; completed 1586. Charles V.'s remains conveyed there 1574. Philip II. died there 1598. [Refer A. F. Calvert, *The Escorial*.]

Esperanto. An attempt to form an international language, invented by Dr. L. Zamenhof (*b.* 1859), a Russian physician, in 1887. Supplanted its predecessor Volapük, which appeared in 1880.

"Essays and Reviews." By six clergymen and one layman of the Church of England, published Mar. 1860; condemned for heterodoxy by Convocation, June 24, 1864.

Essex, Kingdom of. Abolished at the Norman Conquest 1066. The following are the Kings of Essex:—

Exwine *circa* 527	Sigehere (?)
Sleda *circa* 587	Stebbe *circa* 665
Sebert (?)-616	Sigeheard (?)-694
Seward and Sigebert 616-17	Swoefred 694-704
Sigebert the Little 617-53	Offa (?)
Sigebert the Good 653-60	Selred 709-46

[Refer Freeman, *Old English History*.]

Estates of Scotland. *See* Scotland.

Estates, The Committee of the. Appointed by Scotch Parliament 1640; dissolved 1648. *See* Scotland.

Etaples, Treaty of. Signed between Henry VII. of England and Charles VIII. of France, Nov. 9, 1492.

Eton College (Windsor, England). Fd. 1440 by Henry VI. under the title of *The College of the Blessed Mary of Eton beside Windsor*. Supplementary charter granted 1441, when building was commenced. The old custom of "Montem," procession held annually to collect money to send the captain of the school to Cambridge, was abolished 1846. [Refer Cust, *History of Eton College*.]

H

Etruria. A country in Central Italy. Origin uncertain. The Etruscans became subject to Rome after their decisive defeat by Cornelius Dolabella 283 B.C. Received Roman franchise 91 B.C. [Refer Dennis, *Cities of Etruria*.]

European Association. Fd. in London by Mazzini and others to promote Republican movement on the Continent 1855

Evacuation Day. Anniversary of the evacuation of New York city by the British, Nov. 25, 1783.

Evangelical Alliance. (*a*) Formed by the Protestant states of Germany 1608; opposed by Holy Alliance fd. 1609. (*b*) Undenominational alliance of all Protestant Christians to oppose Romanism and infidelity, 1845.

Evangelic League. Fd. by certain Lutherans and Calvinists in 1613 against the Emperor Mathias.

Evil May Day. May 1, 1517. A riot of the London apprentices which arose out of a conspiracy against foreigners, occurring on April 30, 1517. [Refer *Cambridge Modern History*, vol. i.]

Evora, Convention of. Brought an end to civil war in Portugal (*q.v.*); signed 1834.

Examiner of Stage Plays. *See* Drama.

Exchange, Royal (London). Fd. by Sir Thomas Gresham, June 7, 1566. Queen Elizabeth visited it in Jan. 1571, since when it has been called *Royal*. Destroyed by fire 1666; rebuilt by Nicholas Hawksmoor 1668; again destroyed by fire, Jan. 10, 1838; present building was rebuilt 1840-4. [Refer Taylor, *Historical Guide to London*.]

Exchequer, Court of the (*Curia Regis*). Fd. by William I. 1079; separated from Court of Common Pleas 1215; sat for last time, July 10, 1875. Chancellor of the E. office fd. 1221; E. office fd. 1399. [Refer Stubbs, *Constitutional History of England*.]

Excise (Great Britain). System intro. by Long Parliament in 1643. Sir Robert Walpole attempted in 1733 to pass his E. scheme, but had to withdraw it owing to the strong opposition with which it was met. Duty on spirit, imposed 1746, was withdrawn owing to stampive smuggling. E. department amalgamated with that of extenss and taxes and Board of Inland Revenue formed 1849.

Excise (U.S.A.). Bill to impose tax on liquors intro. into Congress 1791; caused rioting 1794. [Refer Harper, *Encyclo. U.S. History*, vol. iii.]

Exclusion Bill, disabling the Duke of York (afterwards James II.), a Roman Catholic, from succeeding to the throne 1679; again passed by Commons, Oct. 1680, but thrown out by the Lords. [Refer Macaulay, *Hist. of England*.]

Exeter (England). Orig. *Caer Wisc*. Captured by Sweyn 1003; made a bishopric 1046; captured by William the Conqueror 1067; cathedral commenced 1112; captured by Prince Maurice 1642; retaken by Fairfax 1646. [Refer Freeman, *Exeter* (Historic Towns Series).]

Exeter Hall (Strand, London). Built 1830-1; used for meetings, concerts, oratorios, etc., till 1880; pulled down 1909.

Exhibition, The Great (London). Royal Commission appointed and building commenced, Jan. 3, 1850; opened by Queen Victoria, May 1, 1851. *See* Crystal Palace.

Extradition Laws (Great Britain and general). Early act passed between William of Scotland and Henry II. of England 1174. Court of Exchequer declared a form of E. L. 1749. Treaty with U.S.A. (Ashburton) 1842 (enlarged 1890); with France 1843. New convention with France, when exception was made with regard to political offences 1852. E. Act 1870; since this many treaties have been made with various countries. [Refer Clarke, *Law of Extradition*.]

F

Fabian Society. A socialist association fd. in London in 1883.

Factory Acts (Great Britain). The first F. A. intro. by Sir Robert Peel the elder passed 1802, providing inspectors for factories [refer Fletcher, *Introductory Hist. of England*, vol. iii.]. The second F. A. passed 1819, relating to cotton mills. Lord Althorpe's act, passed 1833, intro. *half-time* principle, and provided for education of children engaged in factories. Sir Robert Peel's F. A., passed 1844, provided a 10-hours' limit for women and children. Mining Act 1842 prohibited female and child labour in mines (*see* Mining). F. A. Extension and Workshop Regulation Acts passed 1867, by which *all* factories were included in previous acts. Government inspectors for factories appointed by law 1871. Cross's F. and Workshop Act, amending previous acts, 1878; again amended 1901, 1902; further modifications 1908. *See* Shop Hours Act. [Refer Von Plener, *English Factory Legislation.*]

Falaise (France). Treaty of, between Henry II. of England, his son Henry, and Louis VII. of France 1174; besieged by Henry V. of England 1417; captured from England 1450. [Refer Fletcher, *Intro. History of England*, vol. i.]

Falczi (Turkey). Peace of, between Russia and Turkey, July 21, 1711.

Falkland Islands. (S. America). Discovered by John Davis 1592. Great Britain in possession 1765; English expelled by Spanish 1767; Spanish withdrew 1771; new settlement by English effected 1832. [Refer Lucas, *Historical Geog. of British Empire.*]

Family Compact. (1) An agreement made in 1733 between Louis XV. of France and Philip V. of Spain against English commerce; (2) a treaty between France and Spain of perpetual alliance, signed at Fontainebleau, Oct. 25, 1743; (3) between the Bourbons of France and Spain, Aug. 15, 1761. [Refer Fletcher, *Intro. History of England*, vol. ii.]

Faneuil Hall. *See* "Cradle of Liberty."

Farmers' Alliance. Formed in the U.S.A. to protect agricultural classes 1873. [Refer Harper, *Encyclo. U.S. History.*]

"Farmer's Letters, The." A series of letters written by John Dickinson against English ministerial measures; first appeared in *Pennsylvania Chronicle*, Dec. 2, 1767. [Refer Harper, *Encyclo. U.S. History.*]

Farnley Wood Plot. An attempt to overthrow government of Charles II. 1663; leaders tried and executed, Jan. 19, 1664.

Farringdon Market (London). Bill for establishment of, June 21, 1824; opened Nov. 20, 1826. *See* Smithfield.

Farthing. " Edward I. (1272-1307) coined for the first time half-pennies and farthings, instead of having pennies cut into halves and quarters, as had been the custom till that time " [" A Brief Survey of the English Coinage," by Bernard Roth, in *A Literary and Historical Atlas of Europe* (Everyman's Lib.)].

Fashoda Question. The French under Major Marchand occupied Fashoda in the Upper Nile valley, July 10, 1898. Great Britain demanded the French to evacuate, and after much correspondence, which nearly resulted in war, Major Marchand left, Dec. 11, 1898.

Fathers of the Church (*Patres Ecclesiastici*). Great bishops and eminent Christian teachers of the earlier centuries of unimpeachable orthodoxy and eminent sanctity, and accepted by the Church as qualified exponents of her doctrines. The principal ante-Nicene Fathers are:—

Justin Martyr c. A.D. 100-165.	Origen 185-254.
Irenæus c. 130-c. 202.	Cyprian c. 200-258.
Clement of Alexandria c. 150-c. 216.	Gregory Thaumaturgus c. 213-c. 270.
Tertullian c. 155-c. 222.	

The principal post-Nicene Fathers are:—

Eusebius of Cæsarea c. 270-340.	Epiphanius c. 330-403.
Hilary of Poitiers 305-366.	Chrysostom c. 344-407.
Athanasius c. 296-373.	Jerome 331-420.
Basil 329-379.	Augustine 354-430.
Cyril of Jerusalem 315-386.	Cyril of Alexandria -444.
Gregory of Nazianzus 328-c. 390.	Leo the Great -c. 461.
Gregory of Nyssa 351-c. 395.	Gregory the Great -604.
Ambrose 340-c. 397.	John of Damascus.

[Refer McClintock and Strong, *Encyc. of Biblical and Eccles. Lit.*]

Faversham (Kent, England). Abbey fd. 1147-9.

Fawkes, Guy, Conspiracy of. *See* Gunpowder Plot.

Feast of Reconciliation. Held in London on Jan. 25, 1555, by order of Queen Mary I. to celebrate the return of England to the See of Rome. [Refer Gardiner, *History of England*.]

Federal Convention (U.S.A.). Representatives of twelve states assembled at Philadelphia 1787 to prepare a constitution for U.S.A. *See* United States. [Refer Harper, *Encyclo. U.S. History*, vol. iii.]

Federalists (U.S.A.). Advocates of National Constitution 1788. Defeated 1800 by election of Jefferson as president; disbanded 1820. *See* Anti-Federalists. [Refer Harper, *Encyclo. U.S. History*, vol. iii.]

Federal Union. *See* United States.

Fenian Association. Led by James Stephens. Fd. in Ireland about 1858. Its object was to make England's rule impossible in Ireland. Attempted a raid into Canada 1866; rebellion in Ireland and England 1867; attempted to blow up Clerkenwell gaol, Dec. 13, 1867; further raids into Canada 1870; plot of " Irish Invincibles " 1883. [Refer McCarthy, *History of our own Times*.]

Fernando Po (W. coast of Africa). Discovered by a Portuguese explorer, Fernao do Po, 1486; an English settlement 1827-34; now colonised by Spaniards.

Ferrara (Italy). Built and walled in by Ravenna 659. The famous family of Este become hereditary rulers of 1240. Taken by French 1796; res. to the Pope 1814; held by an Austrian garrison 1849-59; annexed to Sardinia, Mar. 1860. [Refer vol. on *Ferrara* in Mediæval Towns Series.]

Ferrars' Arrest. George F., M.P. for Plymouth, became security for a man who failed to settle at the time appointed. F. arrested by sheriffs of the City of London, Mar. 1542. Commons demanded release of F., which was refused. The sheriffs on Mar. 28, 1542, appeared before the bar of the House of Commons to answer to the charge. They were imprisoned, but released on Mar. 30. [Refer Low and Pulling, *Dicty. of English History*.]

Fettmilch Insurrection. Between 1612 and 1616, led by Vincent F. and others, at Frankfort-on-Maine, against the mismanagement of municipal affairs. Leaders executed in 1616. It was not until 1801 that the insurrection was finally suppressed. [Refer Janssen, *History of the German People* (Eng. trans.), vol. x.]

Feudalism. Intro. partly by the Saxons into England about 600, but it was William the Conqueror (1066) who brought in the complete feudal laws. Feudal government prevailed in England during Stephen's reign 1135-54. Act for abolishing feudal tenures 1660. [Refer Stubbs, *Constitutional History of England*.]

Feuillants' Club, The. Fd. by the moderate Jacobins 1790; so called from their meeting-place, a disused convent of the F.; disbanded Nov. 1791. [Refer *Cambridge Modern History*, vol. viii.]

Fiery Chamber. *See* Chambre Ardente.

Fieschi's Plot, to assassinate Louis Philippe of France, July 28, 1835. F. executed with his accomplices, Feb. 19, 1836. [Refer *Annual Register*, 1835.]

" Fifteen," Insurrection of (Great Britain), 1715. An attempt to place James Stuart, the Young Pretender, on the throne after the death of Queen Anne, 1714. John Erskine, Earl of Mar, set up James's standard at Braemar, Sept. 6, 1715; met the Duke of Argyll in battle at Sheriffmuir, Nov. 12; result indecisive. James Stuart landed at Peterhead, Dec. 22, but owing to the suppression of Mar's army by Argyll, re-embarked and took Mar with him to Avignon in France, Feb. 1716. Many of the leaders executed. [Refer Fletcher, *An Intro. Hist. of England*, vol. ii.]

Fifth-Monarchy Men A religious sect fd. in England about 1645. Their preachers, Feake and Powell, attacked Oliver Cromwell, 1653, calling him " the dissemblingest perjured villain in the world." They were brought before the Council, Dec. 21-24, 1653, and warned. Repeated the offence, and were imprisoned, Jan. 1654. They rose in revolt in 1661, were defeated and their leaders executed. [Refer Gardiner, *History of the Commonwealth and Protectorate*.]

Fifty-one, Committee of. Formed in New York in 1774; favoured a general congress.

Figueras (Spain). Fd. by Ferdinand VI. 1746-59; captured by French, Nov. 24, 1794; finally res. to Spain by Treaty of Paris 1814.

Fiji Islands (Australasia). Discovered by Tasman 1643; Capt. Cook at 1773; ceded to Great Britain 1874. [Refer Williams, *Fiji and the Fijians*.]

Finland (N. Europe). About the commencement of the 8th century the Finns took possession of their present position on the continent of Europe. They were continually oppressed by the Swedes, who in 1293 subdued their country. In 1809 F. was united to Russia, and has remained so ever since. In 1898 Russia interfered with the constitution of the Finns, with the result that troubles have resulted ever since; exiles recalled and diet opened 1904; scheme for reform of representation 1906. [Refer Fisher, *Finland and the Tsars*.]

Firearms (*see also* under titles of various weapons). In 1247 Seville was defended by a species of cannon which hurled stones. In 1327 some of the mercenaries in the English army of Edward III. employed cannon (*q.v.*). In 1471 culverin or hand-cannon were used by the soldiers of Edward IV. of England. The wheel-lock, as a substitute for the match-lock, was invented in Germany during the latter half of the 16th century; the firelock or flintlock about 1625 in Spain, and was in general use until about 1842 (*see* Rifles). Pistols were first made at Pistoja in Italy about 1542, and were used with great success at the b. of Renty 1554 (*see* Revolver). [Refer Grose, *Military Antiquities*.]

Fire Brigades (Great Britain). The various fire insurance companies in London had F. B. of their own. In 1825 several united, and in 1833 practically all united [refer Walford, *Insurance Encyclopædia*]. The Metropolitan F. B. estab. by Act of Parliament 1865. [Refer art. on " Fire " in *Chambers's Encyclopædia*.]

Fire Engine. Hautsch of Nuremberg constructed a machine 1657. Flexible hose intro. by Jan Vanderheide 1672. Newsham's engine patented 1700. The first steam engine invented by Braithwaite 1829; Ericsson in New York produced a similar one 1840. They were not generally used until 1860. Engines driven by motor power first used 1905. [Refer Young, *Fires, Fire Engines, and Fire Brigades*.]

Fire of London, Great. Broke out accidentally near London Bridge, Sept. 2, extinguished Sept. 6, 1666.

Five Hundred, Council of the. In 1795 the French legislation was governed by two councils—the Council of Ancients, consisting of men of forty-five years and upwards, and the Council of the Five Hundred, consisting of five hundred deputies of no age limit. This latter council had the management of all taxation and financial matters; elected Napoleon Bonaparte's brother Lucien as their president, Oct. 22, 1799; disbanded by Napoleon, Nov. 10, 1799. [Refer Morse Stephens, *Revolutionary Europe*.]

Five Members, Pym, Hampden, Haselrig, Strode, and Holles; connected with the Long Parliament. Attempted arrest of by Charles I., Jan. 2, 1642. [Refer Hallam, *Constitutional History*.]

Five Mile Act. *See* Nonconformists.

Flagellants. A religious sect fd. in Europe about A.D. 1260. In 1348 they again appeared during the ravages of the " Black Death " (*q.v.*). In 1417 a long train of them wandered through Italy, France, and Spain under the leadership of St. Vincent Ferreri, a Spaniard. Many were condemned as heretics and burnt. [Refer Kurtz, *Hist. of the Christian Church to the Reformation* (Eng. trans.).]

Flammock's Rebellion, 1497, led by Thomas F., Michael Joseph, and Lord Audley, encamped on Blackheath and were met and defeated by Henry VII. June 22, 1497. The leaders were executed, June 28, 1497. [Refer Bacon, *History of Henry VII.*]

Flanders (Europe). Colonised by Saxons 802; annexed to France 843; famous for woollen manufacture 962; part given to Holland 1256. By Treaty of Westphalia, Dutch F. transferred to United Netherlands, East and West F. incorp. with Belgium. *See* Holland, Belgium. [Refer Motley, *United Netherlands*.]

Fleet Prison (London). Its origin uncertain; known to have been a debtors' prison as early as 1290. Burnt by Wat Tyler. The Star Chamber prisoners incarcerated in, 1641, after which it was again a debtors' prison. Burned during Great Fire of London 1666. Parliamentary investigation into abuses at 1726. Burnt by Gordon rioters 1780. Prison abolished in 1842, and the buildings demolished 1845-6. The notorious Fleet marriages were abolished by the Marriage Act (*q.v.*) 1753. [Refer Ashton, *The Fleet, its River, Prison, and Marriages*.]

Flemings. *See* Weaving.

Fleur-de-Lis. The national emblem of France; first used by Clovis A.D. 496, until 1789, when the tricolour was substituted for it.

Florence (Italy). " The beginnings of Florence are lost in cloudy legend " [Gardner, *Story of Florence* (Mediæval Towns Series)]. According to Villani, F. was fd. by Julius Cæsar about 62 B.C. Independent republic A.D. 1198. Suffered defeat by Sienese 1260. Partly burnt through the bickerings of the " Blacks " and " Whites " 1304. Defeated by English mercenaries employed by the town of Pisa 1363. Repelled papal invasion 1375. Cosmo de Medici fd. university 1433; fd. library 1444. Reign of Lorenzo Medici (*the Magnificent*) 1470-92. Lorenzo fd. Platonic Academy 1476. The Pazzi conspiracy against the Medici, Julian killed, Lorenzo escaped, April 1478. Expulsion of the Medici 1494. Death of Savonarola 1498. Restoration of the Medici 1512; again expelled and Florence declared a republic 1527; res. Oct. 28, 1530. Academy Della Crusca fd. 1582. F. presented by Napoleon I. to his sister Elise 1808; provisional capital of Italy 1864-71. [Refer vol. in Mediæval Towns Series.]

Florida (U.S.A.). Discovered 1512 by Ponce de Leon. Conquered by Narvaez and possessed by Spain 1528, and by De Soto 1539. City of St. Augustine in F. captured by Sir Francis Drake 1586. F. exchanged by Spaniards with Great Britain for Cuba by Treaty of Paris 1763; again ceded to Spain 1783; possessed by U.S. Government 1811; returned to Spain 1812; purchased from Spain 1819; admitted to the Union as a state, Mar. 8, 1845. [Refer Harper, *Encyclo. U.S. History.*]

Florin. First struck in gold in Florence in the 11th century. Silver F. first struck 1181. In England Edward III. coined a gold F. in 1337 value 6s. A silver coinage of F. value 2s. struck in 1849; it is known as the " godless or graceless F." because the words *Dei Gratia* were omitted. [Refer art. on " English Coinage " by Bernard Roth in *A Literary and Hist. Atlas of Europe.*]

Flushing (Holland). Taken by revolted Netherlanders 1572 [refer Motley, *Dutch Republic*]; bombarded by English, Aug. 15, 1809. *See* Walcheren Expedition.

Flying Shuttle. *See* Weaving.

Flying Squadron. A political party fd. in Scotland about 1705, led by Lord Tweeddale; secured settlement of Union question 1706. [Refer Burton, *History of Scotland.*]

Fommanah, Treaty of, between Great Britain and the King of Ashanti, signed Feb. 13, 1874.

Fontainebleau, Decree of. Issued against British commerce in 1810 by Napoleon. Treaty of F. (1) between Napoleon and Godoy, the minister of Charles IV. and the *de facto* King of Spain 1807; (2) between Napoleon and the allied powers, signed April 4, 1814, by which the former abdicates.

Fool's Cap Livery, The. The Earl of Egmont in 1563 dressed his servants in a livery resembling a monk's cowl and fool's cap. This was done in mockery of Cardinal Granvelle. The livery became the fashion, and many of the Dutch nobles wore it as well as their servants. [Refer Motley, *Dutch Republic.*]

Foraker Act. Intro. by Joseph Benson Foraker. Passed by U.S. Congress in 1900, establishing self-government in Porto Rico, and providing for a tariff. The tariff provisions repealed in 1901. [Refer Harper, *Encyclopædia of U.S. History.*]

Force Act. Passed by U.S. Congress in 1870; granted rights to Federal authorities to intervene in certain cases regarding law and order in individual states. [Refer Harper, *Encyclopædia of U.S. History.*]

Foreign Enlistment Act (Great Britain). Passed 1819, forbidding British subjects to enlist in foreign services which were at war with any other nation friendly to Great Britain.

Forest Laws. First intro. into England by William the Conqueror, who destroyed several towns to make the New Forest 1079-85. Courts for trying offences against not held since 1632. Surveyor-

General of Crown Land Revenues and the Surveyor-General of Woods and Forests amalgamated under one board called Commissioners of Woods, Forests, and Land Revenues, June 9, 1810. [Refer Gardiner, *History of England* ; Green, *Making of England.*]

Forests, Charter of. Granted by Henry III. of England in 1217, mitigating severity of Forest Laws (*q.v.*). [Refer Green, *Making o England.*]

Formosa, Island of (E. coast of China). Known to the Chinese before Christian era. Colonised by the Dutch 1624; expelled by Chinese 1661; invaded by Japanese 1874; ceded to Japan 1895. *See* under Literary Forgeries for the false descriptions of Formosa by George Psalmanazar. [Refer Guillemard, *Cruise of the " Marchesa."*]

Forth and Clyde Canal (Scotland). Commenced July 10, 1768; navigation opened July 28, 1790.

Forty-five, Rebellion of. Led by Charles Edward Stuart, the Young Pretender, in 1745. Gained victory at Prestonpans, Sept. 21; defeated at Culloden by the Duke of Cumberland (" Butcher " Cumberland), April 16, 1746.

Forty-two Articles, of the Reformed Church of England issued in 1552; afterwards reduced. *See* Thirty-nine Articles, England, Church of, etc.

Fotheringay Castle (Northamptonshire, England). Fd. 1066. Richard III. *b.* at 1452. Mary Queen of Scots executed at, Feb. 8, 1587. Demolished by order of James I. 1604.

Foundling Hospitals. (1) London, projected by Thomas Coram, incorp. by royal charter, Oct. 1739; (2) Dublin, instit. 1704; parliamentary inquiry into abuses at, 1835.

Fourth of July. The birthday of the U.S.A. Independence signed July 4, 1776; also known as Independence Day. *See* U.S.A.

Fourth Party. A body fd. by Lord Randolph Churchill amongst the Conservatives in 1880.

France. Orig. known as *Gaul*. Conquered by Romans 121-48 B.C. Reign of the Emperor Augustus 27 B.C.-A.D. 14. Invasion of the Franks about A.D. 250. Aëtius defeated the Hunnish invaders under Attila at Châlons 450 [refer Creasy, *Decisive Battles*]. End of Roman rule 476. Clovis, King of the Salian Franks 481. Clovis embraced Christianity 496, *d.* 510. Pepin became King of France, July 28, 752. Charlemagne (" the Great ") sole King of the Franks 771; defeated at Roncesvalles, Aug. 15, 778; is crowned Emperor of the Roman Empire at Rome 800; *d.* Jan. 28, 814. Treaty of Verdun, which split up Charles's empire 843. The great siege of Paris by Northmen 886. Election of Hugh Capet 987. Invasion of England by William of Normandy 1066 (*see* England). The First Crusade 1095 (*see* Crusades). " The accession of Louis VI., who reigned from 1108 to 1137, marks a new starting-point and the beginning of a progressive period in French history. Under him and his successors the concentration of France into a great state

FRANCE (*continued*)—

was slowly and steadily effected " [Hassall, *History of France* (The Temple Primers)]. The statutes of the order of the Templars drawn up by St. Bernard 1130. Conquest of Normandy by Philip Augustus 1204. Philip won the b. of Bouvines 1214, which assured his hold over the greater part of France. The Albigensian Crusades 1208-29. "The special work of Philip was the making of France into a great state. And he succeeded" [Hassall, *op. cit.*]. Death of Philip 1223. Reign of Louis IX. (St. Louis) 1226-70, who at "the end of his reign was first prince of Europe" [*op. cit.*]. Royal domain extended to the Mediterranean by Treaty of Meaux 1229. Philip IV. "the founder of Modern France" 1285-1314. Alliance with Scotland, which lasted until time of Mary Stuart 1295. Philip quarrelled with Pope Boniface VIII. 1295, and seized him at Anagni 1302. Pope Clement V. crowned Pope at Lyons 1305; fixed his residence at Avignon 1309, which began the "Babylonish captivity." Order of the Templars suppressed 1312. Beginning of the Hundred Years' War with England 1338. B. of Creçy, Aug. 26, 1346. Calais captured by English 1347. B. of Poitiers, Sept. 19, 1356; King John captured and taken to England by the Brack Prince. Treaty of Brétigny 1360. Truce of Bruges 1375. B. of Agincourt, Oct. 25, 1415. By the Treaty of Troyes, May 21, 1420, Henry V. of England *m.* Katherine, daughter of Charles VI. Siege of Orleans 1428. Treaty of Arras, Sept. 21, 1435. Capture of Paris from the English 1436. B. of Châtillon and end of Hundred Years' War 1453. The Italian expedition under Charles VIII. 1494-6. "With the Italian expedition of Charles VIII. mediæval history ends and modern history begins" [*op. cit.*]. Charles entered Naples, Feb. 22, 1495; expulsion of the French from Naples 1504. League of Cambrai 1508. The Holy League against France, Oct. 1511. Louis XII. assumed title of *Pater Patriæ* 1513. Peace and alliance with England 1514. Accession of Francis I. 1515. Concordat of Bologna between Francis I. and Pope Leo X. Aug. 1516. Summary of the wars of France with the Hapsburgs from 1521-59:—

1. 1521-26, ending with Treaty of Madrid (b. of Pavia 1525).
2. 1527-29, ending with Treaty of Cambrai.
3. 1535-38, ending with Treaty of Nice.
4. 1542-44, ending with Treaty of Crespy.
5. 1552-59, ending with Treaty of Cateau Cambrésis.

[From Hassall, *op. cit.*] Calais captured from the English, Jan. 1558.

The opening of the Religious Wars 1562 (between Huguenots and Catholics):—

The First War 1562-63, ending with Peace of Amboise.
The Second War, 1567-68, ending with Peace of Longjumeau.
The Third War, 1569-70, ending with Peace of St. Germains.
The Fourth War, 1572-73, ending with Peace of La Rochelle (Massacre of St. Bartholomew 1572).
The Fifth War, 1574-76, ending with Peace of Monsieur.
The Sixth War, 1577, ending with Peace of Bergerac.

FRANCE (*continued*)—

The Seventh War, 1579-80, ending with Peace of Fleix.
The Eighth War, 1585-89, when Henry III. *d*., and was succeeded by Henry IV.

Henry of Guise murdered 1588. " The Civil Wars did not end until 1595, but the country did not secure tranquillity till the Peace of Vervins 1598 " [from Hassall, *op. cit*.]. [Refer also Cambridge Modern History, *The Wars of Religion*]. Bourbon monarchy fd. by Henry IV. 1589. Edict of Nantes (*q.v.*), April 15, 1599. War with Savoy 1600. Henry IV. assassinated by François Ravaillac, April 14, 1610. Rebellion of Condé 1614. Ascendancy of Cardinal Richelieu 1624-42. Peace of Westphalia, with the Hapsburgs, 1648. The First or Parliamentary Fronde 1648-9. The Second or Aristocratic Fronde 1650-3 (*see* Fronde). English Alliance (Treaty of Westminster) 1655. Final peace with Spain (the Peace of the Pyrenees) 1659. Death of Cardinal Mazarin, 1661. Colbert became finance minister 1661. French East India Company fd. 1664. The War of Devolution against the Spanish Netherlands 1667-8. Dutch War 1672. Revocation of the Edict of Nantes 1685. Spanish Succession War 1702-13. Death of Louis XIV. Sept. 1, 1715. Triple Alliance (England, France, and Holland), Jan. 1717. Quadruple Alliance (England, France, Austria, and Holland), Aug. 2, 1718. End of Anglo-French Alliance 1740. Treaty of Aix-la-Chapelle, April 1748. Loss of Canada 1760 (for French Revolutions *see* special article). The Napoleonic era 1799-1815. B. of Marengo, June 14, 1800. Napoleon crowned emperor in the presence of Pope Pius VII. at Paris, Dec. 2, 1804. " From 1804-15 the history of France is the history of Europe " [Hassall, *op. cit*.]. B. of Trafalgar, Oct. 21, 1805. Napoleon defeated Russians and Austrians at Austerlitz, Dec 2, 1805. Confederation of the Rhine formed 1806. Russian War 1812. War of Liberation 1813. Wellington proclaimed Louis XVIII. at Bordeaux, Mar. 1814. Napoleon signed an act of abdication, and was exiled to Elba, April 11, 1814. First Treaty of Paris 1814. Napoleon escaped from Elba and entered Paris in triumph, Mar. 20, 1815. B. of Waterloo, June 18, 1815. Napoleon banished to St. Helena 1815. Second Treaty of Paris, Nov. 15, 1815. Louis XVIII. res. to the throne (*see* special article for Second French Revolution). Death of Napoleon 1821. Republic 1848. Establishment of second empire, Dec. 2, 1852. Napoleon III. emperor. Crimean War 1854-6. War with Austria 1859. Franco-German War 1870-1. Paris capitulated, Jan. 28, 1871. Peace signed, Feb. 1871. Commune set up, Feb. 1871; repressed May 1871. Death of Napoleon III. at Chislehurst, England, Jan. 9, 1873. Republican Constitution promulgated 1875. Franco-Russian Alliance 1891, 1896, 1900; Anglo-French Alliance (Entente Cordiale), April 8, 1903; Anglo-French Treaty regarding Morocco affairs 1904. Rupture with Vatican 1904. [Refer Hassall, *History of France* (Temple Primers), a useful little work, which gives various books of reference for each period.] The following is a list of the presidents of the French Republic since 1871:—

FRANCE (*continued*)—

> Louis Adolphe Thiers 1871.
> Marshal M. E. Patrice Maurice MacMahon 1873.
> François Paul Jules Grévy 1879.
> Marie—François Sadi—Carnot 1887.
> Jean Pierre Paul Casimir-Perier 1894.
> François Felix Faure 1895.
> Emile Loubet 1899.
> Armand Fallières 1906.

Franchise, Elective. In the reign of Edward I. the members of the House of Commons were elected by freeholders in counties, certain electors in boroughs, and the clergy. An act was passed limiting rights of voting in counties to resident holders of free land of annual value of 40s., 1430. In cities and boroughs the franchise was not determined by any general statute until 1832. New Reform Act 1867; Reform Bill intro. by Gladstone 1884, followed by Redistribution Act 1885. Franchise granted to all males of 21 and over with one of following qualifications:—(1) Must be resident householders, or rated occupants of dwelling-houses; (2) lodgers, in rooms of yearly value unfurnished not less than £10; (3) persons living in houses occupied by others, but not occupying separate tenements or apartments, to vote under " service franchise." Persons disqualified: females, aliens, infants, peers, imbeciles. [Refer Low and Pulling, *Dicty. of Eng. Hist.*]

Franciscans (monastic order of). Called also Minorites. Fd. by St. Francis of Assisi (1182-1226) in 1208; solemnly approved by Pope Innocent 1216. First came to England 1220, where they fd. monasteries at Canterbury and Northampton. [Refer Jessopp, *Coming of the Friars*.]

Franco-American Treaty. Signed 1778, by which France recognised independence of the U.S.A.

Franco-Prussian War. War declared July 15, 1870. Treaty of peace signed at Frankfort-on-Maine, May 10, 1871. Cost of the war to France estimated at £395,400,000.

Franco-Siamese Treaty. (1) Signed 1893, by which Siam ceded France certain territories east of the Mekong; (2) signed 1902, ceded further territories to France; (3) agreement signed 1907.

Frankfort-on-Maine (Germany). First mentioned by Charlemagne's biographer Einhard in A.D. 793. Diets held at in 822 and 823, 951, 1015, 1069, 1109, etc. Placed under an interdict by the Pope during the dispute with Louis the Bavarian and the papacy 1329-49. By the *Golden Bul* (*q.v.*) was declared the principal seat of the imperial elections (*see* Diets) 1356. Joins League of Schmalkalden 1536 (*see* Fettmilch Insurrection). Garrisoned by Gustavus Adolphus 1631; bombarded by French 1796; made capital of Grand-duchy of Frankfort 1810; entered by Prussians, July 16, 1866. Frankfort Peace signed 1871. [Refer art. in *Ency. Britannica*.]

Franking of Letters (Great Britain). Members of parliament had the right from A.D. 1660; abolished on institution of penny postage, Jan. 10, 1840.

Frederickshald, Siege of. Charles XII. of Sweden killed at, Dec. 11, 1718. [Refer Voltaire, *Charles XII.*]

Free Church of Scotland. *See* Scotland, Church of.

Freemasonry (Great Britain and general). Its origin is lost in obscurity. The first grand lodge in England was estab. 1717; in Ireland 1730; in Scotland 1736. Freemasons' Hall, London, built 1775. Pope Clement XII. issued a bull of excommunication against them in 1738. [Refer Gould, *History of Freemasonry*.]

Freemasonry (U.S.A.). It is uncertain when F. was intro. into America. In 1733 a lodge was estab. at Boston by Henry Price. First masonic hall built at Philadelphia 1754. [Refer Harper, *Encyclo. U.S. History*.]

Free Soil Party (U.S.A.). Fd. on Aug. 9, 1848, against extension of slavery in various territories; disbanded 1854. [Refer Harper, *Encyclo. U.S. History*, vol. iii.]

French Fury, The. Francis, Duke of Anjou, in Jan. 1583 occupied Antwerp. The citizens resisted and massacred two thousand of his troops, besides many officers and nobles. [Refer Motley, *Dutch Republic*.]

French Literature. " French Literature dates its birth from the hour that the French race, after having spoken the Celtic tongue for a prolonged period and the Latin for a somewhat briefer one, began once again to use a tongue, or rather many tongues, distinguishable from the speech in common use in Germany, England, Italy, and Spain, that gradually developed into the French language. This moment of transformation must be assigned to the 9th century, certainly not earlier " [E. Faguet, *The Literary History of France* (Eng. trans.)]. In Gaul " Low Latin " was displaced by " Romance," a corrupted form of Latin, and gradually became a new language. The earliest records of the Romance tongue are found in A.D. 842 in the *Glossary of the Abbey of Reichenau* and the *Oath of Louis the German*. In the 13th century, the French literature was recognised as *the literature* of the civilised world, and many came " to France to study, to think, to get known, and to be heard, to win true glory " [*op. cit.*]. The Académie Française was fd. by Cardinal Richelieu in 1635. The following is a list of the principal French writers:—

Abelard, Pierre (philosopher), famous also for his letters written to Héloïse, the niece of a canon of Paris, 1079-1142.
About, Edmond (novelist and journalist), 1828-85.
Adam de la Halle (*the Hunchback of Arras*) (dramatist), (?)-1286.
Alembert or D'Alembert (philosopher, etc.), *c.* 1717-83.
Amiel, Henri Frédéric (philosopher), 1821-81.
Amyot, Jacques (translator), 1513-93.
Andrieux, François Guillaume Jean-Stanislas (dramatist, etc.), 1759-1833.

FRENCH LITERATURE (*continued*)—

Ariosto, Ludovico (dramatist) 1474-1533.

Arnault, Vincent Antoine (dramatist, etc.), 1767-1834.

Assoucy, Charles Cuypeau d' (poet), 1604-*c*. 1679.

Aubigné, Théodore Agrippa d' (historian, poet, etc.), 1550-1630.

Augler, Emile (dramatist), 1820-89.

Aymeric of Peyrac (chronicler) (?)-1400.

Baïf, Jean Antoine de (poet), 1532-89.

Balzac, Honoré de (novelist), 1799-1850.

Balzac, Jean Louis Guez, Baron of (miscellaneous writer), 1594-1654.

Barante, Amable Guillaume Prosper Brugière, Baron (historian), 1782-1866.

Baron, Michel Boyron (dramatist), 1653-1729.

Barthélemy, Abbé Jean Jacques (miscellaneous writer), 1716-95.

Barthélemy, Nicolas (dramatist), 1478-*c*.1535.

Basselin, Olivier (" inventor of the modern *chanson* "), (?)-1419.

Bayle, Peter (philosopher, critic, and historian), 1647-1706.

Beaumarchais, Pierre Augustin Caron de (dramatist), 1732-99.

Belleau, Remi (poet), 1528-77.

Belloy, Pierre Laurent Beyrette de (dramatist), 1727-75.

Benoist de St. Maure, 12th-century poet.

Benoist de St. More (poet), lived in. 1135.

Benserade, Isaac de (poet), 1613-91.

Béranger, Pierre Jean de (ballad writer), 1780-1857.

Bercheure, Pierre (translator) (?)-1362.

Bernis, François Joachim de Pierre de (Cardinal) (miscellaneous verse and prose writer), 1715-94.

Bertaut, Jean (satirical and religious poet). 1552-1611.

Beze, Théodore de (historian and poet), 1519-1605.

Billard, Claude (Lord of Courgenay) (poet), (?)-1618.

Blanc, Louis (historian), 1813-82.

Blondel de Nesles (ballad writer), living in, 1193.

Bodin, Jean (sociologist), 1530-96.

Boileau, Nicolas Despréaux (historian and satirist), 1636-1711.

Boissier, Gaston (classical scholar), 1823-1908.

Bossuet, Jacques Bénigne (Bishop) (historian and miscellaneous writer), 1627-1704.

Bouquet, Dom Martin (principal author of *Recueil des Historiens des Gaules et de la France*), 1685-1754.

Bourdaloue, Louis (preacher), 1632-1704.

Boursault, Edme (satirist), 1638-1701.

Brébeuf, Guillaume de (poet), 1618-61.

Broglie, Achille Victor, Duc de (political writer), 1785-1870.

Broglie, Albert, Duc de (political and historical writer), 1821-1901.

Brosses, Charles de (historian and archæologist), 1709-77.

Brueys, David Augustine de (dramatist), 1640-1723.

Bude, Guillaume (Hellenist), 1469-1540.

Buffon, Jean Louis Leclerc, Count (scientific writer), 1707-88.

Calmet, Don Augustin (divine), 1672-1757.

Calvin, Jean Cauvin (divine), 1509-63.

FRENCH LITERATURE (*continued*)—

Caro, Edme (philosopher), 1826-87.

Chamfort, Sebastien Roch Nicolas (dramatist and miscellaneous writer), 1741-94.

Chapelain, Jean (poet), 1595-1674.

Charles of Orleans (Count of Angoulême and Blois) (poet), 1391-1445.

Charron, Pierre (philosopher), 1541-1603.

Chartier, Alain (poet, historian, etc.), *c.* 1390-1457.

Chateaubriand, François Auguste, Vicomte de (miscellaneous writer), 1768-1848.

Chénier, André Marie de (poet), 1762-94.

Chénier, Marie-Joseph de (historian and critic), 1764-1811.

Cherbuliez, Victor (novelist), 1829-99.

Choiseul-Gouffier, Marie Gabriel Florent Auguste, Comte de (diplomatist and scholar), 1752-1817.

Chrétien de Troyes (translator), (?)-1195.

Christine de Pisan (poet, historian, etc.), 1363-1430.

Collé, Charles (poet and dramatist), 1709-83.

Collin d'Harleville, Jean François (dramatist), 1755-1806.

Commines or Commynes, Philip de (diplomatist and historian), 1455-1509.

Comte, Auguste (philosopher), 1798-1857.

Condillac, Abbé Etienne Bonnet de (philosopher), 1715-80.

Condorcet, Jean Antoine Nicolas de Caritât, Marquis de (biographer), 1743-94.

Constant de Rebecque, Benjamin (novelist and philosopher), 1767-1830.

Coppée, François (poet), 1842-1908.

Coquillart, Guillaume (satirist), 1450-1510.

Cormenin, Vicomte de (" Timon ") (jurist and pamphleteer), 1788-1868.

Corneille, Pierre (dramatist), 1606-84.

Crébillon, Claude-Prosper Jolyot de (novelist), 1707-77.

Crébillon, Prosper Jolyot de (dramatist), 1674-1762.

Crétin, Guillaume (poet), (?)-1525.

Cyrano de Bergerac (novelist and dramatist), 1619-55.

Dacier, André (translator), 1651-1722.

Dacier, Mdme. (wife of the above) (translator), 1654-1720.

Daudet, Alphonse (artist, poet, and novelist), 1840-79.

Delavigne, Casimir (dramatist), 1793-1843.

Delille, Abbé Jacques (poet and translator), 1738-1813.

Descartes, René (scientific and philosophical writer), 1596-1650.

Deschamps, Eustache (called Morel) (poet), 1340-1410.

Desfontaines, Pierre François (called Guydot), 1685-1745.

Desmarets de Saint-Sorlin, Jean (philosopher), 1595-1666.

Desperiers, Bonaventure (translator, etc.), (?)-1544.

Desportes, Philippe (poet and translator), 1545-1606.

Destouches, Philippe Nericault (dramatist), 1680-1754.

Diderot, Denis (miscellaneous writer), 1713-84.

Dolet, Etienne (printer and translator) (?)-1546.

I

FRENCH LITERATURE (*continued*)—

Du Bartas, Guillaume de Saluste, Baron (poet), 1544-90.
Du Bellay, Joachim (poet and antiquarian) *c.* 1524-60.
Ducis, Jean François (dramatist), 1733-1816.
Duclos (called Charles Pineau) (historian), 1704-72.
Dufresny (called Charles Rivière) (dramatist), 1648-1724.
Dumas, Alexandre Davy (père) (novelist and dramatist), 1803-70.
Dumas, Alexandre (fils) (novelist and dramatist), 1824-95.
Du Perron, Jacques Davy (Bishop) (essayist and poet), 1556-1618.
Durandus, Guillaume (Bishop) (theological writer), 1230(?)-96.
Duruy, Victor (historian), 1811-94.
Du Ryer, Pierre (dramatic poet and translator), 1606-68.
Estienne. The name of a family of printers and scholars who
    lived in the 16th century.
Félelon, François de Salignac (Archbishop) (miscellaneous writer),
    1651-1715.
Feuillet, Octave (novelist), 1821-90.
Flaubert, Gustave (novelist), 1821-80.
Fléchier, Esprit (miscellaneous writer), 1632-1710.
Florian, Jean Pierre Claris de (novelist and poet), 1755-94.
Fontenelle, Bernard Le Bovier de (philosopher, etc.), 1657-1757.
François de Sales (St.) (theologian), 1567-1622.
Froissart, Jean (chronicler), 1337-1411.
Fromentin, Eugène (critic, novelist), 1820-76.
Furetière, Antoine (novelist), 1620-88.
Fustel de Coulanges, Numa-Denis, 1830-89.
Gaguin, Robert (poet and historian), 1433-1501.
Garnier, Robert (dramatist), 1534-90.
Gassendi, Pierre (philosopher), 1592-1655.
Gautier, Théophile (poet, novelist, and dramatist), 1811-72.
Genlis, Félicité Ducrest, Comtesse de (romantic writer), 1746-1830.
Gentil-Bernard (called Joseph Bernard) (dramatist and poet),
    1710-75.
Gerson, Jean Charlier (divine), 1363-1429.
Gilbert, Nicholas Joseph Laurent (poet), 1751-80.
Godeau, Antoine (Bishop) (religious poet), 1605-72.
Gombauld, Jean Ogier de Lussac (poet), 1570-1666.
Gomberville, Marin Le Roy de (romantic writer), 1600-74.
Goncourt, Edmond, 1822-96) novelists
Goncourt, Jules de, 1830-70 ∫ collaborated.
Gregory of Tours (St.) (historian).
Gresset, Jean Baptiste Louis (poet), 1709-77.
Grévin, Jacques (poet), 1538-70.
Gringore (called Pierre Gringon) (poet), *c.* 1475-*c.* 1545.
Guillaume de Nangis (historian) (?)-*c.* 1300.
Guimond de la Touche, Claud (dramatist), 1729-60.
Guizot, François (historian), 1787-1874.
Héloïse, 1101-1171. *See* Abelard.
Helvétius, Claude Adrien (philosopher), 1715-71.
Holbach, Paul Henri Thiry, Baron d' (philosopher), 1723-89.
Huet, Pierre Daniel (Bishop) (scholar), 1638-1721.

FRENCH LITERATURE (*continued*)—

Hughues de la Bachelerie (poet), -12th century.

Hugo, Victor-Marie, Vicomte (novelist and poet), 1802-85.

Huysmans, J. K. (novelist), 1848-1907.

Jacques de Guise (chronicler) (?)-1399.

Jacques de Vitry (Bishop) (chronicler), (?)-1240.

Jean de Meung (called Jean Clopinel) (translator), *c.* 1280-(?).

Jean de Troyes (chronicler), living in, 1480.

Jean le Bel (chronicler), (?)-1370.

Jodelle, Etienne (dramatist), 1532-73.

Joinville, Jean, Sire de (historian), (?)-1319.

Joubert, Joseph (philosopher), 1754-1824.

Jouffroy, Théodore Simon (philosopher), 1796-1842.

Jouy, Victor Joseph Etienne (novelist and dramatist), *c.* 1764-1846.

Juvénal or Jouvenal des Ursins (Archbishop) (historian), 1380-1422.

Labé, Louise (*La Belle Cordonnière*) (biographer and poetess), 1526-68.

Labiche, Eugène (humorist), 1815-88.

La Boëtie, Etienne de (translator and poet), 1530-63.

La Bruyère, Jean de (philosopher, etc.), 1645-96.

La Calprenède, Gautier de Costes de (novelist and dramatist), (?)-1663.

La Chaussée, Pierre Claude Nivelle de (dramatist), 1692-1754.

La Fontaine, Jean de (fable writer and poet), 1621-95.

La Harpe, Jean François de (dramatist), 1739-1803.

Lamartine, Alphonse Marie Louise Prat de (historian and miscellaneous writer), 1790-1869.

La Motte, Antoine Houdart (miscellaneous writer), 1672-1731.

La Popelinière, Henri Lancelot Voisin de (historian) (?)-1608.

La Rochefoucauld, François, Duc de (writer on morals), 1613-80.

La Salle, Antoine de (romantic writer), 1398-1462.

Le Braz, Anatole (poet, tale writer, etc.), 1859-

Le Brun, Ponce-Denis Ecouchard (poet, etc.), 1729-1807.

Le Maire de Belges, Jean (historian and poet, etc.), 1473-1524(?).

Leconte de Lisle (poet), 1820-94.

Lemaître, Jules, (poet and dramatist), 1853-

Le Pays, René (Lord of Plessis-Villeneuve) (traveller), 1634-(?).

Leroux, Pierre (philosopher and economist), 1798-1871.

Le Sage, Alain-René (novelist, author of *Gil Blas*), 1668-1747.

Lorens or Laurent (Fière) (writer on morals), 13th century.

Maintenon, Françoise d'Aubigné, Marquise de (miscellaneous writer), 1635-1719.

Malebranche, Nicholas (philosopher), 1638-1715.

Malherbe, François de (poet, etc.), 1555-1628.

Marguerite de Valois-Angoulême (Queen of Navarre) (romantic writer), 1492-1549.

Marie de France (poetess), 12th century.

Marivaux, Pierre Carlet de Chamblain de (novelist and dramatist), 1688-1763.

FRENCH LITERATURE (*continued*)—

Marmontel, Jean François (dramatist, poet, etc.), 1723-99.

Marot, Clément (poet), 1497-1544.

Mary Stuart, Queen of Scots (poetess), 1542-87.

Massillon, Jean Baptiste (orator and professor rhetoric), 1663-1742.

Maupassant, Guy de (novelist and short story writer), 1850-93.

Maynard, François de (poet, etc.), 1582-1646.

Mendès, Catulle (poet, novelist, dramatist), 1843-1909.

Mérimée, Prosper (novelist), 1803-70.

Meschinot, Jean (poet), *c*. 1415-91.

Mézaray, François Ender de (critic), 1610-83.

Michelet, Jules (historian), 1798-1874.

Mignet, François Auguste (historian), 1796-1884.

Mirabeau, Victor Riquetti, Marquis de (economist), 1715-89.

Molière, Jean Baptiste Poquelin (dramatist), 1622-73.

Montaigne, Michel Eyquem Sieur de (essayist), 1533-92.

Montesquieu, Charles de Secondat, Baron de (sociologist), 1689-1755.

Musset, Alfred de (poet and dramatist), 1810-57.

Necker, James (statesman and miscellaneous writer), 1732-1804.

Nodier, Charles (miscellaneous writer), 1780-1844.

Palissot de Montenoy, Charles (miscellaneous writer), 1730-1814.

Pascal, Blaise (philosopher and poet), 1623-62.

Pasquier, Etienne (historian), 1529-1615.

Perrault, Charles (poet), 1628-1703.

Picard, Louis Benoît (dramatist), 1769-1828.

Pigault-Lebrun, Charles Antoine Guillaume Pigault de Epinoy (novelist), 1753-1835.

Piron, Alexis (poet, dramatist, and translator), 1689-1773.

Ponsard, François (dramatist), 1814-67.

Prevost, Antoine François Prevost d'Exiller (called l'Abbé) (historian and translator of English novels, etc.), 1697-1763.

Prudhomme, M. Sully. *See* Sully-Prudhomme.

Quinault, Philippe (dramatist), 1633-88.

Quinet, Edgar (philosophical historian), 1803-75.

Rabelais, François (story writer), 1495-1553(?).

Racan, Honorat de Bueil, Marquis de (poet, dramatist, and biographer), 1589-1670.

Racine, Jean (poet and dramatist), 1639-99.

Regnard, Jean François (poet and dramatist), 1655-1709.

Régnier, Mathurin (poet), 1573-1613.

Renan, Ernest (historian and philosopher, etc.), 1823-95.

Retz, Jean François Paul de Gondi, Cardinal de (writer of memoirs and " pensées "), 1614-79.

Rivarol, Antoine de (scholar), 1753-

Robert de Sorbon (philosopher, fd. the Sorbonne (*q.v.*)), 1201-74.

Roland, Marie-Jeanne Philippe, Mdme. (writer of memoirs and letters), 1754-93.

Rollin, Charles (historian), 1661-1741.

Ronsard, Pierre de (poet orator), 1524-85.

FRENCH LITERATURE (*continued*)—

Rotrou, Jean (dramatist), 1609-50.

Rousseau, Jean Baptiste (epigrammist), 1670-1741.

Rousseau, Jean-Jacques (novelist, philosopher, etc.), 1712-78.

Royer-Collard, Pierre Paul (philosopher and politician), 1763-1845.

Saint-Amant, Marc Antoine Gerard, Sieur de (poet), 1594-1661.

Saint-Beuve, Charles Augustin (critic, poet, moralist, historian, etc.), 1804-69.

Saint-Evremond, Charles de Marquetel de Saint-Denis, Sieur de (miscellaneous writer), 1613-1703.

Saint-Gelais, Melin de (translator and epigrammist), 1487-1558.

Saint-Gelais, Octavien de (Bishop) (poet), 1466-1502.

Saint-Pierre, Charles Renée Castel, Abbé de (sociologist), 1658-1743.

Saint-Pierre, Jacques Henri Bernardin de (novelist and traveller), 1737-1814.

Saint-Simon, Louis de Rouvray, Duc de (historian), 1675-1755.

Sand, Armandine Lucile Aurore, Baronne Dudevant (" George Sand ") (novelist), 1804-76.

Sandeau, Jules (novelist), 1811-83.

Sardou, M. Victorien, 1831-1908.

Scaliger, Jules-Cæsar (philologist), 1484-1558.

Scarron, Paul (novelist and satirist), 1610-60.

Scribe, Eugène (dramatist), 1791-1861.

Scudéry, Georges de (dramatist), 1601-67.

Scudéry, Madeleine de (sister of the above) (novelist), 1627(?)-81.

Sedaine, Michel Jean (dramatist), 1719-97.

Segrais, Jean Regnauld de (poet, memoir, and story writer), 1624-1701.

Sève or Scève, Maurice (poet), 1510-64.

Sévigné, Marie de Rabutin-Chantal, Marquise de (letter writer, etc.), 1626-96.

Simon-Suisse, Jules (philosopher and journalist), 1814-96.

Sismondi, Jean Charles Léonard Sismonde de (historian), 1773-1842.

Sorel, Albert (historian), 1842-

Sorel, Charles (novelist), 1602-74.

Staël-Holstein, Baroness Necker (novelist), 1766-1817.

Stendhal, Henri-Marie Beyle (novelist), 1783-1842.

Sue, Eugène (novelist), 1804-57.

Sully, Maximilien de Béthune, Baron de Rosny, Duc de (memoir writer), 1560-1641.

Sully-Prudhomme (poet), 1839-1907.

Taine, Hippolyte (positivist philosopher), 1828-93.

Thierry, Augustin (historian), 1795-1856.

Thiers, Adolphe (historian, critic, and statesman), 1796-1877.

Thou, Jacques Auguste de (historian), 1553-1617.

Thyard, Pontus de (Bishop) (poet), 1521-1605.

Tocqueville, Alexis Cherel de (historian), 1805-59.

Tristan L'Hermite (François) (poet), 1601-55

French Literature (*continued*)—

Turgot, Anne Robert Jacques, Baron de l'Aulne (philosopher and political economist), 1727-81.

Urfé, Honoré d' (novelist), 1568-1625.

Vatable, François Wastebled (Hebrew scholar), (?)-1547.

Vauban, Sebastian Le Prestre, Sieur de (political economist), 1633-1707.

Vauvenargues, Luc Clapiers, Marquis de (moralist), 1715-47

Verlaine, Paul (poet), 1844-96.

Verne, Jules (novelist), 1828-1905.

Viau, Théophile de (called Théophile) (poet), 1590-1626.

Vigny, Alfred, Comte de (poet), 1797-1863.

Villehardouin, Geoffroi de (historian), 1155(?)-1213(?).

Villemain, Abel (historian), 1790-1870.

Villon, François de Montcorbier, called (poet), 1431-80(?).

Voisenon, Claude Henri de Fuzée, Abbé de (novelist and dramatist), 1708-55.

Voiture, Vincent (poet and letter writer), 1598-1648.

Volney, Constantin François Chassebœuf, Comte de (philosopher and naturalist), 1757-1820.

Voltaire, François Marie Arouet de (poet, dramatist, philosopher, letter writer, etc.), 1694-1778.

Zola, Emile (novelist), 1840-1902.

[Refer Faguet, *A Literary History of France* (Eng. trans.).]

French Revolution, The Great. It has been said that Jean Jacques Rousseau (1712-78) did much to prepare France for the Great Revolution by his work *Social Contract*, which stated that all citizens should have a voice in the government. Meeting of the States-General, May 5, 1789, when the Third Estate demanded that the assembly should be composed of one order instead of three. The Third Estate met and took title of National Assembly, June 17, 1789. Louis XVI. ordered Three Estates to separate. Led by Mirabeau they refuse, June 23, 1789. Royal troops sent to Paris, July 1789. Necker dismissed by Louis XVI. July 12, 1789. The Bastile (*q.v.*) captured by the mob, July 14, 1789. Mob marched to Versailles and forced royal family to go to Paris, Oct. 5, 1789. Death of Mirabeau, April 2, 1791. Massacre of the Champ de Mars, July 17, 1791. New Constitution formed called the Legislative Assembly, Sept. 30, 1791, and the National Assembly is dissolved. Mob invaded the Tuileries, June 20, 1792. The monarchy overthrown, Aug. 10, 1792. Dumouriez defeated the Prussians, who issued a manifesto against the French people, at the b. of Valmy, Sept. 20, 1792 [refer Creasy, *Decisive Battles*]. National Convention took place of Legislative Assembly, and declares France a republic, Sept. 20, 1792. England, Holland, Spain, Portugal, Tuscany, Naples, and the Holy Roman Empire joined against France, Feb. 1, 1793. Louis XIV. executed, Jan. 21, 1793. Committee of Public Safety formed, Jan. 1793. Girondists overthrown, June 2, 1793. Robespierre triumphant, Mar. 1794, but executed July 28, 1794. Mob demanded bread of the Convention, April 1, 1795. Napoleon Bonaparte fired on the mob, Oct. 1795. The Directory (*q.v.*) formed 1795-9. The Revolution of the 19th Brumaire, Nov. 10, 1799. The Directory destroyed and Napoleon formed a Consulate with himself as First Consul. [Refer Cambridge Modern History, *The French Revolution,* etc.]

French Revolution of 1830. Three days' War of the Barricades. in Paris, July 27-29, 1830; people victorious. Charles X. abdicated, Aug. 2, 1830, and Louis Philippe was proclaimed king, Aug. 7, 1830.

French Revolution of 1848. Louis Philippe abdicated, Jan 24, 1848. Provisional government formed, Jan. 25. Republic proclaimed, Jan. 26. Meeting of National Assembly, May 4. Communist invasion repressed, May 15. Insurrection and barricades June 23. Archbishop of Paris killed, June 25. Insurrection quelled with great bloodshed, June 26. Decree for electing president by universal suffrage, Oct. 7. Louis Napoleon elected president, Dec. 20. The " Clubs " abolished, Mar. 20. *See* France. [Refer Lamartine, *History of French Revolution of* 1848 (Eng. trans.).]

Friedewald, Treaty of, between the Protestant princes under Maurice of Saxony and Henry II. of France, Jan. 1552. [Refer Tanner, *Reformation and the Renaissance.*]

Friends, Society of. *See* Quakers.

" Friends of the Constitution." A society fd. in Ireland by Henry Grattan in Dec. 1792, under the presidency of the Duke of Leinster, " intended to promote in every way Catholic emancipation and parliamentary reform, while resisting all republican innovations." [Refer Lecky, *Hist. of Ireland in the* 18*th Century,* vol. iii.]

" Friends of the People." A society fd. in 1792 to obtain parliamentary reform by constitutional means. [Refer Cambridge Modern History, *The French Revolution.*]

Friesland (Netherlands). Independent until 1744, when it became subject to Prussia. Napoleon annexed it to Holland 1806; regained by Prussia 1814.

Frobisher's Straits (Arctic Ocean). Discovered by Sir Martin Frobisher 1576.

Fronde, The. The First or Parliamentary F. orig. in the Paris Parliament, June 1648, against abuses in the government. Closed with the Treaty of Rueil, April 1, 1649. The Second or Aristocratic F. led by certain nobles under Condé, principally against Cardinal Mazarin 1650; suppressed in 1653. [Refer Hassal, *History of France* (Temple Primers).]

Fugitive Slave Circular, etc. *See* Slavery.

G

Gabelle. A word to indicate certain taxes levied in France, especially on salt; first levied 1286; finally abolished 1789. [Refer Guizot, *History of France.*]

Gadsden Purchase. In 1853 the U.S. Government bought certain lands from Mexico. The negotiations were managed by Gen. James Gadsden (1788-1858), hence the name. [Refer Harper, *Encyclo. of U.S. History*, vol. iv.]

Gaeta (W. Central Italy). Besieged by Alphonso V. of Aragon 1435; by Austrians 1707; by Charles of Naples 1734; by French 1806; by Austrians 1815; by Italian National Party 1861. Pope Pius IX. took refuge here 1848-9.

Gainsborough (Lincs. England). Marriage of Alfred the Great at A.D. 868. Destroyed by the Danes 1013. Church fd. by Templars 1209. Captured from parliamentarians 1643. [Refer Lewis, *Topographical Dicty. of England.*]

Galicia (Austria). Formerly part of Poland. Invaded by Austrians 1793, and annexed by them in 1794; part of Grand-duchy of Warsaw 1809; recovered by Austria 1815.

Galicia (Spain). A kingdom from A.D. 411-585. In 1072 it was incorp. with Leon and Castile. [Refer Meakin, *Galicia, the Switzerland of Spain.*]

Galistan, Peace of, between Persia and Russia, signed Oct. 12, 1813.

Gallican Church. Owing to its independent attitude towards the Roman See, the Church in France in former years was often called the Gallican Church. In 1269 the Pragmatic Sanction (*q.v.*) provided that the laws of the Church should conform with the common law. Philippe le Bel in 1302 opposed the Pope Boniface VIII. and imprisoned him; and again in 1438 the Pragmatic Sanction of Bourges aimed at the encroachments of Rome. This last was superseded by an agreement called the Concordat of Bologna, between Pope Leo X. and the King Francis I. The famous declaration of the French clergy in 1682 is regarded as the charter of the G. C. By this the Pope was declared invalid to interfere in civil affairs. Condemned by Pope Alexander VIII. 1690; by Clement XI. 1706; and by Pius VI. 1794. After many changes the declaration of 1682 was again put into force by Napoleon in 1810. In 1826 the French bishops confirmed this. The French bishops, however, at the Vatican Council 1869-70 again declared for papal infallibility. [Refer Jervis, *History of the Church of France from the Concordat of Bologna* A.D. 1516.]

Gallican Confession. Profession of faith of the French Reformed Church adopted at the Synod of La Rochelle 1571. [Refer Tanner, *The Renaissance and the Reformation.*]

Gallipoli (Turkey). Captured by Turks 1357. British and French armies landed at, April 1854, and proceeded against the Russians.

Galvanism. *See* Electricity.

Galway (Ireland). Fortified 1124; surrendered to parliamentary forces, July 10, 1691. Gavazzi riots at, Mar. 1859. [Refer Hardiman, *History of Town and County of Galway*.]

Galway Election. In May 1872 a petition was presented to unseat Capt. Nolan, the member for Galway, owing to the alleged intimidation of certain Irish Roman Catholics. The petition was granted, and the Bishop of Clonfert and others were tried but acquitted. [Refer Jennings, *Anecdotal History of the British Parliament*.]

Gambia (N.W. Africa). Settlement fd. by English on initiative of Portuguese in London 1588. English factory estab. at, 1620. English right to confirmed by Treaty of Paris 1815; separated from Sierra Leone 1842. [Refer R. W. Martin, *British Colonies*.]

Game Laws (Great Britain). The earliest were passed in 1389, forbidding those who possessed land under value of 40*s.* to keep dogs for hunting. Another law in 1494 forbade poaching. In 1604 a law was passed forbidding the use of gun or cross-bow for shooting game. Hawking and trapping of various birds forbidden during certain months 1609. All previous acts repealed 1831, and new laws made regarding poaching, etc. Ground Game Act 1880. [Refer Low and Pulling, *Dicty. of Eng. History*.]

Gaming and Gambling, Laws against (Great Britain). Act of Charles II. by which persons losing more than £100 at one time were not compelled to pay. In Anne's reign an act provided that bonds and other securities won at play were not recoverable, and any person losing more than £10 might sue and recover this amount from the winner 1710. Act to amend previous laws passed, Aug. 1845. *See* Betting, Lotteries. [Refer Ashton, *History of Gambling in England*.]

Gandamak, Treaty of, between Great Britain and Afghanistan 1879.

Garter, Order of the. Fd. by King Edward III. of England, probably on Jan. 18, 1344. [Refer Nicolas, *History of British Orders of Knighthood*.]

Gas (Coal). Described by Rev. Dr. John Clayton *c.* 1691. Illumination by first attempted in Cornwall 1792. First used to replace candles and lamps at a factory in Manchester 1805. In London it was introduced in 1807, and generally used in 1814. [Refer art. in *Chambers's Encyclopædia*.]

Gas, Illumination by (U.S.A.). First in streets of Boston 1823.

Gastein, Treaty of, between Austria and Prussia at close of Schleswig-Holstein War, signed 1865.

Gaul. *See* France.

Gaza (Palestine). An ancient town mentioned in Genesis (x. 19) and other biblical books. Captured by Alexander the Great 332 B.C.; by Turks 1170; by Napoleon 1799; by Ibrahim Pasha 1831.

"Gazette, London." *See* Newspapers.

Gelnhausen, Compact or **Agreement of,** by the electors of Germany to resist the innovations of the Emperor Maximilian, June 1502. [Refer Johnson, *Europe in the 16th Century*.]

General Assembly of the Church of Scotland. *See* Scotland, Church of.

Geneva (Switzerland). Republic fd. 1512; allied with Fribourg 1519, and Berne 1526; adopted Lutheran doctrines 1535. John Calvin (*see* Calvinists) exiled from, 1538; recalled, Sept. 1541. Calvin *d.* at 1564. Joins Swiss Confederation 1815. [Refer Johnson, *Europe in the 16th Century*.]

Geneva Convention. (1) Signed by the representatives of twelve foreign countries first in 1864, and dealt with the treatment of wounded during war time. The U.S.A. did not sign the convention. A second conference was held in 1868, but no effect was ever given to the articles signed. On July 6, 1906, a third convention was signed. [Refer art. in *Encyclopædia Britannica*.]

Genoa (Italy). Orig. *Genua*. Submitted to Romans 115 B.C.; a free state A.D. 1000; sacked by Spaniards and Italians under Colonna 1522; bombarded by French 1684; by British 1745; blockaded by British and Austrians 1800; annexed to France 1800; surrendered to British 1814; proclaimed a republic after a revolt, April 3, 1849; surrendered to Gen. La Marmora, April 11, 1849.

Gentlemen-at-arms. Bodyguard of the British sovereign, fd. by Henry VIII. 1509.

Geographical Society, American. Estab. 1852.

Geographical Society, Royal, of London. Estab. 1830.

Georgia (W. Asia). Called by Russians *Gruzia*. Invaded by Tartars 1235; conquered by Timour 1388, who was driven out in 1403; invaded by Persians 1618. The last king was George XIII., who resigned the crown in favour of Paul, Emperor of Russia, 1799; formally annexed to Russia 1801. [Refer Wardrop, *The Kingdom of Georgia*.]

Georgia (Southern state, U.S.A.). Fd. by royal charter granted June 9, 1732; named after George II.; state constitution adopted by convention, Feb. 5, 1777. [Refer Harper, *Encyclopædia U.S. History*.]

German Catholics. A religious body who separated from the Roman Church in 1844, immediately caused by the exhibition of the Holy Coat at Treves, which was deemed by them to be idolatry. First met in council 1845. Movement gradually died out, and was succeeded by " Old Catholics " (*q.v.*). [Refer art. in *Chambers's Encyclopædia*.]

Germanic Confederation (*Der Deutsche Bund*). (1) June 8, 1815, against French aggression after the b. of Waterloo. (2) During Franco-German War 1871.

Germanic League. Constituted at Congress of Vienna in 1815.

German Literature. " The dialectical separation between the North and South German had been accomplished previous to the date of any extant literary remains. High German gained the supremacy as a literary language; it continued to develop down to the 11th century, and is known as High German. No remains of German poetry have come down to us from the first seven centuries, but there are references to the existence of such. The Goths were the first among the German tribes to embrace Christianity. From them we have one of the earliest monuments of interest as regards its bearing on the history of the German language " [Marian Edwardes, *A Summary of the Literatures of Modern Europe*]. The following are the principal German writers:—

Abbt, Thomas (historian), 1738-66.
Alexis, Willibald (novelist), 1798-1871.
Anzengruber, Ludwig (dramatist), 1839-89.
Arndt, Ernst Moritz (poet), 1769-1860.
Arnim, Bettina von (poetess), 1785-1859.
Arnim, Ludwig Achim von (miscellaneous writer), 1781-1831.
Auersperg, Graf Anton Alexander von (poet), 1806-76.
Bauernfeld, Eduard von (dramatist), 1802-90.
Beer, Michael (dramatist), 1800-33.
Bodenstedt, Friedrich (poet), 1819-92.
Bodmer, Jakob (miscellaneous writer), 1698-1783.
Böhme, Jakob (philosopher), 1575-1624.
Börne, Ludwig or Löb Baruch (journalist, etc.), 1786-1836.
Brant, Sebastian (satirist), 1457-1521.
Breitinger, Johann Jakob (miscellaneous writer), 1701-76.
Büchner, Georg (dramatist), 1813-37.
Bunsen, Chr. Carl J. (antiquarian), 1791-1860.
Bürger, G. A. (poet), 1748-94.
Chamisso, Adelbert von (poet), 1781-1838.
Curtius, Ernst (archæologist), 1814-96.
Dach, Simon (poet), 1605-59.
Dalm, Felix (antiquary and historian), 1834.
David of Augsburg (mystic) (?)-1272.
Droste-Hülshoff, Annette von (poetess), 1797-1848.
Ebers, Georg (romance writer), 1837-98.
Eilhart von Oberge (poet), *circa* 1170.
Ekkehard of St. Gall (poet), *circa* 930.
Fichte, Immanuel Hermann (philosopher), 1797-1879.
Fichte, Johann Gottlieb (philosopher), 1762-1814.
Fischart, Johann (satirist), *circa* 1550-90.
Fontane, Theodor (novelist), 1819-98.
Forster, Johann Georg (writer on travel), 1754-94.
Fouqué, Friedrich de la Motte (novelist), 1777-1843.
Freidank or Vrîdanc (poet), *circa* 1215-30.

GERMAN LITERATURE (*continued*)—

Freiligrath, Hermann Ferdinand (poet), 1810-76.

Freytag, Gustav (novelist), 1816-95.

Gaudy, Franz von (poet), 1800-40.

Geibel, Emanuel (poet), 1815-84.

Geiler von Kaisersberg, Johann (mystic), 1445-1510.

Gellert, Christian Fürchtegott (poet), 1715-69.

Gervinus, G. G. (philosopher), 1805-71.

Gessner, Salomon (romantic writer), 1730-88.

Göckingk, Leopold F. G. von (poet), 1748-1828.

Goethe, Johann Volfgang von (poet), 1749-1832.

Gotter, Frederich W. (dramatist), 1746-97.

Gottfried von Strassburg (poet), *circa* 1210.

Gottsched, Johann Christoph (poet and dramatist), 1700-66.

Gotz, Johann N. (poet), 1721-81.

Grillparzer, Franz (poet), 1791-1872.

Grimm, Jacob, 1785-1863 } philologists and writers of fairy
Grimm, Wilhelm, 1786-1859 } tales; brothers who collaborated.

Grimmelshausen, Johann Jakob Christoffel von (romantic writer),
circa 1624-76.

Gunther, Johann Christian (poet), 1695-1723.

Gutzkow, Karl F. (novelist), 1811-78.

Hagedorn, Friedrich von (poet), 1708-54.

Haller, Albrecht von (poet), 1708-77.

Hardenberg, Friedrich von (poet), 1772-1801.

Häring, W. H. *See* Alexis, W.

Hartman von Aue (poet), 1170-1215.

Hauff, Wilhelm (novelist), 1802-27.

Hebbel, Christian Friedrich (poet), 1813-63.

Hegel, G. W. F. (romantic philosopher), 1770-1831.

Heine, Heinrich (poet and dramatist), 1797-1856.

Heinrich von Meissen (Frauenlob), *circa* 1250-1318.

Heinrich von Morungen (poet), end of 12th century.

Heinrich von Veldeke (poet), *circa* 1170.

Herder, Johann Friedrich (poet and philosopher), 1744-1803.

Herwegh, Georg (poet), 1817-75.

Hoffmann, Ernst Theodor Wilhelm (romanticist), 1776-1822.

Hillebrand, Joseph (philosopher), 1788-1862.

Hoffmann von Fallersleben, A. H. (poet), 1798-1874.

Hofmann von Hofmannswaldau, C. N. (poet), 1617-79.

Holderlin, Friedrich (poet), 1770-1843.

Hölty, Ludwig H. C. (poet), 1748-76.

Hrotsuith of Gandersheim (dramatist), *circa* 930-1000.

Humboldt, Wm. von (critic and philologist), 1767-1835.

Iffland, August Wilhelm (dramatist), 1759-1814.

Immermann, Karl Leberecht (dramatist), 1796-1840.

Kant, Immanuel (philosopher), 1724-1804.

Kastner, A. G. (poet), 1719-1800.

Keller, Gottfried (novelist), 1819-90.

Kerner, Justinus A. C. (poet), 1786-1862.

Kinkel, Gottfried (poet), 1815-82.

GERMAN LITERATURE (*continued*)—

Kleist, Ewald Christian von (poet), 1715-59.
Klinger, Maximilian (novelist), 1752-1831.
Klopstock, Friedrich Gottlieb (poet), 1724-1803.
Konrad von Wurzburg, Rudolf von Ems (poet) (?)-1287.
Körner, Karl Theodor (dramatist and poet), 1791-1813.
Kotzbue, August F. F. (novelist), 1761-1819.
Kurz, Hermann (poet, translator, and novelist), 1813-73.
Laroche, Sophie von (novelist), 1730-1807.
Laube, Heinrich (essayist), 1806-84.
Lavater, Johann Kaspar (poet), 1741-1801.
Leibnitz, Godfrey (philosopher), 1646-1716.
Leisewitz, J. A. (dramatist), 1753-1806.
Lenz, Jakob Michael Reinhold (dramatist), 1751-92.
Lessing, Gotthold Ephraim (dramatist and critic), 1729-81.
Leuthold, Heinrich (poet), 1827-79.
Logau, Friedrich von (epigrammist), 1605-55.
Lohenstein, D. C. von (dramatist), 1635-83.
Ludwig, Otto (poet and dramatist), 1813-65.
Luther, Martin (humanist and theologian), 1483-1546.
Manuel, Niklaus (poet), 1484-1530.
Mayer, Karl F. H. (poet), 1786-1870.
Miller, J. M. (poet and novelist), 1750-1814.
Mommsen, Theodor (historian), 1817-1903.
Moritz, Karl Philipp (novelist), 1757-93.
Möser, Justus (historian), 1720-94.
Müller, Mahler (poet), 1749-1825.
Müller, Wilhelm (poet), 1794-1827.
Müllner, Adolf (dramatist), 1774-1829.
Murner, Thomas (satirical poet), 1457-1537.
Neidhart von Reuenthal (poet), *circa* 1180-1250.
Nestroy, Johann (dramatist), 1801-62.
Nietzsche, Friedrich Wilhelm (philosopher), 1844-1900.
Opitz, Martin (poet), 1597-1639.
Oswald von Wolkenstein (poet), 1367-1445.
Platen-Hallermunde, August Graf von (poet and critic), 1796-1835.
Rabener, Gottlieb Wilhelm (satirist), 1714-71.
Raimund, Ferdinand (dramatist), 1790-1836.
Ramler, Karl Wilhelm (poet), 1725-98.
Ranke, Leopold (historian), 1795-1886.
Rebhun, Paul (poet), 1500-46.
Richter, Johann Paul (novelist, etc.), 1763-1825.
Rittershaus, Friedrich Emil (poet), 1834-97.
Rückert, Friedrich (poet and translator), 1788-1866.
Sachs, Hans (dramatist), 1494-1578.
Scheffel, Joseph Victor von (poet), 1826-86.
Schelling, F. W. J. von (romantic philosopher), 1775-1854.
Schiller, Johann Friedrich (poet and dramatist), 1759-1805.
Schlegel, August Wilhelm (poet, essayist, and translator), 1767-1845.

GERMAN LITERATURE (*continued*)—

Schlegel, Friedrich (novelist, dramatist, and critic), 1772-1829.
Schlosser, F. C. (historian), 1776-1861.
Schopenhauer, Arthur (philosopher), 1788-1860.
Schröder, Friedrich Ludwig (dramatist), 1744-1816.
Schubart, C. F. D. (poet and musician), 1739-91.
Storm, Theodor W. (poet and novelist), 1817-88.
Sybel, Heinrich von (historian), 1817-95.
Tauler, Johannes (mystic), 1300-61.
Tieck, Johann Ludwig (dramatist), 1773-1853.
Treitschke, Heinrich von (historian), 1834-96.
Uhland, Johann Ludwig (poet), 1787-1862.
Uz, Johann Peter (German), 1720-96.
Voss, Johann Heinrich (poet), 1751-1826.
Wackenroder, W. H. (romanticist), 1773-98.
Wagner, Richard (dramatist and musician), 1813-83.
Walther von der Vogelweide (poet), 1170-1228.
Weisse, C. F. (dramatist), 1726-1804.
Werner, Zacharias (dramatist), 1768-1823.
Wieland, Christoph Martin (novelist and translator), 1733-1813.
Winckelmann, Johann Joachim (art historian), 1717-68.
Wolfram von Eschenbach (poet), *circa* 1170-1220.
Zedlitz, J. C. von (poet), 1798-1862.

[Refer John G. Robertson, *A History of German Literature*.]

Germany. The victory of Arminius over the Roman legions in the Teutoburg Forest A.D. 9 secured the independence of the Teutonic, and Germany advanced from that time [refer Creasy, *Fifteen Decisive Battles ;* Tacitus, *Germania* (Eng. trans. Everyman's Lib.)]. From the reign of Clovis A.D. 481 to the end of the reign of Charles the Great, Germany and France were united (*see* France). Louis the Pius divides the empire 817. German provinces assert their independence, and Conrad of Franconia reigns 911-18. Henry I. conquers the Hungarians 919. Otto I. crowned by the Pope 962. Henry III. deposes three popes and conquers Bohemia 1039-56. Henry IV. excommunicated by Pope Gregory VII. (Hildebrand) 1106. The Golden Bull (*q.v.*) 1356. Sigismund elected emperor 1414. Hussite War 1420-31. Albert II. first emperor of the House of Hapsburg 1438-93. Reign of the Emperor Maximilian I. 1493-1519. Diet of Worms 1495; Diet of Augsburg 1500. Maximilian takes title of " Roman Emperor Elect " 1508. Reign of Charles V. 1519-58. Luther condemned at Diet of Worms 1521. War with France (Francis I.) 1521-25. Peasants' War (*q.v.*) 1525. Renewal of war with France 1527-29. Sack of Rome by imperial troops 1527. Augsburg Confession 1530. Opening of Council of Trent 1545. Death of Luther 1546. Abdication of Charles V. 1555. The Protestant Union 1608. Outbreak of Thirty Years' War 1618; ended by Peace of Westphalia 1648. Rise of the Prussian Monarchy under Leopold I. 1658-1705. Prussia made a kingdom under Frederick I. 1701 (*see* Prussia). Invasion of Saxony by Charles XII. of Sweden 1706. George I. of Hanover became King of England

1714. Maria Theresa, Queen of Hungary and Archduchess of Austria 1740-80. First Silesian War 1740-42. Austrian Succession War 1741-48. Second Silesian War 1744-45. Emperors of the Lorraine-Hapsburg line 1745-1806. Seven Years' War 1756-63. War between Austria and Prussia, and France 1792. B. of Valmy 1792. Second war against France 1798-1802; third ditto 1805-7. Dissolution of German Empire and formation of the Confederation of the Rhine, July 12, 1806. The German Confederation (*q.v.*) 1815-48. Zollverein fd. 1828-42. Revolution in G. 1848-50. German Diet resumes sessions 1851. Franco-German War 1870, till Peace of Frankfort-on-Maine, May 10, 1871. First German Imperial Parliament, Mar. 1871. New code of laws 1877. [Refer Henderson, *Short History of Germany*.] For later sovereigns, *see* Prussia.

Gertruydenberg. Conference at, an unsuccessful attempt to end the War of the Spanish Succession (*q.v.*) 1710. [Refer Stanhope, *Reign of Queen Anne*.]

Ghent (Belgium). Said to have been fd. in the 5th century. Given to Count Baldwin IV. 1007; capital of Flanders (*q.v.*) 12th century; John of Gaunt *b.* at 1340. Insurrection of Jacob von Artevelde at 1379; rebels against the Emperor Charles V. 1539; surrenders to Spaniards 1584; taken by Louis XIV. of France 1698; by Duke of Marlborough 1706; seized by French 1793; incorp. with Netherlands 1814; becomes part of Belgium 1830 (*see* Flanders). [Refer art. in *Encyclopædia Britannica*.]

Ghent, Treaty of, between U.S.A. and Great Britain, ratified Feb. 17, 1815. Convention of, granted the Groote Privilegie to the Netherland provinces 1477. Pacification of, agreed to the expulsion of the Spaniards and the establishment of the Reformed religion 1576.

Gibraltar (S. Spain). Taken by Moors 1410; captured by Spaniards 1462; formally annexed to Spain 1502; surrenders to combined English and Dutch fleet under Sir George Rooke 1704; finally ceded to Great Britain by Treaty of Utrecht 1713; frequently besieged by Spaniards, most famous attempt 1779-83. [Refer Martin, *British Colonies*.]

Gilbertines. A religious order fd. in England by St. Gilbert of Sempringham, 1148; suppressed at the time of the Reformation.

Gilbert's Workhouses Act. Passed 1782, appointing paid guardians of the poor. [Refer G. B. Smith, *History of English Parliament*.]

Gin Act (Great Britain). Passed 1736, imposing duty on gin sold by retail; repealed 1743. [Refer G. B. Smith, *History of the English Parliament*.]

Gipsies, Acts against (Great Britain). Banished from England 1531; from Scotland 1541. In 1562 an act was passed forbidding intercourse with gipsies. Acts repealed 1783. [Refer art. in *Chambers's Encyclopædia*.]

Girondists or **Girondins.** A party of moderate republicans formed during the French Revolution 1791. The earliest members of the party were returned by the votes of the Gironde district of France, hence the name. Louis XVI. forms a G. ministry 1792. They attempt to save the king's life, but fail. On Oct. 1, 1793, many of the members were tried before the National Convention for conspiracy, and several were executed. [Refer Lamartine, *History of the Girondists* (Eng. trans.).]

Girton College (England). A college for women. Fd. at Hitchin 1869; removed to Girton 1873.

Gisors, Treaty of, between Henry I. of England and Louis VI. of France, signed 1113.

Gladstone Administrations (Wm. Ewart Gladstone, 1809-94). (1) Dec. 9, 1868—Feb. 17, 1874; (2) April 28, 1880—June 9, 1885; (3) Feb. 2, 1886—July 20, 1886; (4) Aug. 15, 1892—Mar. 3, 1894. [Refer Lord Morley, *Life of Gladstone*.]

Glamorgan Treaty, The, between the Roman Catholics and Charles I., negotiated on the king's side by the Earl of Glamorgan 1644. [Refer Low and Pulling, *Dicty. of Eng. Hist.*]

Glasgow (Scotland). The date of foundation uncertain. The cathedral was commenced in 1181. Made into a royal burgh 1190; incorp. by James II. 1450. University fd. by Bishop Turnbull 1450-1; endowed by James, Earl of Hamilton, 1460, and a new charter was granted by James VI. 1577; new buildings opened 1864. [Refer Macgregor, *History of Glasgow*.]

Glassites, The. A religious body in Scotland led by John Glass; originated about 1730.

Glastonbury Abbey. Said to have been fd. by St. Joseph of Arimathea about A.D. 63. The Chapel of St. Joseph built 1101-20; destroyed by fire 1184. The last abbot, Richard Whiting, was hanged for opposing the commissioners of Henry VIII. Nov. 15, 1539. [Refer Warner, *History of Glastonbury*.]

Glencoe, The Massacre of. The government issued a proclamation in Scotland promising pardon to all who before Dec. 31, 1691, would lay down their arms and promise to live peaceably. One of the heads of clans, MacIan of Glencoe, was late in doing so, and he and all his clan were ruthlessly slaughtered on Feb. 13, 1692. [Refer Macaulay, *History of England*.]

Globe Theatre (London). Erected by Burbage Bros. 1599; associated with William Shakespeare; burnt 1613; rebuilt shortly afterwards; destroyed by Puritans 1644.

Glorious Fourth. *See* Fourth of July.

Gloucester (Gloucestershire, England). Orig. *Glevum*. Fd. A.D. 96-8; Abbey of St. Peter fd. 681; cathedral fd. by Abbot Serlo (1072-1104); first charter granted by Henry II. 1155; incorp. by Richard III. 1483; restoration of cathedral 1873-90, and 1897. [Refer art. in *Encyclopædia Britannica*.]

Gobelin Tapestry. Called after a family of dyers Gobelins, who set up a tapestry works in Paris in 1662.

Godolphin Administration. After Lord Godolphin, First Lord. (1) Formed 1684; (2) 1690.

God's Truce. An instrument for suspending hostilities on holy days and seasons used during the Middle Ages, probably instit. about 988; confirmed by Council of Clermont 1095, and other councils. [Refer Semichon, *La Paix et la Trève de Dieu*.]

Gold Coast (W. Africa). Possessed by Portuguese 1481-2; by Dutch 1642; war between English and Dutch over settlements 1664-5; Dutch forts and territory purchased by Great Britain 1871; created a separate Crown colony 1874. [Refer Lucas, *Historical Geog. of British Empire*, vol. iii.]

Golden Bull, The, of Charles IV. So called from the golden seals attached to it. The Emperor Charles IV. of Germany in 1356 called a diet (*q.v.*) at Nuremberg, and published the first part of the G. B. on Jan. 10, the remainder in the following December. This act confirmed the powers of the diets (*q.v.*) and remained in force until 1806. [Refer Stubbs, *Germany in the Later Middle Ages*, A.D. 1200-1500.]

Golden Fleece, Order of the. Military order of knighthood fd. by Philip the Good, Duke of Burgundy, A.D. 1429. An exhibition connected with the various antiquities connected with this order was held at Bruges, June-Sept. 1907. [Refer De Lettenhove, *La Toison d'Or*.]

Goldsmiths' Company of London. Incorp. by Richard II. 1392.

Gold Standard Act (U.S.A.), to fix value of coinage, etc., passed senate, Mar. 6, 1900. [Refer Harper, *Encyclo. U.S. History*, vol. iv.]

Good Parliament, during the reign of Edward III. of England, sat 1376, reformed numerous abuses and intro. beneficial laws. [Refer Stubbs, *Const. History*.]

Goorkha War, between Great Britain and the Indian tribesmen, the Goorkhas, lasted from 1814 till a treaty of peace was signed, Dec. 2, 1816. [Refer Wilson, *History of India*.]

Gordon Riots. Caused by a bill which parliament intro. in 1778 to repeal certain harsh laws against Roman Catholics. On June 2, 1780, a large number of people assembled together in London to protest against this repeal. Lord George Gordon headed the mob, which forced its way into the House of Commons. During the next few days much property was destroyed by the rioters, and on June 6, Newgate prison was attacked and many prisoners released. The military soon dispersed the mob, and many of the ringleaders were executed. Lord George Gordon was imprisoned and *d.* in Newgate, 1793. [Refer *Annual Register*, 1780, *et seq.*]

Gothic Architecture. The transition stages leading from Roman to pure Gothic are given in the following chronological table. After middle of the 16th century the practice of Gothic Architecture died out gradually, but its influence extended to the end of the 17th century, and was partially revived in the 18th.

Norman, or Romanesque, 1066-1154.
Transitional from Norman to Pointed, 1154-1189.
Early English, First Pointed, or Lancet, 1189-1272.
Trans. from Early to Complete Pointed, 1272-1307.
Geometrical Pointed, 1307-1327.
Flowing, or Curvilinear, 1327-1377.
Trans. from Geometrical and Flowing (sometimes classed together as Decorated, or Middle Pointed) to stiff and hard lines 1377-1399.
Third Pointed, Rectilinear, or Perpendicular, 1399-1546.
[Refer art. in *Ency. Brit.*].

Goths. " The Emperor Decius (in A.D. 249) . . . was summoned to the banks of the Danube by the invasion of the Goths. This is the first considerable occasion in which history mentions that great people " [Gibbon, *Rome*, ch. x.]. Defeated by Claudius A.D. 269. After the fall of the Roman Empire in 410 the Goths became masters of Italy until A.D. 553, when they were conquered by Justinian's general, Narses (*see* Rome). [Refer Gibbon, *Rome*.]

Göttingen (Germany). Joins Hanseatic League about 1360; captured by Tilly 1626; recaptured by Saxons 1632; university fd. 1734, opened 1737.

Gowrie Conspiracy. Instigated in 1600 by the Earl of Gowrie and his brother, Alexander Ruthven, who persuaded James VI. of Scotland to visit Gowrie House near Perth, on some pretext, and attempted to murder him. An alarm was raised, however, and the two brothers were killed. The affair is surrounded with an air of mystery. [Refer Lang, *James VI. and the Gowrie Mystery*.]

Granada (Spain). Of very early origin, but dates are uncertain. Part of kingdom of Murcia 1229-38. Falls into hands of Abu Abdullah Mahommed Ibn al Ahmar, who forms the kingdom of Granada 1238. Moors finally expelled, Jan. 2, 1494. [Refer Calvert, *Granada*.]

Grand Alliance. Concluded at the Hague, Sept. 7, 1701, between England, Holland, and the Empire; joined by Prussia, Jan. 20, 1702; by Portugal, May 16, 1703; by Savoy, Oct. 25, 1703. It dealt mainly with the conquest of Spain. *See* Spanish Succession, War of.

Grand Remonstrance. *See* Remonstrance.

Grantham (England). Supposed to have been fd. 303 B.C. Incorp. by Edward IV. 1463; captured by Royalists, Mar. 22, 1642.

Grattan's Parliament. The name given to the Irish Parliament which was declared independent in May 1782 through the exertions of Henry Grattan (1746-1820). It came to an end on July 2, 1800. [Refer Froude, *English in Ireland*.]

Gravelines (France). Fd. by Henry, Count of Flanders, 1160. Defeat of French by Spaniards at 1558; taken by French 1658, and ceded to them, Nov. 7, 1659.

Gravesend (England). Mentioned in Domesday Book. Attacked and burnt by French 1380; incorp. by Queen Elizabeth, July 22, 1562.

Great Britain. The following is a list of the sovereigns of Great Britain since the Union of England and Scotland in 1603 (for those previous *see* England):—

James I. 1603-25; *m.* Anne of Denmark 1589. Hampton Court Conference (*q.v.*) 1604; Gunpowder Plot (*q.v.*), Nov. 5, 1605; the Addled Parliament 1614; execution of Sir Walter Raleigh 1618; departure of the *Mayflower* for New Plymouth 1620.

Charles I. 1625-49; *m.* Henrietta Maria of France 1625. Petition of Right drawn up 1628; assassination of the Duke of Buckingham 1633; Short Parliament met 1640; Long Parliament met 1640; impeachment of the Earl of Strafford 1641; Grand Remonstrance passed 1641; Civil War broke out 1642-45 (*see* under Battles); Charles surrendered to Scottish 1646.

The Commonwealth and Protectorate 1649-60. Oliver Cromwell made Lord Protector 1653; war with Dutch 1652-54; capture of Jamaica from Spanish 1656; death of Oliver Cromwell 1658; Gen. Monk declared for a free parliament, the Convention Parliament, 1660, and Charles II. declared king.

Charles II. 1660-85; *m.* Katherine of Portugal 1662. The " Clarendon Code " passed 1661; war against Holland 1665-67; the Great Plague 1665; the Great Fire 1666; the Triple Alliance, between England, Holland, and Sweden against France 1668; Test Act passed 1673; the Popish Plot 1678; Habeas Corpus Act 1679; Exclusion Bill 1679; Rye House Plot 1683.

James II. 1685-88; *m.* Anne Hyde 1660, Mary of Modena 1673. Monmouth's Rebellion (*q.v.*) 1685; revolution to depose James succeeded 1688.

William III. of Orange and Mary 1689-94; William alone -1702. Meeting of Convention Parliament, Jan. 22, 1689; Triennial Act (*q.v.*) passed 1694; death of Mary 1694; Darien Scheme (*q.v.*) 1698; Act of Settlement (*q.v.*) passed 1701; Grand Alliance (*q.v.*) passed 1701.

Anne 1702-14; *m.* Prince George of Denmark 1683. War of Spanish Succession (*q.v.*) 1702, which was ended by Treaty of Utrecht 1713; Union of Parliaments of England and Scotland 1706.

George I. 1714-27; *m.* Sophia of Brunswick 1682. Riot Act (*q.v.*) passed 1715; first Jacobite Rebellion 1715 (*see* " Fifteen," Rebellions of); South Sea Bubble burst 1720.

George II. 1727-60; *m.* Caroline of Anspach 1705. War with Spain 1739; War of Austrian Succession 1741-48; second Jacobite Rebellion 1745 (*see* " Forty-five," Rebellion of); Clive's campaign in India 1751-57; Wolfe's campaign in Canada 1755-59; Seven Years' War commenced 1756.

GREAT BRITAIN (*continued*)—

George III. 1760-1820; *m.* Charlotte Sophia of Mecklenburg-Strelitz 1761. End of Seven Years' War by Treaty of Paris 1763; American War of Independence (*see* U.S.A.) 1775-83; Treaty of Versailles acknowledged U.S. independence 1783; French Revolution commenced 1789; Union with Ireland 1801; death of Lord Nelson at Trafalgar 1805; commencement of Peninsular War (*q.v.*) 1805, which ended after b. of Waterloo, June 18, 1815.

George IV. 1820-30; *m.* Caroline of Brunswick 1795. Cato Street Conspiracy (*q.v.*) 1820; repeal of Test and Corporation Acts 1828.

William IV. 1830-37; *m.* Adelaide of Saxe-Meiningen 1818. Opening of Liverpool and Manchester Railway 1830; the Reform Bill 1832; Poor Laws reformed 1833; slavery abolished in British colonies 1833; General Registration Act for births, deaths, and marriages 1836.

Victoria 1837-1901; *m.* Albert of Saxe-Coburg 1840. Introduction of penny postage 1839; repeal of Corn Laws 1846; Navigation Laws repealed 1849; Irish famine 1849; Russian (Crimean) War 1854-56; Indian Mutiny 1857; East India Company abolished 1858; American Civil War 1861-65; second Reform Bill 1867; Fenian Riots 1867; Disestablishment of the Irish Church, 1869; first Irish Land Act 1870; Education Act 1870; Queen Victoria proclaimed Empress of India 1876; death of Gen. Gordon 1885; third Reform Bill 1885; Irish Home Rule propositions by Gladstone 1886; Royal Commission to inquire into charges against Parnell 1888-89; treaty with Germany regarding African possessions 1890; Home Rule Bill rejected 1893; conquest of the Sudan 1896-99; troubles with France concerning Fashoda question 1898; Diamond Jubilee of Queen Victoria 1897; commencement of the Boer War 1899; death of Queen Victoria, Jan. 22, 1901.

Edward VII. 1901-10; *m.* Alexandra of Denmark 1863. End of Boer War by Peace of Pretoria, May 31, 1902; Anglo-French Agreement 1904; Anglo-German Arbitration Treaty signed, July 1904; Arbitration Treaty with U.S.A. Dec. 12, 1904; new treaty with Japan, Aug. 1905.

George V. 1910; *m.* Princess Victoria Mary of Teck 1893. Extension of Anglo-Japanese Treaty, July 1911. Passing of the Parliament Bill, Aug. 1911.

Great Contract, The. The treasurer of James I. of England, the Earl of Salisbury, in 1610 entered into an agreement with parliament to obtain money. The king by this *Great Contract* forfeited certain feudal rights, and obtained a permanent grant of £200,000 a year. [Refer Cambridge Modern History, vol. iii. *The Wars of Religion*.]

Great Council of the Peers (Great Britain). Summoned by Charles I. at York, Sept. 24, 1640, in place of a parliament.

Great Intercourse. A commercial treaty between Philip of Burgundy and Henry VII. of England 1495.

Great Privilege (*Groot Privilegie*). On Feb. 3, 1477, a congress of the Netherlands met at Ghent, which was the first regular assembly of the States-General of the Netherlands. The Duchess Mary, then ruler, granted to this assembly a charter known as the G. P. on Feb. 11, 1477. It has been called the " Magna Charta of Holland," and was a restoration of ancient rights, not a creation of new ones. [Refer *The Historian's History of the World*, vol. xiii.]

Greece (S. of Europe). Conquest of Peloponnesus by the Dorians (chiefly legendary) *c.* 1104 B.C. Lycurgus, the great legislator of Sparta, flourished 776. First Messenian War 743-724; second Messenian War 685-668. Institution of Annual Archons 683. Legislation of Dracon at Athens 621. Attempt of Cylon to make himself master of Athens 620. Democratic legislation of Solon 594. Usurpation of Pisistratus 560-527; succeeded by his sons Hipparchus and Hippias; assassination of the former 514; expulsion of Hippias by the Alcmæonidæ and the Lacedæmonians 510. Democratic reforms of Clisthenes 510. The Persian Wars begun, capture of Sardis by Cyrus, King of Persia 646; conquest of Thrace and Macedonia by Persians 510; defeat of the Ionian fleet at Ladé 495; Miltiades, the Athenian general, defeated Persians at Marathon 490; Xerxes set out to invade Greece 480; battles of Thermopylæ and Artemisium; Athenians deserted their city, which was taken by Xerxes, but destroyed the Persian fleet at Salamis 480. Maritime supremacy of Athens lasts for about seventy years. Pericles at the head of public affairs in Athens 461. Egyptian War 460-455. Thirty years' truce made between Athens and Sparta in 445. The Peloponnesian Wars 431-404. Athenian democracy abolished and government entrusted to the Thirty Tyrants. Trial and death of Socrates 399. Expedition of the Greeks under Cyrus and the retreat of the Ten Thousand 401-400. Supremacy of Sparta 404-371. Supremacy of Thebes 371-361. Philip of Macedon invaded Thessaly 352; defeated Athenians at Chæroneia 338, and became master of Greece. Accession of his son, Alexander the Great 336; began his conquest of Asia Minor, Egypt, Syria in 336; died at Babylon 323. Lamian War 323-2. Capture of Athens by Demetrius 296. Accession of Philip V. 220. War between Philip and Rome 216; b. of Cynoscephalæ, victory to Rome 197. Greece declared free by Flamininus 196. Antiochus III. defeated by the Romans at the b. of Thermopylæ 191. Greece made a Roman province 146. Invaded by the Goths under Alaric A.D. 396; plundered by Normans 1146; the Latin conquest 1204; annexed to Turkish Empire in 1456 by Mahommed II. From the year 1770 and onwards there were continual attempts to throw off Turkish rule. War of independence commences April 1821, and is practically ended by the b. of Navarino, Oct. 20, 1828, when the Egyptian fleet was destroyed by Great Britain, France, and Russia. On May 7, 1832, Greece is declared an independent kingdom under British, French, and Russian protection. New constitution adopted 1843. War with Turkey, April 10, 1897, ended by Treaty of Constantinople, signed Dec. 1897. The following are the sovereigns of Greece since the declaration of independence:—

Otho I. 1832.   George I. 1863.

[Refer art. in *Encyclopædia Britannica*.]

Greek Church. First signs of disunion between the Greek and Roman Churches in A.D. 385, when celibacy of the priests was enforced, and a demand that the Pope of Rome should be recognised as supreme, and doctrinal differences were raised. In A.D. 484 the two Churches separated for a period of 40 years. In 734 the Greeks condemned image worship. The date of the final separation may be said to be in 1054, when Pope Leo IX. excommunicated the patriarch, as the ecclesiastical head of Constantinople was called. Several attempts were made to bring about a reconciliation, but without success. The " Orthodox Confession " was drawn up in 1643. [Refer Dean Stanley, *Lectures on the History of the Eastern Church ;* Gibbon, *Rome.*]

Greek Literature:—

Homer (epic poet), *c.* 9th-10th century B.C.
Hesiod (epic poet), *c.* 850.
Simonides (poet), *fl. c.* 664.
Sappho (poetess), *c.* 610-565.
Æsop (fabulist), *c.* 550.
Pythagoras (philosopher), *fl.* 536-2.
Anacreon (lyric poet), *fl. c.* 536-520.
Æschylus (tragedian), 525-456.
Pindar (poet), 518, alive after 446.
Bacchylides of Ceos (poet), *c.* 507-430 (?).
Heraclitus of Ephesus (philosopher), *c.* 504.
Sophocles (tragedian), *c.* 496-406.
Herodotus (historian), 484-443.
Euripides (tragedian), 480-406.
Antiphon (orator), 480-411.
Thucydides (historian), *c.* 471-404.
Democritus (natural philosopher), 460-351.
Aristophanes (comedian), *c.* 444-380.
Xenophon (historian), 443-359.
Isocrates (rhetorician), 436-338.
Plato (philosopher), 427 or 429-347.
Isæus (orator), *b.* 420.
Lysæus (orator), *fl.* 403-380.
Critias of Athens (poet and orator), *d.* 403.
Aristotle (philosopher), 384-322.
Demosthenes (orator), 384-322.
Theopompos of Chios (historian), *c.* 378-305 (?).
Menander (poet and comedian), *b.* 342, *fl.* 321-*c.* 291.
Demetrius of Phalerum (poet and philosopher), born *c.* 345.
Epicurus (philosopher), 342-270.
Theophrastus (philosopher), *d.* 288-284, at a great age.
Theocritus (pastoral poet), *c.* 312, *fl.* 285-247.
Callimachus of Cyrene (poet and grammarian), *c.* 310-*c.* 240.

GREEK LITERATURE (*continued*)—

   Zeno (philosopher), began his teaching in the Stoa, 294, *d.* 264-263.
   Bion (poet), born *c.* 280.
   Moschus (poet and grammarian), fl. *c.* 250.
   Apollonius of Rhodes (poet), *fl.* 222-181.
   Aristophanes of Byzantium (grammarian), born *c.* 260.
   Polybius (historian), born *c.* 210-206.
   Aristarchus of Samothrace (grammarian), *fl.* 156.
   Apollodorus of Athens (grammarian), *fl. c.* 140.
   Strabo (geographer), born *c.* 54.
   Diodorus Siculus (historian), born *c.* 40.
   Dionysius of Halicarnassus (rhetorician), born *c.* 29-25.
   Epictetus (philosopher), born *c.* A.D. 90.
   Arrian (philosopher), born *c.* 90.
   Plutarch (historian and biographer), *fl.* second half of 1st century A.D.
   Lucian (satirist), *c.* 120-200.
   Alciphron (epistolary writer), fl. *c.* 200-220 (?).
   Marcus Aurelius, 120-180.
   Pausanias (traveller and geographer), *fl.* 2nd century A.D.
   Dion Cassius (historian), *c.* 200.
   Diogenes Laertius (biographer), *c.* 200-250.

Greenland (N. America). Discovered 980. Visited by Frobisher 1577. Danish settlements fd. 1721. [Refer art. in *Chambers's Encyclopædia*.]

Green Thursday (*Dies Viridium*) or Holy Thursday, the day before Good Friday. Name first used about 1200.

Greenville, Treaty of, between the U.S.A. and the North-western Indian tribes, Aug. 3, 1795. [Refer Harper, *Encyclo. U.S. History*.]

Greenwich Hospital (England). Fd. 1694; opened 1705. Became a Royal Naval College 1873.

Greenwich Observatory (London). Built 1674 by Christopher Wren; opened 1675-76.

Gregorian Calendar. *See* Calendar.

Gregorian Chants. Named after Pope Gregory I. (A.D. 540-604), who (A.D. 600) added extra tones to the Ambrosian chants then in use.

Grenada (West Indies). Discovered by Columbus 1498; colonised by French 1650; ceded to England by Treaty of Paris (*q.v.*) 1763; recaptured by French 1779; res. to England by Treaty of Versailles (*q.v.*) 1783. [Refer Martin, *British Colonies*.]

Grenadiers. Orig. soldiers for throwing hand grenades. A few of these men were first attached to every French regiment in 1667. Formed into companies in 1670. Evelyn in 1678 mentions that he saw certain soldiers, who were called grenadiers, and who were dexterous in throwing hand grenades. The British Grenadier Guards, formerly the First Foot Guards, were organised in 1660. They received their present name in 1815 after Waterloo. [Refer art. in *Ency. Brit.*]

Grenville Administration (George Grenville, First Lord). Formed after dissolution of Bute Administration (*q.v.*), April 16, 1763; dissolved, July 10, 1765.

Gresham College (London). Fd. by Sir Thomas Gresham 1575. Present college opened, Nov. 2, 1843.

Gretna Green (Scotland). After the abolition of Fleet marriages (*q.v.*) in 1754, those in England wishing to marry clandestinely crossed the border to G. G. to take advantage of the Scotch marriage laws. By a law passed in 1856 these marriages were invalid unless one of the parties had resided in Scotland for three weeks. [Refer art. in *Chambers's Encyclopædia*.]

Greyfriars. A monastery estab. in London by Henry III. 1216-72; afterwards Christ's Hospital (*q.v.*).

Griqualand West. Made a British colony 1867; province of Cape Colony 1877. [Refer Low and Pulling, *Dicty. of Eng. History*.]

Groats were supposed to have been issued first in England by Edward I. (1272-1307). They fell into disuse, but were revived in William IV.'s reign (1830-37), when they were sometimes called " Joeys " after Mr. Joseph Hume, who suggested their revival. In Scotland they were first issued in 1358; in Ireland in 1460. Last coined in Great Britain 1856. [Refer Thorburn, *Coins of Great Britain and Ireland*.]

Grocers, according to a statute of Edward III. dated 1363, orig. meant " ingrossers " or " monopolisers." Grocers' Company fd. 1345; incorp. 1429. [Refer Rees, *History of the Grocery Trade*.]

Groningen (Holland). Joins Hanseatic League 1282; becomes part of the United Netherlands 1594. [Refer Motley, *Dutch Republic*.]

Guadaloupe (West Indies). Discovered by Columbus 1493; colonised by France 1635; captured by Great Britain 1759; res. to France 1763; ceded to Sweden 1813; res. to France 1814.

Guadulupe-Hidalgo, Treaty of, between U.S.A. and Mexico, signed Feb. 2, 1848. [Refer Harper, *Encyclo. of U.S. History*, vol. iv.]

Guatemala (Central America). Declared independent from Spain 1821. Joins in Confederation of C. American States 1824. The capital attacked by Salvadorians 1827; Jesuits expelled from 1871.

Guelphs and Ghibellines. Two mediæval factions caused by the rivalry between emperor and pope, after the death of Henry V. in 1125. The Ghibellines, or the emperor's party, took their name from Waiblingen, a castle in Augsburg, Italianised into Ghibellino. The Guelphs or papal party had their name from Welf or Guelfo, which was the title of many princes of the House of Bavaria. The first outbreak of hostilities between the two parties occurred in 1154, when the Emperor Frederick Barbarossa made an expedition into Italy. [Refer Browning, *Guelphs and Ghibellines*.]

Guernsey (Channel Islands). Granted by Childebert to a Saxon bishop in 550; French made ineffectual attempts to land 1779 and 1780.

Gueux (" Beggars "). During the revolt of the Netherlands against Spanish rule a confederacy of the nobles drew up in 1565 a " Compromise " (*q.v.*) binding themselves to reform various abuses. In April 1566 they marched through the streets of Brussels and presented a petition to the regent, Margaret of Parma. The demonstration caused the latter some alarm, but she was reassured by the words of a councillor, " Madam, is your highness afraid of these beggars (*ces gueux*)? " After that the party opposed to Spain were known as " beggars." [Refer Motley, *Dutch Republic*.]

Guildhall (London). Fd. 1411; destroyed by fire 1666; present building built 1789.

Guillotine. An instrument of decapitation, supposed to have been invented by Joseph Ingace Guillotin (1738-1814), but it is more likely that he merely recommended the use of the instrument as a humane mode of ending life. It was first used to execute a highwayman in Paris on April 25, 1792. [Refer art. in *Chambers's Encyclopædia*.]

Guineas. Gold coinage; first used in England in 1663; last issued in 1813. [Refer Thorburn, *Coins of Great Britain and Ireland*.]

Guines, Treaty of. *See* Cloth of Gold, Field of the.

Gun. *See* Firearms, Cannon, etc.

Gun-cotton. Discovered by Braconnot 1832. Put to practical use by Schönbein, a German chemist, in 1845. First manufactured in England 1847. [Refer Cundill, *Dictionary of Explosives*.]

Gunpowder. " The precise era of the invention and application of gunpowder is involved in doubtful traditions and equivocal language, yet we may clearly discern that it was known before the middle of the 14th century, and that before the end of the same, the use of artillery in battles and sieges, by sea and land, was familiar to the states of Germany, Italy, Spain, France, and England " [Gibbon, *Rome*, ch. lxv.]. G. is said to have been discovered by Michael Schwartz of Brunswick about A.D. 1320, although Roger Bacon mentions its composition in a work published 1216. *See* Firearms, etc. [Refer also Hallam, *Europe during Middle Ages*.]

Gunpowder Plot. Said to be originated by Robert Catesby early in 1604, to blow up the Houses of Parliament. In July 1605 Guido Fawkes was commissioned to commit the deed, and Nov. 5, 1605, the day on which Parliament was to meet, was the day chosen. Catesby was killed during the course of his flight from the government officers. Fawkes and other leaders were executed in Jan. and Feb. 1606.

Guy's Hospital (London). Fd. by Thomas Guy 1722; opened 1725. [Refer Wilks and Bentley, *History of Guy's Hospital*.]

Gwalior (Central India). Under British protection 1803. Visited by Prince of Wales (King Edward VII.) Jan. 1876, Duke and Duchess of Connaught Jan. 1903, and King George when Prince of Wales Feb. 1906.

H

Haarlem (E. Holland). Besieged by Duke of Alva and the Spaniards, Dec. 1572—July 12, 1573. [Refer Motley, *Dutch Republic.*]

Habeas Corpus Act (Great Britain). Passed 1679 to prevent illegal imprisonment; extended to other cases than criminal ones 1816. It has been suspended in times of national emergency. In Scotland the Wrongous Imprisonment Act, passed 1701, is equivalent to the English act; Irish act passed in 1783. [Refer Hallam, *Constitutional History.*]

Hackney Coaches. First used in London in 1625. Laws regarding hire of them passed 1831, 1853, 1869.

Hadfield's (James) attempt to assassinate George III. at Drury Lane Theatre, May 15, 1800; trial and acquittal, June 26, 1800.

Hadrianople or **Adrianople** (Turkey). Received present name from the Emperor Hadrian, who rebuilt and embellished the town. Besieged by Goths A.D. 378; by Emperor Frederick I. of Germany 1190; captured by Turks 1360; capital of Ottoman Empire 1366 until capture of Constantinople 1453 [refer Gibbon, *Rome*]; entered by Russian army, Aug 20, 1829; Treaty of, between Russia and Turkey, signed Sept. 1829.

Hadrian's Wall (England). Supposed to have been built by the Emperor Hadrian about A.D. 121. Extended from the Tyne to the Solway Firth; repaired by Severus 207. [Refer Collingwood Bruce, *The Roman Wall.*]

Hague, The, or **Gravenhage** (Holland). Fd. 1250. Spanish supremacy abjured at 1580 [refer Motley, *Dutch Republic*]; the De Witts killed 1672; captured by French, Jan. 19, 1795. For treaties of, *see* next article.

Hague, The, Treaties of. (1) Between England, France, and Holland to enforce Peace of Roskeld (*q.v.*), May 21, 1659; (2) between England and Holland, July 1659; (3) between England, France, and Holland, Aug. 1659; (4) between Great Britain and Holland, Jan. 23, 1668: receives name of Triple Alliance after Sweden joins, April 25, 1668; (5) between Portugal and Holland, May 7, 1669; (6) between the Emperor, Holland, and Spain against France, July 25, 1672; (7) Grand Alliance (*q.v.*) renewed 1696; (8) second Triple Alliance (*q.v.*), Jan. 4, 1717; (9) between Spain, Savoy, and Austria, Feb. 17, 1717; (10) convention between Great Britain, Austria, Holland, and Sardinia against France and Spain, Jan. 26, 1748; (11) France and Holland, May 16, 1795.

Hague, The, Peace Conferences at. (1) Met May 18, 1899: Arbitration Court instit. April 1899; (2) met June 15—Oct. 18, 1907.

Haileybury College (Herts. England). Fd. 1809 by the East India Company as a training home for their cadets. When the company in 1858 was taken over by the Crown the college fell into neglect. In 1862 it was reopened as a public school. [Refer Higgen, *Old and New Haileybury*.]

Hair-powder, Tax on, in Great Britain 1795; act repealed 1869.

Half-crown. *See* Crown.

Half-pay in British Army and Navy. In the army *permanent* half-pay first granted 1698; abolished for *retired* half-pay 1884.

Halifax Administration (Lord Halifax, First Lord of the Treasury). Formed Oct. 5, 1714. Halifax *d.* May 19, 1715, and was succeeded by the Earl of Carlisle. [Refer McCarthy, *Reign of Queen Anne*.]

Halifax Fisheries Award. One of the articles of the Treaty of Washington (*q.v.*) provided for a commission to inquire into the value of the fishery privileges allowed to the U.S. by the treaty; met at Halifax, Nova Scotia, June 5, 1877. Great Britain awarded $5,500,000 for fishing privileges for 12 years. [Refer Harper, *Encyclo. U.S. History*.]

Halley's Comet. Named after Edmund Halley (1656-1742), who observed it in 1680. He predicted its reappearance in 1759, which proved to be the case; again appeared in 1835 and in 1909-10. [Refer art. in *Chambers's Encyclopædia*.]

Hamburg (Germany). Fd. by Charlemagne A.D. 808; made a bishopric in 831, archbishopric 834; with Lübeck laid foundations of Hanseatic League (*q.v.*) 1241; made an imperial town by Emperor Maximilian I. 1510; Bank of fd. 1619; Peace of 1762; occupied by French 1806; annexed to France 1810; evacuated by French on approach of Russians 1813; freed from French 1814; joined German Confederation (*q.v.*) 1815; one-third of the town destroyed by fire 1842. [Refer art. in *Chambers's Encyclopædia*.]

Hampton Court Conference. Held at Hampton Court, Jan. 12-18, 1604, between the High Church party and the Puritans. The only good result was the decision to translate the Bible (*q.v.*). [Refer Gardiner, *History of England*.]

Hampton Court Palace (Middlesex, England). Built by Cardinal Wolsey, and presented by him to King Henry VIII. 1525; Edward VI. born there, Oct. 12, 1537; enlarged by Christopher Wren for William III. 1694, when the famous chestnut avenue was planted; vine planted 1769; excavation of ancient moat completed and restoration, Oct. 14, 1910. [Refer Law, *Hampton Court in Tudor, Stuart, Orange, and Guelph Times*.]

Hanaper Office. A department of the Court of Chancery, fd. in Charles II.'s reign, and abolished in 1842.

Hanover, Treaties of, between England, France, and Prussia signed Sept. 3, 1725, to oppose the secret Treaty of Vienna (April 20, 1725) between Spain and Austria, who pledged themselves to assist in the restoration of the Stuarts [refer Lecky, *History of Eng-*

land during 18th Century]; joined by Holland, Aug. 9, 1726; by Sweden, Mar. 26, 1727; by Denmark, April 18, 1727; (2) between George II. and Maria Theresa, June 24, 1741; between Hanover and England 1834.

Hanover (Germany). Made an electorate 1692, and the Elector George made King of England as George I. in 1714; made a kingdom 1814; occupied by Prussians 1866, and joined to Prussia, Sept. 26, 1866. [Refer A. W. Ward, *Great Britain and Hanover.*]

Hanover, House of. *See* Great Britain.

Hanoverian Succession. Estab. by law, June 12, 1701; arranged that the Princess Sophia of Hanover and her heirs should succeed to the British throne after the death of Queen Anne, provided the latter died without issue. [Refer Macaulay, *History of England.*]

Hanseatic League. Formed by Hamburg and Lübeck in Germany in 1241 for political and commercial purposes; other towns joined at intervals. Dissolved in 1630, but some of the towns retained the privileges gained from the league, until absorbed into the German Empire in 1871. [Refer Zimmern, *History of the Hanseatic League.*]

Hapsburg or **Habsburg, House of.** Rudolph, Count of Habsburg, became Emperor of Germany 1273.

Hardwicke's Act. *See* Marriage Acts.

Harfleur (France). Captured by Henry V. of England, Sept 22, 1415; English expelled 1433, but again masters of the town in 1440; driven out by Dunois 1449; pillage by Huguenots 1562.

Harleian Library. Collected by Robert Harley, afterwards Earl of Oxford and Mortimer, who *d.* 1724. The collection is now in the British Museum.

Harleian Society. Fd. 1869.

Harrow School. Fd. by John Lyon 1571. The original red brick school-house built 1608-15; chapel built 1857. [Refer Pitcairn, *Harrow School.*]

Hartford (U.S.A.). Conventions: (1) Oct. 20, 1779, to inquire into the depreciation of continental paper money; (2) Dec. 15, 1814, to deliberate upon " means of security and defence " during the Civil War. [Refer Harper, *Encyclo. U.S. History.*]

Hartford (Connecticut, U.S.A.). Settled by English 1635. First named Newtown, but changed to H. in honour of the birthplace in England of Samuel Stone, one of the leaders of the settlers. [Refer Harper, *Encyclo. U.S. History.*]

Harvard University (U.S.A.) (*see also* Cambridge, U.S.A.). Fd. 1638. Named after Rev. John Harvard, who went out to America in 1637, and bequeathed in 1638 the whole of his library and a sum of money for the foundation of a university at Cambridge, Mass. Charter granted in 1650. Under control of state until 1865, since when it has been self-governing. [Refer Thayer, *An Historical Sketch of Harvard University.*]

Harwich (Essex, England). Danes defeated off, A.D. 885; incorp. 1318, and charter further extended 1604; Isabel, queen of Edward II., lands at 1326; Dutch fleet defeated by Duke of York near, June 3, 1665. Parkeston Quay erected 1882. [Refer Lewis, *Topograph. Hist. of England.*]

Hastings (Sussex, England). One of the cinque ports, supposed to have been fd. by Hastings, a Danish pirate, about A.D. 593. William, Duke of Normandy, lands at 1066; burned by French 1377 and 1380.

Hastings, Warren, Trial of. Commenced before the bar of the House of Lords, Feb. 12, 1788, and lasted until April 23, 1795. [Refer Malleson, *Life of Warren Hastings.*]

Hatfield, Council of (England). Held to declare the orthodoxy of the English Church regarding Monothelite heresy; also accepted the decrees of the five first general councils, Sept. 17, 680. [Refer Low and Pulling, *Dicty. of English History.*]

Hatfield House (Herts. England). Built by Sir Robert Cecil 1611. [Refer Brewer, *English Studies.*]

" Hats." *See* " Caps and Hats."

Hatteras Expedition. The Confederate forts at Hatteras Inlet (U.S.A.) attacked by Federal army, under Gen. Butler and a small fleet, Aug. 28, 1861; Confederates, under Major W. S. G. Andrewes, surrendered on following day. [Refer Harper, *Encyclo. U.S. History.*]

Hatti Humayun, Edict of. Passed by the Sultan Abdul Mejid of Turkey in 1856, granting equal rights to his Christian and Mohammedan subjects.

Havre (France). Orig. *Havre de Notre Dame de Grace.* Fd. by Louis XII. 1509; given to Queen Elizabeth by Huguenots 1562; besieged and captured by Montmorency 1563; bombarded unsuccessfully by English 1678, 1694, 1759, 1794, 1795.

Hawaiian or Sandwich Islands. Discovered by Gaetano 1542; and again by Capt. Cook 1778. Cook was murdered by the natives here in 1779. Constitution granted by reigning king 1840; independence guaranteed by Great Britain and France 1844; revolution at 1893; formed into a republic 1894; annexed to U.S.A. 1898. [Refer art. in *Chambers's Encyclopædia.*]

Hawkers or Pedlars, acts respecting in Great Britain. Pedlars Act passed 1871, by which they were placed under surveillance of the police; extended 1881. Hawkers Act of 1888, by which a half-yearly licence had to be taken out. [Refer art. in *Chambers's Encyclopædia.*]

Hay-Pauncefote Treaty, between Great Britain and U.S.A., signed 1901, to amend Clayton-Bulwer Treaty (*q.v.*), regarding canal scheme between Atlantic and Pacific Oceans.

Hayti or **Haiti** (W. Indies). Discovered by Columbus, Dec. 6, 1492. Colonised by negro slaves 1505; ceded to France by Treaty of Ryswick 1697; independent republic, July 22, 1801; Dessalines proclaims himself emperor, Oct. 1804; republic again proclaimed 1859; frequent disturbances since. [Refer St. John, *Hayti, or the Black Republic*.]

Head Act (Ireland). Proclaimed in Ireland 1465; it permitted wholesale murder of the natives. [Refer Taaffe, *History of Ireland*.]

Hearth or **Chimney Money**. A tax first levied in England in 1663 on every hearth; abolished 1689.

Hearts of Steel. A society formed in Ireland in 1772 by the Protestant tenants of Tyrone and Antrim. [Refer Lecky, *Ireland in the 18th Century*.]

Heidelberg (W. Germany). University fd. by the Elector Rupert I. in 1385; reconstituted by Charles Frederick, Grand-Duke of Baden, 1803. H. plundered by Count Tilly in 1622, the Swedes in 1633, and by the Imperialists in 1635; sacked by the French 1688 and 1693.

Helena, St., Island of. (South Atlantic Ocean). Discovered by the Portuguese on St. Helena's Day, May 21, 1501; possessed by East India Company 1651; Napoleon *d.* at 1821; certain Boer prisoners during S. African War sent there 1900-2; British troops withdrawn from, which causes protest from inhabitants, Oct. 29, 1906. [Refer Martin, *History of British Colonies*.]

Heligoland (island N.W. of Germany). Ceded to Great Britain 1814; exchanged with Germany for certain East African possessions 1890. [Refer Black, *Heligoland*.]

Helsingfors (Finland). Fd. by Gustavus I. of Sweden in 16th century; made capital of Finland in 1819; bombarded by allied fleets, Aug. 1855. *See* Finland.

Helvetian Republic, *see* Switzerland.

Helvetic Confession. Drawn up in 1536 by the Swiss theologians assembled at Basel. [Refer Cambridge Modern History, vol. i. *The Reformation*.]

Heralds' College of Arms. Fd. by Richard III. of England 1484.

Heretics, Laws concerning (England). In 1382 provided that sheriffs should arrest " persons certified by the bishops to be heretics." By the *De Hæretico Comburendo* Act, passed 1401, the bishops themselves were empowered to arrest and punish H. This act was enlarged in 1414. In 1533 an act declared that offences against the See of Rome were not heresy. The Bill of the Six Articles 1539 defined various heretical acts. Punishment of death for heresy abolished 1677. [Refer art. in Low and Pulling, *Dicty. of English History*.]

Heritable Jurisdictions Act. Passed in 1747, abolishing hereditary jurisdictions in Scotland.

Herzegovina (Austria-Hungary). United with Bosnia 1326; ceded to Turkey 1699 by Peace of Carlowitz; rebels against Turkish rule 1875; occupied by Austrians, Aug. 1878; formally annexed to Austria-Hungary, Oct. 7, 1908.

Hibbert Lectures. Dealing with theology. Fd. by trustees of Robert Hibbert in 1878.

High Church Party. This term first appeared in England about 1703, and referred to the party who vigorously opposed the Dissenters (*see* Noncomformists), and enforced the laws made against them. [Refer art. in Low and Pulling, *Dicty. of English History.*]

High Commission, The Court of. Estab. by Queen Elizabeth in 1559 to investigate ecclesiastical cases; abolished by act of the Long Parliament, July 1641. James II. in 1686 revived it, but it was finally abolished by the Bill of Rights in Oct. 1689. [Refer Macaulay, *History of England.*]

Highland Garb Act. Passed 1746, after rebellion of " '45." It forbade the wearing of the Highland dress.

High Treason. *See* Treason.

Holland (Europe) (*see also* Netherlands). Orig. peopled by the Batavi, a people of Germany. Sovereignty fd. by Thierry A.D. 868; governed by counts of Hainault 1299; became part of Spain through succession of Charles I. 1519; rebels against Spanish yoke 1572; renounces Spain by solemn declaration, signed July 1581; assassination of William I. of Orange 1584; war with England 1653; French Republican army march into Holland 1793; William V. expelled, Jan. 15, 1795; declared a kingdom with Louis Bonaparte as king, June 5, 1806; abdication of Louis, July 1, 1810; united to France, July 9, 1810; House of Orange res. (William Frederick) and Belgium annexed, Nov. 15, 1813; separates from Belgium (*see* Belgium), July 12, 1831; peace finally concluded between Holland and Belgium, April 19, 1839. William Frederick abdicated; William II. succeeded 1840; William III. 1849; Wilhelmina crowned (after Queen Mother's regency) 1898. [Refer Motley, *Rise of the Dutch Republic.*]

Holy Alliance. Signed at Paris, Sept. 26, 1815, between the rulers of Russia, Prussia, and Austria. It was offered for signature to the other powers, and all except Great Britain signed. [Refer Cambridge Modern History, vol. x. *The Restoration.*]

Holy Leagues, The. (1) Formed in 1511 between Pope Julius II., the Emperor, Maximilian I., Henry VIII. of England, and Ferdinand King of Aragon, to crush France; dissolved in 1513 [refer Cambridge Modern History, vol. i. *The Renaissance*]; (2) formed by Pope Clement VII. in 1526 against the Emperor Charles V.; France, Venice, and Milan were also in the league [refer Robertson, *Emperor Charles V.*]; (3) formed by Pope Pius V., Spain, and Venice against the Turks 1570 [refer Prescott, *Philip II.*]; (4) formed by the Catholic party against the Huguenots in 1576, also known as the Catholic League [refer Cambridge Modern History, vol.

iii. *The Wars of Religion*]; (5) formed by Catholic princes of Germany under Maximilian of Bavaria in 1609 as a counterblast to Protestant Union of 1608 (*q.v.*) [refer S. A. Dunham, *Hist. of Germanic Empire*]; (6) formed by Pope Innocent XI., the Emperor, Poland, Venice, and Russia, against the Turks in 1684 [refer Wakeman, *The Ascendancy of France*].

"Holy Maid of Kent." Elizabeth Barton during Henry VIII.'s reign was so called, urged on by the Catholic party. She prophesied the violent death of the king if he married Anne Boleyn. She and her confederates were executed, April 20, 1534.

Holyrood Abbey and Palace (Edinburgh). Abbey fd. 1128 by King David I. of Scotland. The palace, apart from the abbey, was built in 1501 by James IV. of Scotland; destroyed by English 1544, but immediately rebuilt; Rizzio murdered at, 1566; burned by Cromwell's troops 1650; rebuilt by Charles II. 1671-79.

Homestead Act (New Zealand). (1) Passed 1885, providing land for emigrants free of charge; (2) Western Australia, similar act 1893.

Homestead Act (U.S.A.). Passed by congress 1862, by which every U.S. citizen of the age of 21 years was entitled to claim a certain portion of unappropriated land.

"Homilies, Book of." The Convocation of 1542 decided to publish a volume of H. for the guidance of preachers. They were first published 1547; reprinted in 1560. Second book published 1563.

Honduras (Central America). Discovered by Columbus 1502; throws off Spanish yoke 1821; becomes independent of the Confederation of Central America 1839; up to 1876 frequent wars with other states. [Refer Lombard, *The New Honduras*.]

Honduras, British (Central America). Visited by Columbus 1502; England's right to, acknowledged by Spain 1670; several times attacked by Spaniards; made a Crown colony 1870; separated from Jamaica 1884.

Hong-Kong (China). Occupied by British 1840; formally ceded to Great Britain by Treaty of Nanking 1842.

Hops. First intro. from the Netherlands into England A.D. 1524. Their use was prohibited in 1528, owing to the representations of certain physicians, who stated that the herb was harmful.

Horse Guards (Royal). Instit. 1550 during reign of Edward VI. Their headquarters in Whitehall, London, erected 1758.

Hospitallers, The Knights, or **Brethren of St. John at Jerusalem.** Military order of Crusaders, fd. about 1092. [Refer art. in Low and Pulling, *Dicty. of English History*.]

Houghers, The. Rioters in Ireland, who first appeared in 1711, and were suppressed by means of rewards offered in 1713. They appeared again, and a special act was passed against them in 1784. [Refer Lecky, *Hist. of Ireland during 18th Century*.]

L

Hubertsberg, Treaty of, between Prussia and Austria at conclusion of Seven Years' War, signed 1763. *See also* Treaty of Paris. [Refer Carlyle, *Frederick the Great*.]

Hudson's Bay Territories or **Prince Rupert's Land** (N.W. America). Discovered by Cabot 1517; revisited by Hudson 1610; Hudson's Bay Company formed 1670; English factories at, captured by French 1685; res. by Peace of Utrecht 1713; part of territory united with British Columbia, remainder incorp. with Canada 1858. [Refer Martin, *English Colonies*.]

Huguenots. The name originated between 1510 to 1535 at Geneva, when those in favour of an alliance with Fribourg were called *Eidgengossen* or *Eidnots*, literally " partakers of an oath." They joined themselves with the Bernese, who had declared for the Reformed religion. The name gradually became to be attached to the French Protestants. *See* Bartholomew, St.; France, etc. [Refer Stone, *Reformation and Renaissance*.]

Humane Society, Royal. Fd. 1774 by several Englishmen, including Drs. Hawes and Cogan.

Humble Petition and Advice. The second paper constitution of the English Protectorate 1657. It arranged for the future government of England in the event of the death of Cromwell. The petition collapsed on the dissolution of parliament by Cromwell in 1658. [Refer Ranke, *History of England*.]

Hundred Associates, The. Cardinal Richelieu in 1627 annulled a charter of the Trading Company of New France in America belonging to a family of Huguenots, and organised a company known as the H. A., who were to drive out the Huguenots and colonise the district. [Refer Harper, *Encyclo. U.S. History*.]

Hundred Years' War, between England and France 1338-1453, started by Edward III. of England attempting to force his claims to the French throne. England lost all her French conquests except Calais. [Refer Michelet, *History of France* (Eng. trans.).]

Hungarian Refugee Question. Kossuth, the leader of the revolution in Hungary, visited England in 1851, and asked for an interview with Lord Palmerston, which was refused owing to the representations of Austria. [Refer *Annual Register*, 1851.]

Hungary. Little known of the early history of H. The Hungarians, who gave the country its present name, crossed the Carpathians in A.D. 889 and conquered the ancient *Pannonia* and *Dacia* of the Romans. Invaded by Mongols 1226; Albert of Austria succeeds to the throne 1437; Vienna made capital 1485 (*see* Austria); invaded by Turks 1526; rebellion against Austrian rule, Sept. 28, 1848—Sept. 28, 1849. New electoral system granted 1906; ratified 1907.

Hussites. The followers of John Huss (*b.* 1369), the reformer, who was ordered to be burned alive by the Council of Constance in

July 1415. John Ziska in 1419 with a large following took up arms to avenge the death of Huss, and a formidable party was formed. In 1420 they defeated the Emperor Sigismund. They were, however, themselves finally defeated in 1438. [Refer Ranke, *History of the Reformation in Germany*.]

Hyde Park (London, W.). Originally belonged to the Abbey of Westminster; after the dissolution in 1535, became Crown property. Serpentine formed 1730-33. Famous for political demonstrations.

Hydrogen. A gas discovered by Paracelsus about 1500; experiments by Boyle in 1672; proved to be an element by Cavendish 1766; its presence in water was discovered by Watt and Cavendish in 1781.

I

Iceland. Discovered by Irishmen or Scotsmen at the beginning of 9th century. Seventy years later was colonised by Norwegians. Inhabitants acknowledge sovereignty of Norway 1262-64. United to Denmark with Norway 1388; at separation of Norway and Denmark in 1814 becomes part of Denmark. New constitution granted 1874.

"Ich Dien." Orig. motto of John of Luxemburg, King of Bohemia, found on his helmet after the b. of Crecy, Aug. 26, 1346. It was adopted as the motto of the Prince of Wales by Edward the Black Prince. The explanation of the motto as " Eich Dyn " *i.e.*, " your man," is doubtful.

Iconoclasts or **Image Breakers.** The name was given in the 8th century to those who opposed the use of images in the church. The Emperor Leo Isauricus issued edicts against the use of images in A.D. 726 and 736. The worship of images res. in 780. This schism in the Church caused the Second Council of Nice 782. [Refer Finlay, *Byzantine Empire.*]

Iglau, Treaty of, between the Hussites and the Emperor Sigismund, signed 1436, putting an end to the Hussite War. [Refer Cambridge Modern History, *Wars of Religion.*]

Illinois (U.S.A.). Explored by Marquette and Joliet, French missionaries, in 1673. By treaty passed under the jurisdiction of the English 1763; ceded to United States 1783; admitted into the Union as a state, Dec. 3, 1818. [Refer Harper, *Encyclo. of U.S. History.*]

Illuminati. Certain mystic religious sects were known by this name. The chief were the *Alombrados*, who originated in Spain about 1520, and finally crushed by the Inquisition; and the *Guérinets* in France, who existed between 1623 and 1625. The most famous, however, of a later date were known as the Order of the I., instit. at Ingolstadt 1776 by Adam Weishaupt (1748-1830). The society was denounced in 1784 and 1785 and Weishaupt banished. [Refer art. in *Chambers's Encyclopædia.*]

"Imitatio Christi" (*The Imitation of Christ*). Appeared about 1441; supposed to be the work of Thomas à Kempis (1379-1471). It had a great influence on religious life and ideals. Translated into English about 1460, eighty editions had appeared before 1500. [Refer Bruce, *Age of Schism.*]

Impeachment. The first in Great Britain was in 1376, when an attack was made on Richard Lyons and Lord Latimer by the " Good Parliament." In 1386 the Earl of Suffolk was impeached, and this latter act seems to be more in accordance with those of later times. [Refer art. in Low and Pulling, *Dicty. of Eng. Hist.*]

Imperial Institute (Kensington, London). Built to commemorate Queen Victoria's Jubilee 1887; opened by Queen Victoria 1893; used as part of London University 1899; management of transferred to Board of Trade 1902.

Imperial Service Order. Conferred on members of the Imperial Civil Service; instit. 1902.

" Incident, The." The name given to a supposed plot to assassinate the Earls of Hamilton, Argyll, and Lanark in 1641. It was a mysterious affair altogether, and nothing seems to have been discovered as to its origin. [Refer S. R. Gardiner, *History of England.*]

" In Cœna Domini." A papal bull published annually on Holy Thursday.

Income Tax (Great Britain). Parliament during the great Civil War levied a tax on property and incomes 1642. William Pitt intro. a system of income tax to assist the war with France, Dec. 1798; finally revived by Sir Robert Peel in 1842. Law passed by which all incomes under £160 were exempt from taxation and deductions on other amounts 1898. Law regarding earned and unearned incomes 1898. Budget of 1909 intro. abatement of incomes under £500 for every child under 16 years old.

Income Tax (U.S.A.). First enacted by congress, July 1, 1862, taxing all incomes over $600 and under $10,000, 3 per cent., and over $10,000 5 per cent. Act of Mar. 3, 1865, increases tax to 5 and to 10 per cent. on the excess over $5000. Act of Mar. 2, 1867, exemption increased to $1000, and rate fixed at 5 per cent. on all excess above $1000; tax to be levied until 1870. Bill renewed for one year, July 14, 1870; repealed, Jan. 26, 1871. [Refer Harper, *Encyclopædia of U.S. History.*]

Incumbered Estates (Ireland) Bill. Passed in parliament, July 28, 1849; first court of commissioners held in Dublin, Oct. 24, 1849.

Indemnity Bill. By which a minister of the Crown was relieved from the responsibility of measures passed in urgent cases without consent of parliament. Originated in 1715. On April 19, 1801, a Bill of Indemnity was passed during the suspension of the Habeas Corpus Act.

Independence Day (U.S.A.). Observed as a holiday every July 4, to celebrate signing of Declaration of Independence 1776.

Independents or **Congregationalists.** A religious body distinct from the Established Church, who had their first meeting-house in England, under headship of Henry Jacobs, in 1616. *See* Nonconformists.

" Index Expurgatorius." Part of the Prohibitory Roman Index (*see* following entry); a list of books to be expurgated before being sanctioned to be read. Quiroga first printed the list in his Salamanca volume of 1601.

"**Index Librorum Prohibitorum.**" Official list of books of which the reading is forbidden to members of the Roman Catholic Church. Drawn up by a committee of the Council of Trent, submitted for Papal approval, and published 1564; it is kept revised and brought up to date by the "Congregation of the Index," and underwent modifications under Leo XIII. An early list of forbidden works had been previously drawn up by the University of Louvain, and the first Roman Index was issued in 1557, and 1559 under Paul IV.

India (*see also* East India Company and under various provinces). Invasion of Alexander the Great, during the reign of Sandracothus 315 B.C. Conquered by the Mahommedans under Mahmud Gazni A.D. 1000. Afghan Empire fd. 1205. Invasion by Tamerlane 1398. Passage to India discovered by Vasco da Gama 1497. Baber's invasion 1525. Persian invasion under Nadir Shah 1738. Gen. Clive wins b. of Plassey, June 20, 1757, and England gains Bengal and Behar. Patna conquered by British, Nov. 6, 1763. India Bill passed in British Parliament, June 16, 1773 (*see* Hastings, Warren, Trial of). Burmese War, Dec. 23, 1825—Feb. 24, 1826; Scinde War 1843; Sikh War 1845-49; second Burmese War 1851. Great Indian Mutiny breaks out 1857. Queen Victoria declared empress, Jan. 1, 1877. Frontier War 1897-98. Prince and Princess of Wales (now George V. and Queen Mary) tour through India 1905-6. *See* Afghan War. The following are the governor-generals of India, with the dates of their appointments:—

Warren Hastings 1774	Earl of Auckland 1836
Sir John Macpherson 1785	Earl of Ellenborough 1842
Marquis Cornwallis 1786	Viscount Hardinge 1844
Sir John Shore 1793	Marquis of Dalhousie 1848
Sir Alured Clarke 1798	Earl of Canning 1856
Marquis Wellesley 1798	Earl of Elgin 1862
Marquis Cornwallis 1805	Sir John Lawrence 1864
Sir George Barlow 1805	Earl of Mayo 1869
Earl of Minto 1807	Lord Northbrook 1872
Marquis of Hastings 1813	Earl Lytton 1876
Hon. John Adam, Jan. 1— Aug. 1, 1823	Marquis of Ripon 1880
	Earl of Dufferin 1884
Lord Amherst 1823	Marquis of Lansdowne 1888
Hon. W. Butterworth Bayley 1828	Earl of Elgin 1894
	Lord Curzon 1899
Lord William Bentinck 1828	Earl of Minto 1905
Sir Charles Metcalfe 1835	Baron Hardinge 1910

[Refer art. in Low and Pulling, *Dicty. of English History*.]

Indiana (U.S.A.). First explored by French missionaries about 1700; ceded to English 1763; treaty of 1783 included the territory in the U.S.; admitted into the Union, Dec. 11, 1816. [Refer Harper, *Encyclopædia of U.S. History*.]

Indulgence, Declarations of. (1) Proclaimed by Charles II. in 1662, and again in 1672, permitting free worship to both Nonconformists and Roman Catholics; (2) James II. again passed a similar law in 1687, and this caused the famous trial of the seven bishops, who refused to allow their clergy to read the declaration. [Refer Macaulay, *History of England*.]

Indulgences. Commenced in the Roman Catholic Church about A.D. 800 by Pope Leo III. In the 12th century they were given principally as rewards to the Crusaders. Clement V. in 1313 instit. the public sale of I. Leo X.'s abuse of the issue of I. led amongst other things to the Reformation (*q.v.*). [Refer Lea, *History of Auricular Confession and Indulgence*.]

Infallibility. *See* Papacy.

Ingolstadt (Germany). University fd. at 1472; town fortified in 1539.

Innsbruck (Tyrol). Captured by Maurice of Saxony 1552; by Bavarians 1703; by French and Bavarians 1805.

Inns of Court and of Chancery (London). The Temple, made up of three societies, the Inner, Middle, and Outer, fd. by the Knights Templars (*see* Templars) 1185. Inner and Middle Temple made law associations about 1340; the Outer Temple in 1560. The following are the principal inns, with the dates when they were fd.:—

Barnard's Inn 1445	New Inn 1485
Clement's Inn 1478	Old Serjeants' Inn (Fleet Street)
Clifford's Inn 1345	1429
Furnivall's Inn 1563	Serjeants' Inn (Chancery Lane),
Gray's Inn 1357	now abolished, 1411
Lincoln's Inn 1310	Staple Inn 1415
Lyon's Inn 1420	Thavies' Inn 1519

Some of the above dates are not absolutely certified. The Inner and Middle Temple, with Lincoln's Inn and Gray's Inn, were Inns of Court; the others Inns of Chancery.

Inoculation. *See* Vaccination.

Inquisition. Arose during the persecution of the Albigenses and Waldenses in the 12th century. The first court was instit. by Pope Innocent III. in 1203. In 1248, under Innocent IV., the direction of the court was given to the Dominican order. Estab. in France in 1226; afterwards its operations were mainly directed in Spain. In 1483 Thomas de Torquemada was appointed chief inquisitor, and the court was firmly estab. It was not finally abolished in Spain until 1835. In Rome it still exists, but only in a very modified form. [Refer H. C. Lea, *History of the Inquisition of the Middle Ages*.]

Instrument of Government. Passed by English Parliament, Dec. 1653, constituting Oliver Cromwell Lord Protector of England. It also arranged that parliaments should be triennial. [Refer Ranke, *History of England*.]

Insurance (Great Britain). The earliest record of any life policy being issued was on June 15, 1583, at the " Office of Insurance within the Royal Exchange." The oldest insurance company is the " Hand in Hand," started in 1696 under the name of the " Amicable." The oldest *life* insurance office was the " Society of Assurance for Widows and Orphans," started in 1699. Life Assurance Companies Act passed 1870, by which all companies before starting had to deposit a sum of £20,000 with the Court of Chancery.

Insurance (U.S.A.). The first insurance company was estab. in Boston, Mass., by the Sun Insurance Company (English) in 1728. The first fire insurance policy was issued in Hartford, Conn. 1794. First accident insurance company estab. at Hartford, Conn. 1863. [Refer Harper, *Encyclopædia of U.S. History*.]

Interdict. The most famous in history are those issued (1) against Scotland by Pope Alexander III. 1180; (2) against Poland by Gregory VII. after the murder of Stanislaus; (3) against England under King John by Innocent III. 1208; (4) against England under Henry VIII. by Leo X. 1535.

Interest. *See* Usury Laws.

Interim of Augsburg. A system of doctrine issued by Charles V. in May 1548, attempting to reconcile the religious differences dividing the world.

Invasions of Great Britain. From the Norman Conquest, the following are the principal invasions of the British Isles :—

William the Conqueror 1066	Perkin Warbeck 1495
The Irish 1069	Ireland, by Spaniards and Italians 1580
The Scots 1091	
Robert of Normandy 1103	Ireland, by Spaniards 1601
The Scots 1136	Duke of Monmouth 1685
Empress Maud 1139	William of Orange 1688
Ireland, by Fitz-Stephen 1169	Ireland, by James II. 1689
Ireland, by Edward Bruce 1315	James Stuart the old Pretender 1708
Queen Isabel 1326	
Duke of Lancaster 1399	Second invasion of Pretender 1715
Queen Margaret 1462	
Earl of Warwick 1470	Young Pretender 1745
Edward IV. 1471	Ireland 1760
Queen Margaret 1471	Wales, by the French 1797
Earl of Richmond 1485	Ireland, by the French 1798
Lambert Simnel 1487	

Inventions and Discoveries. *See* under their various titles.

Investiture, Ecclesiastical. The act of a sovereign towards an ecclesiastic by which the former claimed the right to grant ecclesiastical privileges. This, of course, encouraged simony, and tended to lessen the power of the Church. Pope Gregory VII. (Hildebrand) in 1075 condemned the practice; Pope Urban II. in 1095 extended this rule, and forbade any bishop or other ecclesiastic from taking an oath of homage to any lay person. By the Concordat of Worms 1122 the emperor agreed to surrender his right of investiture, and the struggle between pope and emperor was brought to a close. [Refer Hallam, *Europe during the Middle Ages*.]

Iodine. Discovered in 1811 by M. de Courtois at Paris.

Ionian Islands (Mediterranean). Included Corfu, Paxo, Santa Maura, Ithaca, Cephalonia, Zante, and Cerigo. In 1081 Corfu and Cephalonia were seized by Robert Guiscard. Corfu becomes Venetian property 1386. Ceded to France 1797. Seized by Russia and Turkey 1799, when they were formed into the Republic of the Seven United Islands. Res. to France by Treaty of Tilsit 1807. After Napoleonic Wars, Nov. 5, 1815, formed into the United States of the Ionian Islands under British protectorate. Incorp. with Greece by treaty, Nov. 14, 1863. [Refer Kirkwall, *History of Ionian Islands.*]

Iowa (U.S.A.). Orig. part of Louisiana (*q.v.*). Ceded to U.S. 1803; made a separate territory on June 12, 1838; admitted to the Union, Dec. 28, 1846; present constitution framed 1857. [Refer Harper, *Encyclo. U.S. History.*]

Ipswich (Suffolk, England). Pillaged by Danes A.D. 991 and 1000. First charter granted by King John 1199.

Ireland. Until the arrival of St. Patrick from Rome in A.D. 432 the history of Ireland is not at all authentic. The five chief kingdoms of Ireland in the 5th century were: Ulster, Leinster, Meath, Connaught, and Munster. According to Celtic tradition Tara was the chief residence of the Irish kings in ancient times, a central monarchy being established here, and 150 monarchs reigned till it was destroyed in 563 (refer Cusack, *History of the Irish Nation*). In the 10th century the famous Brian Boru brought the country into subjection to his rule; he was killed at Clontarf, where the Scandinavian power in Ireland was finally destroyed, 1014. After his death various dynasties disputed the over-lordship of Ireland. Roderick O'Connor was high king when Henry II. in 1172 entered Ireland to receive homage from him and the under-kings. By this time the Anglo-Normans, under Strongbow, were conquering all the most fertile parts of the country, resisted only by a few of the stronger tribes. The territories of the invaders were divided into palatinates, the rule of the lord palatinate being almost absolute. They were virtually independent kingdoms. [Refer Lawless, *Story of the Nations Series.*] Division of English pale into counties by King John 1212. Richard II. landed with armed force 1394. Insurrection of Tyrone 1601. Maguire's rebellion (Ulster Civil War) to expel English, great massacres, Oct. 23, 1641. Oliver Cromwell subdues the whole land 1649-56. Landing of the deposed James II. 1689. Landing of William III. June 14, 1690. B. of Boyne 1690. Treaty of Limerick (*q.v.*), Oct. 3, 1691. Irish Parliament declared independent (*see* Grattan's Parliament) 1782. Act of Union which joins English and Irish Parliaments, Jan. 1, 1801; followed by Robert Emmet's insurrection, July 23, 1803. Daniel O'Connell's great agitation for repeal of Act of Union commences 1842; trial of O'Connell, Jan. 15, 1844. Murder of Lord Frederick Cavendish, secretary to lord lieutenant, and Mr. Burke, permanent under-secretary, May 1882. Mr. Gladstone's first Home Rule Bill brought and defeated, Mar. 1886; Mr. Gladstone's second Home Rule Bill passed by Commons but thrown out by Lords 1893. Mr. Augustine Birrell's Irish Council Bill thrown out 1907. *See* Fenian Association, etc.; Ireland, Lords Lieutenants of. [Refer Ball, *Hist. Review of the Legislative Systems in Ireland from Invasion of Henry II. to the Union*, 1889.]

Ireland, Church of (*see also* previous article). First missionary visit of St. Patrick, " the apostle of Ireland," A.D. 432. Opposition to papal claims ceases after Synods of Kells 1152 and Cashel 1172. Dissolution of Irish monasteries 1528-38. Act of Catholic Emancipation passed 1829. Act of Disestablishment, July 26, 1869. Irish Presbyterianism dates from 1613. Church organised, June 10, 1642. [Refer art. in *Chambers's Encyclopædia*.]

Ireland, Lords Lieutenants and Lords Deputies of:—

- 1172. Hugh de Lacy.
- 1173. Richard, Earl of Pembroke.
- 1176. Raymond le Gros.
- 1177. Prince John.
- 1184. Lords Justices, no Lord Deputy.
- 1189. Hugh de Lacy.
- 1199. Meyler Fitz-Henry.
- 1203. Hugh de Lacy.
- 1204. Meyler Fitz-Henry.
- 1205. Hugh de Lacy.
- 1215. Geoffrey de Marisco.
- 1308. Piers Gaveston.
- 1312. Edmund le Botiller.
- 1316. Roger de Mortimer.
- 1320. Thomas Fitzgerald.
- 1321. John de Bermingham.
- 1327. Earl of Kildare.
- 1328. Prior Roger Outlow.
- 1332. Sir John d'Arcy.
- 1337. Sir John de Cherlton.
- 1340. Prior Roger Outlow.
- 1344. Sir Raoul de Ufford.
- 1346. { Sir Roger d'Arcy. / Sir John Moriz.
- 1348. Walter de Bermingham.
- 1355. Maurice, Earl of Desmond.
- 1356. Thomas de Rokeby.
- 1357. Almeric de St. Amand.
- 1359. James, Earl of Ormonde.
- 1361. Lionel, Duke of Clarence.
- 1367. Gerald, Earl of Desmond.
- 1369. William de Windsor.
- 1376. { Maurice, Earl of Desmond. / James, Earl of Ormonde.
- 1380. Edmund Mortimer, Earl of March.
- 1385. Robert de Vere, Earl of Oxford.
- 1389. Sir John Stanley.
- 1391. James, Earl of Ormonde.
- 1393. Thomas, Duke of Gloucester.

IRELAND, Lords Lieutenants and Lords Deputies of (*continued*)—

1395. Roger de Mortimer.

1398. { Reginald Grey
        Thomas de Holland } Lords Justices.

1398. Sir John Stanley.
1401. Thomas, Earl of Lancaster.

1413. { Sir John Stanley.
        Sir John Talbot.

1420. James, Earl of Ormonde.
1423. Edmund de Mortimer, Earl of March.
1425. Sir John Talbot.
1427. Sir John Grey.
1428. Sir John Sutton.
1431. Sir Thomas Stanley.
1438. Lord de Wells.
1446. John, Earl of Shrewsbury.
1449. Richard, Duke of York.
1461. George, Duke of Clarence.
1470. Earl of Worcester.
1478. John de la Pole, Earl of Suffolk.
1483. Gerald, Earl of Kildare,
1484. John de la Pole, Earl of Lincoln.
1488. Jasper Tudor, Duke of Bedford.
1494. Henry, Duke of York (afterwards Henry VIII.)
1496. Gerald, Earl of Kildare.
1521. Thomas Howard, Earl of Surrey.
1529. Henry, Duke of Richmond.
1560. Thomas, Earl of Sussex.
1599. Robert, Earl of Essex.
1603. Lord Mountjoy.
1623. Lord Falkland.
1629. Lord Strafford.
1643. James, Marquis of Ormonde.
1647. Philip, Lord Lisle.
1649. Oliver Cromwell.
1657. Henry Cromwell.
1662. James, Duke of Ormonde.
1669. Lord Roberts.
1670. Lord Berkeley.
1672. Arthur, Earl of Essex.
1677. James, Duke of Ormonde.
1685. Henry Hyde, Earl of Clarendon.
1687. Earl of Tyrconnel.
1690. Lord Sydney.
1695. Lord Capel.
1700. Laurence, Earl of Rochester.
1703. James, Duke of Ormonde.
1707. Thomas, Duke of Pembroke.
1709. Earl of Wharton.
1710. Thomas, Duke of Ormonde.
1713. Charles, Duke of Shrewsbury.

IRELAND, Lords Lieutenants and Lords Deputies of (*continued*)—

1717. Duke of Bolton.
1721. Duke of Grafton.
1724. John, Lord Carteret.
1731. Lionel, Duke of Dorset.
1737. William, Duke of Devonshire.
1745. Earl of Chesterfield.
1747. Earl of Harrington.
1751. Duke of Dorset.
1755. William, Duke of Devonshire.
1757. Duke of Bedford.
1761. Earl of Halifax.
1763. Earl of Northumberland.
1765. Earl of Hertford.
1767. George, Viscount Townshend.
1772. Simon, Earl of Harcourt.
1777. John, Earl of Buckinghamshire.
1780. Frederick, Earl of Carlisle.
1782. { Duke of Portland.
       { Earl Temple.
1783. Robert, Earl of Northington.
1784. Duke of Rutland.
1787. Marquis of Buckingham (Earl Temple).
1790. John, Earl of Westmoreland.
1795. { William, Earl Fitzwilliam.
       { John, Earl Camden.
1798. Marquis Cornwallis.
1801. Earl of Hardwicke.
1806. Duke of Bedford.
1807. Duke of Richmond.
1813. Earl Whitworth.
1817. Earl Talbot.
1821. Richard, Marquis of Wellesley.
1828. Henry, Marquis of Anglesey.
1829. Duke of Northumberland.
1830. Henry, Marquis of Anglesey.
1833. Richard, Marquis of Wellesley.
1834. Earl of Haddington.
1835. Marquis of Normanby.
1839. Earl Fortesque.
1841. Earl de Grey.
1844. Lord Heytesbury.
1846. Earl of Bessborough.
1847. Earl of Clarendon.
1852. Earl of Eglinton.
1853. Earl of St. Germans.
1855. Earl of Carlisle.
1864. John, Lord Wodehouse (Earl of Kimberley).
1866. James, Marquis of Abercorn.
1868. John, Earl Spencer.
1874. James, Duke of Abercorn.

IRELAND, Lords Lieutenants and Lords Deputies of (*continued*)—

    1874. Duke of Marlborough.
    1880. Earl Cowper.
    1882. Earl Spencer.
    1885. Earl of Carnarvon.
    1886. Earl of Aberdeen.
    1886. Marquis of Londonderry.
    1889. Earl of Zetland.
    1892. Lord Houghton (Earl of Crewe).
    1895. Earl of Cadogan.
    1902. Earl of Dudley.
    1905. Earl of Aberdeen.

[Refer Low and Pulling, *Dicty. of Eng. Hist.*]

Iron Crown of Italy. Said to have been made for the King of the Longobards in 591. Charlemagne and all succeeding emperors who were also kings of Lombardy were crowned with it. Napoleon, who fd. the Order of the Iron Crown, was crowned at Milan with it on May 26, 1805. The order was abolished 1814, but revived two years later.

Iron Mask, The Man with the. An unknown prisoner of the Bastille, supposed to have been imprisoned on Sept. 18, 1698, and it is almost certain that he *d.* on Nov. 19, 1703. The first public notice was brought to the famous case by the publication of *Mémoires Secrets pour servir a l'Histoire de Perse*, published in Amsterdam 1745-6.

Irvingites. *See* Catholic Apostolic Church.

Italian Literature. Italian was the latest developed of the Romance languages. Its use for literary purposes was delayed by the adoption of the Italians of foreign forms, language, and subjects for their earliest non-Latin works. Early in the 13th century, however, the Italian dialects prevailed, and the first period of Italian literature dates from 1220. The Sicilian school of poetry and transition school of poetry in Tuscany were followed by that of the " Dolce Stil nuovo," which carries us down to the close of the 13th century, and to Petrarch and Boccaccio, the two great writers of the 14th century. The following are the principal authors with their dates:—

    Alamanni, Luigi (poet and satirist), 1495-1556.
    Alberti, Leone Battista (humanist), 1404-72.
    Aleardi, Aleardo (poet), 1812-78.
    Alfieri, Vittorio (Count) (poet and dramatist), 1749-1803.
    Algarotti, Francesco (critic), 1712-64.
    Amari, Michele (Orientalist and historian), 1806-89.
    Ammirato, Scipone (historian), 1531-1601.
    Angioleri, Cecco (poet), *c.* 1250-*c.* 1312.
    Aretino, Pietro (dramatist), 1492-1556.
    Ariosto, Lodovico (poet and dramatist), 1474-1533.
    Arnaboldi, Alessandro (poet), 1827-98.
    Azeglio, Massimo d' (novelist), 1798-1866.

ITALIAN LITERATURE (*continued*)—

Bandello, Matteo (novelist), 1480-1561.

Baretti, Giuseppe (miscellaneous writer), 1719-89.

Basile, Giovanni (Count of Morone) (writer of stories), 17th century.

Beccaria, Cesare (legist), 1735-94.

Belli, Groacchino (poet), 1791-1863.

Bello, Francesco (poet), 15th century.

Bembo, Pietro (Cardinal) (poet and historian), 1470-1547.

Bentivoglio, Guido (Cardinal) (historian), 1579-1644.

Berchet, Giovanni (poet), 1783-1851.

Berni, Francesco (poet), *c.* 1497-1535.

Bisticci, Vespasiano di (biographer), 1421-98.

Boccaccio, Giovanni (novelist and poet), 1313-75.

Boiardo, Matteo Maria (poet), *c.* 1434-94.

Bruni, Leonardo (biographer), 1369-1414.

Bruno, Giordano (poet), 1548-1600.

Campanella, Tommaso (poet), 1568-1639.

Carducci, Giosuè (poet), 1835-1907.

Caro, Annibale (poet and translator), 1507-66.

Casti, Giovanni Battista (poet), 1721-1803.

Castiglione, Baldassare (author of *The Book of the Courtier*), 478-1529.

Cavalcanti, Guido (poet), *c.* 1250-1300.

Cellini, Benvenuto (artist and autobiographer), 1500-71.

Chiabrera, Gabriello (poet), 1552-1637.

Cino da Pistoia (poet), 1270-1336.

Cinthio, Giovanni Battista Giraldi (novelist), 1504-73.

Colletta, Pietro (historian), 1775-1831.

Colonna, Vittoria (poetess), 1490-1547.

Compagni, Dino (chronicler), (?)-1324.

Coppetta, Francesco (poet), 1510-54.

Costanzo, Angelo di (poet and historian), 1507-*c.* 1591.

Dante Alighieri (poet), 1265-1321.

Filicaja, Vincenzo (poet), 1642-1707.

Fogazzaro, Antonio (novelist), 1842-1911.

Foscolo, Ugo (poet), 1778-1827.

Giannone, Pietro (historian), 1676-1748.

Gioberti, Vincenzo (philosopher), 1801-52.

Giordani, Pietro (miscellaneous writer), 1774-1848.

Giusti, Giuseppe (poet), 1809-50.

Goldoni, Carlo (dramatist), 1707-93.

Gozzi, Carlo (dramatist), 1720-1806.

Guarini, Giovanni Battista (poet and dramatist), 1537-1612.

Guicciardini, Francesco (historian), 1483-1540.

Guidiccioni, Guido (poet), 1500-41.

Lanzi, Luigi (art historian), 1732-1810.

Latini, Brunetto (poet), 1210-94.

Leopardi, Giacomo (philologist, poet, and philosopher), 1798-1837.

Lorenzo de' Medici (poet and patron of letters), 1449-92.

Machiavelli, Niccolo (historian and political writer), 1469-1527.

ITALIAN LITERATURE (*continued*)—

    Maffei, Count Scipione (archæologist), 1675-1755.
    Mamiani, Terenzio (miscellaneous writer), 1799-1885.
    Manzoni, Alessandro (poet), 1785-1873.
    Marini, Giovanni Battista (poet), 1569-1625.
    Mazzini, Giuseppe (patriot), 1808-72.
    Meli, Giovanni (poet), 1740-1815.
    Metastasio, Pietro (poet and dramatist), 1698-1782.
    Molza, Francesco Maria (poet), 1489-1544.
    Monti, Vincenzo (poet), 1754-1828.
    Muratori, Lodovico Antonio (editor and historian), 1672-1750.
    Parini, Giuseppe (poet), 1729-99.
    Petrarca, Francesco (poet), 1304-74.
    Pellico, Silvio (poet and dramatist), 1788-1854.
    Pindemonte, Ippolito (poet), 1753-1828.
    Pius II., Pope (Enea Silvio Piccolomini) (critic), 1405-64.
    Poliziano (Angelo Ambrogini) (poet and dramatist), 1454-94.
    Polo, Marco (traveller), *c.* 1250-1324.
    Pontano, Giovanni (statesman, diplomatist, and poet), 1426-1503.
    Prati, Giovanni (poet), 1815-84.
    Pulci, Luca (poet), 1431-70.
    Pulci, Luigi (poet), 1432-84.
    Redi, Francesco (physician and naturalist), 1626-98.
    Romagnosi, Giovanni Domenico (philosopher), 1761-1835.
    Rossetti, Gabriele (translator), 1783-1854.
    Sacchetti, Franco (novelist), *c.* 1330-1399.
    Sannazaro, Jacopo (poet), 1458-1530.
    Sarpi, Pietro (natural philosopher), 1552-1623.
    Stampa, Gaspara (poetess), 1523-54.
    Tasso, Bernardo (poet), 1493-1568.
    Tasso, Torquato (poet), 1544-95.
    Tassoni, Alessandro (poet), 1565-1635.
    Telesio, Bernardo, 1509-88.
    Testi, Count Fulvio (poet), 1593-1646.
    Tiraboschi, Girolamo (historian), 1731-94.
    Tommaseo, Niccolo (essayist), 1802-74.
    Trissino, Giovanni Giorgio (poet and diplomatist), 1478-1549.
    Troya, Carlo (historian), 1784-1858.
    Uberti, Fazio degli (poet), *c.* 1310-*c.* 1370.
    Valle, Pietro della (traveller), 1586-1652.
    Vanini, Giulio Cesare (poet), *c.* 1585-1619.
    Vasari, Giorgio (biographer), 1511-74.
    Verri, Count Alessandro (poet), 1741-1816.
    Vico, Giovanni Battista (philosopher), 1668-1744.
    Villani, Giovanni (historian), *c.* 1275-1348.
    Zanella, Giacomo (poet), 1820-88.
    Zeno, Apostolo (dramatist), 1668-1750.

[Refer Garnett, *Italian Literature*.]

    Italy. The early history of I. is so closely associated with that of Rome that under the latter heading will be found all the principal dates. Invasion of I. by Theodoric, King of the Ostrogoths, A.D. 489. Reign of Theodoric 489-526. Power of Goths overthrown 553. Lombard invasion under Alboin 568. Charlemagne's invasion 774; he is crowned Emperor of the West at Rome 800. Hildebrand (Gregory VII.) becomes pope, and the great struggle between Guelph and Ghibelline (*q.v.*) commences 1073. During the 14th and 15th centuries I. was split up between five principal powers (*see* under titles of various duchies, Ferrara, Venice, etc.). Invasion of Charles VIII. of France 1494. Napoleon Bonaparte enters I. 1796 (*see* Napoleon); is crowned King of I. 1805. By Congress of Vienna 1815 I. was reorganised, and French rule ended. States of Central I. annexed to kingdom of Victor Emmanuel, Mar. 1860. First Italian Parliament meets at Turin, Feb. 1861, and Victor Emmanuel proclaimed King of I. Emancipation of I. completed by Victor Emmanuel's triumphal entry into Rome, Sept. 20, 1870. Assassination of King Humbert, July 29, 1900, by an anarchist. [Refer to works mentioned under art. on Rome.]

M

J

Jacobins. Members of a political club which was formed during French Revolution, orig. known as *Club Breton*, fd. at Versailles 1789, by members of States-General (*q.v.*). It was practically dissolved at the death of Robespierre 1794; formally closed, Nov. 9, 1794. [Refer Carlyle, *French Revolution.*]

Jacobites. Followers of the exiled Stuarts. Name first adopted after revolution of 1688 (*see* "Fifteen" and "Forty-five" Rebellions). The last Jacobite to be executed was Dr. Archibald Cameron, June 7, 1753. [Refer Macaulay, *History of England.*]

Jacquerie. A rebellion of French peasants in 1358. Word taken from "Jacques Bonhomme," the name given by the nobles to the peasants; finally suppressed at b. of Meaux, June 9, 1358. [Refer Hallam, *Europe during the Middle Ages.*]

Jamaica (W. Indies). Orig. *Xaymaca*, "Land of Springs." Discovered by Columbus 1494; possessed by Spaniards 1509; British expedition sent out under Oliver Cromwell conquers the island 1655; ceded to England by Treaty of Madrid 1670; insurrection of negroes, Oct. 1865; new constitution framed 1866; great earthquake at Kingston, destroying practically whole town, Jan. 14, 1907. [Refer art. in *Chambers's Encyclopædia.*]

Jameson Raid. An invasion of the Transvaal by the forces of the British South Africa Company, Jan. 1896. The leader was Dr. Jameson, who was tried in July 1896 under the Foreign Enlistment Act, and sentenced to imprisonment. [Refer Bryce, *South Africa.*]

James's Palace, St. (London). Built by Henry VIII. 1530-6. Extended by Charles II. 1668; by George IV. 1827. [Refer Sheppard, *Memorial of the St. James's Palace.*]

Jamestown (Virginia). Named after James I. of England by some English settlers, who landed May 13, 1607. *See* Virginia.

Janissaries. An order of infantry in the Turkish army, fd. by Amurath I. 1361; insurrection of, June 14, 1826 [refer Gibbon, *Rome*, ch. lxiv., for interesting account of the origin of these soldiers]; abolished same year.

Jan Mayen Land (island, Arctic Ocean). Discovered by Jan Mayen, the Dutch navigator, 1611; station for Austrian Polar expedition 1882-3. [Refer Dufferin, *Letters from High Latitudes.*]

Jansenists. A religious sect fd. after the death of Cornelius Jansen (1585-1638), opposed to the Jesuits. It grew up through the controversy raised by Jansen's work, *Augustinus, seu Doctrina, S. Aug. de Hum. Naturæ Sanitate, Ægritudine, Medicina adversus*

179

Pelagianos et Massilienses, which was published in 1640. Work condemned by Inquisition 1642. Many well-known theologians supported the work, including Pascal, Arnaud, and Nicole, who fd. the Port Royal Community (*q.v.*). The controversy resulted in Pascal's *Provincial Letters*, published in 1656-7. The movement in France was practically dissolved in 1719; but they are still strong in Utrecht. [Refer art. in *Chambers's Encyclopædia*.]

Japan (Asia). Early history legendary up to A.D. 500. Buddhism intro. 552, and estab. by government 624. Great expedition against Korea 1592. Portuguese landed in J. and estab. trade there 1543. Foreigners forbidden to land 1624, and Portuguese finally expelled 1638. U.S. fleet under Commodore Parry enforced trading treaty, Mar. 31, 1854, and since then other countries have enacted similar treaties. Japanese expedition to Formosa against piracy 1874. Popular constitution proclaimed 1889. First parliament met 1891. War with China 1894-5. Formosa ceded 1895. Treaty with Great Britain 1902. War with Russia opened, Feb. 1904; Port Arthur surrendered, Jan. 2, 1905; peace concluded, Sept. 5, 1905. Further treaty with Great Britain 1905; extended, July 1911. [Refer Murray, vol. in Stories of the Nations Series.]

Jarrow (Durham, England). The Venerable Bede was associated with the Benedictine abbey fd. here in A.D. 682 by Benedict Biscop. [Refer Jewitt, *Jarrow Church*.]

Java (island, Dutch E. Indies). Dutch rule commences in 1610; occupied by British 1811; regained by Dutch 1817. [Refer art. in *Chambers's Encyclopædia*.]

Jedburgh (Roxburghshire, Scotland). Abbey fd. by David I. 1118-47; burned by English 1544-5. [Refer Watson, *Jedburgh Abbey*.]

Jena (Germany). University fd. 1547-58 by the Elector John Frederick of Saxony. *See also* under Battles.

Jersey (Channel Islands). Futile attempts by the French to capture in 1779 and 1781.

Jerusalem (Palestine). 1050 B.C. taken by David from Jebusites and made his capital. Destroyed by Babylonians under Nebuchadnezzar 588 B.C. Rebuilt 536; completed 512. Great siege by the Emperor Titus A.D. 70. New city rebuilt by the Emperor Adrian 130. Walls rebuilt 437. Captured by Persians 614; by Saracens 637 (*see* Crusades); by French under Napoleon, Feb. 1799. [Refer Smith, *Jerusalem, the Topography, Economics, and History*.]

Jervaulx Abbey (Yorkshire, England). Fd. 1156; dismantled 1539; ruins excavated 1803.

Jesuits (Society of Jesus). A religious order fd. by Ignatius Loyola (1491-1556) 1534. Loyola with his associates visited Rome and submitted their rules to Pope Paul III. 1539. Order approved by papal bull of 1540. First colleges opened in Portugal 1540; in Paris 1542. Expelled from France 1594, but res. in 1603; again suppressed in France 1764; and again res. 1814; and finally expelled 1880. Expelled from England 1579, 1581, 1586, 1602, 1829. The following is a list of the generals of the order since its foundation:—

Ignatius Loyola 1541-56	Michele Angelo Tamburini 1706-30
Diego Laynez 1558-65	
Francesco Borgia 1565-72	Franz Retz 1730-50
Everard Mercurian 1573-80	Ignazio Visconti 1751-55
Claudio Acquaviva 1581-1615	Alessandro Centurioni, 1755-57
Mutio Vitelleschi 1615-45	Lorenzo Ricci 1758-75
Vincenzio Caraffa 1646-49	Thaddæus Brzozowski 1805-20
Francesco Piccolomini 1649-51	Aloysio Fortis 1820-29
Alessandro Gottofredi 1652	Johannes Roothaan 1829-53
Goswin Nickel 1652-64	Peter Johannes Beckx 1853-84
Giovanni Paolo Olivia 1664-81	Antoine Anderledy 1884-92
Charles de Noyelle 1682-86	Luis Martin 1892-1906
Tirso Gonzalez 1687-1705	Francis Xavier Wernz 1906

[Refer McClintock and Strong, *Cyc. of Theo. and Eccles. Lit.*]

" **Jeunesse Dorée** " (" Gilded Youth "). The name given to a party of youths in Paris after Robespierre's death, July 27, 1794, who attempted to bring about a counter-revolution. [Refer Carlyle, *French Revolution.*]

Jews in England. Mentioned in ecclesiastical documents as early as A.D. 740. Riots against them in 1189 at coronation of Richard I. Owing to frequent oppression, in 1253 they begged permission to leave the country. Driven from England by an edict of Edward I. 1290; readmitted by Cromwell 1652. Bill passed to naturalise J. 1753; repealed 1754. Allowed to obtain freedom of the City of London 1832. Act to relieve J. elected to municipal offices from taking oaths 1845; extended when they were admitted to parliament 1858. Universities Tests Act 1871 enables J. to graduate at the universities. First admitted to House of Lords 1885. [Refer Goodman, *History of the Jews* (Temple Cyclopædic Primers).]

Johannesburg (Transvaal). Fd. 1887. Jameson Raid (*q.v.,*) organised at 1896.

John, St., Knights of. *See* Malta, Knights of.

John o' Groat's House. Ancient house situated on the most northerly point of Great Britain. Name said to be derived from a Dutch family who settled here about 1489.

Joint High Commission. Appointed in 1871 by the U.S. and Great Britain to settle various claims of the former against the latter by the depredations of the *Alabama*. The commissioners first met at Washington on Feb. 27, 1871. Treaty agreed to and signed May 8, 1871, which provided for settlement by arbitration. [Refer Harper, *Encyclopædia of U.S. History.*]

Joinville, Treaty of. A religious compact between Philip II. of Spain and Henry of Guise, signed Jan. 1585. [Refer Johnson, *Europe in the 16th Century.*]

Juan Fernandez, Island of (Pacific). Discovered by Juan Fernandez in 16th century. The famous Alexander Selkirk lived here from 1704-9. Occupied by Spaniards 1750.

Jubilee, Year of. This name was adopted by the Roman Catholic Church after the Jewish festival, and celebrated at intervals. The first such festival was instit. by Pope Boniface VIII. in 1300. This was to be held every 100 years, but in 1343 Clement VI. reduced the period to 50 years. Paul II. again in 1470 reduced it to every 25 years.

Judicature Acts, constituting the English Supreme Court, passed 1873-76.

Judiciary of the U.S.A. Supreme Court organised 1789; Court of Claims estab. and organised by Congress 1855; Circuit Court of Appeals estab. and organised by Congress 1891. Women were admitted to practise in the Supreme Court by Act of Congress, Feb. 15, 1879. [Refer Harper, *Encyclo. U.S. History.*]

" Junius, Letters of." A series of seventy political letters signed *Junius*, which appeared in the *Public Advertiser* between Jan. 21, 1769, and Jan. 21, 1772; reprinted in two vols. Mar. 1772. The printer and publisher, H. S. Woodfall, was prosecuted in Dec. 1769 for a certain letter which appeared against the king, George III., but he was acquitted. [Refer H. R. Francis, *Junius Unveiled.*]

Jury, Trial by. Modern system intro. into England during Alfred's reign A.D. 871-901. Act for trial by jury in civil cases intro. into Scotland 1815. Act to amend laws relating to juries in Ireland 1833. [Refer Forsyth, *History of Trial by Jury.*]

Justice of the Peace. Name first used in England 1264. Appointment of special *custodes pacis* by Act of Parliament 1327. Local Government Act of 1888 defines jurisdiction of. [Refer art. in *Chambers's Encyclopædia.*]

" Justification," The, of William of Orange. In 1567 the Council of Blood (*q.v.*) in Spain declared William of Orange an outlaw if he did not surrender himself for trial to their court. William's reply was his " Justification," published in 1568, and sent to all the Courts of Europe. [Refer Motley, *Rise of Dutch Republic.*]

Justinian Code. Drawn up by a commission, which was appointed by the Roman Emperor Justinian in A.D. 528; promulgated 529.

Juvenile Offenders Acts. Act for instit. a prison for the correction of juvenile offenders, passed 1838. Act for committal to reformatories 1854. The Juvenile Offenders Act passed 1901. By the act of 1908 separate courts were set apart for the trial of children.

K

Kabul or **Cabul** (Afghanistan). Captured by Tamerlane A.D. 1394; by Nadir Shah 1702; made capital of Afghanistan (*q.v.*) 1774; taken by Pollock, Sept. 1842. *See* Afghanistan.

Kaffirs. A race inhabiting Swaziland, Zululand, etc. First Kaffir War with Great Britain 1834; second ditto 1846-48. Colony known as British Kaffraria from 1847 to 1875, when the district was joined to Cape Colony.

Kandahar (Afghanistan). Supposed to have been fd. by Alexander the Great (334-324 B.C.). Made capital of Afghanistan 1747 In 1774, however, Kandahar ceased to be the capital, which was transferred to Kabul. Held by British, Aug. 7, 1839—May 22, 1842; finally evacuated by British, April 1881. *See* Afghanistan.

Kansas, State of (U.S.A.). Part of Louisiana purchase in 1803; territory estab. by Act of Congress 1854; admitted to Union as a state, Jan. 29, 1861. [Refer Harper, *Encyclopædia of U.S. History*.]

Kamtschatka or **Kamchatka** (Asia). Discovered by Morosco A.D. 1690; in Russian possession 1697; visited by Behring 1728; unsuccessful attempt made on fort of Petropavlovsk by combined British and French fleets 1854.

Kappel (Switzerland). First Peace of, between the Forest Cantons and the Zwinglian party, June 1529; second Peace of, Oct. 11, 1531. [Refer Tanner, *The Renaissance and the Reformation*.]

Katrine, Loch (Scotland). Has supplied Glasgow with water since 1859. The works were started in 1854. Further works to increase supply completed 1896.

Keeper of the Great Seal. *See* Seal.

Kenilworth (Warwickshire, England). Castle fd. by Geoffrey de Clinton about 1120. Crown possession until 1563, when it was given by Queen Elizabeth to the Earl of Leicester. [Refer Scott, *Kenilworth*.]

Kenilworth, Dictum of. Passed during Henry III.'s reign 1266, and enacted that all who took up arms against the king should pay the value of their lands for five years. [Refer Low and Pulling, *Dicty. of English History*.]

Kensington (London). The palace was presented to the nation in 1899. Orig. the seat of Lord Chancellor the Earl of Nottingham. Bought by William III. in 1689. The Museum (the Victoria and Albert) was estab. in 1857; enlarged 1899, Queen Victoria laying the foundation stone of the new buildings.

Kentish Petition, The. Drawn up by William Colepepper, chairman of the Quarter Sessions at Maidstone, in 1701, protesting against the peace policy of the Tory party during a threatened French invasion. It was signed by the deputy lieutenants, twenty justices, and a large number of freeholders. [Refer Burnet, *History of his own Times.*]

Kentucky, State of (U.S.A.). Received its present name in 1776; made a separate territory from Virginia 1790; admitted to the Union as a state, June 1, 1792. [Refer Harper, *Encyclopædia of U.S. History.*]

Ket's Rebellion. Instigated by Robert Ket, a Norfolk tanner, in July 1549. The rioters met at Norwich, but were soon disbanded. Ket was executed in Aug. 1549. [Refer Russell, *Ket's Rebellion.*]

Kew (Surrey, England). Royal Botanic Gardens fd. 1760; open to the public since 1840.

Khartoum (Soudan). Fd. in 1823 by Mehemet Ali; defended against the Mahdi by Gen. Gordon 1884-5, who was killed there, Jan. 26, 1885; after the b. of Omdurman, Sept. 2, 1898, Khartoum was again made the capital of the Eastern Soudan.

Khyber Pass (Afghanistan). Twice crossed by British army during First Afghan War 1841, 1842, and again in the Second Afghan War, Nov. 1878. The Treaty of Gandamak 1879 stipulated that the pass should be fully controlled by the British authorities.

Kiel, Treaty of, ceding Norway to Sweden, between Great Britain, Sweden, and Denmark, signed Jan. 14, 1814. [Refer Alison, *History of Europe.*]

Kilkenny, Statutes of. Forbade amongst other things (1) marriage between English and Irish; (2) Englishmen to use Irish names or wear Irish apparel; passed 1367. [Refer Hallam, *Constit. History.*]

Kimberley (S. Africa). Relieved after siege of three months during Transvaal War (*q.v.*), Feb. 15, 1900.

King or Queen's Bench, Court of. Said to have originated in 1178, when five judges sat to hear the complaints of the people; sat for the last time 1875.

King's Bench Prison (London). Burnt down during Gordon Riots, June 7, 1780; rebuilt 1781; buildings demolished 1880.

King's College (London). Fd. by royal charter 1828; confirmed by Act of Parliament 1882. [Refer *The Celebration of the College Jubilee,* 1881.]

King's Counsel. Title first granted in England by James I. in 1604 to Sir Francis Bacon.

King's Evil or Scrofula. Supposed to have been cured by the touch of the sovereign. The custom seems to have originated with Edward the Confessor in 1058. It fell into disuse with George I. in 1714.

Kings of Great Britain. *See* under England, Great Britain.

Kingston (Jamaica). Fd. 1693-1703. Almost totally destroyed by an earthquake, Jan. 14, 1907. *See also* Jamaica.

Kingston-on-Thames (Surrey). Incorp. 1206. Saxon kings crowned here. Castle captured by Henry III. during Barons' War 1264. Headquarters of Gen. Fairfax during Civil War 1647. [Refer Lewis, *Topographical History of England*.]

Kit-Cat Club. Fd. by thirty-nine noblemen and gentlemen in London, about 1703. The members were all staunch supporters of the Hanoverian succession; dissolved about 1720.

Knighthood, Orders of (Great Britain and Ireland). The following are the principal orders, with the dates of their foundations:—

Bannerets 1360; renewed 1485.
Bath 1399; renewed 1725.
Carpet 1553.
Garter 1350.
Merit, Order of, 1901.
Round Table 528.
Royal Victorian Order 1896.
St. Andrew, Scotland, 809; renewed 1452; again 1605.
St. George 1349.
St. Michael and St. George 1861.
St. Patrick, Ireland, 1783.
Star of India 1878.
Thistle 812; revived 1540.

Many of the above are described under their various titles.

Knighthood. The following are the principal orders of K. in Europe, with the dates of their foundation:—

Albert (Saxony), 1850.
Albert the Bear (Anhalt), 1382.
Alcantara (Spain), 1156.
Alexander Newsky (Russia), 1722.
Amaranta (Sweden), 1645.
Andrew, St. (Russia), 1698.
Anna, St. (Bavaria), 1784.
Anne, St. (Russia), 1735.
Annunciada (Italy), 1355.
Anthony, St. (Bavaria), 1382.
Apostolic Order of St. Stephen (Hungary), 1764.
Avis, St. Benedict of (Portugal), 1147.
Bavarian Crown (Bavaria), 1808.
Bear (Austria), 1213.
Belgian Lion (Belgium), 1815.
Black Eagle (Prussia), 1701.
Blood of Our Saviour (Austria), 1608.
Calatrava (Spain), 1158.
Catherine, St. (Russia), 1714.
Charles III. (Spain), 1771.
Charles XIII. (Sweden and Norway), 1811.

KNIGHTHOOD (*continued*)—

Charles Frederic (Baden), 1807.
Christ (Portugal), 1317.
Compostella or Santiago (Spain), 1175.
Crescent (Turkey), 1801.
Danebrog (Denmark), 1219.
De la Scaura (Spain), 1320.
Ducal House (Oldenburg), 1838.
Elephant (Denmark), 1458.
Ernest (Saxe-Coburg), 1690.
Faustin, St. (Hayti), 1849.
Ferdinand, St. (Spain), 1811.
Fidelity (Denmark), 1732.
Francis Joseph (Austria), 1849.
Frederick (Wurtemburg), 1830.
George, St. (Austria), 1470.
George, St. (Bavaria), 1729.
George, St. (Russia), 1769.
George d'Alfaura, St. (Spain), 1201.
Golden Fleece (Spain and Austria), 1429.
Henry the Lion (Brunswick), 1834.
Hermingilde, St. (Spain), 1814.
Hubert, St. (Bavaria), 1444.
Iron Cross (Prussia), 1813.
Iron Crown (Austria), 1805.
Iron Helmet (Hesse), 1814.
Isabella, St. (Portugal), 1804.
Isabella the Catholic (Spain), 1815.
James, St. (Portugal), 1310.
James of Compostella, St. (Spain), 1175.
John, St. (Prussia), 1812.
Lady of Mercy (Spain), 1218.
Legion of Honour (France), 1802.
Leopold (Belgium), 1832.
Lily of Aragon (Spain), 1410.
Louis (Bavaria), 1827.
Louisa, St. (Prussia), 1814.
Malta, St. John of (Austria), 1043.
Maria Louisa, St. (Spain), 1792.
Maria Theresa (Austria), 1757.
Maurice, St. (Italy), 1434.
Maximilian (Bavaria), 1853.
Medjidie (Turkey), 1852.
Mercy (Spain), 1261.
Merit (Prussia), 1740.
Michael, St. (Bavaria), 1693.
Military Merit (Russia), 1792.
Nicani-Iftihar (Turkey), 1831.
Olaf, St. (Norway), 1847.
Our Lady of the Conception (Portugal), 1818.
Our Lady of Montesa (Spain), 1317.

KNIGHTHOOD (*continued*)—

Palatine Lion (Bavaria), 1768.
Polar Star (Sweden), 1748.
Red Eagle (Prussia), 1734.
Redeemer (Greece), 1833.
Rosary of Toledo (Spain), 1212.
Saviour (Spain), 1118.
Saviour of the World (Sweden), 1561.
Savoy (Italy), 1815.
Seraphim (Sweden and Norway), 1280.
Sincerity (Prussia), 1705.
Slaves to Virtue (Austria), 1662.
Stanislaus (Russia), 1765.
Starry Cross (Austria), 1668.
Swan (Prussia), 1449.
Sword (Sweden and Norway), 1525.
Teutonic Order (Austria), 1191.
Theresa (Bavaria), 1827.
Tower and Sword (Portugal), 1459.
Ulrica (Sweden), 1734.
Vasa (Sweden and Norway), 1772.
White Eagle (Russia), 1634.
White Falcon (Saxe-Weimar), 1732.
William (Netherlands), 1815.
Wing of St. Michael (Portugal), 1172.
Wolodomir (Russia), 1782.

Knights of Labour. A labour association fd. at Philadelphia, U.S.A., in 1869. First general assembly held 1878. [Refer Harper, *Encyclopædia of U.S. History*.]

Knights of the Round Table. An order said to have been fd. by King Arthur of England about A.D. 528. The order was revived by Edward III. in 1344, but fell into disuse shortly afterwards.

Knights Templars. A military order of knighthood fd. in A.D. 1119 by Hugues de Payen and Geoffroi de Saint-Adhémar for the protection of pilgrims to the Holy Land. Statutes drawn up in 1128 at the Council of Troyes. Rendered independent of any bishop's authority by a bull dated 1172. By order of Philip the Fair, Oct. 1307, the order was persecuted in France with great cruelties, and the knights were abolished in 1312 by the Council of Vienne. *See also* Temple Church (London).

Knights' War, The, 1522-3, between the knights of Germany under Franz von Sickingen and Ulrich von Hutten, who espoused the Lutheran cause, against the empire. [Refer Tanner, *The Renaissance and the Reformation*.]

" Know-Nothings." A political party fd. in the U.S. about 1854. Its objects were to secure American government by Americans; disbanded in 1856 after a brilliant meteoric career. [Refer Harper, *Encyclopædia of U.S. History*.]

Königsberg (Germany). Original town fd. by the knights of the Teutonic order 1255. University fd. 1544; rebuilt 1844.

Königsberg, University of. Fd. 1544.

Koran. The Bible of the Mohammedans, written about A.D. 612 (*see* Mohammedism); translated into Latin 1143. [Refer Gibbon, *Rome* ; Irving, *Life of Mahomet*.]

Korea (E. Asia). Originally Chinese territory, now a Japanese protectorate. Anti-foreign riots which nearly resulted in war with Japan 1882; treaty with Great Britain 1883; treaty with Russia 1888; invasion by Japan 1894; independence proclaimed 1895; Russo-Japanese treaty to maintain the independence of Korea 1897; Anglo-Japanese treaty concerning the independence of Korea 1902; Russo-Japanese War waged in great part in Korea 1904; annexed by Japan 1910.

Ku-Klux-Klan. A secret society said to have been fd. in Tennessee in 1869. It gradually came to have far-reaching powers, and did a great deal of harm; disbanded, Mar. 1869. [Refer Harper, *Encyclopædia of U.S. History*.]

Kutchuk-Kainardji, Treaty of, between Catherine II. of Russia and the Sultan Abdul Hamed, signed 1774. By this treaty Turkey gave up the Crimea, Azov, and Taganrog. [Refer Alison, *History of Europe*.]

Kyrle Society. Fd. 1877, and named after John Kyrle (Man of Ross).

L

Labour Exchanges. Registries for the distribution of labour. Established by R. Owen in England 1832-4. Previously established at Cincinnati by J. Warren.

Labour Party (Great Britain). Independent Labour Party held first conference at Bradford, Jan. 1893; held every year since 1905.

Labrador (N. America). Visited by Norsemen about A.D. 1000; by the Portuguese navigator, Cortereal, 1500; explored by Frobisher 1576; rediscovered by Hudson 1610; colonised 1750; incorp. with Dominion of Canada 1868. [Refer art. in Low and Pulling, *Dicty. of English History*.]

Lack-learning or **Unlearned Parliament.** A name given to the parliament of 1404, which met at Coventry, so called because no lawyers were amongst its members. [Refer Low and Pulling, *Dicty. of English History*.]

Ladies' Colleges. Tennyson's *Princess* written in derision of higher education for women 1847. First schools of London University were Bedford and Queen's, fd. in 1848. Since then have sprung up:—

Cheltenham, 1854.
Girton, Cambridge, 1869.
Newnham, Cambridge, 1875.
Royal Holloway, London, 1876.
Lady Margaret Hall ⎫ Oxford, 1879.
Somerville Hall　　⎬
Westfield, London, 1882.
St. Hugh's Hall, Oxford, 1886.
St. Hilda's Hall, Oxford, 1893.
University Hall, Liverpool, 1895.
University Women's Hostel, Durham, 1895.

Ladrones or **Mariana Islands** (Pacific Ocean). Discovered by Magellan about 1521. Guam ceded to U.S.A. by Spain 1898; remainder sold to Germany 1899.

Lady Day is on Mar. 25 of each year. One of the quarter-days in England and Ireland.

Ladysmith (Natal, S. Africa). During Transvaal War was besieged for 121 days, and relieved by Sir Redvers Buller on Feb. 28, 1900.

Lagos (Guinea, Africa). Created a separate government 1863; part of British West African settlements from 1866; of Gold Coast 1874; made a colony in 1886; together with Southern Nigeria Protectorate renamed the Colony of Southern Nigeria 1906. [Refer Low and Pulling, *Dicty. of English History*.]

Lahore (India). British Council of Regency estab. at 1846; becomes capital of the Punjab 1849; great earthquake at 1905.

Lambeth Articles. Drawn up by Archbishop Whitgift 1595. They embraced the doctrines of Calvinism and were disapproved by parliament; at the Hampton Court Conference in 1604 they were again rejected.

Lambeth Palace (London). Official residence of the Archbishops of Canterbury since 1197, when it was built by Hubert Walter, then Archbishop of Canterbury. Many valuable books and papers were destroyed on June 14, 1381, by the followers of Wat Tyler, and the archbishop, Dr. Sudbury, put to death. [Refer Cave-Browne, *Lambeth Palace*.]

Lammas-Day. Half-quarter day in England on Aug. 1 of each year.

Lancaster (Lancashire, England). Castle supposed to have been built by Agricola A.D. 124; res. by John of Gaunt in the 14th century; burnt by Scots 1322 and 1389; incorp. 1199. [Refer Lewis, *Topographical Dicty. of England*.]

Lancaster, Duchy of. Settled on John of Gaunt and his heirs for ever by royal charter 1362. By consent of parliament was annexed to the Crown by Edward IV. 1461. The court of the county was abolished by the Judicature Act of 1873.

Land League. Fd. in Ireland by Michael Davitt 1879, for the purchase of land; suppressed by Act of Parliament 1881.

Land Taxes. First tax on land levied in 1690, as an annual grant; made perpetual in 1798. Mr. Lloyd George's Budget of 1909 taxed land values.

Laocoön, The. A famous work of ancient sculpture discovered at Rome in 1506, and placed in the Vatican by Julius II. Napoleon brought it to Paris in 1796. It was res. in 1814. [Refer H. B. Walter, *The Art of the Greeks*.]

Laon (N.W. France). Seat of a bishop 515-1790. Present cathedral fd. in 12th century. Napoleon repulsed at, by Blücher and Bülow, Mar. 1814; surrendered to Germans, Sept. 9, 1870.

La Plata. Capital of Buenos Ayres; fd. 1882.

Lateran, Church of St. John (Rome). Rebuilt on the site of the palace of Plautius Lateranus about the middle of the 12th century.

In 1586 Pope Sixtus V. entirely rebuilt the church. [Refer Wey, *Rome*.]

Latin Authors. The following are the principal authors, with their dates:—

Plautus (comic poet), *c.* 254-184 B.C.
Ennius (poet), *c.* 239-169.
Terence (comic poet), 196-159.
Cato the Elder (historian and moralist), 234-149.
Lucilius (satirist), 180-102.
Accius (Attius) (tragic poet), 170-94 (?).
Varro (miscellaneous writer), 116-28.
Cicero (orator), 106-43.
Lucretius (poet), 100-55.
Julius Cæsar (historian), 100-44.
Catullus (poet), 87-54 (?).
Sallust (historian), 86-34.
Virgil (poet), 70-A.D. 19.
Horace (poet), 65-8.
Vitruvius (architect), *fl.* end 1st century B.C.
Tibullus (poet), 54 (?)-18.
Propertius (poet), *c.* 51-15.
Livy (historian), 59-18.
Ovid (poet), 43-A.D. 18.
Seneca (philosopher), 7-A.D. 65.
Celsus (author of treatise on Medicine), *fl.* A.D. 17.
Persius (poet), A.D. 34-62.
Quintilian (rhetorician), 35 (?), died *c.* end of 1st century.
Lucan (poet), 39-65.
Statius (poet), *c.* 40 (?)-*c.* 100.
Martial (poet), 43-102 (?).
Pliny the Elder (natural historian), 23-79.
Pliny the Younger (letter writer), 61-(?).
Tacitus (historian), *fl.* second half of 1st century.
Juvenal (satirist), *d.* 125 (?).
Valerius Flaccus (poet), *fl.* 1st century.
Aulus Gellius (grammarian), *fl.* 169.
Suetonius (historian), died *c.* 120.
Apuleius (romance writer), *c.* 114, *d.* after 173.
Ammianus Marcellinus (historian), *fl.* last half of 4th century.
Claudian (poet), *fl.* last half of 4th century.
Cassiodorus (historian, etc.), 477-569.
Boethius (philosopher), 481-525.
Macrobius (grammarian), *fl.* end 4th-5th century.

Latin Kingdom. *See* Rome.

Latitudinarians. A school of theologians in England advocating " as a party on matters of belief and practice, within certain limits, considerable latitude, hence their name." The party grew up after the year 1688. [Refer Spence, *History of the English Church*.]

Laureate, Poet. The first P. L. proper was appointed by Queen Elizabeth in 1591. The following is a list of the names with the dates:—

Edmund Spenser 1591-99	Laurence Eusden 1718-30
Samuel Daniel 1599-1619	Colley Cibber 1730-57
Ben Jonson 1619-37	William Whitehead 1757-85
Vacant from 1637-60	Thomas Warton 1785-90
Sir William Davenant 1660-68	Henry James Pye 1790-1813
John Dryden 1670-89	Robert Southey 1813-43
Thomas Shadwell 1689-92	William Wordsworth 1843-50
Nahum Tait 1692-1715	Alfred Tennyson 1850-92
Nicholas Rowe 1715-18	Alfred Austin 1896

[Refer Kenyon West, *The Laureates of England*.]

League and Covenant, Solemn. Drawn up by the Scottish nation in 1638, protesting against the religious interference of Charles I.'s minister, Archbishop Laud. The English Parliament under the guidance of Pym signed the Covenant in 1643; declared illegal by parliament 1661. [Refer Macaulay, *History of England*.]

League of Cognac. Concluded between Francis I. of France and the Italian states, May 22, 1526. [Refer Ranke, *History of Reformation in Germany*.]

League of Schmalkalde. Formed by the Protestants of Germany, who met at the town of Schmalkalde on Dec. 22, 1530. It was finally organised in Dec. 1531. It split Germany up into two separate parties. [Refer Ranke, *History of Reformation in Germany*.]

League of Torgau, between the Elector of Saxony and the Landgrave of Hessen to uphold the opinions of Martin Luther, concluded at Gotha, Feb. 1526. [Refer Ranke, *History of Reformation in Germany*.]

Leeds (Yorkshire, England). Captured by parliamentary forces under Gen. Fairfax 1643; incorp. 1627, and again in 1673 after the charter had been forfeited.

Legion of Honour. An order of merit fd. by Napoleon in 1802 as a reward for civil or military services.

Leicester (Leicestershire, England). Said to have been fd. by King Lear, hence its original name, *Legerceastre*. Seized by the Danes A.D. 874. Cardinal Wolsey *d.* at the Abbey of Black Canons (fd. 1143), 1530. Captured by royalist forces, May 1645, when the castle was dismantled; retaken by parliamentary forces under Fairfax, June 1645; incorp. by King John 1199. [Refer Bateson, *Records of the Borough of Leicester*, 3 vols.]

Leipzig (Germany). First mentioned in 1015. University fd. 1408. Leipzig Conference between Luther, Eck, and Carlstadt 1519. Leipzig Book Fair instituted 1545. During the *Thirty Years' War* (1618-48) it was five times besieged and taken; captured by Prussian army 1756; allied armies enter the city after defeat of Napoleon, Oct. 16 and 18, 1813.

Lent. The forty days' fast from Ash Wednesday to Easter Monday. Pope Felix III. in A.D. 487 fixed the number of days as forty. Previously there had been no uniformity in the duration of the fast.

Leon (Spain). An ancient kingdom fd. in the 10th century A.D. United to Castile 1037; finally in 1230. [Refer Calvert, *Spain*, 2 vols.]

Letters of Marque. Licences first granted in 1295 permitting seizure of an enemy's ships or property. By the Treaty of Paris 1856 these licences were abolished by common consent.

Lettres de Cachet. Warrants of imprisonment granted by the kings of France. The practice was condemned and abolished by the National Assembly, Nov. 1, 1789. [Refer Carlyle, *French Revolution*.]

Leukas. *See* Ionian Islands.

Levellers. A party which originated in the parliamentary army during the Civil War in 1647. In 1649 it brought about a meeting, but it was suppressed. The leader was a certain Lieut.-Colonel John Lilburne (1618-57). [Refer art. in Low and Pulling, *Dicty. of English History*.]

Leyden (Holland). University fd. 1575 by William of Orange in commemoration of the citizens' defence of the town against the Spaniards from Oct. 1573—Oct. 1574.

Liberals. The Covenanters were termed "Whigamores" in 1679; and the name Whig came to be fastened on all the Scottish Presbyterian zealots, then on English politicians who opposed the court and treated Nonconformists leniently. The terms Whig and Tory came into use in 1679-80, and the more advanced Whigs and reformers were first named Liberals in 1828.

Liberia (W. Africa). A negro republic, orig. of liberated slaves. Fd. by the American Colonising Society 1821; republic constituted 1847. [Refer Johnston, *Liberia*, 1906.]

Liberty of Conscience. James II. permitted religious liberty for political purposes 1687.

Libraries. The following are the most famous libraries of Europe, with the dates of their foundations:—

Austria. Vienna, Imperial Library, fd. by Frederick III. about 1440.

France. Paris, Royal Library, now the Bibliothèque Nationale, fd. by Francis I. about 1520.

Germany. Berlin, Royal Library, fd. 1659. Dresden, Royal Library, fd. 16th century. Munich, Royal Library, fd. by Albert V., Duke of Bavaria, in middle 16th century. Stuttgart, Royal Library, fd. 1765.

Great Britain and Ireland. Library Association of the United Kingdom fd. Oct. 2, 1877. Cambridge, University Library, fd. 16th century, enlarged by George I. 1720. Dublin, King's Inn Library, fd. 1787; Trinity College Library, fd. 1601. Edinburgh, University Library, fd. 1580; Faculty of Advocates Library, fd. 1682. Oxford, Bodleian Library, fd. 1598; Radcliffe Library, fd. by the will of Dr. Radcliffe 1714, opened 1749. London, British Museum: the Library is made up of several bequests (*see* under British Museum); London Institution Library, fd. 1805; London Library, fd. 1840; University of London Library, fd. 1839.

Italy. Florence, Library, fd. by Niccolo Nicoli 1436; Mediceo-Laurenziana 1571; Nazionale (amalgamation of Maglia-Vechiana and Palatina) 1861; Marucelliana 1703. Rome, Vatican Library, fd. by Pope Nicholas V. 1446, enlarged by Sixtus V. 1588; Vittore Emmanuele Library, joined to Bibliotheca Casanatense, fd. 1700.

Portugal. Oporto, Municipal Library, fd. 1833.

Spain. Madrid. The Escurial Library, fd. 1562; Salamanca, University Library, fd. 1254.

See also under various towns and universities.

Libraries, Ancient. Chaldean libraries said to have existed as early as 1700 B.C. First public library fd. at Athens by Pisistratus 540. Founding of the great Alexandrian library by the first of the Ptolemies 284; partially destroyed when Julius Cæsar set fire to the city in 47. First library in Rome brought from Macedonia by Æmilius Paulus 167. Library at Constantinople fd. by Constantine *c.* A.D. 355.

Libraries in U.S.A. American Library Association fd. 1876. The following are the principal libraries of the U.S.A., with the dates of their foundations:—

Baltimore, John Hopkins University, 1876; Peabody Institute Library 1857; Enoch Pratt Free Library 1857.

California, Leland Stanford University Library, 1891.

Chicago, University Library 1892; Newberry Library, 1887; John Crearar Library, 1894.

Harvard, University Library, 1638.

Massachusetts, Amherst College Library 1821.

Michigan, University Library, 1837.

New Haven, Yale College Library, 1701.

New Jersey, Princetown University, 1746.

New York, Columbia University, 1763; Astor Library, opened 1854; Lenox Library 1870.

Pennsylvania, Lehigh University Library, 1877; University of Pennsylvania, 1749; State Library, 1777.

Washington, Library of Congress, 1800; Bureau of Education, 1868; Geological Survey, 1882; House of Representatives Patent Office, 1836.

Licensing, Laws regarding (Great Britain). The present law fd. on the Consolidation Act of 1826. In 1830 an act was passed empowering publicans to take out beer licences without applying to the magistrates, thus amending a previous licensing act 1828. The act of 1904 made county licences valid only on confirmation by quarter sessions. Wine and Beer House Act of 1869 regulated " off licence " houses. Act of 1872, amended in 1874, restricted issue of new licences, and shortened the hours for the sale of liquor. Act of 1902 increased penalties for drunkenness, convicted habitual drunkards, and compelled clubs to be registered. Act of 1904 mainly deals with the question of compensation for withdrawal of licences. Children's Bill preventing the sale of liquor to children under age passed. The principal licensing act in Scotland was the one passed in 1903 embodying all previous ones. It provides for shorter hours, and the closing of licensed houses on certain days. [Refer art. in *Chambers's Encyclopædia*.]

Lichfield (Staffordshire, England). The Mercian See fd. here in 656. Cathedral dates from 13th century. Besieged by parliamentary army 1643. Statue of Dr. Samuel Johnson erected 1838.

Lick Observatory (California). Fd. by James Lick (1796-1876), who left a sum of money for the purpose. Interesting discoveries made here concerning the Jupiter satellites 1905.

Liége (Belgium). Cathedral fd. 712. Captured by Charles the Bold 1467; by the French 1691; by the English under Marlborough 1702; by French 1794. [Refer Hénaux, *Histoire de Liége*.]

Lifeboat. The first L. was patented in Nov. 1785 by Lionel Lukin, an Essex coachbuilder. Henry Greathead about 1789 also patented one, and is generally credited as the inventor of the L.

Lifeboat Institution, Royal. Fd. in 1823 as *The Royal National Institution for the Preservation of Life from Shipwreck*, through the exertions of Sir William Hilary and Thomas Wilson, M.P. for the City of London.

Lighthouses. Several were in existence at a very early date. The first L. proper in England was erected 1758-60. The Northern Lighthouse Board, instit. by Act of Parliament in 1786, provided for the building of several L. In America an Act of Congress dated 1789 provided for the building of L.

Lille (France). Fd. in the 11th century by counts of Flanders. Mortgaged to France 1305; became part of Burgundy 1369; captured by Louis XIV. 1667; by the Duke of Marlborough 1708; res. 1713; bombarded by Austrians 1792. [Refer Van Heude, *Histoire de Lille*.]

Lima (Peru). Fd. by Pizarro 1534, who was murdered here in 1541. University fd. 1551. [Refer Prescott, *Conquest of Peru*.] *See also* Peru.

Limerick (Ireland). Incorp. 1195. Taken by Ireton 1651; invested by English and Dutch, Aug. 1691. The Protestant Cathedral of St. Mary fd. 1180; rebuilt 1490.

Lincoln (Lincolnshire, England). Castle commenced by William the Conqueror 1086. Cathedral built between 1075 and 1501. Fight known as " Fair of Lincoln " 1217. Five parliaments held here between 1301-86. Besieged by parliamentary army under the Earl of Manchester 1644. [Refer Sympson, *Lincoln*.]

Lincolnshire Insurrection, The. Was the outcome of the dissolution of the monasteries. It was originated by the priests in Oct. 1536. The surrender and submission of the rebels on Oct. 19, 1536, led to their general pardon. [Refer Burnet, *History of the Reformation*.]

Linnean Society (London). Fd. 1788 by Sir J. E. Smith; incorp. 1802; named after Carl Linnæus, the Swedish botanist (1707-87).

Lion League. Formed by the Order of Knights, protesting against the tax instead of personal service levied by Albert IV. of Bavaria 1488. [Refer Ranke, *History of Reformation in Germany*.]

Lisbon (Portugal). Conquered by the Moors in A.D. 716, who are said to have given it the name of *Lisboa*. Made the capital of Portugal 1506. The cathedral built in 1147; res. 1756. The Monastery and Church of Belem, built on the spot where Vasco da Gama embarked in 1497, was commenced in 1500. Seized by the Duke of Alva for Spain 1580; recaptured 1640 by the Duke of Braganza; almost entirely destroyed by earthquake, Nov. 1, 1755; held by the French 1807-8. *See also* Spain and works quoted under.

Literary Fund, Royal (Great Britain). Fd. by Rev. David Wilkins 1790, for relief of literary men of all nations; incorp. 1818.

Lithography. Printing from stone, invented by Aloys Senefelder (1771-1834) in 1796. *See* Printing and Engraving.

Liturgy. *See* Prayer Book.

Liverpool (Lancashire, England). Name occurs in a deed dated A.D. 1190; made a free burgh by Henry III. 1229; besieged by Prince Rupert, June 26, 1644; King's Dock constructed 1785; Queen's Dock 1786; Clarence Dock completed, Sept. 1830; Waterloo Dock opened 1834; Victoria and Trafalgar Docks opened, Sept. 8, 1836; University College fd. 1880; Mersey Railway Tunnel opened 1886.

Livery Companies of London. The following are the principal L. C. of London in the order of precedence, and the dates of their institution:—

1. Weavers .	.	. 1164	12. Cordwainers	.	. 1410
2. Parish clerks	.	. 1232	13. Cutlers .	.	. 1417
3. Saddlers .	.	. 1280	14. Vintners .	.	. 1437
4. Bakers .	.	. 1307	15. Brewers .	.	. 1438
5. Barber Surgeons		. 1308	16. Drapers .	.	. 1439
6. Skinners .	.	. 1327	17. Leather-sellers	.	. 1442
7. Goldsmiths	.	. 1327	18. Haberdashers	.	. 1447
8. Carpenters	.	. 1344	19. Girdlers .	.	. 1448
9. Grocers .	.	. 1345	20. Armourers and Bra-		
10. Fishmongers	.	. 1384	ziers .	.	. 1463
11. Mercers .	.	. 1393	21. Tallow-chandlers	.	. 1463

LIVERY COMPANIES OF LONDON (*continued*)—

22. Ironmongers	.	1464
23. Merchant Tailors		1466
24. Dyers	.	1469
25. Pewterers	.	1474
26. Cooks	.	1481
27. Clothworkers	.	1482
28. Wax-chandlers	.	1484
29. Lorimers	.	1488
30. Plasterers	.	1500
31. Coopers	.	1501
32. Poulterers	.	1503
33. Inn-holders	.	1515
34. Fletchers	.	1536
35. Watermen	.	1550
36. Glovers	.	1556
37. Stationers	.	1556
38. Salters	.	1558
39. Joiners	.	1564
40. Tilers and Bricklayers		1568
41. Blacksmiths	.	1577
42. Paper-stainers	.	1580
43. Embroiderers	.	1591
44. Butchers	.	1604
45. Fruiterers	.	1604
46. Musicians	.	1604
47. Turners	.	1604
48. Felt-makers	.	1604
49. Curriers	.	1605
50. Shipwrights	.	1610
51. Plumbers	.	1611
52. Founders	.	1614
53. Scriveners	.	1616
54. Gardeners	.	1616
55. Apothecaries	.	1617
56. Bowyers	.	1620
57. Gold and silver wire-drawers	.	1623

58. Upholders	.	1627
59. Silk-throwsters	.	1629
60. Card-makers	.	1629
61. Spectacle-makers	.	1630
62. Starch-makers	.	1632
63. Clock-makers	.	1632
64. Pin-makers	.	1636
65. Glaziers	.	1637
66. Horners	.	1638
67. Hatband-makers	.	1638
68. Soap-makers	.	1638
69. Gunmakers	.	1638
70. Comb-makers	.	1650
71. Needle-makers	.	1656
72. Tobacco-pipe makers		1663
73. Framework-knitters	.	1664
74. Glass-sellers	.	1664
75. Tinplate-workers	.	1670
76. Wheelwrights	.	1670
77. Patten-makers	.	1670
78. Farriers	.	1673
79. Masons	.	1677
80. Coach and Harness-makers	.	1677
81. Fishermen	.	1687
82. Fan-makers	.	1709
83. Porters	.	* *
84. Carmen	.	* *
85. Wood-mongers	.	* *
86. Bowstring-makers	.	* *
87. Distillers	.	* *
88. Silkmen	.	* *
89. Paviors	.	* *
90. Basket-makers	.	* *
91. Woolmen	.	* *

Livingstonia Mission. Suggested by Dr. David Livingstone, the explorer (1813-73), for the abolition of slavery on the east coast of Africa; expedition first fitted out in 1875, and settled at Cape Maclear; moved in 1883 to Bandawé. [Refer Johnston, *Livingstone and the Exploration of Central Africa*.]

Lloyd's Marine Intelligence Department. Was orig. in a coffee-house kept by Edward Lloyd in the 17th century; moved from Tower Street to Lombard Street in 1692; to Royal Exchange 1774; parliamentary inquiry into management of the concern 1810; incorp. 1871. [Refer Grey, *Lloyd's Yesterday and To-day*.]

Local Government (United Kingdom). By the reform of municipal corporations between 1832-35 town councils were made elective. The act of 1894 extended previous acts.

Local Government Board. Estab. 1871, and superseded the old Poor Law Board.

Lollards. A name given in England to the followers of Wyclif (1324-84). The origin of the name is uncertain. In 1395 they presented a petition to parliament protesting against abuses in the Church. The movement grew so strong that in 1401 the statute *De Hæretico Comburendo* was passed against them, with the result that on Feb. 12, 1401, William Sawtree, the first victim, was burnt at the stake for his views. The persecution continued through several reigns, Sir John Oldcastle being one of the most famous victims, executed in 1414. [Refer Trevelyan, *England in the Age of Wycliffe ;* also art. in Low and Pulling, *Dicty. of English History.*]

Lombardy (Italy). Conquered by the Romans A.D. 222. Joined by Charlemagne to his empire 772. From 843 ruled by its own kings until 1337, when it passed to the dukes of Milan. Became part of Spain under Charles V. 1529, who held it until 1714, when it fell to Austria. After Napoleon's campaign and his downfall it was res. to Austria 1815. Given by Napoleon to Victor Emmanuel 1859. [Refer Sismondi, *History of Italian Republics.*]

London, City of (England). Said to have been fd. about A.D. 43 during the Roman governorship of Aulus Plautius. Burned by Boadicea 61. Wall built between 350 and 369. Destroyed by the Danes 839. First charter granted by William the Conqueror 1079. Aldermen appointed 1242. Divided into wards 1285. Black Death 1348-9, 1361-2, 1369. Law passed preventing further building 1580. Great Plague (*q.v.*) 1665. Great Fire (*q.v.*) 1666. Streets first lighted by lamps 1677. Charter declared forfeited 1682; res. 1689. Mint finished 1811; Bank of England 1821. Various buildings and occurrences in L. under their respective headings.

London, Bishopric of. Supposed to have been fd. as early as A.D. 179. The names of the bishops of London before the Conquest and their dates are very uncertain. The following is a list after 1044, with the dates of their appointments:—

William 1051	Henry de Wenghham 1260
Hugh d'Orivalle 1075	Henry de Sandwich 1263
Maurice 1086	John de Chishull 1274
Richard de Belmeis I. 1108	Richard Gravesend 1280
Gilbert Universalis 1128	Ralph de Baldock 1306
Robert de Sigillo 1141	Gilbert Segrave 1313
Richard de Belmeis II. 1152	Richard de Newport 1317
Gilbert Foliot 1163	Stephen de Gravesend 1319
Richard Fitzneal 1189	Richard de Bintworth 1338
William de Santa Maria 1199	Ralph de Stratford 1340
Eustace de Fauconberg 1221	Michael de Northburg 1355
Roger Niger 1229	Simon de Sudbury 1362
Fulk Basset 1244	William Courtenay 1375

LONDON, BISHOPRIC OF (*continued*)—

Robert de Braybroke 1382	George Abbot 1610
Roger Walden 1405	John King 1611
Nicholas Bubwith 1406	George Mountain 1621
Richard Clifford 1407	William Laud 1628
John Kemp 1421	William Juxon 1633
William Gray 1426	Gilbert Sheldon 1660
Robert FitzHugh 1431	Humfrey Henchman 1663
Robert Gilbert 1436	Henry Compton 1675
Thomas Kemp 1450	John Robinson 1714
Richard Hill 1489	Edmund Gibson 1723
Thomas Savage 1496	Thomas Sherlock 1748
William Wareham 1502	Thomas Hayter 1761
William Barons 1504	Richard Osbaldeston 1762
Richard FitzJames 1506	Richard Terrick 1764
Cuthbert Tunstall 1522	Robert Lowth 1777
John Stokesley 1530	Beilby Porteous 1787
Edmund Bonner 1540	John Randolph 1809
Nicholas Ridley 1550	William Howley 1813
Edmund Bonner 1553	Charles James Blomfield 1828
Edmund Grindal 1559	Archibald C. Tait 1856
Edwin Sandys 1570	John Jackson 1869
John Aylmer 1577	Frederick Temple 1885
Richard Fletcher 1595	Mandell Creighton 1896
Richard Bancroft 1597	Arthur F. Winnington-Ingram
Richard Vaughan 1604	1901
Thomas Ravis 1607	

[Refer Milman, *Annals of St. Paul's Cathedral*.]

London Bridge. Orig. built of wood in 1014. A new one was commenced in 1176, and completed 1209. It suffered from fire frequently, and was res. Toll was discontinued Mar. 27, 1782. The present bridge was commenced Mar. 15, 1824, and was opened by William IV. Aug. 1, 1831; widened 1901-3; reopened Mar. 28, 1904. [Refer *London* (Mediæval Towns Series).]

London, County of. Defined by Local Government Act of 1888, and a county council formed. Formed into 28 municipal boroughs by London Government Act 1899.

London, Lord Mayors of. First mayor appointed 1189. Since 1354 known as " Right Honourable the Lord Mayor." First Lord Mayor's Show 1453.

London, Tower of. Said to have been fd. by Julius Cæsar 54 B.C., but this is extremely doubtful. The present White Tower, the earliest part of the structure, was built by William the Conqueror about 1078. In 1140 Stephen used the Tower as a residence. In Henry III.'s reign (1216-72) the regalia was removed to the Tower. The famous attempt to steal the Crown jewels by Col. Blood from the Tower, May 9, 1671. [Refer Stirling-Taylor, *Historical Guide to London*.]

London, Treaties of. (1) Between England and Holland, signed 1674, ending war of 1672; (2) between England, France, and Russia, during Greek War of Independence: contracting parties bound themselves to take action for the purpose of securing the independence of Greece under Turkish suzerainty: signed 1827; (3) between Great Britain, France, and Holland, providing for the erection of the Flemish and Walloon provinces into an independent kingdom, signed 1833; (4) between Austria, France, Great Britain, Prussia, and Russia, confirming the treaty of 1833; (5) between England, France, Russia, Austria, and Turkey, after conclusion of Syrian War: it provided that the Bosphorus and Dardanelles should be closed to ships of war (also known as the Treaty of Dardanelles): signed 1841; (6) between Austria, France, Great Britain, Prussia, Russia, and Sweden, settling the succession to the Danish throne, signed 1852.

London University. Seven professorships endowed by Sir Thomas Gresham in Bishopsgate 1548. Institution in Gower Street (now University College) fd. as the University of London 1828. Charters granted by William IV., both to University and to University College, Nov. 28, 1836. The following are the principal schools of the University with the dates of their foundations:—

University College 1828.
King's College 1829.
King's C. (Women's Dept.) 1881.
Imperial C., Royal C. of Science, and Royal C. of Mines, 1851.
City and Guilds C. 1878.
Royal Holloway C. 1886.
Bedford C. for Women 1849.
East London C. 1892.
London School of Economics 1895.
South-Eastern Agricultural C.
Westfield C. 1882.
London Day Training C. (admitted) 1910.
Regent's Park C. 1810.
King's C. (Theological Dept.) (admitted) 1910.
Wesleyan C., Richmond, 1843.
St. John's Hall, Highbury, 1863.
St. Bartholomew's Hospital Medical School 1123.
St. George's H. Med. School c. 1752.
London H. Med. School 1741.
London Sch. of Medicine for Women 1874.
University C. H. Med. School 1828.
London Sch. of Tropical Medicine 1898.
Royal Army Med. C. 1902.
Goldsmith's C. 1891.
Lister Institute of Preventive Medicine (incorporated) 1905.
King's C. H. Med. School (admitted) 1909.

Londonderry (Ireland). Grew up round a monastery fd. in A.D. 546 by St. Columba. The famous 105 days' siege lasted from April-Aug. 1689. [Refer Hempton, *Siege and History of Londonderry.*]

Long Parliament. The fifth parliament summoned by Charles I.; met Nov. 3, 1640 (*see* Pride's Purge); dissolved forcibly by Oliver Cromwell, April 20, 1653; recalled twice, and finally dissolved, Mar. 16, 1660. [Refer Macaulay, *History of England ;* and art. in Low and Pulling, *Dicty. of English History.*]

Lord Lieutenant of Ireland. *See* Ireland.

Lord of the Isles. A title borne by the rulers of the Western Isles of Scotland. The first was Somerled, Lord of Argyll, who in 1135 was conferred these islands by David I. of Scotland. Norway obtained forcible possession frequently, but in 1266 they were surrendered to Scotland, and the Lords of the Isles became vassals of the Scottish Crown. Finally annexed to Scottish Crown 1540, since when the Prince of Wales has been possessor of the title of Lord of the Isles. [Refer art. in *Chambers's Encyclopædia.*]

Lords, House of. " There is a point in English history at which the historian can fairly say, ' Here the House of Commons began,' but the House of Lords was always with us from the first moment when England could be described as a united nation " [J. Wylie, *The House of Lords* (Fairbairns)]. The earliest writ summoning the peers is dated 1265. House of Lords abolished by Commons, Feb. 6, 1649; revived April 25, 1649. Voting by proxy abolished in, Mar. 31, 1868. Mr. Asquith's Veto Bill first brought in, April 14, 1910; passed finally Aug. 15, 1911. [Refer work quoted above.]

Loretto (Italy). Famous for the *Santa Casa* or House of the Virgin Mary, which is reputed to be the house in which the Virgin lived at Nazareth, which was miraculously transferred to Loretto in 1295. The French seized Loretto in 1796, and the famous holy image was taken to France, but returned with great pomp on Jan. 5, 1803.

Lorraine. Old kingdom of Lotharingia; fd. A.D. 855; the Duchy of Lorraine was ceded to the King of Poland 1738; finally incorp. with France 1766. *See* Alsace-Lorraine.

Lotteries in England were declared illegal by an act passed Oct. 1826. In Aug. 1836 another act was passed prohibiting the advertising of foreign or other L. in the British newspapers. *See* Gambling. [Refer J. Ashton, *History of English Lotteries.*]

Louis-d'or. Gold coin intro. into France in 1641 and issued until 1795.

Louisiana (U.S.A.). Orig. claimed for France by the explorer La Salle (1643-87), who named the territory after Louis XIV. Handed over to the Mississippi Company (*see* Mississippi Scheme) 1719. Ceded to Spain by England 1762; to France 1800. Sold to U.S. by Napoleon 1803; admitted as a state 1812. [Refer Harper, *Encyclopædia of U.S. History.*]

Lourdes (France). Famous for its pilgrimages to the rock where the Virgin Mary is said to have appeared to a peasant girl, Bernadette Soubirons, on Feb. 11, 1858. The basilica over the miraculous spring which is said to have suddenly come to light at the time of the miracle was erected in 1876. [Refer Emile Zola, *Lourdes.*]

Louvain (Belgium). University fd. 1426; suppressed 1797; re-founded 1817.

Louvre, The (Paris). Erected in 1541 by Francis I. Formerly a royal palace, now a museum and picture gallery; enlarged during reign of Louis XIV. (1638-1715). *See* Paris.

Lübeck (Germany). Fd. by Saxons A.D. 1143; held by French 1806-14; joined North German Confederation 1866.

Lucca (Italy). Orig. *Luca*. Made a Roman colony 177 B.C.; independent republic from 1369-1797; made a principality by Napoleon 1805; passed to Spain 1815; ceded to Tuscany 1847.

Lucknow (India). Ancient capital of the state of Oudh 1732; besieged during the Indian Mutiny, July 1, 1857; relieved by Sir Colin Campbell, Nov. 10, 1857. [Refer Innes, *Lucknow and Oude in the Mutiny*.]

Luddite Riots. Broke out first in Nottinghamshire in Nov. 1811. The rioters were enraged at the introduction of machinery, which lessened the amount of labour. The name Luddite originated with one Ned Ludd, a worker who had broken some machinery some years before. The riots were renewed in July 1816, and much damage was done before the disturbances were quelled. [Refer Peel, *Risings of the Luddites*, etc.]

Lunéville, Peace of. Signed between Germany and France, Feb. 9, 1801, confirming the Treaty of Campo-Formio (*q.v.*). [Refer Alison, *History of Europe*.]

Lutterworth (Leicestershire, England). Wyclif was rector at the church here from 1374-84. The church, containing many relics of the reformer, was carefully restored 1867-69.

Lutzen (Germany). Wallenstein defeated by Gustavus Adolphus 1633; allies by Napoleon 1813. [Refer Alison, *History of Europe*.]

Luxemburg, town and grand-duchy (Europe). From its position on the map has changed hands many times. From 1659-1713 it belonged to the French, and again, after a memorable siege of town on June 7, 1795, it reverted to France. Created a separate state by Congress of Vienna 1815, but only as a member of the German Confederation. In 1867, by Treaty of London, it was declared an independent grand-duchy, and the Prussians withdrew. The famous fortifications were at the same time demolished. [Refer Passmore, *In the Further Ardennes*.]

Lyons (France). Roman colony fd. 43 B.C. Destroyed by fire A.D. 59; by the Romans 197. Made capital of Burgundy 478. United to French Crown 1312. Francis I. intro. silk manufacturing 1515. In 1793 refused to acknowledge National Convention, and was besieged for 70 days and destroyed. Its name was also changed to Ville-Affranichie. Capitulated to Austrians, Mar. 1814 and July 1815. [Refer Michelet, *History of France* (Eng. trans.).]

M

Macadamisation of Roads. A process named after John L. Macadam (1756-1836). First used in England between 1810 and 1816.

McAll Mission. A Protestant mission in France fd. by Rev. R. W. McAll (1821-93) in 1871.

Macao (China). Portuguese obtain permission from China to settle at 1557; declared a free port 1845; British and Chinese prevent coolie trade at 1873.

Madagascar (Africa). Very little known about island previous to 1823-25, but said to have been discovered by Lorenzo Almeida 1506, when Captain Owen, R.N., surveyed the coasts; explored by Grandicher between 1865 and 1870; conquered by French in 1895. [Refer art. in *Chambers's Encyclopædia*.]

Madeira (an island off N.W. coast of Africa). Date of discovery doubtful, probably in the 14th century; was colonised by Portuguese 1431; occupied by British troops 1801 and from 1807-14, when it was held in trust for the Portuguese Crown. [Refer Biddle, *Madeira*, 2 vols.]

Madras (seaport on E. coast of India). City and presidency. English established themselves in 1640; city captured by French 1746; res. to English 1749; besieged by French, Dec. 12, 1758. *See also* India, Seringapatam, and next art.

Madras Mutiny, among the European officers of the East India Company's army, broke out in 1809; by Aug. 16 of the same year it ended. [Refer art. in Low and Pulling, *Dicty. of English History*.]

Madrid (Spain). Known in 10th century as *Medina Magerit*, " belonging to the Moors." Retaken by Ramiro II., King of Leon and the Asturias, 939, but not permanently conquered until 1083. First charter granted 1202. Cortes first held there 1309. Treaty between Charles V. and Francis I. 1526. Declared capital of Spain by Philip II. 1560. Captured from French by allied forces under Wellington 1812. Figured largely during revolutionary wars. *See* Spain.

Mad Parliament. Met in 1258 under Henry III. Its chief work was the appointing of the Commission which drew up the Provisions of Oxford (*q.v.*). [Refer Pearson, *History of England*.]

Madrigal Society of London. Claims to be the oldest musical association in Europe, fd. by John Immyus 1741. [Refer Grove, *Dicty. of Musicians*.]

Mafeking (Cape Colony). Jameson raid (*q.v.*) starts from 1896; relieved after siege of seven months during Transvaal War, May 17, 1900. [Refer Innes, *History of the Boer War*.]

Magdeburg (Prussia). Fd. by Charlemagne A.D. 805; destroyed by the Wends 924, and refounded shortly afterwards by Editha; made seat of a bishopric 968; joined Luther, July 17, 1524; joined League of Schmalkalde 1531 (*q.v.*); surrendered to Maurice of Saxony, Nov. 1551; besieged in vain by Wallenstein 1629; burnt by Tilly 1631; annexed by French to kingdom of Westphalia 1803; res. to Prussia 1813. [Refer Ranke, *Hist. of Reformation in Germany*.]

Magna Charta. The Great Charter of England granted by King John, who was forced to sign it by the barons at Runnymede, June 19, 1215. It was reproduced in facsimile by Records Commissioners in 1865. [Refer McKechnie, *Magna Charta*.]

Mahrattas. A race inhabiting Western and Central India. First mentioned in history about the middle of the 17th century; defeated by the Afghans, Jan. 1761; from 1780-1818 they were at continual warfare with the British, who finally occupied the territory in 1818. [Refer Grant-Duff, *History of the Máráthás*.]

Maine (U.S.A.). Settled by English 1607. Western territory, known as province of Maine 1635, from 1651-1820 a detached part of Massachusetts. The present state of Maine fd. 1820; boundary dispute settled with Great Britain 1842. [Refer Harper, *Encyclopædia of U.S. History*.]

Mainz or **Mayence** (Germany). Of Roman origin; dates from 13 B.C.; cathedral built 978-1009; head of the confederacy of the Rhenish cities 13th century; in French possession 1797-1814; by Congress of Vienna 1814-15 ceded to Hesse-Darmstadt; declared a federal fortress 1870.

Major-General. This rank was instit. in the British army by Oliver Cromwell in 1655, after he had quarrelled with his first parliament. Each major-general was to govern a military district. This original scheme was dropped in 1657. [Refer Cromwell, *Letters and Speeches*.]

Malacca (Malay Peninsula). Settled by Portuguese in 1511, who held it until 1640, when the Dutch seized it, who in turn held it until 1795, when the English took possession; res. to the Dutch by the Peace of Amiens 1801; exchanged with Britain for the island of Sumatra 1825; made part of Straits Settlements 1867. [Refer Martin, *History of English Colonies*.]

Malta (Mediterranean). Count Roger of Sicily drove Arabs from, 1090; conquered by Spain 1282; given by the Emperor Charles V. to the Knights of the Order of St. John of Jerusalem 1530, who owned the island until 1798, when the French took possession; the Maltese rebelled, and after much fighting the island was recognised as British by the Congress of Vienna 1814-15. Constitution granted 1887; revised 1903. [Refer Martin, *History of English Colonies*.]

Malta, Knights of. Religious order of knighthood, known also as the Order of the Knights of St. John of Jerusalem, the Knights of Rhodes, and the Hospitallers; fd. about A.D. 1048 in a hospital at

Jerusalem; sanctioned by Pope Paschal II. 1113; Frederick Barbarossa took the order under his protection 1185; captured Rhodes 1310, which they held until 1523; Charles IV. presented them with the island of Malta (*q.v.*) 1530, which they surrendered in 1798. The English Order of the Knights of St. John is an English survival of the old order. [Refer art. " Hospitallers," in *Chambers's Encyclopædia*.]

Man, Isle of (Great Britain). History lost in obscurity previous to 6th century. From then till near the end of 9th century ruled by Welsh kings, when the Norwegians conquered the island; ceded to the kings of Scotland 1266; inhabitants placed themselves under protection of Edward I. of England 1290; granted to Sir John Stanley 1406; surrendered to parliamentary army 1651; fell by inheritance to the Duke of Athol 1765, from whom it was purchased by the British Government. [Refer Scott, *Peveril of the Peak;* also art. in *Chambers's Encyclopædia*.]

Manchester (Lancashire, England). Fd. about the year A.D. 79 during Agricola's conquest; orig. called *Mancunium*, Saxon *Manceastre*. After departure of the Romans was captured by the Saxons about 488; captured by Edwin, Duke of Northumbria, 620; first charter granted, May 14, 1301; during Civil War Fairfax captured it 1643; walls and fortifications removed 1652; Owens College fd. 1851; Victoria University fd. 1880 by royal charter; Manchester Ship Canal built 1887-94. [Refer Saintsbury, *Manchester*.]

Manchuria (Asia). *See* China and Japan.

Mandalay (Burma, India). Fd. 1860 as capital of independent Burma; captured by British 1885.

Manhattan Island (U.S.A.). Purchased for the Dutch West India Company by Peter Minuit 1626. [Refer Harper, *Encyclopædia of U.S. History*.]

Manila or **Manilla** (Philippine Islands). Fd. 1571 by Miguel Lopez de Legazpi; invaded by British 1762; blockaded by U.S. navy during Spanish-American War, May 1898. [Refer Harper, *Encyclopædia of U.S. History*.]

Mansion House (London). The official residence of the Lord Mayor; building begun 1739.

Mantua (Italy). Taken by French 1797; by Austrians 1814; surrendered to Italy 1866.

Maori Wars. (1) Between the settlers at New Zealand and the natives 1843-47; it resulted in the definition of boundaries; (2) boundary disputes cause war 1863—Aug. 1864; (3) in consequence of a massacre of whites by natives, July 1869—Jan. 1870. [Refer art. in Low and Pulling, *Dicty. of English History*.]

Marathon (Attica). Site of a battle between the Greeks under Aristides, Miltiades, and Themistocles and the Persians in which the latter were defeated 490 B.C.

Marine Corps (U.S.A.). Estab. by congress in Nov. 1775; became a permanent arm of the service by the act of July 11, 1798. [Refer Harper, *Encyclopædia of U.S. History*.]

Marlborough, Parliament of. Met in 1267 for restoring good order after the Barons' War (*q.v.*).

Marprelate Controversy. Caused by certain writings against episcopacy by Elizabethan Puritans; supposed to have been written by John Penry, who was executed in 1593. [Refer Burnet, *History of the Reformation*.]

Marriage Laws (Great Britain). Lord Hardwicke's Act of 1753 provided that marriages must be performed in the parish church, with the exception of those of Jews or Quakers. Dissenters Marriage Bill 1836, by which Dissenters could marry in their own chapels or churches or enter into a civil contract by giving notice to the registrar of the district. Marriage Act of 1886 extended hours of marriage from 12 to 3 p.m. Marriage Act Amendment passed, Aug. 6, 1900. Marriage with Deceased Wife's Sister Act passed, Aug. 26, 1907. [Refer art. in *Encyclopædia Britannica*.]

Marrow Controversy. Took place in Scotland, and was caused by the publication, by an illiterate barber, of a book entitled *Marrow of Modern Divinity*, in 1645.

Marseillaise, The, national anthem of the French Republic, was partly written and composed in 1792 by Rouget de Lisle, an officer stationed at Strasburg. Orig. called *Chant de l'Armée du Rhin*. Brought to Paris by certain soldiers from Marseilles, and sung by them as they advanced to the storming of the Tuileries, July 30.

Marseilles (France). One of the oldest towns in France, orig. known as *Massalia* or *Massilia*. Captured by Julius Cæsar 49 B.C.; became a republic A.D. 1112; treacherously surrendered to Henri IV.; shortly after it finally lost its independence.

Marston Moor (Yorks). Cromwell's troops defeated Prince Rupert's army here, after the latter had attempted to raise the siege of York 1644.

Maryland (U.S.A.). First settled by Capt. William Claiborne 1631. It was named after Queen Henrietta Maria, Queen of Charles I. Representative government estab. 1639; parliamentary commissioners take possession of the government 1652, but it was res. to the governor 1658; a Protestant association overthrow the government, which was Roman Catholic, 1689; declared a free state 1776; Confederate army enters Maryland after crossing the Potomac, Aug. 30, 1862. [Refer Harper, *Encyclopædia of U.S. History*.]

Mashonaland (S. Africa). Placed under British protection 1888; powers of administration granted to British S. Africa Company 1889.

Massachusetts (U.S.A.). Explored by Gosnold 1602; Champlain 1604; John Smith 1614. Settled by English Nonconformists,

Nov. 1620, who sailed over in the *Mayflower*. First constitution formed 1780; amended 1820. Constitution of United States adopted 1788. [Refer Harper, *Encyclopædia of U.S. History*.]

Matterhorn. Peak in the Swiss Alps. Summit first reached in July 1865, by a party of Englishmen, four of whom lost their lives.

Maundy Thursday. The Thursday before Good Friday, also known as Holy Thursday, on which day alms are still given to the poor in the form of " maundy money," James II. being the last English sovereign who personally assisted in the presentation.

Mauritius (Indian Ocean). Discovered by Pedro Mascarenhas, a Portuguese navigator, in 1507; occupied by the Dutch, and named Mauritius after Prince Maurice of Orange 1598; abandoned by Dutch 1712; occupied by French 1715; captured by English 1810; formally ceded to England by Treaty of Paris 1814. [Refer Martin, *Hist. of Eng. Colonies*.]

Mayflower Descendants, Society of. Fd. in New York, Dec. 22, 1894, by the lineal descendants of the *Mayflower* Pilgrims.

Maynooth College (Ireland). Fd. 1795 for the education of candidates for the Irish Roman Catholic priesthood. Endowment granted by parliament 1845. This was stoutly opposed in parliament, and in 1871 the endowment ceased.

Meal-tub Plot. A pretended conspiracy against the Duke of York originated by Dangerfield in 1679; when arrested, Dangerfield declared his papers were concealed in a meal-tub, hence the name.

Medici Family. Chiefs of the Florentine Republic from 1434. Contributed to the restoration of literature and the arts in Italy. Cosmo de Medici was the first chief. Lorenzo de Medici ruled 1469-1492; he was the father of Pope Leo X. Cattarina de Medici became Queen of France 1547. The family became extinct 1743.

Melrose Abbey (Scotland). Celebrated in Scott's *Abbot* and *Lay of the Last Minstrel*. Fd. by David I. in 1136; rebuilt after destruction by English between 1322 and 1505.

Memorial or **Decoration Day.** Generally observed by the citizens of the U.S. on every 30th day of May; in the Southern states the 20th of May is observed as the day. On this anniversary the graves of Union soldiers and sailors are decorated with appropriate ceremonies.

Mennonites. A religious sect deriving its name from Simon Menno, who lived in the 16th century. They condemn war as sinful, and also lawsuits and oaths. Their Confession of Faith was first published in 1626, and in 1649 they adopted a system of Church policy. Theological seminary estab. at Amsterdam 1735. In 1871, owing to their most valued privilege, exemption from military duty, being taken away, most of the sect emigrated to the U.S.

Merchant Adventurers, The. A guild of traders estab. in Brabant 1296. The branch in England received the title by patent of Henry VII. 1505; incorp. 1564.

Merchant Taylors' School (London). Fd. 1561; schoolhouse destroyed during great fire of 1666; rebuilt 1671-74; rebuilt on new site 1873-74.

Merchants, Charter of. Granted in 1303 by Edward I. to foreign merchants.

Merchants, Statute of. Passed in 1283 by Edward I. providing for the registration and recovery of merchants' debts.

Merciless (or Wonderful) Parliament. Summoned in 1388 by the Lords Appellant after the defeat of the young Richard II. It condemned eight of Richard's supporters to death. [Refer Stubbs, *Constitutional History*.]

Methodists. Name first given to followers of John and Charles Wesley at Oxford in 1729; Wesleyan Methodist Society fd. by John Wesley 1739; first conference held 1744; conference constituted the supreme authority 1784; Dr. Coke constituted "bishop" of the American Methodist body 1784; death of Wesley 1791, after which the sect split up; union of many of the divisions into the "United Methodist Church" 1907. [Refer Smith, *History of Wesleyan Methodism*.]

Methuen Treaty. Negotiated by Paul Methuen, English ambassador in Portugal, in 1703. It reduced the duty on Portuguese wines to the detriment of French wines; annulled in 1835. [Refer Smith, *Wealth of Nations*.]

Mexico (S. America). The city of Mexico or Tenochtitlan was fd. by a tribe known as the Aztecs about A.D. 1325. In 1519 Hernando Cortes (1485-1547), the Spanish adventurer, landed at Vera Cruz, and conquered the land 1521. In 1540 Mexico was united with other American territories and called by the name of New Spain [refer Prescott, *Conquest of Mexico*]. Declares itself independent of Spain, and Gen. Iturbide is made emperor, May 1822. Formed into a republic, Oct. 1823. War with the U.S. regarding boundary dispute, June 4, 1845, to May 19, 1848, when a peace treaty was signed. War with France 1862-67. Emperor Maximilian shot 1867. [Refer Frost, *History of Mexico*.]

Michael (St.) and St. George, Order of. An order of knighthood fd. by George III. of England in 1818 to celebrate acquisition of Malta and the Ionian Islands.

Michaelmas Day. One of the four quarter days in England and Ireland. Feast of St. Michael and All Angels, Sept. 29; instit. A.D. 487.

Michigan (U.S.A.). Discovered and settled by French missionaries 1668. Fort Mackinaw estab. 1671; Detroit fd. 1701; possessed by British 1763; by Americans 1796; erected into an independent territory 1805; fell into the hands of the British, Aug. 1812; reconquered by Gen. Harrison 1813; admitted to the Union as a state, Jan. 1837; new constitution adopted 1850. [Refer Harper, *Encyclopædia of U.S. History*.]

Microscope, The. Early history obscure. The first compound M. said to have been made by Jansen, a Dutchman, in 1590. It was not, however, of much practical use until the achromatic lens was invented.

Midwives Act (Great Britain), 1902, provided that after April 1, 1905, no woman should use the title of midwife without being certified, and after April 1, 1910, no woman, except in cases of emergency, should attend cases of childbirth unless under the direction of a qualified medical man.

Milan (Italy). Latin *Mediolanum.* Taken from Gauls by Romans 222 B.C.; Constantine's edict in favour of Christians 313; sacked by Huns A.D. 452; by Goths 539; head of Lombard League from 1167; from 1555-1713 under the rule of Spain, then of Austria; after Napoleonic wars res. to Austria 1815; capital of Austro-Italian kingdom until 1859, when it became part of Italy; present cathedral fd. 1386, and completed by order of Napoleon 1805-13.

Military Academy (U.S.). A government institution at West Point, New York, estab. by Act of Congress, Mar. 16, 1802. [Refer Harper, *Encyclopædia of U.S. History.*]

Militia (Great Britain). During Alfred's reign (872-901) all subjects were made to join the military; militia raised 1122, 1176, 1557; militia statutes 1661-3; general militia act passed 1802; Militia Reserve Act 1867; Militia Enlistment Act 1875; title of militia abolished on introduction of Territorial and Reserve Force Act 1907.

Militia (U.S.A.). Bill for the organisation of the militia passes House of Representatives, Mar. 27, 1792. [Refer Harper, *Encyclopædia of U.S. History.*]

Millbank Prison (London). Commenced 1812; completed 1821; closed 1890; demolished 1891; on present site is the National Gallery of British Art. *See* Tate Gallery.

Minnesota (U.S.A.). Explored by two Huguenots, Groselliers and Radisson, 1659; formally possessed by French 1669; visited by Jonathan Carver 1763; part of territory, lying west of Mississippi, included in territory of Indiana 1800; purchased by U.S. 1803; territory of Minnesota created 1849; admitted to the Union as a state, May 11, 1858. [Refer Harper, *Encyclopædia U.S. History.*]

Minorca (Mediterranean). Captured by English 1708 during War of Spanish Succession; ceded to England by Treaty of Utrecht 1713; recaptured by French 1756; res. to England by Treaty of Paris 1762; recaptured by French and Spaniards 1781; ceded to Spain 1782; retaken 1798, but finally res. to Spain by Treaty of Amiens 1802. [Refer art. in Low and Pulling, *Dicty. of Eng. History.*]

Mint (Great Britain). Regulations for the government of the M. were made by King Athelstan about A.D. 928; by an Act of Parliament dated 1810 the present M. was fd. on Tower Hill; in 1815 a new constitution was fd. on the report of the Hon. Mr. Wellesley Pole; in 1851 a complete change was made in the administration, when a master, deputy-master, and comptroller were appointed; in 1869 the office of Chancellor of the Exchequer carried with it the position of master, and the offices of deputy-master and comptroller were made one. M. were estab. at Sydney, Australia, in 1853, and in Melbourne, Australia, 1869.

Mint (U.S.A.). The earliest colonial coinage was in Massachusetts, when a M. house was estab. at Boston, May 27, 1652. " The power of coinage was exercised by several of the independent states from 1778 until the adoption of the National Constitution." M. estab. at Rupert, Vt. 1785. Estab. of a M. by Act of Congress, 1795, at Philadelphia. [Refer arts. on " Mint " and " Coinage " in Harper, *Encyclopædia of U.S. History.*]

Mississippi (U.S.A.). The river discovered by La Salle 1682, and includes the surrounding country; territory of Mississippi created, April 7, 1798; admitted to the Union as a state 1817; new constitution adopted 1832. [Refer Harper, *Encyclopædia of U.S. History.*]

Mississippi Scheme. A proposal to develop resources of Louisiana (*q.v.*), the country on the borders of the Mississippi. The scheme was the idea of John Law (1671-1729), who floated a company for this purpose in 1717. The scheme was not a success, and in July 1720 the bubble broke.

Missouri (C. state, U.S.A.). Orig. known as Upper Louisiana. Town of St. Genevieve fd. 1755; by Treaty of Paris 1763 territory passed into the hands of the English; ceded to U.S. 1803; admitted into the Union as a state, Aug. 10, 1821 (*see* next art.); suffered from dissensions during Civil War of 1861; new constitution framed, Jan. 6, 1865. [Refer Harper, *Encyclopædia of U.S. History.*]

Missouri Compromise, The. In 1817 the inhabitants of the Missouri territory petitioned for admission into the Union as a state; subsequently a bill was intro. into congress on Feb. 13, 1819. A question of the abolition of slavery in the territory caused the bill to be delayed until a compromise was agreed to, Mar. 2, 1820; this, however, still led to much discussion, and it was not until Feb. 27, 1821, that a final compromise was adopted, and this led to the admission of Missouri to the Union as a state. [Refer Harper, *Encyclopædia of U.S. History.*]

Moabite Stone, The. Now in the Louvre, Paris. Discovered by Rev. F. Klein at Dhibän in 1868.

Modena (Italy). Made a duchy 1452; duke expelled by French 1796; res. 1814; finally expelled and the duchy incorp. with kingdom of Italy 1860.

Mohammedanism. The religious belief fd. by Mohammed (A.D. 570(?)-632); between the years 600-610 Mohammed started to preach his doctrines; the Mohammedan era dates from A.D. 622, when the prophet went to Medina, and was recognised by large numbers as a lawgiver and prophet. [Refer Washington Irving, *Life of Mahomed.*]

Mohawks or **Mohocks, The.** A club which existed in London in 1711. They caused so much mischief and damage by their outlawry that on Mar. 18, 1712, they were the cause of a royal proclamation. [Refer the *Spectator*, No. 347.]

Molly Maguires. A secret society formed by Irishmen which terrorised Pennsylvania between 1867 and 1877; many of the leaders were tried and executed in 1877, and the society disbanded.

Monaco (N.W. Italy). A principality acquired by the Grimaldi family in A.D. 968; made a French protectorate 1644; Mentone and Roquebrune annexed by Sardinia 1846; became part of Italy 1859; Mentone and Roquebrune sold to Napoleon III. 1861. [Refer Pemberton, *Monaco, Past and Present*.]

Monasteries (Great Britain). The first monastery in England appears to have been erected about A.D. 596 by St. Augustine [refer Stanley, *Memorials of Canterbury*]. A large number of these religious houses grew up in England. In 1535 during Henry VIII.'s reign a commission was issued for the visitation of the monasteries. In 1536 an act was passed for the suppression of the religious houses whose income did not exceed £200 a year. The larger houses were suppressed in 1539. [Refer Stone, *Reformation and Renaissance*.]

Monmouth's Rebellion. Originated by James, Duke of Monmouth (1649-85), who landed in England on June 11, 1685, at Lyme Regis. He was defeated by the royal troops at Sedgemoor, July 8, 1685, and executed July 15, 1685. [Refer Macaulay, *History of England*.]

Monopolies. A right claimed by the Crown of England to issue patents conferring exclusive rights for the sale of certain commodities. In 1597 parliament protested to Elizabeth against this right. The parliaments of Charles I. protested still more strongly, and by an act of 1624 most of these monopolies were abolished, and in 1639 the whole system was done away with. [Refer art. in Low and Pulling, *Dicty. of English History*.]

Monroe Doctrine. Proclaimed by President James Monroe (1759-1831) of the U.S. in his message to congress on Dec. 2, 1823. In the words of Monroe himself, the doctrine was that the U.S. " should consider any attempt on their [the foreign powers'] part to extend their system to any portion of this [the American] hemisphere as dangerous to our peace and safety." [Refer Harper, *Encyclopædia of U.S. History*.]

Montana (N. state, U.S.A.). By Act of Congress the territory was taken from the eastern portion of Idaho and organised as a separate territory; admitted to the Union as a state, Nov. 8, 1889. [Refer Harper, *Encyclopædia of U.S. History*.]

Mont Blanc (France). In 1760 Saussure offered a reward for the discovery of a practicable route to the summit of Mont Blanc. Two guides in June 1786 gained the reward. Saussure reached the top himself the following year.

Mont de Piété (French) or **Monte di Pietà** (Italian). Institutions fd. for lending money to the poor at a low rate of interest, first estab. at Orvieto 1463.

Montenegro (Europe). The history of Montenegro as an independent state begins with the b. of Kossova 1389; Cettinge is made capital 1484; conquered by Turks 1526; captured by the Turks 1623, 1687, and 1714; fresh war with Turkey 1852; peace finally res. Nov. 1858; Turkish supremacy recognised, Sept. 1862; declared independent of Turkey by Treaty of San Stefano, Mar. 3, 1878; first Montenegrin Parliament assembled at Cettinge, Oct. 1906; Prince Nicholas assumed title of king, Aug. 28, 1910. [Refer Wyon and Prance, *The Land of the Black Mountain*.]

Montevideo (Uruguay). First settlement made 1726; taken by the English 1807; in 1828 it was made the capital of Uruguay or Banda Oriental (*q.v.*).

Montreal (Canada). Orig. called *Ville Marie*. Fd. by French settlers 1642; captured by British, Sept. 8, 1760; by Americans, Nov. 12, 1775; recaptured by British, June 15, 1776. McGill College fd. 1813; made a university by royal charter 1821; new charter granted 1852. Bishopric fd. 1850. Cathedral destroyed by fire, Dec. 10, 1856. [Refer art. in *Chambers's Encyclopædia*.]

Montyon Prizes. Rewarded each year by the French Academy for examples of disinterested goodness. The fund for this purpose was bequeathed by the Baron de Montyon (1733-1820).

Moors. *See* Spain, Morocco, Granada, etc.

Moravian Brethren or **Moravian Church.** A religious sect fd. in the east of Bohemia about 1457; first synod held 1467. It grew out of the Hussites or followers of John Huss; the sect flourished principally in Moravia, hence the name. In 1749 the British Parliament passed acts to encourage their settlement in the English-American colonies. [Refer Hutton, *History of the Moravian Church*.]

Mormons, The, or **Latter-day Saints.** A religious sect fd. by Joseph Smith (1805-44). The *Book of Mormon* was first published at New York in 1830. The first church was fd. on April 6, 1830, at Fayette; moved to Kirkland, Ohio, Jan. 1831. Their headquarters at Salt Lake City fd. 1847. [Refer art. in *Encyclopædia Britannica*.]

Morocco (N. Africa). Early in possession of the Romans; seized by the Vandals A.D. 429; conquered by Belisarius 533; invaded by Arabs 680, who have possessed it practically ever since; town of Morocco fd. 1072; war with Spain 1859-60; conference of the European powers at Algeciras concerning Moroccan affairs 1906; anti-European riot at Casablanca 1907; agreement between Germany and France recognising independence of M. signed 1909.

Mortmain, Statute of. Issued by Edward I. of England on Nov. 15, 1279. It forbade " any person whatsoever, religious or other, to buy or sell or under colour of any gift, term, or other title, to receive from any one any lands or tenements in such a way that such lands and tenements should come into *mort main.*" A second Statute of Mortmain was passed under Richard II. in 1391, which extended the former one. [Refer Reeves, *History of English Law.*]

Moscow (Russia). Fd. 1156; captured by Tamerlane 1382; burned by the Khan of the Crimea 1571; the city was burned by the inhabitants in 1812, when Napoleon entered, and he was forced to leave it. [Refer Gerrare, *The Story of Moscow.*]

Muckers. A religious sect which originated at Königsberg in 1835.

Muggletonians. A religious sect which was fd. in England about 1651 by John Reeve and Lodovick Muggleton. [Refer essay in Jessopp, *Coming of the Friars,* etc.]

Munich or **Munchen** (Germany). Supposed to have been fd. A.D. 962 by Henry of Saxony; taken by Gustavus Adolphus of Sweden 1632; by Austrians 1704, 1741, 1746; by French, July 2, 1800; university fd. 1826.

Münster (Germany). Orig. a monastery; by 1186 had grown into a town; declared for the Reformed faith 1532; famous during 1535 for the Anabaptist disturbances, when the Roman Catholic bishop was expelled, but returned after besieging the city the same year. [Refer Ranke, *History of the Reformation in Germany.*]

Münster, Treaty of, between France, Germany, and Sweden against Spain. The theory of the balance of power was first recognised in this treaty, which was signed Oct. 24, 1648. Also known as the Treaty of Westphalia.

Musical Composers. The following are the most celebrated of the world's musical composers with their dates:—

Abbatini, Antonio Maria (Italian), *c.* 1595-1677.
Abt, Franz (German), 1819-85.
Arditi, Luigi (Italian), 1822-1903.
Arne, Thomas Augustine (English), 1710-78.
Attwood, Thomas (English), 1765-1838.
Auber, Daniel François Esprit (French), 1782-1871.
Bach, Johann Sebastian (German), 1685-1750.
Balfe, Michael William (English), 1808-70.
Barnby, Joseph (English), 1838-96.
Barthélémon, François Hippolyte (French), 1741-1808.
Bazzini, Antonio (Italian), 1818-97.
Beaulieu, Marie Désiré Martin (French), 1791-1863.
Beethoven, Ludwig van (German), 1770-1827.
Bellini, Vincenzo (Italian), 1801-35.
Benedict, Julius (English), 1804-85.
Bennett, William Sterndale (English), 1816-75.
Benoist, François (French), 1794-1878.
Benoit, Peter Léonard Leopold (Flemish), 1834-1901.
Berger, Ludwig (German), 1777-1839.
Berlioz, Hector (French), 1803-69.

MUSICAL COMPOSERS (*continued*)—

Bertini, Henri (French), 1798-1876.
Best, William Thomas (English), 1826-97.
Bishop, Henry Rowley (English), 1786-1855.
Bizet, Georges (French), 1838-75.
Blangini, Giuseppe Marco Maria Felice (Italian), 1781-1841.
Blumenthal, Joseph von (German), 1782-1856.
Boccherini, Luigi (Italian), 1743-1805.
Bochsa, Robert Nicholas Charles (French), 1789-1856.
Boieldieu, François Adrien (French), 1775-1834.
Brahms, Johannes (German), 1833-97.
Bruckner, Anton (Austrian), 1824-96.
Brunetti, Gaetano (Italian), 1753-1808.
Bülow, Hans Guido von (German), 1830-94.
Burney, Charles (English), 1726-1814.
Byrd or Bird, William (English), 1538-1623.
Caccini, Giulio (Italian), *c.* 1546-1615.
Callcott, John Wall (English), 1766-1821.
Campra, André (French), 1660-1744.
Carey, Henry (English), *c.* 1690-1743.
Carissimi, Giacomo (Italian), 1604-74.
Cavalli, Francesco (Italian), *c.* 1599-1676.
Cellier, Alfred (English), 1844-91.
Cherubini, Maria Luigi Zenobio Carlo Salvatore (Italian), 1760-
    1842.
Chiaromonte, Francesco (Italian), 1809-86.
Chopin, Frédéric François (French), 1810-49.
Cimarôsa, Domenico (Italian), 1749-1801.
Clark, Jeremiah (English), 1670-1707.
Clementi, Muzio (Italian), 1752-1832.
Corelli, Arcangelo (Italian), 1653-1713.
Cornelius, Peter (Dutch), 1824-74.
Coupeius, François (French), 1668-1733.
Czerny, Karl (Austrian), 1791-1857.
Damrosch, Leopold (German), 1832-85.
Delibes, Leo (French), 1836-91.
Deprès, Josquin (Dutch), *c.* 1450-1521.
Ditters, Karl (Austrian), 1739-99.
Donizetti, Gaetano (Italian), 1797-1848.
Dorn, Heinrich Ludwig Egmont (German), 1804-92.
Durante, Francesco (Italian), 1864-1755.
Dvorak, Anton (Bohemian), 1841-1904.
Ellerton, John Lodge (English), 1807-73.
Elvey, George Job (English), 1816-93.
Flotow, Friedrich Freiherr von (German), 1812-83.
Franz, Robert (German), 1815-92.
Frescobaldi, Girolamo (Italian), 1583-1644.
Gabrieli, Andrea (Italian), 1510-86.
Gabrieli, Giovanni (Italian), 1557-1612.
Gade, Niels Wilhelm (Danish), 1817-90.
Gagliano, Marco Zanobi da (Italian), (?)-1642.

MUSICAL COMPOSERS (*continued*)—

Gallus, Jacobus (German), 1550-91.
Geminiani, Francesco (Dutch), 1680-1762.
Genée, Franz Fr. Richard (German), 1823-95.
Gesius, Bartholomäus (German), 1555-1613.
Giardini, Felice de (Italian), 1716-96.
Gibbons, Orlando (English), 1583-1625.
Giovanelli, Ruggiero (Italian), *c.* 1560-*c.* 1620.
Glinka, Michail Iwanowitsch (Russian), 1804-57.
Gluck, Christoph Wilibald (German), 1714-87.
Godard, Benjamin Louis Paul (French), 1849-95.
Gomez, Antonio Carlos (Portuguese), 1839-96.
Gossec, François Joseph (French), 1734-1829.
Gounod, Charles François (French), 1818-93.
Gouvy, Ludwig Théodore, 1819-98.
Graun, Karl Heinrich (German), 1701-59.
Graupner, Christoph (German), 1683-1760.
Grell, Eduard August (German), 1800-86.
Grétry, André Erneste Modeste (French), 1741-1813.
Grieg, Edvard Hagerup (Norwegian), 1843-1907.
Grisar, Albert (Dutch), 1808-69.
Guglielmi, Pietro (Italian), 1727-1804.
Gumpeltzhaimer, Adam (German), 1559-1625.
Halévy, Jacques Fromental Elie (French), 1799-1862.
Hallström, Ivar (Swedish), 1826-1901.
Hammerschmidt, Andreas (German), 1611-75.
Handel, Georg Friedrich (German), 1685-1759.
Hanssens, Charles Louis (the younger) (Belgian), 1802-71.
Hartmann, Johann Peter Emil (Danish), 1805-1900.
Hasler, Hans Leo (German), 1564-1612.
Hasse, Johann Adolf (German), 1699-1783.
Hässler, Johann Wilhelm (German), 1747-1822.
Haydn, Franz Joseph (German), 1732-1809.
Heller, Stephen (German), 1815-88.
Herbeck, Johann (German), 1831-77.
Hérold, Louis Joseph Ferdinand (French), 1791-1833.
Hervé, Florimond Ronger (French), 1825-92.
Herzogenberg, Heinrich von (German), 1843-1900.
Hignard, Jean Louis Aristide (French), 1822-98.
Hiller, Johann Adam (German), 1728-1804.
Hiller, Ferdinand von (German), 1811-85.
Himmel, Friedrich Heinrich (German), 1765-1814.
Hoffmann, Ernst Theodor Amadeus (German), 1776-1822.
Holstein, Franz von (German), 1826-78.
Hullah, John Pyke (English), 1812-84.
Hummel, Johann Nepomuk (German), 1778-1837.
Isaak, Heinrich (Netherlander), 1450-1517.
Isouard, Niccolò (French), 1775-1818.
Jadassohn, Salomon (German), 1831-1902.
Jannequin, Clément (Belgian), 16th century.
Jensen, Adolf (German), 1837-79.

MUSICAL COMPOSERS (*continued*)—

Jommelli, Nicola (Italian), 1714-74.
Joncières, Félix Ludger (French), 1839-1903.
Kapsberger, Johann Hieronymus von (German), 1604-*c.* 1650.
Kastner, Johann Georg (German), 1810-67.
Keiser, Reinhard (German), 1674-1739.
Kiel, Friedrich (German), 1821-85.
Kirchner, Theodor (German), 1824-1903.
Klein, Bernhard (German), 1793-1832.
Köhler, Chr. Louis Heinrich (German), 1820-86.
Kotzeluch, Leopold Anton (German), 1738-1818.
Krebs, Karl (German), 1804-80.
Kreutzer, Konradin (German), 1780-1849.
Kücken, Friedrich Wilhelm (German), 1810-82.
Kusser, Johann Siegmund (German), 1657-1727.
Lachner, Franz (German), 1804-90.
Lacombe, Louis Trouillon (French), 1818-84.
Lajarte, Théodore Edouard Dufaure de (French), 1826-90.
Lalo, Edouard (French), 1823-92.
Lange, Samuel de (Dutch), 1840-.
Lanner, Joseph Franz Karl (German), 1801-43.
Lapicida, Erasmus (nationality unknown), 16th century.
Lassen, Eduard (Belgian), 1830-1904.
Lasso, Orlando di (Italian), 1520-94.
Legrenzi, Giovanni (Italian), 1625-90.
Leo, Leonardo (Italian), 1694-1746.
Lesueur, Jean François (French), 1764-1837.
Liszt, Franz (German), 1811-86.
Litolff, Henry Charles (English), 1818-91.
Lobe, Johann Christian (German), 1797-1881.
Logroscino, Nicolà (Italian), 1700-63.
Lortzing, Gustav Albert (German), 1803-51.
Lotti, Antonio (German), 1667-1740.
Löwe, Johann Karl Gottfried (German), 1796-1869.
Lully, Jean Baptiste (French), 1633-87.
Mabellini, Teodulo (Italian), 1817-97.
Macfarren, George Alexander (English), 1813-87.
Mangold, Karl Ludwig Amand (German), 1813-89.
Marcello, Benedetto (Italian), 1686-1739.
Marchetti, Filippo (Italian), 1835-1902.
Marenzio, Luca (Italian), *c.* 1550-99.
Marmontel, Antoine François (French), 1816-98.
Marschner, Heinrich August (Germany), 1795-1861.
Méhul, Etienne Nicolas (French), 1763-1817.
Meinardus, Ludwig Siegfried (German), 1827-96.
Mendelssohn-Bartholdy, Jakob Ludwig Felix (German), 1809-47.
Mercadante, Giuseppe Saverio Raffaele (Italian), 1795-1870.
Merulo, Claudio (Italian), 1533-1604.
Métra, Jules Louis Olivier (French), 1830-89.
Meyerbeer, Giacomo (German), 1791-1864.
Molique, Wilhelm Bernhard (Germany), 1802-69.

MUSICAL COMPOSERS (*continued*)—

Monsigny, Pierre Alexandre (French), 1729-1817.
Monteverde, Claudio (Italian), 1567-1643.
Morlacchi, Francesco (Italian), 1784-1841.
Morley, Thomas (English), 1557-1604.
Moscheles, Ignaz (Germany), 1794-1870.
Mosonyi, Michael Brandt (Hungarian), 1814-70.
Mottl, Felix (Germany), 1856-1911.
Mouton, Jean (French), (?)-1522.
Mozart, Wolfgang Amadeus (German), 1756-91.
Mussorgski, Modest Petrowitsch (Russian), 1839-81.
Nanino, Giovanni Maria (Italian), 1540-1607.
Nares, James (English), 1715-83.
Naumann, Emil (German), 1827-88.
Naumann, Johann Gottlieb (German), 1741-1801.
Nessler, Victor E. (German), 1841-90.
Neukomm, Sigismund (German), 1778-1858.
Nicolai, Otto (German), 1810-49.
Offenbach, Jacques (French), 1819-80.
Onslow, George (English), 1784-1852.
Otto, Ernst Julius (German), 1804-77.
Ouseley, Sir Frederick Arthur Gore (English), 1825-89.
Pacini, Giovanni (Italian), 1796-1867.
Paër, Ferdinando (Italian), 1771-1839.
Paganini, Niccolo (Italian), 1782-1840.
Paine, John Knowles (American), 1839-1906.
Palestrina, Giovanni Pierluigi (Italian), *c.* 1515-94
Parry, Joseph (English), 1841-1903.
Pergolesi, Giovanni Battista (Italian), 1710-36.
Piccinni, Nicola (Italian), 1728-1800.
Pinsuti, Ciro (Italian), 1829-88.
Pitoni, Guiseppe Ottavio (Italian), 1657-1743.
Planquette, R. (French), 1851-1903.
Pleyel, Ignaz Joseph (Austrian), 1757-1831.
Poniatowski, Joseph M. X. F. J. (Prince of Monte Rotundo), 1816-73.
Purcell, Henry (English), 1658-95.
Raff, Joseph Joachim (German), 1822-82.
Rameau, Jean Phillipe (French), 1683-1764.
Reher, Napoleon Henri (French), 1807-80.
Rossini, Gioacchino Antonio (Italian), 1792-1868.
Rubinstein, Anton von (Russian), 1830-94.
Sacchini, Antonio Maria Gasparo (Italian), 1734-86.
Saldoni, Don Balthasar (Spanish), 1807-90.
Salieri, Antonio (Italian), 1750-1825.
Sarasate, Pablo de (Italian), 1844-1910.
Sarti, Giuseppe (Italian), 1729-1802.
Scarlatti, Alessandro (Italian), 1659-1725.
Scarlatti, Domenico (Italian), 1685-1757.
Schubert, Franz Peter (German), 1797-1828.
Schultz, Heinrich (German), 1585-1672.

MUSICAL COMPOSERS (*continued*)—

Schumann, Robert (German), 1810-56.
Smart, George Thomas (English), 1776-1867.
Smetana, Friedrich (Bohemian), 1824-84.
Spohr, Ludwig (German), 1784-1859.
Spontini, Gasparo Luigi Pacifico (Italian), 1774-1851.
Stainer, Sir John (English), 1840-1901.
Steffani, Agostino (Italian), 1655-1730.
Steibelt, Daniel (German), 1765-1823.
Stradella, Alessandro (Italian), 1645-81.
Strauss, Johann (German), 1825-99.
Strungk, Nikolaus Adam (German), 1640-1700.
Sullivan, Arthur (English), 1842-1900.
Suppé, Franz von (Austrian), 1820-95.
Tartini, Giuseppe (Italian), 1692-1770.
Telemann, Georg Philipp (German), 1681-1767.
Thalberg, Sigismund (German), 1812-71.
Thomas, Charles Louis Ambrose (French), 1811-96.
Traetta, Tommasso (Italian), 1727-79.
Tschaikowsky, Peter Iljitoch (Polish), 1840-93.
Vecchi Orazio (Italian), *c.* 1550-1605.
Verdelot, Philippe (Belgian), *c.* 1530-67.
Verdi, Giuseppe (Italian), 1813-1901.
Viadana, Ludovico (Italian), 1564-1645.
Vicentino, Nicola (Italian), 1511-*c.* 1576.
Vittoria, Tomaso Ludovico da (Italian), *c.* 1540-*c.* 1608.
Vogler, Georg Joseph (German), 1749-1814.
Volkmann, Friedrich Robert (German), 1815-83.
Wagner, Wilhelm Richard (German), 1813-83.
Weber, Karl Maria Friedrich Ernst (German), 1786-1826.
Zimmermann, Anton (German), 1741-81.
Zingarelli, Nicola Antonio (Italian), 1752-1837.

[Refer Riemann, *Dictionary of Music*; Baker, *Biog. Dict. of Musicians.*]

Mutiny Act (Great Britain). Passed in 1697 owing to a mutiny at Ipswich. It was to be in force for six months, but was continued. *See* Army, British.

N

Namur (Belgium). Captured by Louis XIV. in 1692; recaptured in 1695 by William III.; in French possession 1701-12; bombarded by allies 1704; subsequently in possession of different powers, and assigned to Belgium 1831.

Nancy (France). Captured by Charles the Bold, Nov. 29, 1475; lost by him, Oct. 5, 1476; captured by French 1633 and 1670; res. to Duke Leopold 1697; became French possession 1766; put up to ransom by the Prussians 1870. [Refer Pfister, *Histoire de Nancy.*]

Nantes (France). Of Roman origin. In possession of Clotaire I. A.D. 560; held by Normans 843-936; communal constitution granted by Francis II. 1560; scene of Carrier's " Noyades " and other atrocities 1793. [Refer art. in *Encyclopædia Britannica.*]

Nantes, Edict of. By which the Huguenots were permitted to exercise their own religion, was published on April 15, 1598, by Henry IV. of France. Its revocation on Oct. 24, 1685, by Louis XIV. drove many of the Protestants into exile. [The full text of the edict is given in Tanner, *The Renaissance and the Reformation.*]

Naples (Italy). The Romans subdued the territory in 328 B.C.; it fell into the hands of the Goths, but they were driven out by Belisarius in A.D. 536; Charles of Anjou in possession 1266; great massacre of the French at Palermo known as the Sicilian Vespers (*q.v.*) 1282; united with Sicily (*q.v.*) 1442; annexed to Spain 1504; insurrection headed by Masaniello 1647; possessed by Austria 1707; recovered by Spain 1734; invaded by French Republican army 1789; by Napoleon 1806; restoration of the Bourbons 1815; incorp. in the kingdom of Italy 1861. [Refer Norway, *Naples, Past and Present.*]

Napoleon Bonaparte, Emperor of the French, *b.* Aug. 15, 1769, *d.* May 5, 1821. The following are the principal battles associated with Napoleon in chronological order:—

Millesimo, April 13, 1796	Nile, The, Aug. 1, 1798
Dego, April 14, 1796	Marengo, June 14, 1800
Ceva, 1796	Austerlitz, Dec. 2, 1805
Mondavi, 1796.	Jena, Oct. 14, 1806
Borghello, May 27, 1796	Auerstädt, Oct. 14, 1806
Lonato (1), July 31, 1796	Eylau, 1806
Lonato (2), Aug. 3, 1796	Friedland, June 14, 1807
Castiglione, Aug. 5, 1796	Vimiera, 1808
Bassano, Sept. 1796	Aspern, May 1809
Arcola, 1796	Wagram, July 5 and 6, 1809
Rivoli, Jan. 14, 1797	Borodino, Sept. 6, 1812
Capture of Malta, May 19, 1798	Retreat from Moscow, Oct. 18,
Chebreïss, July 24, 1798	1812

NAPOLEON BONAPARTE (*continued*)—

Lutzen, May 2, 1813	Montmirail, Feb. 11, 1814
Bautzan, May 20 and 21, 1813	Chateau-Thierry, Feb. 12, 1814
Gross-Bearen, Aug. 23, 1813	Vauchamps, Feb. 13, 1814
Katzbach, Aug. 26, 1813	Craonne, 1814
Dresden, Aug. 27, 1813	Laon, 1814
Leipzig, Oct. 1813	Ligny, June 16, 1815
Champaubert, Feb. 10, 1814	Waterloo, June 18, 1815.

[Refer art. in *Encyclopædia Britannica*.]

Narbonne (France). A considerable time before the Roman invasion of Gaul, N. was a famous city. In 118 B.C. the first Roman colony in Gaul was fd. under the name of *Narbo Martius*; seized by the Visigoths A.D. 462; by Saracens after a two years' siege 719; retaken by Pepin le Bref 759; Cinq-Mars arrested at for conspiracy 1642; united to French crown 1507. [Refer art. in *Chambers's Encyclopædia*.]

Nassau (Germany). Early occupied by the Alamanni, who were defeated by Clovis towards the close of the 5th century; becomes part of German kingdom 843; annexed to Prussia 1860.

Natal (S. Africa). Discovered by Vasco da Gama on Christmas Day 1497, hence the name; declared part of British dominions 1843; formally annexed to Cape Colony, May 31, 1844; declared a separate colony, July 15, 1856; Zululand annexed to 1897; Boers finally driven from, 1900. *See* Ladysmith, Transvaal War, etc. [Refer Russell, *The Garden Colony. The Story of Natal and its Neighbours*.]

National Anthem (Great Britain). Is of uncertain origin; first printed in the *Harmonia Anglicana* 1742; both words and music have been attributed to Henry Carey, 1740; they were printed in *Gentleman's Magazine* for Oct. 1745.

National Anthem (U.S.A.). *The Star Spangled Banner*, composed and written in 1814, words by F. S. Key, music by J. S. Smith. *Hail, Columbia*, was produced about 1798, words by Joseph Hopkinson, music by Fyles.

National Debt (Great Britain). Originated in the reign of William III., and was intro. by Charles Montagu, Earl of Halifax (1661-1715), on Dec. 15, 1692. [Refer Macaulay, *History of England*.]

National Gallery (London). Present building completed 1838; enlarged 1861, 1869, 1876, 1887; National Portrait Gallery fd. in 1856, estab. at S. Kensington 1869; removed to Bethnal Green Museum 1885; transferred to new buildings adjoining National Gallery 1896. *See also* Tate Gallery.

National Gallery of British Art. *See* Tate Gallery.

National Guard (France). Intro. into Paris during French Revolution, July 1789; superseded by present military system 1870.

Naturalisation Act (Great Britain). Passed 1870; a treaty with U.S.A. was entered into the same year, by which both countries pledged themselves to recognise claims of naturalisation. [Refer Cutler, *Law of Naturalisation*.]

Navigation Laws (Great Britain). The first to adopt the navigation system as a policy was Oliver Cromwell, who in 1650 excluded all foreign ships without a licence from trading with the plantations of America. The Navigation Act of Cromwell was passed in 1651. Act providing that all colonial produce should be exported in English vessels 1660. Colonies prohibited from receiving goods in foreign vessels 1663. Act of 1672, the Navigation Act of Charles II., extends Cromwell's act and ruins the Dutch navy. Navigation Act repealed 1826, but a new code of regulations still prevents free trade. These laws abolished 1842, 1846, and 1849. Coasting trade of Great Britain thrown open to foreign vessels 1854. [Refer art. in Low and Pulling, *Dicty. of English History*.]

Navy (U.S.A.). On Oct. 13, 1775, Congress authorised the fitting out of a gun-carrying vessel. This was the beginning of the U.S. Navy. Board of Admiralty estab. 1779. Other vessels fitted out 1775. In 1794, the navy having fallen into neglect, Congress voted a sum of money "for creating a small navy." In Jan. 1813 an act was passed authorising the building of four gunboats and six frigates. In March 1813 another act provided for the building of six sloops of war. After that date the navy has steadily increased. [Refer art. in Harper, *Encyclopædia of U.S History*.]

Nebraska (U.S.A.). Made a territory, May 30, 1854; state government formed 1866; admitted to the Union as a state, Mar. 1, 1867. [Refer Harper, *Encyclopædia of U.S. History*.]

Netherlands (Europe). *See* Flanders, Holland, and Belgium.

Neuchâtel (Switzerland). Orig. *Novum Castellum*, whose original possessors took the name of count from the middle of the 12th century; under Prussian rule from 1707 to 1857, with the exception of the years 1806-14, when Napoleon granted it to Marshal Berthier; becomes a full republican member of the Swiss confederation 1857. [Refer art. in *Chambers's Encyclopædia*.]

Nevada (U.S.A.). Territory created by Act of Congress, Mar. 2, 1861; admitted to the Union as a state, Oct. 31, 1864. [Refer Harper, *Encyclopædia of U.S. History*.]

New Brunswick (N. America). Discovered by Cabot 1497; colonised by French 1630 and 1672; by British North American Act is incorp. with the Dominion of Canada 1867.

New Caledonia (Pacific Ocean). Discovered by Captain Cook 1774; closely explored by D'Entrecasteaux 1793; claimed by France 1843; it was not until 1853, however, that the British withdrew their claim to the island.

Newcastle-on-Tyne (England). Named after a castle which was erected in 1080 by Robert Curthose; besieged by William Rufus 1095; present castle built between 1172 and 1177; besieged by Scotch under Gen. Leslie 1644; bishopric fd. 1882.

New England (U.S.A.). Visited by Sir Humphrey Gilbert 1583, and by Bartholomew Gosnold 1602; Puritans sail in the *Mayflower*, and fd. settlement 1620. *See* Massachusetts, Maine.

New Forest (Hampshire, England). Laid out by William the Conqueror 1079. *See* Forest Laws.

Newfoundland (N. America). Discovered by John Cabot, June 24, 1497; visited by Portuguese 1500; formally possessed by England, Aug. 1583; ceded wholly to England by Treaty of Utrecht 1713, but French retain certain fishing privileges which were renounced under the Anglo-French Convention 1904. [Refer Prowse, *A History of Newfoundland*.]

Newgate Prison (London). Orig. built 1218; destroyed during Great Fire 1666; rebuilt 1780; largely destroyed during Gordon Riots (*q.v.*) 1780 [refer Dickens, *Barnaby Rudge*, and description in Boswell, *Johnson*]; again rebuilt 1857; demolished 1902-3. [Refer Gordon, *The Old Bailey and Newgate*.]

New Hampshire (U.S.A.). Settled in 1623; permanent settlement in 1629; formed into an independent state government, Jan. 5, 1776; state constitution formed, June 12, 1781. [Refer Harper, *Encyclopædia of U.S. History*.]

New Haven (Connecticut, U.S.A.). Orig. called by its Indian name of *Quinnipiac;* was first settled by a band of Puritans from England in 1637; in 1716 the Collegiate School of Connecticut was removed here, and it afterwards grew into Yale University (*q.v.*); invaded by British, July 5, 1779; incorp. 1784. [Refer Harper, *Encyclopædia of U.S. History*.]

New Jersey (U.S.A.). One of the 13 original colonies; settlements made in 1623; National Constitution adopted, Dec. 1787; ratified, Aug. 13, 1844; admitted to the Union as a state. [Refer Harper, *Encyclopædia of U.S. History*.]

New Jerusalem Church or **New Church.** Fd. by the followers of Emmanuel Swedenborg (1688-1772). Its origin may be traced to the foundation of the " Theosophical Society " in 1783, an association of the admirers of Swedenborg's writings. The New Jerusalem Church was fd. on May 7, 1787, and the original society dissolved. First conference held, April 1789. In the U.S.A. the first society for worship was held in 1792 at Baltimore; and the first general convention met at Philadelphia in 1817. [Refer art. in *Encyclopædia Britannica*.]

New Mexico (U.S.A.). In 1598 it was first successfully colonised by Spaniards; independent of Spain 1822; ceded to U.S.A. by Treaty of Guadulupe-Hidalgo 1848; admitted to the Union as a state, June 1910. [Refer Harper, *Encyclopædia of U.S. History*.]

New Model. The name given to the Parliamentary Army as new modelled in April 1645.

New Netherland (U.S.A.). Fd. by a charter of the states-general of Holland, Oct. 11, 1614; made a province of Holland 1623; passed into the hands of the English 1664; name changed to New York 1664 after James, Duke of York, brother of Charles II. *See* New York. [Refer Harper, *Encyclopædia of U.S. History*.]

New Orleans (U.S.A.). Fd. 1718; possessed by Spain, Aug. 8, 1769; attacked by British, Dec. 1814, who were repulsed, Jan. 8, 1815; surrendered to the Federals, April 1862. [Refer Harper, *Encyclopædia of U.S. History*.]

New South Wales (Australia). Name given by Capt. Cook 1770; colony estab. 1788 by transported prisoners; transportation ceases 1840; gold first discovered at Bathurst 1851. *See* Australia.

Newspapers. The origin of N. may be traced to ancient Rome, when accounts of the various armies were sent to the imperial officers stationed in the provinces. In the 15th century in some of the German towns news-sheets were issued in the form of letters. The first official paper was issued in Venice in 1566, and was known as the *Notizie Scritte*, published by order of the Venetian government. This was followed by others of a similar nature, and they were exhibited at various places, where on payment of a coin called a *gazetta* they could be read. This is the origin of the word *gazette*. The first English N. proper was the *Weekly News*, published in 1622, followed in the same year by the *London Weekly Courant*. The *Public Intelligencer*, first issued in 1663 by Sir Roger L'Estrange, is worthy of note. It was discontinued on the appearance of the *London Gazette* on Nov. 7, 1665. In 1662 a press censorship was started and continued until its abolishment in 1695. The first daily paper in England was the *Daily Courant*, first published in 1702. A tax of one halfpenny on N. intro. in 1712 increased by various stages to fourpence in 1815. In 1836 it was reduced to one penny, and the tax was abolished altogether in 1855. The *Times* N. was started in 1788. *See* Advertisements. [Refer Grant, *Newspaper Press*.]

Newspapers (U.S.A.). The first N. issued in America was in 1690 at Boston. Its title was *Public Occurrences*. It, however, only lasted a day owing to its too outspoken nature. The first permanent paper was the *Boston News-Letter*, which was issued in April 1704. The first daily paper was the *Pennsylvania Packet or General Advertiser*, afterwards known as the *Daily Advertiser*, first issued in 1784. [Refer Harper, *Encyclopædia of U.S. History*.]

New York City (U.S.A.). Settled by the Dutch and named New Amsterdam 1614; captured by English and the name changed to New York, Aug. 27, 1664; surrendered to the English during War of Independence, Sept. 15, 1776; British evacuate, Nov. 25, 1783; made capital of New York state 1784. [Refer Harper, *Encyclopædia of U.S. History*.]

New York, State of (U.S.A.). Discovered by Henry Hudson 1609. For early history *see* New Netherland. Constitution adopted and state government estab. April 20, 1777; slavery abolished 1817. [Refer Harper, *Encyclopædia of U.S. History*.]

New Zealand. Discovered by Tasman 1642; surveyed by Capt. Cook 1769; ceded to Great Britain by Treaty of Waitangi 1840, and it was colonised the same year; self-government granted 1852; Wellington made capital 1865; called Dominion of N.Z. 1907. [Refer Martin, *British Colonies*.]

Nicaragua (C. America). Discovered by Columbus in 1502; explored by Gil Gonzalez Dakla 1522; declared itself independent 1821; joined Federal Union of the five Central States 1823; independence acknowledged by Spain 1850; present constitution estab. Aug. 19, 1858; war with Honduras, Feb.-April 1907. [Refer Belt, *The Naturalist in Nicaragua ;* art. in *Encyclopædia Britannica*.]

Nice (France). Fd. by the Phocæans of Marseilles about 2000 years ago; Saracens repulsed 729; burnt by Saracens 880; attacked by Francis I. and Barbarossa 1543; captured by Duke of Guise 1600; by Catinat 1691; res. to Savoy 1696; besieged by French 1705 and captured; by Treaty of Utrecht is again res. to Savoy 1713; again captured by French 1795, who owned it until 1814, when it reverted to Sardinia; finally ceded to France 1860 by treaty. [Refer art. in *Encyclopædia Britannica*.]

Nice, Truce of. Of ten months' duration arranged in June 1538 between Charles V. and Francis I. [Refer Tanner, *The Renaissance and the Reformation*.]

Nicene Creed, or **Constantinopolitan Creed.** Based on creed of Eusebius 325, and revised by Council of Nicæa 325.

Nigeria (Africa). Includes what was formerly the Niger Coast Protectorate, constituted Jan. 1, 1900; Lagos added 1906.

Nile. *See* Bruce's Travels.

Nobel Prize. Awarded annually for excellence in various branches of learning and the furtherance of universal peace; fd. by Alfred Nobel (1833-96); first awards made in 1901.

Non-Compounders. A section of the Jacobite party formed about 1692; they expressed their willingness to restore James II. without any conditions whatsoever.

Nonconformists. Name taken by Puritans after Act of Uniformity was passed, Aug. 24, 1662. The following are the principal acts passed against the Nonconformists:—

Conventicle Act, forbidding assemblies for worship other than those of the Established Church 1664.

Five Mile Act forbade expelled ministers except those who would subscribe to the Act of Uniformity to reside within five miles of any corporate town 1665.

Corporation Act, ordering all holders of municipal office to renounce the Covenant and take the sacrament according to the Established Church form 1661.

These acts were all known as the Clarendon Code. Charles II. in 1672 proclaimed the Declaration of Indulgence, which suspended all these acts and those against Roman Catholics. Again proclaimed by James II. 1687.

The Toleration Act passed in 1689 allowed freedom of worship to Nonconformists.

Occasional Conformity Bill in 1711 prevented Nonconformist ministers from accepting any municipal office, although they might have taken the sacrament according to the Established Church form; repealed 1718.

Schism Act prevented any person keeping a public or private school unless he was a member of the Church of England and licensed by the bishop of the diocese; repealed 1718.

Test and Corporation Acts repealed 1828.

University Test Act allowed Nonconformists and Roman Catholics to take degrees at Oxford and Cambridge Universities 1871.

Nonjurors. Clergy in England and Scotland who refused to take the oath of allegiance to William and Mary. An act passed Aug. 1, 1689, required them to take the oath within six months or else suffer deprivation. In Scotland all the bishops refused the oath, and Episcopacy was abolished. [Refer Overton, *The Nonjurors*.]

Norham, Conference of. Between Edward I. and the English barons and the competitors for the Crown of Scotland, June 1291. The question of the disposal of the Scottish Crown was settled, Nov. 1292.

Normandy (France). Rollo appointed first duke A.D. 912; becomes a province of England under William the Conqueror (Duke of Normandy) 1066; united to Crown of France 1204; English claim formally renounced 1259; conquered by Edward III. 1346; by Henry V. 1418; English finally driven out 1450. [Refer Palgrave, *History of Normandy and of England*.]

North Administration, Jan. 1770. Lord North, First Lord, resigned Mar. 30, 1782; succeeded by Coalition Ministry (*q.v.*).

North, The Council of the. Instit. in 1536 by Henry VIII. orig. to try persons connected with the Pilgrimage of Grace (*q.v.*); abolished by Long Parliament 1641. [Refer Gardiner, *History of England*.]

North Briton Newspaper. Instit. by John Wilkes. " Number 45," the issue dated April 23, 1763, was publicly burnt by the hangman, Dec. 3, 1763, as containing a libel against the king. *See* Wilkes Case.

North Carolina (U.S.A.). Coasts said to have been discovered by Cabot 1498; named after Charles II. of England, who in 1663 granted the region to certain of his courtiers; settled by English 1670; made a royal province 1729; declared itself independent of Great Britain, May 1775; state constitution adopted, Dec. 1, 1776; admitted to the Union as a state 1868. [Refer Harper, *Encyclopædia of U.S. History*.]

North Dakota (U.S.A.). Colonised by French 1780; claimed by the U.S. 1823; admitted to the Union as a state, Nov. 3, 1889. [Refer Harper, *Encyclopædia of U.S. History*.]

North Sea Fisheries Convention. Entered into by Great Britain, Germany, Holland, Belgium, and France, on May 6, 1882; supplementary convention signed, Nov. 16, 1887.

North Sea Outrage. On the night of Oct. 21, 1904, the Russian Baltic fleet fired on some English fishing boats in the North Sea. An International Commission of Inquiry was held on the affair from Nov. 22, 1904, to Feb. 25, 1905. [Refer *Annual Register*.]

North-West Frontier Province (India). Created Oct. 25, 1901.

Norway (Europe). Origin lost in obscurity. Olaf Trætelia, expelled from Sweden, estab. a colony in Vermeland A.D. 630; Christianity intro. 998; Norway divided between Kings of Sweden and Denmark 1000; reunited as one kingdom 1016; after this date it was frequently united and disunited with Sweden and Denmark; ceded to Sweden by Frederick VI. of Denmark 1814; recognised by King Oscar of Sweden as a separate state, Oct. 1905; Prince Charles of Denmark became king under title of King Haakon VII. Nov. 18, 1905.

Norwich (Norfolk, England). Mentioned in Saxon Chronicle; cathedral fd. 1096; dedicated 1101; charter granted to the city 1158 by Henry II.; further extended by Richard I. 1194. [Refer Hudson, *Records of the City of Norwich*.]

Nova Scotia (Canada). Discovered by John Cabot 1497; partly colonised by the French 1598; French settlements destroyed by English from Virginia 1614; granted by James I. to William Alexander, Earl of Stirling, 1621; ceded to France by Treaty of Breda 1667; captured by English 1689; res. to France by Treaty of Ryswick 1697; Port Royal captured by English under Gen. Nicholson 1710; formally ceded to England by Treaty of Utrecht 1713; became part of the Dominion of Canada 1867. [Refer Martin, *British Colonies*.]

Noyon, Treaty of. Between Charles of Spain and Francis I. signed 1516; by it Francis gave up all claims to Naples, and France's right to Milan was acknowledged. [Refer Tanner, *The Renaissance and the Reformation*.]

O

Oaths, Parliamentary. First imposed in 1679, when it was stated that no member could take his seat until the oaths of allegiance, supremacy, and abjuration were taken; by the act of 1829 Roman Catholics could use a special form of oath; in 1866 the three oaths were combined in one, and in 1868 the form included all religious denominations. [Refer art. in Low and Pulling, *Dicty. of English History*.]

Occasional Conformity Act, and bill against. *See* Nonconformists.

October Club. Instit. in England in 1710. It was Tory in politics and attacked the Whig policy.

Ohio (U.S.A.). First explored by La Salle about 1680; north of the O. river was held by French until 1763, when it was surrendered to the English; admitted to the Union as a state, April 30, 1802. [Refer Harper, *Encyclopædia of U.S. History*.]

Oklahoma (U.S.A.). Territory set apart by Congress 1834; repurchased from Indian tribes 1889; admitted to Union as a state, Nov. 16, 1907. [Refer Harper, *Encyclopædia of U.S. History*.]

Old-Age Pensions (Great Britain). First proposed in 1772 by Francis Maseres, and again in 1787 by Mr. Mark Rolle, M.P.; other schemes were proposed, notably when Mr. W. E. Gladstone referred the matter to a royal commission in 1893, but nothing was done in the matter until 1908, when the Old-Age Pension Act was passed, which came into force on Jan. 1, 1909. [Refer art. in *Encyclopædia Britannica*.]

Old Catholics. Those Roman Catholics who refused to accept the decrees of papal infallibility passed by the Vatican Council of 1870. *See* Jansenists.

Oldenburg (Germany). An independent state in 1180; after 1667 it passed into the hands of the Danish royal family until 1773, when it passed to Grand-Duke Paul of Russia; shortly afterwards it became a duchy until 1866, when it became part of Prussia. [Refer art. in *Encyclopædia Britannica*.]

Olive Branch Petition. Drawn up in July 1775 by the American colonies previous to the War of Independence. It was presented to the government, but no notice was taken of it. [Refer Bancroft, *Hist. of American Revolution*.]

Olympia (Greece). The site of the famous Olympic games. The earliest building on the site is the temple of Hera, which dates from about 1000 B.C. After the year A.D. 393 the festival of the games was discontinued. [Refer Smith, *Classical Dicty*.]

Oneida Community (or Bible Communists). A religious sect fd. in Oneida (U.S.A.) by John Humphrey Noyes (1811-86); in 1834 he began to preach his religious views; a conference of several ecclesiastical bodies held at Syracuse University on Feb. 14, 1879, denounced the movement, but it flourished nevertheless. [Refer art. in *Encyclopædia Britannica*.]

Ontario (Canada). Fd. by emigrants from the U.S. after the latter had declared its independence; made into a separate province in 1791 and known as Upper Canada, but in 1867 it again received its original name. [Refer to works quoted at end of art. on Canada.]

Oporto (Portugal). Of very early origin; captured by Visigoths A.D. 540; by the Moors 716; recaptured by Christians 997; captured by the Duke of Wellington, May 12, 1809; besieged by Dom Miguel, 1832-3. *See* Portugal.

Orange Free State (S. Africa). Inhabited by the Dutch Boers 1836; annexed to British Crown 1848; given up to the Boers 1854; became part of British empire after Boer War as the Orange River Colony 1902; granted responsible government 1907; joined Union of 1910 as the Orange Free State.

Orangemen, The. A term applied to the upholders of revolution principles in Ireland in 1689; the first orange lodge instit. Sept. 21, 1796; dissolved in 1825; in 1836, however, they were exceedingly strong, and in 1869 their grand-master was arrested for violating the Party Procession Act. [Refer McCarthy, *History of Our Own Times*.]

Oratory of St. Philip Neri, Congregation of the (or Oratorians). A Roman Catholic order fd. by Philip Neri (1515-95); the order was confirmed by papal bull in 1575, and again in 1612; their first congregation in England was estab. in 1848. [Refer Schaff-Herzog, *New Encyclopædia of Religious Knowledge*.]

Ordainers, The Lords. Consisted of earls, barons, and bishops appointed in Mar. 1310; they were formed for the purpose of reforming the laws of the realm.

Ordeal, Trial by. Was introduced into England at the very earliest times; it was abolished in 1215. [Refer Stubbs, *Constitutional History*.]

Orders in Council (Great Britain). Issued by the sovereign on the advice of the privy council; first issued in the 18th century; orders in council were issued by George III. in 1807 in reply to Napoleon's Berlin decree (*q.v.*); owing to fear of famine in Sept. 1766, orders in council were issued to prohibit exportation of wheat. [Refer art. in Low and Pulling, *Dicty. of English History*.]

Orders of Knighthood. *See* Knighthood, Orders of.

Oregon (U.S.A.). Columbia River discovered by Captain Gray, May 7, 1792; fur-trading post estab. at head of river in 1811; provisional government formed 1843; created a territory 1848; disputes with Indians 1855-6; admitted to Union as a state, Feb. 14, 1859. [Refer Harper, *Encyclopædia of U.S. History*.]

Oregon Question, The. A dispute which occurred between England and the U.S.A. with reference to the boundary line between Canada and the U.S. eastwards from the great lakes and also westwards from the Rocky Mountains; convention regarding the matter concluded, Nov. 1818, for ten years, and renewed, Aug. 6, 1827; The matter was finally settled by arbitration in 1872. [Refer Molesworth, *Hist. of England.*]

Orkney Islands (N. of Scotland). Possessed by Northmen in 9th century; granted to the Earls of Angus 1231; pledged by Christian I. of Denmark for the payment of the dowry of his daughter Margaret, betrothed to James III. of Scotland in 1470; the money was never paid, so the islands passed to the Scottish Crown. [Refer Barry, *History of Orkney.*]

Orleanists. A French political party who supported the royal claims of the House of Orleans, fd. shortly after the French Revolution; after the revolution of 1848 the party practically ceased to exist.

Orleans (France). Orig. *Aurelianum.* Vainly besieged by Attila the Hun A.D. 451; captured by Clovis 498; first ecclesiastical council assembled at 511; entered by Joan of Arc, April 29, 1429; besieged by the Duke of Guise 1563; held by Huguenots 1567-8; surrendered to Henry IV. of France 1594; occupied by Prussians 1815 and 1870. [Refer art. in *Encyclopædia Britannica.*]

Orsini Question. Caused by the attempt of Felix Orsini and his gang on the life of the French emperor on Jan. 14, 1858; these men came from London, where they had arranged their plot; this caused the French minister of foreign affairs to write a very strong letter of protest to the French ambassador in London, resulting in the resignation of the government, who saw fit to introduce a bill propitiating the French government; the matter was settled under the next Derby administration. [Refer *Life and Letters of Queen Victoria.*]

Orthodox Eastern Church. *See* Greek Church.

Orvieto (Italy). Captured by Belisarius A.D. 539; Pope Hadrian IV. resided at, 1157; cathedral commenced before 1285; town became part of kingdom of Italy 1866. [Refer Hutton, *Cities of Umbria.*]

Osborne House (Isle of Wight). Purchased by Queen Victoria from Lady Isabella Blackford 1845; Queen Victoria died 1901; presented to the nation by Edward VII. as a convalescent home for officers of the army and navy 1902; the Royal Naval College at Osborne was opened in 1903.

Ottawa (Canada). Discovered by Champlain 1613; first permanent settlement made 1800; orig. known as *Bytown*; the name was changed to Ottawa in 1854, when it was incorp. as a city; made capital of Canada 1858; first parliament opened at 1865. *See* Canada.

Owens' College (Manchester). Fd. by John Owens, who left on his death in 1846 a sum for the institution of a college; opened in 1851; new buildings constructed 1873. [Refer Thompson, *Owens' College*.]

Oxford (Oxfordshire, England). Mentioned in the English Chronicle A.D. 912; Canute held a national council at, 1017; charter granted by Henry II. 1199; Mad Parliament (*q.v.*) held at 1258; captured by Charles I. 1644. [Refer C. W. Boase, *Oxford*.]

Oxford, Provisions of. The schemes drawn up by the Mad Parliament of Henry III.'s reign in 1258 for the reorganising of the affairs of the realm; they were annulled in 1261 by the king himself. [Refer Stubbs, *Constitutional History of England*.]

Oxford, University of. Fd. early in the 12th century; frequent charters granted, the most notable being in 1523 by Henry VIII.; reorganised during reign of Elizabeth 1571; privileges confirmed 1635; the following are the colleges and halls, with the dates of their foundation, together with their founders:—

All Souls' College, fd. by Archbishop Chichele in 1437.

Balliol College, fd. by John Balliol and Devorguilla Balliol, mother of John Balliol, King of Scotland, about 1268.

Brasenose College, fd. by William Smyth, Bishop of Lincoln, and Sir Richard Sutton 1509.

Christ Church College, projected by Cardinal Wolsey and fd. by Henry VIII. in 1546.

Corpus Christi College, fd. by Richard Foxe, Bishop of Winchester, in 1516.

Exeter College, fd. by Walter de Stapledon, Bishop of Exeter, in 1314.

Hertford College, orig. fd. by Dr. Richard Newton 1740; dissolved 1805; refounded by T. C. Baring, M.P., in 1874.

Jesus College, fd. by Queen Elizabeth 1571; endowed further by Sir Leoline Jenkins 1661.

Keble College, fd. in memory of John Keble in 1870.

Lincoln College, fd. by Richard Fleming, Bishop of Lincoln, in 1427; refounded by Thomas Rotherham, Archbishop of York, in 1478.

Magdalen College, fd. by William Waynflete, Bishop of Winchester, in 1458.

Merton College, fd. at Malden, Surrey, 1264; transferred to Oxford by Walter de Merton, Bishop of Rochester, in 1274.

New College, fd. by William of Wykeham, Bishop of Winchester, 1379.

New Inn Hall, fd. about 1369; closed in 1887.

Oriel College, fd. nominally by King Edward II., but really by Adam de Brome in 1326.

Pembroke College, fd. by Thomas Tesdale and Richard Wightwick in 1624.

Queen's College, fd. by Robert de Eglesfeld, Chaplain to Queen Philippa, consort of Edward III., in 1340.

Ruskin Hall, 1899.

St. Alban Hall, fd. about 1230, united to Merton College 1882.

St. Catharine's Hall (non-collegiate) 1868.

St. Edmund Hall, fd. about 1229.

St. John's College, fd. by Sir Thomas White in 1555.

St. Mary Hall, fd. by Oriel College 1333; united to Oriel Coll. 1882.

Trinity College, fd. by Sir Thomas Pope in 1554.

University College, orig. in an endowment left by William of Durham in 1249; supposed to have been fd. by Alfred 872.

Wadham College, fd. by Dorothy and Nicholas Wadham in 1612.

Worcester College, fd. by Sir Thomas Cookes of Worcestershire 1714; originally Gloucester Hall.

Other colleges, etc., *not* affiliated to the University of Oxford:—

Private Halls:

Marcon's Hall }
Parker's Hall } Fd. under licence; statute passed in 1882 (a
Pope's Hall } substitution for one of 1855).

Theological Institutions:—

St. Stephen's House, fd. 1876.

Wycliffe Hall, fd. 1878.

Pusey House, fd. 1884.

Mansfield College, transferred to Oxon. 1889.

Manchester College, fd. 1893.

[Refer *Oxford College Histories.*]

Oxygen. First obtained in 1727 by Stephen Hales; it was first described by J. Priestley in 1774; the name " oxygen " was first used by Lavoisier about 1775.

P

Padua (Italy). Orig. the Roman *Patavium*, came under the Roman supremacy 215 B.C.; under rule of the Franks A.D. 774; the university was fd. by the Emperor Frederick II. in 1221, and the present buildings date from 1493-1552; the town was conquered by the Venetians in 1405, who ruled it until 1797, when it was ceded to Austria; incorp. with kingdom of Italy 1866.

Palatinate (Germany). The count palatine of the Rhine was a royal official first mentioned in the 10th century; the P. separated from Bavaria 1294; was devastated by Bavarians and Spaniards 1622; by the French 1688; finally united with Bavaria 1815.

Palermo (Sicily). Orig. *Panormus*. Conquered by Pyrrhus 276 B.C.; by the Romans 254 B.C.; by the Vandals A.D. 440; by the Saracens 832; by Normans 1072; the cathedral built by Archbishop Walter, an Englishman, 1169-85; university fd. 1447; revolts against the Bourbon kings of Naples 1820 and 1848; incorp. with kingdom of Italy 1860. [Refer Freeman, *History of Sicily*.]

Palestine. *See* Crusades.

Palestine Exploration Fund, The. Fd. in 1865 through the exertions of Colonel Sir Charles Wilson and Colonel Sir Charles Warren.

Palmerston Administrations. Henry John Temple, Viscount Palmerston (1784-1865), at the head. (1) Feb. 1855-Feb. 1858, followed by Derby Administration; (2) together with Lord John Russell, June 1859-65; Earl Russell then continued the Administration. [Refer *Letters of Queen Victoria*.]

Pan-American Conference. Arranged by an act passed by the U.S. Congress in 1888; Conference assembled, Oct. 2, 1889; as a result ten of the nations signed an arbitration treaty in April 1890. [Refer Harper, *Encyclopædia of U.S. History*.]

Pan-Anglican Synod. A conference of English, Colonial, and American bishops which first met at Lambeth Palace, London, Sept. 24-27, 1867; a second conference met July 2, 1878; a third, July 7-28, 1888; a fourth, July 1897-Aug. 1897; Pan-Anglican Congress in London, June 1908.

Panama Canal. The scheme for joining the Atlantic and Pacific Oceans by means of a canal through the Isthmus of Panama has been discussed for nearly 500 years; in 1879, through the mediation of Ferdinand de Lesseps, the builder of the Suez Canal, an International Congress was convened to discuss the matter; a company was formed, and in Feb. 1881 the work of surveying was commenced. A large sum of money was subscribed, but owing to complications the company was forced to go into liquidation on

Jan. 1, 1889; during 1892 and 1893, as a result of inquiries, some of the promoters of the scheme were fined and imprisoned; new company formed 1899; on Jan. 22, 1903, the Panama Canal treaty was signed at Washington between the U.S.A. and Columbia; estimated to be completed by 1915.

Papacy, The. The first Pope to claim superiority over Western Christendom was Innocent I. 402-17; the temporal power of the papacy was not, however, estab. until the 8th century, when Pepin le Bref and Charlemagne conferred estates on the Pope; Charlemagne was crowned by Leo III. on Christmas Day, 800, this being the first act indicative of the Pope's temporal power; under Innocent III. (1198-1216) and his immediate successors the papacy reached the summit of its greatness; schism of east and west 1054; right of papal election first vested in the cardinals 1059; the quarrel concerning investiture begun in 11th century under Gregory VII. was terminated in 1122 by Concordat of Worms; it broke out again and did not come finally to an end till Conradin's death 1268; in 1305, due in part to the influence of the French king, the popes removed from Rome to Avignon and did not return till 1377; the schism of the west lasted from 1378-1417, during which period the anti-popes resided at Avignon and elsewhere; in 1799 Pius VI. was carried from Rome as a prisoner of war by the French; Pius IX. (1846-78), owing to the revolution in Rome, escaped from the city in Nov. 1848, and went to Gaeta; he, however, returned in April 1850; the states of the Church were annexed to the kingdom of Italy in 1870; the doctrine of PAPAL INFALLIBILITY was declared part of the faith of the Church on July 18, 1870, by a Vatican Council; the temporal power of the papacy ceased to exist on Sept. 21, 1870, when Victor Emmanuel's army entered Rome; rupture of diplomatic relations between the French government and the Vatican 1904; encyclical on modernism issued 1907; encyclical of 1910 protested against in Germany, and Prussian bishops ordered to and abstain from its publication; the power of the Pope has been limited from time to time: by the Pragmatic Sanction 1438; the Concordat 1516; the Declaration du Clergé de France 1682; and the Concordat of 1801. The following is a list of the Popes and Bishops of Rome:—

42. St. Peter	192. St. Victor
67. St. Linus	202. St. Zephirinus
78. St. Anacletus	218. St. Calixtus
91. St. Clement	222. [Vacant]
100. St. Evaristus	222. St. Urban
109. St. Alexander	230. St. Pontianus
119. St. Sixtus	235. St. Anterus
128. St. Telesphorus	236. St. Fabian
139. St. Hyginus	250. [Vacant]
142. St. Pius	251. St. Cornelius
157. St. Anicetus	252. St. Lucius; *Novatianus*,
168. St. Soterus	antipope
176. St. Eleutherus	253. St. Stephen

PAPACY, THE (*continued*)—

257. Sixtus II.
259. Dionysius
269. Felix I.
275. Eutychianus
283. Caius
296. Marcellinus
304. [Vacant]
308. Marcellus I.
310. St. Eusebius
311. St. Melchiades
314. Silvester
336. Marcus
337. Julius
352. Liberius
356. *Felix II.*, antipope
366. Damasus
384. Siricius
398. Anastasius
402. Innocent I.
417. St. Zosimus
418. St. Boniface I.
422. St. Celestine I.
432. Sixtus III.
440. St. Leo I. (the Great)
461. St. Hilary
468. St. Simplicius
483. St. Felix III.
492. St. Gelasius
496. St. Anastasius II.
498. St. Symmachus
514. *Laurentius*, antipope
514. St. Hormisdas
523. St. John I.
526. St. Felix IV.
530. Boniface II.
533. John II.
535. Agapetus
536. Silverius
537. Vigilius
555. Pelagius I.
560. John III.
573. [Vacant]
574. Benedict I.
578. Pelagius II.
590. Gregory I. (the Great)
604. Sabinianus
606. Boniface III.
607. Boniface IV.
614. Deusdedit
617. Boniface V.

625. Honorius I.
639. [Vacant]
640. Severinus
640. John IV.
642. Theodorus I.
649. Martin I.
654. St. Eugenius I.
657. Vitalianus
672. Adeodatus
676. Domnus I.
678. Agathon
682. Leo II.
683. [Vacant]
684. Benedict II.
685. John V.
686. Conon
686. *Theodore* and *Pascal*, anti-
          popes
687. Sergius
701. John VI.
705. John VII.
708. Sisinnius
708. Constantine
715. St. Gregory II.
731. Gregory III.
741. Zacharias
752. Stephen II.
757. Paul I.
768. Stephen III.
772. Adrian I.
795. Leo III.
816. Stephen IV.
817. Pascal I.
824. Eugenius II.
827. Valentinus
827. Gregory IV.
844. Sergius II.
847. Leo IV.
855. Benedict III.
858. Nicholas I. (the Great)
867. Adrian II.
872. John VIII.
882. Martin II.
884. Adrian III.
885. Stephen V.
891. Formosus
896. Boniface VI.
897. *Romanus*, antipope
897. Stephen VI.
898. Theodorus II.

PAPACY, THE (*continued*)—

898. John IX.	1119. Calixtus II.
900. Benedict IV.	1124. Honorius II
903. Leo V.	1130. Innocent II.
904. Sergius III.	1143. Celestine II.
911. Anastasius III.	1144. Lucius II.
913. Landonius	1145. St. Eugenius III.
914. John X.	1153. Anastasius IV.
928. Leo VI.	1154. Adrian IV.
929. Stephen VII.	1159. Alexander III.
931. John XI.	1181. Lucius III.
936. Leo VII.	1185. Urban III.
939. Stephen VIII.	1187. Gregory VIII.
942. Martin III.	1187. Clement III.
946. Agapetus II.	1191. Celestine III.
956. John XII.	1198. Innocent III.
963. Leo VIII.	1216. Honorious III.
964. Benedict V.	1227. Gregory IX.
965. John XIII.	1241. Celestine IV.
972. Benedict VI.	1241. [Vacant]
974. Boniface VII.	1243. Innocent IV.
974. Domnus II.	1254. Alexander IV.
975. Benedict VII.	1261. Urban IV.
983. John XIV.	1265. Clement IV.
984. John XV.	1268-70. [Vacant]
985. John XVI.	1271. Gregory X.
996. Gregory V.	1276. Innocent V.
999. Silvester II.	1276. Adrian V.
1003. John XVII.	1276. Vicedominus
1003. John XVIII.	1276. John XXI.
1009. Sergius IV.	1277. Nicholas III.
1012. Benedict VIII.	1281. Martin IV.
1024. John XIX.	1285. Honorius IV.
1045. Gregory VI.	1288. Nicholas IV.
1046. Clement II.	1292-94. [Vacant]
1048. Damasus II.	1294. Celestine V.
1048. St. Leo IX.	1294. Boniface VIII.
1054. [Vacant]	1303. Benedict XI.
1055. Victor II.	1304. [Vacant]
1057. Stephen IX.	*1305. Clement V.
1058. *Benedict X.*, antipope	1314-16. [Vacant]
1058. Nicholas II.	*1316. John XXII.
1061. Alexander II.	*1334. Benedict XII.
1073. Gregory VII. (Hildebrand)	*1342. Clement VI.
	*1352. Innocent VI.
1085. [Vacant]	*1362. Urban V.
1086. Victor III.	*1370. Gregory XI.
1088. Urban II.	1378. Urban VI.; *Clement VII.*
1099. Pascal II.	antipope
1118. Gelasius II.	1389. Boniface IX.

*The popes of the Avignon period.

Papacy, The (continued)—

1394. *Benedict XIII.*, antipope	1590. Gregory XIV.
1404. Innocent VII.	1591. Innocent IX.
1406. Gregory XII.	1592. Clement VIII.
1409. Alexander V.	1605. Leo XI.
1410. John XXIII.	1605. Paul V.
1417. Martin V.	1621. Gregory XV.
1431. Eugenius IV.	1623. Urban VIII.
1439. *Felix V.*, antipope	1644. Innocent X.
1447. Nicholas V.	1655. Alexander VII.
1455. Calixtus III.	1667. Clement IX.
1458. Pius II. (Æneas Silvius)	1670. Clement X.
1464. Paul II.	1676. Innocent XI.
1471. Sixtus IV.	1689. Alexander VIII.
1484. Innocent VIII.	1691. Innocent XII.
1492. Alexander VI.	1700. Clement XI.
1503. Pius III.	1720. Innocent XIII.
1503. Julius II.	1724. Benedict XIII.
1513. Leo X.	1730. Clement XII.
1522. Adrian VI.	1740. Benedict XIV.
1523. Clement VII.	1758. Clement XIII.
1534. Paul III.	1769. Clement XIV.
1550. Julius III.	1775. Pius VI.
1555. Marcellus II.	1800. Pius VII.
1555. Paul IV.	1823. Leo XII.
1559. Pius IV.	1829. Pius VIII.
1566. Pius V.	1831. Gregory XVI.
1572. Gregory XIII.	1846. Pius IX.
1585. Sixtus V.	1878. Leo XIII.
1590. Urban VII.	1903. Pius X.

See also Anti-Popes, Rome, Investiture, etc. [Refer Ranke, *History of the Popes ;* Pastor, *History of the Popes.*]

Paraguay (S. America). Discovered by Juan Diaz de Solis 1515; explored by Cabot 1526; first settlement in, by Pedro de Mendoza 1536; declared its independence of Spain 1811; new constitution proclaimed 1844; war with combined forces of Brazil, Argentina, and Uruguay 1865-70, when Lopez the Younger was killed; the present constitution proclaimed 1870; settlement in, of 500 Australian socialists 1893. [Refer art. in *Chambers's Encyclopædia.*]

Paris (France). First mentioned in Cæsar's *Commentaries* under title of *Lutetia*, a settlement of a Gallic tribe known as the Parisii; in 53 B.C. it became a Roman town of some importance; Clovis makes it his capital A.D. 507; between 1180 and 1223 the church of Notre Dame was commenced and the University of Paris fd.; revolution of P. headed by Etienne Marcel 1358; reconstruction of the city under Napoleon III. 1851-70. *See* France, Bastille, etc. [Refer *Paris*, Mediæval Towns Series.]

Paris, Declaration of. Drawn up at the Congress of Paris in 1856. It settled four important points of international law.

Paris, Treaties of. (1) Between France, Spain, and England, by which the Seven Years' War was ended and Canada ceded to England, signed Feb. 1763; (2) between the allies, after the abdication of Napoleon in May 1814; (3) after the close of Napoleon's final campaign in Flanders, Nov. 20, 1815; (4) between Russia, Turkey, England, France, and Sardinia, at the close of the Crimean War, signed Mar. 30, 1856; (5) between England and Persia, amongst other things it abolished the slave trade in the Persian Gulf, signed Mar. 3, 1857; (6) terminating the Spanish-American War, Dec. 10, 1898.

Parliament of Great Britain and Ireland (*see also* Lords, House of, and Commons, House of, and Speakers of the House of Commons). The word is first mentioned in England in the statute of Westminster 1272; by the provisions of Oxford (*q.v.*) in 1258 it was enacted that the parliament should sit three times a year; in Jan. 1265, there was a meeting for the first time of citizens and burgesses together with knights of the shire, but it was not until Nov. 27, 1295, that writs were issued by Edward I. for an assembly, which would properly represent the nation; Acts of Parliament were first printed in 1501; House of Lords (*q.v.*) abolished 1649; first Parliament of Great Britain meets Oct. 23, 1707; Septennial Act brought in, May 7, 1716; first Parliament of the United Kingdom of Great Britain and Ireland 1801; Catholic Emancipation Bill 1829; Reform Bill, 1832; Houses of Parliament destroyed by fire, Oct. 16, 1834; new buildings commenced 1840; new House of Lords completed, April 15, 1845; new House of Commons completed, Nov. 4, 1852; Act for enabling Jews to sit 1858; Parliamentary Elections Act passed, July 31, 1868; closure adopted 1882. [Refer Parry, *Parliaments and Councils*.]

Parnell Commission. Caused through letters published in the *Times* on April 18, 1887, said to have been written by Mr. Charles S. Parnell (1846-91). These letters excused the Phœnix Park murders. Owing to a libel action against the *Times* a commission was appointed, which reported on Feb. 13, 1890. It acquitted Mr. Parnell of all charges. [Refer art. in Low and Pulling, *Dicty. of English History*.]

Partition Treaties. Attempted to settle the question of the Spanish succession, after the death of the King Charles II. (1) Between England, France, and Holland; it appointed the Viceroy of the Spanish Netherlands to be regent during the minority of Charles II., signed Oct. 11, 1698; (2) Charles II. *d.* in Feb. 1699, so a second treaty was signed on Oct. 11, 1700, appointing the Archduke Charles of Austria king; the treaty, however, was not popular and the War of the Spanish Succession resulted (*q.v.*). *See* Spain. [Refer Mahon, *War of Spanish Succession*.]

Passau, Agreement of. Between the Protestant states of the empire and the Roman Catholics signed July 29 and Aug. 15, 1552. [Refer Ranke, *History of the Reformation in Germany*.]

Passionists. A Roman Catholic congregation of priests fd. by St. Paul of the Cross in Rome 1714, when it received the sanction of Pope Benedict XIV.; the brotherhood came to England in 1842, and to America in 1852.

Paston Letters, The. A series of letters written to or by the Pastons, a famous Norfolk family, between 1422-1509; they give an insight into English life of the 15th century, and are invaluable for this reason.

Patagonia (S. America). Since 1881 part of the Argentine Republic (*q.v.*); coasts explored by Magellan in 1520.

Patents, Laws regarding (Great Britain). First granted for exclusive privilege of printing books 1591; properties and rights of inventors first protected in 1623; this law was repealed and a new act passed known as the Patent Act in 1883; amended 1885, 1886, 1888, 1901, 1902, and 1907. [Refer art. in *Ency. Britannica*.]

Patents, Laws regarding (International). A select committee of the House of Commons in 1872 recommended inquiries respecting the international protection of patents; in 1873 at Vienna, and in 1878 at Paris, international congresses met, and on Mar. 20, 1883, an "International Convention for the Protection of Industrial Property" was signed at Paris; most of the civilised countries of the world signed this.

Patents, Laws regarding (U.S.A.). First Patent Act passed by Congress, April 10, 1790; revised 1793; all previous laws repealed and new one passed in 1836. [Refer Harper, *Encyclopædia of U.S. History.*]

Patrick, The Most Illustrious Order of St. An Irish order of knighthood estab. by George III. on Feb. 5, 1783; enlarged 1833.

Paulicians. A religious reforming sect fd. in the 5th century in Asia Minor; they were persecuted as heretics by numerous emperors and ecclesiastics, but notwithstanding they flourished, and in 969 a colony of them settled at Philippolis. [Refer Finlay, *History of Greece.*]

Paul's Cathedral, St. (London). According to tradition was fd. on the site of a temple dedicated to Diana; the early history is, however, doubtful; in 1083 Bishop Maurice undertook the construction of a new cathedral, which was completed about 1284; in 1561 it was burned and Inigo Jones was instructed with the task of restoration; in 1666, however, after its destruction by the Great Fire, Dr. Christopher Wren was entrusted with the scheme of rebuilding the cathedral, and in 1675 the foundation stone of the new building was laid, and the whole edifice was completed 1710. [Refer Stirling Taylor, *Historical Guide to London.*]

Paul's School, St. (London). Fd. by Dean Colet in 1512; the schoolhouse was destroyed by fire 1666, and rebuilt by Wren; removed to Hammersmith, April 1884.

Peace Conferences (International). *See also* Hague. (1) Met at the Hague 1899; arbitration court formed at the Conference, and fd. July 29, 1899; (2) met at the Hague, June 15-Oct. 18, 1907.

Peace Preservation Act. Intro. into Parliament on Mar. 17, 1870, to prevent certain outrages which were occurring in Ireland. It was allowed to lapse in 1880; new act 1881-87.

Peasants' War. *See* Jacquerie.

Peculiar People. A religious faith-healing sect fd. in London by John Banyard and J. W. Bridges in 1838.

Peel Administrations. Sir Robert Peel (1788-1850) at the head. (1) Dec. 1834-April 1835; (2) Sept. 1841-June 1846. [Refer *Life and Letters of Queen Victoria.*]

Peep-of-Day Boys. An Irish Protestant secret society fd. about 1785.

Pekin or **Peking** (China). Captured by Khitan Tartars A.D. 986; recaptured by Chinese in 12th century; again captured by Tartars 1151; first settlement of foreigners in 1860; during 1900 the city was the scene of the Boxer riots and the siege of the Legations. *See* China.

Pelagians. The followers of Pelagius (*circa* 360-420), a British theologian. Pelagius was summoned before a synod of bishops at Lydda 415, who were satisfied with his explanations and refused to pronounce his views as heretical. Pope Innocent, however, in 416 upheld the opponents of Pelagius, amongst whom was St. Augustine. The doctrine of Pelagianism was finally condemned in 418 by the Western Church, and in 431 by the Eastern Church. [Refer Harnack, *History of Dogma.*]

Pelham Administration. Henry Pelham (1696-1754) at the head. Formed Aug. 1743; dissolved at the death of Pelham, Mar. 6, 1754. [Refer Hunt and Poole, *Political History of England.*]

Penang (Straits Settlements). Ceded to East India Company by the Sultan of Kedah 1785; made a penal settlement 1796; incorp. with Singapore and Malacca 1826; made capital of Straits Settlements 1837. [Refer Swettenham, *British Malaya.*]

Peninsular War, The (1808-14). Between France and England, begun in consequence of the alliance signed between Spain and England in July 1808, when the Duke of Wellington, then Sir Arthur Wellesley, was dispatched to Spain with troops; the war commenced with the b. of Vimiera on Aug. 21, 1808, when Wellington defeated Junot, and ended with the b. of Toulouse, April 10, 1814, when Wellington defeated Soult. [Refer Napier, *History of the Peninsular War.*]

Pennsylvania (U.S.A.). Fd. by William Penn, who in 1681 obtained a large grant of land in America from Charles II. In Sept. 1682 Penn himself embarked on the *Welcome* for America, and landed on Oct. 28 of the same year; adopted an independent constitution, Sept. 28, 1776, and admitted to the Union as a state. [Refer Harper, *Encyclopædia of U.S. History.*]

Penny, Common. *See* Common Penny.

Penny. Intro. into England by King Offa 735 and made of silver; halfpennies were first struck in Edward I.'s reign (1272-1307); copper pence first struck in 1797; bronze substituted for copper 1860. [Refer Roth, art. on " The English Coinage " in *A Literary and Historical Atlas of Europe*.]

Pennymite and Yankee War, 1769. Between Connecticut settlers and the Pennsylvanians. [Refer Harper, *Encyclopædia of U.S. History*.]

Pensions Bill. *See* Old Age Pensions.

Perceval Administration. Spencer Perceval (1762-1812) at the head. Formed Oct. 1809; dissolved on assassination of Perceval in the House of Lords, May 11, 1812. [Refer Hunt and Poole, *Political History of England*.]

Persia (Asia). Early history lost in obscurity; revolt of Cyrus against the Medes 553 B.C.; Persians under Darius defeated at Marathon 490; under Xerxes at Salamis and Platæa 480-479; defeated by Alexander the Great at Arbela 331; and then became subject to the Seleucidæ dynasty; invaded by the Romans 3rd and 4th century A.D.; Emperor Julian slain near the Tigris 363; united with Armenia 365; disunited 386; reunited 428; invaded by Arabs 641; by Mongols, who form a dynasty, 1253-1335; Bagdad made capital 1345; invaded by Timour 1380-99; taken by Turcomans 1468; Teheran made capital 1796; war with Russia 1826-29 (for war with England *see* next art.); National Council or Parliament opened by the Shah, Oct. 7, 1906; revolution 1906-09; Shah Mahommed Ali Mirza compelled to abdicate, July 15, 1909; New Parliament opened, Nov. 15, 1909. [Refer art. *Encyclopædia Britannica*.]

Persian War. The Persians took Herat in violation of the treaty of 1853, and behaved insultingly to the British ambassador; war between Great Britain and Persia was declared, Nov. 1, 1856; peace was signed at Paris, Mar. 3, 1857. [Refer *Annual Register*, 1856-7.]

Perth (Scotland). Made a royal burgh by William the Lion 1210; besieged and captured by Robert Bruce 1311; captured by Edward III. 1335; retaken by Scots 1339; after 1437, the year of the murder of James I., Perth was no longer capital of Scotland; captured by Montrose 1644; by Cromwell 1651; Old Pretender proclaimed at, Sept. 16, 1715. [Refer Cowen, *The Ancient Capital of Scotland*.]

Peru (S. America). Conquered by Pizarro for Spain 1553; city of Lima fd. 1535; assassination of Pizarro, June 26, 1541 [refer Prescott, *Conquest of Peru*]; rebellion against Spanish rule 1780-July 1783; independence proclaimed at Lima, July 28, 1821; constitution drawn up, Mar. 21, 1828; joined with Chili in war against Spain, Feb. 1866. [Refer Akers, *History of South America*.]

Perugia (Italy). Orig. *Perusia*. Captured by Pope Leo X. from the Baglioni 1520; occupied by French 1797; by Austrians 1849; united to kingdom of Italy 1860. [Refer Symonds and Gordon, *Perugia*, Mediæval Towns Series.]

Peterborough (Northants, England). Orig. a Saxon village called *Medehamstede.* In 655 Saxulf, a monk, fd. a monastery there, and the name was altered subsequently to *Burgus sancti Petri ;* cathedral fd. 656; destroyed by Danes 870; the present building fd. 1117, and was consecrated, Oct. 4, 1237.

Petersburg, St. (Russia). Fd. by Peter the Great, May 27, 1703; became seat of government 1712; Peace of, between Russia and Prussia, signed May 5, 1762; Treaty of Alliance signed at, between Bernadotte and the Emperor of Russia, Alexander, signed Mar. 24, 1812. *See* Russia.

Peter's Pence. A tax levied by the Popes of Rome; date of origin doubtful; it is mentioned in a letter of Cnut's dated 1031 from Rome to the English clergy; in 1534 the tax was abolished by Henry VIII.

Peter's, St., Rome. Church orig. erected by the Emperor Constantine about A.D. 306; the present church was designed by the architect Bramante, and in 1506 the first stone was laid by Pope Julius II.; the church was consecrated, Nov. 18, 1626. [Refer *Rome* in Mediæval Towns Series.]

Petition of Right. Presented to King Charles I. by the two Houses of Parliament, May 28, 1628; it asked for a reform of various constitutional abuses. [Refer Hallam, *Constitutional History of England.*]

Philippine Islands (Malay Archipelago). Discovered by Magellan 1521; possessed by Mexico on behalf of Spain 1565; ceded to U.S.A. 1899 (*see* Spanish-American War); assembly for self-government opened by Mr. Taft, U.S. secretary for war, Oct. 16, 1907.

Phœnix Park. *See* Ireland and Parnell.

Phosphorus. Discovered 1669 by Dr. Brandt of Hamburg; important experiments and discoveries by John Kunchel about 1670.

Photography. In the 16th century the action of light on chloride of silver was known, but it was not until about 1802 that Thomas Wedgwood (1771-1805) published his account, *An Account of a Method of copying Painting upon Glass, and of making Profiles by the Agency of Light upon Nitrate of Silver ;* Wedgwood is known as "the first photographer"; in 1819 Sir John Herschel improved the method, and in 1824 Louis J. M. Daguerre produced photographic sensitive plates, which were afterwards known as *Daguerreotypes ;* the first *negative* plate was produced by Talbot in 1839, by which any number of copies of the photograph could be reproduced; copyright of photographs secured by Act passed 1862; direct colour photography by the Lumiere Autochrome Plate patented 1904.

Physicians, Royal College of (London). Charter granted through exertions of Dr. Linacre, Henry VIII.'s physician in 1518.

Pilgrimage of Grace. The name given to the insurrection caused by the dissolution of the monasteries; it originated in Yorkshire and Lincolnshire in 1536; the leaders were executed in Mar. 1537.

Pisa (Italy). Early history uncertain; famous leaning tower built 1154; university fd. 1343; subject to Florence 1406; becomes independent 1494; retaken by Florence 1509; mob attempt to destroy cathedral as a protest against execution of Ferrer, Oct. 17, 1909.

Pitt Administrations. William Pitt (1759-1806) at head. (1) Dec. 18, 1783-1801; (2) May 12, 1804-Jan. 23, 1806. [Refer Hunt and Poole, *Political History of England.*]

Plymouth (Devonshire, England). Frequently attacked by the French during the 14th and 15th centuries. First English town to be incorp. by Act of Parliament, Nov. 12, 1439. Witnessed the departure of Drake on his expedition round the world 1577; of the Elizabethan fleet in the encounter with the Spanish Armada 1588; and of the *Mayflower* 1620. With Stonehouse and Devonport forms the " Three Towns," constituting one of the finest ports in England.

Plymouth Brethren. A religious sect fd. about 1830 at Plymouth; John Nelson Darby (1800-82) is generally regarded as the founder of the sect.

Poland (Europe). Formed into a kingdom about A.D. 992, when Christianity was intro.; invaded by Tartars 1081; incorp. with Lithuania 1569; conquered by Swedes and Russians 1654; independent 1660; declared a Russian province 1847. [Refer Morfill, *Poland*, Story of the Nations Series.]

Poll-Tax. First levied in England 1380, and may be said to have caused Wat Tyler's rebellion in 1381; revived 1513; finally abolished 1689. [Refer Hume, *History of England.*]

Pompeii (Italy). Of great antiquity; early history uncertain; entirely destroyed by eruption of Mount Vesuvius, Aug. 24, A.D. 79; in 1750 the excavations were commenced.

Pontefract Castle (Yorkshire, England). Built about 1080; Richard II. murdered at, Feb. 10, 1400; dismantled 1649.

Poor Laws (Great Britain). Present law dates from Elizabeth's time, when in 1601 overseers were appointed for parishes; Poor Law Commission 1832-3; Poor Law Board appointed 1834; dissolved 1846; Poor Law Amendment Bill passed 1834; amended 1836, 1838, 1846; Poor Law Amendment Act passed 1868; New Poor Law Act passed 1889; amended 1890.

Popish Plot, The. An imaginary conspiracy of the Roman Catholics, owed its existence to Titus Oates and others, who in 1678 deposed before a magistrate that he knew of a plot by Roman Catholics against the king; Oates was convicted of perjury in 1685; in 1688 parliament declared Oates' trial illegal, and he was granted a pension. [Refer Macaulay, *History of England.*]

Port Arthur. Massacre of Chinese by Japanese, Nov. 21, 1894; surrendered by Russian garrison to Japan, Jan. 2, 1905.

Porteous Riots. Caused by the hanging of a smuggler in Edinburgh in 1736; Captain Porteous ordered the military to fire on the rioters and killed many; he was sentenced to death, but respited; the mob, however, seized him afterwards and hanged him. [Refer Scott, *Heart of Midlothian.*]

Portland Administrations. William Henry Cavendish, Duke of Portland (1738-1809). (1) Known as Coalition Ministry, April 5, 1783-Dec. 1783; (2) Mar. 25, 1807-09. [Refer Hunt and Poole *Political History of England.*]

Portugal (Europe). Orig. *Lusitania.* Kingdom estab. between 1095 and 1279; Lisbon made capital 1433; seized by Philip II. of Spain 1580; Spanish rule thrown off, 1640; war with Spain 1640-68; by the Treaty of Lisbon signed 1668 Spain acknowledged independence of Portugal; Methuen Treaty, between Great Britain and Portugal, concluded through influence of Paul Methuen, British ambassador at Lisbon, regulated commerce between the two countries, signed Dec. 27, 1703; invasion by France and Spain 1762 (*see* Peninsular War); assassination of King Carlos I. Feb. 1, 1908; revolution, Aug. 1910; expulsion of King Manoel, who escapes to England, Oct. 1910; Dr. Manoel de Arriaga appointed first president of the new republic 1911. [Refer art. in *Encyclopædia Britannica.*]

Post Office (Great Britain). In the 13th century we read of accounts for payments for the conveyance of letters; the first English postmaster of whom there is any account is Sir Brian Tuke, who is mentioned about 1533; in 1619 Matthew de Quester was appointed " Postmaster-general of England for foreign parts "; new postal system organised by the Common Council of London 1650; rates of postage and the rights and duties of postmasters settled by Act of Parliament 1657; act for erecting and estab. a post office passed 1660; this is the origin of the present system. *Penny Post* instit. in London and suburbs by Robert Murray 1681; annexed to the Crown revenues department 1690; new Penny Postage Law intro. through exertions of Rowland Hill 1839; adhesive stamps invented by James Chalmers 1834; new general post office at St. Martin's-le-Grand opened 1891; removed to Newgate Street 1910. [Refer Joyce, *History of British Post Office.*]

Poynings Law. Called after Sir Edward Poynings (1459-1521), lord-deputy of Ireland; passed Sept. 13, 1494; this law made the Irish legislature subordinate and completely dependent on the English Parliament; repealed, April 1782. [Refer Froude, *The English in Ireland.*]

Pragmatic Sanction. An ordinance relating to Church and State affairs; Pragmatic Sanction of Bourges passed in 1438 by Charles VII. of France, imposing limits on the papal authority; Pragmatic Sanction dealing with the succession of the House of Hapsburg passed by the Emperor Charles VI. April 19, 1713; this latter caused the War of the Austrian Succession.

Prague (Bohemia). Fd. about A.D. 759; rebuilt by Charles IV. 1348; captured by Sweden 1648; by French 1741; by Prussians 1744; treaty of Prague signed, Aug. 23, 1866; ends war between Prussia and Austria. [Refer Lutzow, *Prague*, Mediæval Towns Series.]

Prayer, Book of Common. *See* Common Prayer.

Pre-Raphaelite School of Painting. Fd. about 1850 by J. E. Millais (1829-96); Wm. Holman Hunt (1827-1910); Dante Gabriel Rossetti (1828-82); other artists were also in the movement.

Press. *See* Newspapers.

Pride's Purge. The name given to the expulsion and arrest of certain members of parliament who opposed the trial of Charles I. Col. Pride, at the head of the parliamentary army, on Dec. 6, 1648, effected the " purge." [Refer Macaulay, *History of England*.]

Primrose League. A Conservative association fd. in 1884 in memory of Disraeli, Lord Beaconsfield.

Prince Edward Island (Canada). Discovered by Cabot 1497; captured by Great Britain from French 1758.

Printing. Orig. practised by the Chinese in very early times (*see* Engraving); the origin of the present system seems to be very doubtful.

Privateering. Abolished by mutual agreement among civilised nations by the Declaration of Paris 1856; Spain and the U.S. did not sign this.

Privy Council (Great Britain). The council summoned by the sovereign to advise him on matters of state orig. known as the *Curia Regis* is of very early date; by an act passed May 1612 in James I.'s reign, privy councillors took precedence after Knights of the Garter; dissolved on the demise of the Crown; in 1679 the council was remodelled and the privy councillors by this act held office for six months after the sovereign's death.

Probate and Divorce Court (England). Created 1857; by Judicature Acts of 1873 was joined with the Admiralty Court.

Propaganda. An institution of the Roman Catholic Church at Rome consisting of a congregation and college fd. for the propagation of the Roman Catholic faith orig. by Pope Gregory XIII. (1572-84), but more fully developed by Gregory XV. 1622.

Prussia (Germany). The early inhabitants were Slavonic tribes who in A.D. 997 first appear to have been called *Borussi* or *Prussians*; in 1283 the Teutonic knights (*q.v.*) became masters of the country; West Prussia and Ermland ceded by the knights in 1466 by the Treaty of Thorn to Poland; the remainder of Prussia declared to be fiefs of Poland; in 1525 converted into a secular duchy and declared for Lutheranism; made a kingdom 1701. Kings of Prussia:—

    Frederick I. 1701.
    Frederick William I. 1713.
    Frederick the Great 1740.
    Frederick William II. 1786.
    Frederick William III. 1797.
    Frederick William IV. 1840.
    William I. 1861; proclaimed Emperor of Germany 1871.
    Frederick III. 1888.
    William II. 1888.
See Germany.

Puritans. The name first given to those clergymen of the Church of England who refused to conform to the liturgy and ceremonies of the Church of England between 1564 and 1569. *See* Church of England, Nonconformists.

Q

Quadruple Alliance. Between England, France, Austria, and Holland, 1718.

Quakers or Society of Friends. A religious sect fd. by George Fox between 1648-66; the name of *Quaker* was given to the sect by Justice Bennet of Derby in 1650, who was admonished by Fox to tremble at the word of the Lord; in 1650 their first meeting-house was opened in London; in 1696 their " affirmation of the truth " was declared by Act of Parliament to be sufficient in place of the usual oath in courts of justice; and in 1828 they were relieved from oaths qualifying persons to municipal offices, and again in 1837. [Refer Turner, *The Quakers*.]

"Quarterly Review." First published in Feb. 1809 by John Murray, to counteract the Whig opinions of the *Edinburgh Review ;* the first editor was William Gifford (1756-1826), who resigned his position in 1824. [Refer Smiles, *A Publisher and his Friends*.]

Quatre-Bras (Belgium). Battle between the Allies and the French under Ney, June 16, 1815, in which the Duke of Brunswick was killed.

Quebec (Canada). Town and province. Town fd. by Champlain 1608; captured by Great Britain 1626; res. to France 1632; finally captured by British army under Gen. Wolfe, Sept. 13, 1759; formally ceded to Great Britain by Treaty of Paris 1763; the " Quebec Act " of 1774 gave the French-Canadians the right to exercise their customs, laws, and religion. Province united with the other provinces of Canada 1867. [Refer Garneau, *History of Canada*.]

Queen Anne's Bounty. Instit. in 1704 for the relief of the poor clergy. Queen Anne devoted the funds arising from first fruits and tithes which were at her disposal to this object. [Refer Burnet, *History of His Own Times*.]

Queensbury Plot. In March 1703 a general pardon was granted to the Jacobites, who would take the oath of fidelity to Queen Anne and her government; Lord Lovat took advantage of the pardon, but his name was forged to a letter which would have led to disgrace and perhaps death; the fraud was discovered, and the Duke of Queensbury, who was a party, had to resign his office as High Commissioner. [Refer Burnet, *History of His Own Times*.]

Queen's College for Women (London). Estab. 1848; incorp. by royal charter 1853.

Queensland (Australia). Explored 1823; proclaimed a separate colony apart from New South Wales 1859.

Queens of England. The following are the Queens of England since the Norman Conquest. The dates of the deaths of some of the earlier queens are uncertain, in those cases where they survived their husbands:—

Matilda of Flanders, *m.* William the Conqueror 1051, *d.* 1084.

Matilda of Scotland, *m.* Henry I. 1100, *d.* 1119.

†Adelais of Louvaine, *m.* Henry I. 1129, *d.* 1151.

*Matilda, daughter of Henry I., *b.* 1101, *d.* 1167, *m.* (1) Henry V. of Germany 1109 (who *d.* 1125); (2) Geoffrey Plantagenet.

Matilda of Boulogne, *m.* Stephen 1128, *d.* 1151.

Eleanor of France, *m.* Henry II. 1152, *d.* 1204.

Berengaria of Navarre, *m.* Richard I. 1191, *d.* 1230.

Avisa of Gloucester, *m.* John 1189, divorced.

†Isabella of Angoulême, *m.* John 1200.

†Eleanor of Provence, *m.* Henry III. 1236, *d.* 1292.

Eleanor of Castile, *m.* Edward I. 1253, *d.* 1296.

†Margaret of France, *m.* Edward I. 1299.

Isabella of France, *m.* Edward II. 1308.

Philippa of Hainault, *m.* Edward III. 1328, *d.* 1369.

Anne of Bohemia, *m.* Richard II. 1382, *d.* 1395.

†Isabella of France, *m.* Richard II. 1396.

†Joan of Navarre, *m.* Henry IV. 1403, *d.* 1437. The previous wife of Henry IV. *d.* before he was king in 1394.

†Catherine of France, *m.* Henry V. 1420.

†Margaret of Anjou, *m.* Henry VI. 1445, *d.* 1482.

Lady Elizabeth Grey, secret marriage made public 1464.

Anne of Warwick, *m.* Richard III. 1474, *d.* 1485.

Elizabeth of York, *m.* Henry VII. 1486, *d.* 1503.

Catherine of Aragon, *m.* Henry VIII. 1509, divorced 1533, *d.* 1536.

Anne Boleyn, *m.* Henry VIII. 1532, executed 1536.

Jane Seymour, *m.* Henry VIII. 1536, *d.* 1537.

Anne of Cleves, *m.* Henry VIII. Jan. 1540, divorced July 1540, *d.* 1557.

Catherine Howard, *m.* Henry VIII. 1540, *d.* 1542.

†Catherine Parr, *m.* Henry VIII. 1543, *d.* 1548.

*Mary, *m.* Philip II. of Spain 1554 (*d.* 1598), *d.* 1558.

*Elizabeth, unmarried, *d.* 1603.

Anne of Denmark, *m.* James I. 1589, *d.* 1619.

†Henrietta-Maria, *m.* Charles I. 1625, *d.* 1669.

†Catherine of Portugal, *m.* Charles II. 1662, *d.* 1705.

†Mary-Beatrice of Medina, *m.* James II. 1763, *d.* 1718.

*Mary II. *m.* William III. 1677, *d.* 1694.

*Anne, *m.* George of Denmark 1683 (*d.* 1708), *d.* 1714.

The wife of George I., Sophia Dorothea, *d.* before the king's accession 1714.

Wilhelmina Caroline Dorothea of Brandenburg-Anspach, *m.* George II. 1704, *d.* 1737.

* Queens in their own right.   † Survived their husbands.

QUEENS OF ENGLAND (*continued*)—

Charlotte Sophia of Mecklenburg-Strelitz, *m.* George III. 1761, *d.* 1818.

Caroline Amelia Augusta of Brunswick, *m.* George IV. 1795, *d.* 1821.

†Adelaide Amelia Augusta of Saxe-Meinengen, *m.* William IV. 1818, *d.* 1849.

*Victoria, *m.* Albert of Saxe Coburg Gotha 1840, who *d.* 1861. The queen *d.* 1901.

†Alexandra of Denmark, *m.* Edward VII. 1863.

Victoria Mary of Teck, *m.* George V. 1893.

[Refer Strickland, *The Queens of England*.]

Queen Victoria Memorial. Facing Buckingham Palace; unveiled in presence of Kaiser by King George V., May 16, 1911.

R

Radcliffe College (Cambridge, Mass. U.S.A.). A college for women fd. 1878 and made a part of Harvard University; named after Annie Radcliffe, the first woman who left a sum of money for the founding of Harvard University. [Refer Harper, *Encyclopædia of U.S. History.*]

Radical. The word applied to a political party was probably originated by a speech by Charles J. Fox in 1797, when he referred to the necessity for "radical reform." [Refer art. in Low and Pulling, *Dicty. of English History.*]

Rebellion, The Great. *See* Great Britain and under various acts of Cromwell, etc.

Recissary Act. Passed by Scottish Parliament 1661; it was proposed by Sir Thomas Primrose with the object of annulling the Acts establishing Presbyterianism in Scotland. [Refer Burton, *History of Scotland.*]

Record Office (London). Fd. on the recommendation of a committee of the House of Commons, which first met in 1800; the report of this commission was published 1837; the publication of the Calendars of State Papers was commenced in 1856.

Red Cross, American National. Fd. Oct. 1, 1881, for the relief of suffering by war, pestilence, famine, flood, fire, etc.; reincorporated, April 17, 1893. [Refer Harper, *Encyclopædia of U.S. History.*]

Red Sea Expedition. In 1800 the Marquis of Wellesley despatched troops to assist in the expulsion of the French from Egypt; this expedition proceeded up the Red Sea to Cosseir. [Refer Alison, *History of Europe.*]

Reform Bills (Great Britain and Ireland). *See also* Parliament, House of Commons, etc. The first question of Parliamentary Reform was raised by Wm. Pitt in 1785, who proposed to disenfranchise certain rotten boroughs in favour of others which were more deserving; his motion was, however, defeated. On March 1, 1831, Lord John Russell's famous Reform Bill was intro. and the bill was carried by a majority of one; it was, however, defeated on an amendment; in June 1831 the bill was again brought in and passed the House of Commons, but was thrown out by the Lords; in December of the same year a third Reform Bill was brought in by the Commons, but the Lords virtually rejected it; on May 15 of the following year the king was prepared to create new peers if necessary to pass the Reform Bill; the Lords, however, gave way, and the bill was passed on June 4, 1832. Frequent attempts were made to intro. other Reform Bills, when in Feb. 1867 Mr. Disraeli's famous bill was passed which conferred a household and lodger franchise in boroughs. Another Reform Bill was intro. in Mar. 1884 by Mr. Gladstone, and was finally passed Dec. 6, 1884. [Refer Molesworth, *History of the Reform Bill*, etc.]

Reformation, The. *See also* Counter-Reformation. The religious and political revolution of the 16th century. According to Professor J. H. Robinson in the *Encyclopædia Britannica*, " Outwardly the Reformation would seem to have begun when on Dec. 10, 1520, a professor in the University of Wittenberg invited all the friends of evangelical truth among his students to assemble outside the wall at the ninth hour to witness a pious spectacle—the burning of the *godless book of the papal decrees*." In England, however, the R. may said to have been started by the preaching of Wycliffe (1320-84) and his followers (*see* Lollards). Martin Luther (1483-1546), as a protest against the abuses in the Church of Rome, nailed his 95 theses to the church door at Wittenberg, Nov. 1, 1517. Erasmus (1466-1536), although a Roman Catholic, did much to further the cause of the Reformation by his work, *The Praise of Folly*, which showed up the follies and sins of the monasteries. In England, under Henry VIII. (1509-1547), the R. gained much ground. In 1534 the English Church was declared independent of Rome and the payment of annates and of Peter's Pence (*q.v.*) were forbidden. Between 1536 and 1538 the monasteries in England were dissolved. *See also* various acts passed owing to the R. [Refer Stone, *Reformation and Renaissance*.]

Reformed Episcopal Church (U.S.A.). A Protestant community dating from Dec. 1873; fd. by George D. Cummins (1822-76), assistant bishop of Kentucky. The sect was intro. into England in 1877.

Regency Bills (Great Britain). (1) 1751, on the death of Frederick, Prince of Wales, appointing the Princess of Wales regent in the event of George II.'s death before the Prince of Wales was 18; (2) 1765, on the recovery of George III. from his first attack of mental disease; (3) 1788, during the second mental attack of George III. The king, however, recovered; (4) 1810, when the mind of George III. finally gave way; (5) 1830, the Duchess of Kent appointed regent during the minority of Victoria should the latter succeed to the throne before the age of 18; (6) 1837, provided for the carrying on of the government by lords justices in the event of the Duke of Hanover, the heir-presumptive, being abroad; (7) 1840, on the marriage of Queen Victoria with Prince Albert. It enacted that on the event of Victoria's demise, and that any child of hers should succeed to the throne under the age of 18, Prince Albert should act as regent. [Refer May, *Constitutional History of England*.]

Regicides, The. In British history the name was given to those who tried and condemned Charles I. in 1649; the Bill of Indemnity in 1660 ordered severe penalties against the regicides. [Refer Macaulay, *History of England*.]

Regium Donum (royal gift). A grant made every year to Presbyterian and other Nonconformist bodies in Great Britain and Ireland by the king; it was instit. 1672; finally discontinued 1869.

Regulating Act. Intro. by Lord North in 1773 to cause the British government to interfere in the administration of India. [Refer Mill, *History of India*.]

Regulating Act. Passed by parliament 1774 for the subversion of the charter of Massachusetts in America. [Refer Harper, *Encyclopædia of U.S. History*.]

Remonstrance, The Grand. A petition drawn up by parliament protesting against the cruelty and injustice of Charles I.; presented Dec. 1, 1641.

Remonstrants. The name given to the Dutch Protestants who in 1610, after the death of Arminius, presented to the Holland and Friesland states a remonstrance in five articles in which the doctrines of Calvinism were repudiated; their confession of faith was drawn up in 1621; they received official recognition 1795. [Refer Strong and McLintock, *Dicty. of Eccles. Biog.*]

Renaissance, The. A period in the history of Europe during which arts and letters experienced a revival; it is impossible to give a date when this movement started; the artist Giotto (1276–1336) revived the ancient idea of the appeal to nature in art, and his contemporary Dante (1265-1321) revived the same ideal in literature. [Refer Stone, *Reformation and Renaissance*.]

Repeal Agitation. *See* Ireland and O'Connell.

Reproduction. *See* Engraving, etc.

Republican Army. This name was given to the U.S. army which invaded Canada 1776.

Requests, Court of. Supposed to have been fd. 1390; on the suppression of the Star Chamber in 1640 it was abolished; the other courts of requests or courts of conscience, for deciding claims under the amount of 40s., were estab. in Henry VIII.'s reign (1491-1547); abolished by County Courts Acts passed 1846.

Réunion or **Bourbon** (Indian Ocean). Discovered by Portuguese navigator, Pedro Mascarenhas; possessed by French 1638; attacked and captured by British 1810; res. to France, April 1815. Refer art. in *Encyclopædia Britannica*.]

Revolutionary Tribunal, The. Estab. in Paris, Oct. 1793, for the trial of criminal cases; it was suppressed, May 31, 1795. [Refer Carlyle, *French Revolution*.]

Revolutionary War (U.S.A.). *See* U.S.A.

Rheims (France). Built on the site of *Durocortorum*, mentioned by Julius Cæsar as the capital of the *Remi*; Clovis baptised at 496; from 1179 to 1825 the sovereigns of France were crowned here; cathedral built between 1212 and 1430; res. 1877 *et seq.*

Rhine, Confederation of the. *See* Confederation of the Rhine.

Rhode Island (U.S.A.). Supposed to have been the place where the Northmen attempted to fd. a settlement in the 11th century; explored by the Dutch 1614; commonwealth of Rhode Island fd. in 1636 by Roger Williams; further settlements in 1638 and 1643; charter granted 1644; first General Assembly met 1647; charter confirmed by Oliver Cromwell 1655; new charter granted by Charles II. 1663; ratified National Constitution of U.S. May 29, 1790. [Refer Harper, *Encyclopædia of U.S. History*.]

Rhodes (Mediterranean). The island was settled by Dorian Greeks at a very early period; submitted to Persians 490 B.C.; submitted to Alexander of Macedon 322 B.C.; captured by the Knights Hospitallers (*see* Malta, Knights of) 1309; capitulated to Turks 1523. [Refer Torr, *Rhodes in Ancient Times* and *Rhodes in Modern Times*.]

Rhodesia (S. Africa). Named after Cecil Rhodes (1853-1902), who fd. the British South African Colony, which in 1889 had its first charter granted.

Ribbonism. " The name assumed by a group of secret associations among the lower classes in Ireland throughout the half century extending from 1820-70 " (*Chambers's Encyclopædia*).

Ridolphi Conspiracy. A plot against Queen Elizabeth by the Roman Catholics, of which Robert Ridolphi was one of the principal conspirators; it originated in 1571; the Duke of Norfolk was involved in the scheme, and was executed with other plotters in June 1572. [Refer Froude, *History of England*.]

Rights, Declaration of. *See* Declaration of Rights.

Rights of Man, Declaration of the. Adopted by the French National Assembly, Aug. 1789.

Rio de Janeiro (Brazil). Fd. 1566; made the capital of Brazil 1822.

Riot Act (Great Britain). Passed in 1715, during the time when Jacobite risings were feared.

Ripon, Treaty of. Signed 1640; brought to an end the war between England and Scotland; peace finally concluded at London, Aug. 1641.

Rochelle (France). Became part of English possessions by marriage of Henry II. to Eleanor of Aquitaine; taken by Louis VIII. of France 1224; ceded to England 1360; retaken by France 1372; resisted siege as Huguenot stronghold 1573; taken by Richelieu 1628; modern harbour opened 1890.

Rochester (Kent, England). Bishopric fd. 604 by St. Augustine; present cathedral fd. 1077-1107; castle of very early construction, captured by King John 1215; besieged in vain by Simon de Montfort 1264; captured by Wat Tyler 1381.

Rockingham Administrations. Charles Watson Wentworth, Marquis of Rockingham (1730-82), at the head. (1) July 13, 1765—July 30, 1766; (2) March—July 1, 1782.

Rockingham, Council of. March 11-14, 1095, held to discuss the dispute between Pope Urban II. and the anti-popes, and to decide whether Urban could be accepted as the real Pope of Rome. [Refer art. in Low and Pulling, *Dicty. of English History*.]

Roman Catholic Church. *See* Rome, Papacy, etc.

Roman Catholics in England. Absolved from allegiance to the king 1535 by Pope Pius III.; excluded from the throne 1689; laws against them repealed 1780, 1791; Catholic Emancipation Bill passes April 13, 1829; Eucharistic Congress in London, Sept. 1908. *See also* various laws against and for the Roman Catholics.

Rome (Italy). Said to have been fd. by Romulus 753 B.C.; Capitol fd. about 614 B.C.; first dictatorship 501 B.C.; first tribune 494 B.C.; decemvirs instit. 452 B.C.; sacked by Gauls 390 B.C.; Aqua Appia built 311 B.C.; First Punic War 264-241 B.C.; Second Punic War 218-201 B.C.; First Triumvirate 63 B.C.; Julius Cæsar assassinated 44 B.C.; Second Triumvirate 43 B.C.; Aqua Julia built 34 B.C.; Pantheon built 27 B.C; Colosseum begun A.D. 72; Trajan's Column 114; invasion of Goths 250; captured by Alaric 410; pillaged by Genseric 455; taken by Odoacer 476; O. defeated by Theodoric 493; taken by Belisarius 536; by Totila 549; annexed to Eastern empire by Narses 553; Charlemagne crowned at 800; captured by Saracens 846; by the emperor 896; devastated by Guiscard and his Normans 1084; taken by Barbarossa 1167; papacy transferred to Avignon 1309; Rienzi established a republic 1347; return of papacy 1377; St. Peter's begun, 1450; entered by Charles VIII. and French 1494; consecration of St. Peter's, Nov. 1626; walls restored by Benedict XIV. 1749; proclaimed a republic by the French 1798; res. to pope, retaken, and again res. 1799-1801; annexed by Napoleon to Kingdom of Italy 1808; res. to pope 1814; revolution 1848; siege of 70 days by the French 1849; Garibaldi's campaign, Oct.-Nov. 1867; Italian government removed to R. 1870, and a national constitution is proclaimed; R. declared the capital of Italy at the same time. [Refer *Rome*, Mediæval Towns Series.]

Rome-feoh or **Rome-scot.** *See* Peter's Pence.

Röntgen Rays. Discovered by W. K. Röntgen in 1895; Röntgen Society fd. by Prof. S. P. Thompson 1897.

Rosebery Administration. Archibald Philip Primrose, Earl of Rosebery (*b.* 1847), at the head. Mar. 1894—June 21, 1895.

Roses, Wars of the. Between the Lancaster party and the York party in England commenced 1455; ended 1485 by b. of Bosworth.

Rotterdam (Holland). John I. in 1299 granted various privileges to burghers of, and this date marks the origin of the present town; Erasmus *b.* at 1467; plundered by Spaniards 1572.

Rouen (France). Orig. *Ratuma*, Romanised as *Rotomagus*. An archbishop's see in A.D. 260; becomes capital of Normandy 912; death of William the Conqueror at 1087; Joan of Arc burned at

1431; sacked by Huguenots 1562; occupied by Germans, Dec. 1870—July 1871.

Roumania (Europe). The name assumed by the Danube principalities (*q.v.*) in Dec. 1861; declared independent, July 13, 1878.

Royal Academy (London). Orig. the Society of Incorporated Artists, fd. by Hogarth about 1739; first exhibition held, April 21, 1760; the present institution fd. Dec. 1768, with Sir Joshua Reynolds as president; first exhibition held at Burlington House, May 3, 1869. The following are the presidents:—

Sir Joshua Reynolds 1768	Sir Charles Eastlake 1850
Benjamin West 1792	Sir Edwin Landseer } 1866
James Wyatt 1805	Sir Francis Grant }
Benjamin West 1806	Sir Frederick Leighton 1878
Sir Thomas Lawrence 1820	Sir John Everett Millais } 1896
Sir Martin A. Shee 1830	Sir Edward John Poynter }

Royal Exchange (London). Fd. by Sir Thomas Gresham, June 1566; buildings opened by Queen Elizabeth, Jan. 1571; destroyed by fire, Sept. 1666; new building opened 1670; destroyed by fire 1838; present building opened by Queen Victoria, Oct. 28, 1844. [Refer Taylor, *Historical Guide to London*.]

Royal George, a British man-of-war lost off Spithead, Aug. 29, 1872.

Royal Institution of Great Britain. Fd. by several noblemen in London on Mar. 9, 1799; incorp. by Royal Charter, Jan. 13, 1800; extended by Act of Parliament 1810.

Royal Society. Organised in 1660; incorp. April 22, 1662.

Rugby School (Warwickshire, England). Fd. and endowed by Laurence Sheriff 1567; rebuilt 1809.

Rump Parliament. *See* Pride's Purge.

Russell Administrations. Lord John Russell (1792-1878) at the head. (1) July 1846—Feb. 1852; (2) Oct. 18, 1865—June 28, 1866.

Russia (Europe). Invaded by Huns A.D. 376; by Tartars 1223; Moscow made capital 1252; invasion of Tartars 1479; Siberia discovered 1554; war with Sweden 1700; with Turkey 1711; expulsion of Jesuits 1718; war with France, June 22, 1812; retreat of Napoleon from Moscow, Oct. 1812; war with Turkey, Oct. 5, 1853; ended by Treaty of Paris, Mar. 30, 1856; New Commercial Treaty with Great Britain 1859; war with Turkey, April 24, 1877; ended by Treaty of Constantinople, Feb. 8, 1879; war with Japan, Feb. 10, 1904; Peace Treaty signed, Sept. 5, 1905; new constitution granted Oct. 1905. [Refer Morfill, *Russia*, Story of the Nations.]

Russian Literature. The earliest preserved manuscript in the Russian language is the codex of the Slavonic gospels dated 1056-7; they were written by the *diak* Gregory by order of the governor of Novgorod; printing was intro. into Russia in 1553 at Moscow, and the first book printed was The Acts of the Apostles, etc., in 1564.

RUSSIAN LITERATURE (*continued*)—
The following are the principal Russian writers:—

Akssakov, Ivan Serguiéiévitch (poet and miscellaneous writer), 1823-86.

Akssakov, Sergius Timofiéiévitch (novelist), 1791-1859.

Baratinski, Eugène Abramovitch (poet), 1800-44.

Bashkirtsev, Maria (essayist), 1860-84.

Batiouchkov, Constantine Nicolaiévitch (poet and translator), 1787-1855.

Biélinski, Vissarion Grigoriévitch (critic and philosopher), 1810-48.

Delwig, Antony Antonovitch (poet), 1798-1831.

Diérjavine, Gabriel Romanovitch (poet), 1743-1816.

Dmitriev, Ivan Ivanovitch (poet), 1760-1837.

Dobrolioubov, Nicholas Alexandrovitch (miscellaneous writer and critic), 1836-60.

Dolgoroukaïa, Princess Natalia Borissovna (memoir writer), 1713-70.

Dostoïevski, Fiodor Mikhaïlovitch (novelist), 1822-81.

Gogol, Nicholas Vassiliévitch (novelist), 1809-52.

Gontcharov, Ivan Aleksandrovitch (novelist), 1814-91.

Griboiédov, Alexander Serguiéiévitch (dramatist), 1795-1829.

Grigorovitch, Dmitri Vassiliévitch (novelist), 1822-1900.

Herzen, Alexander Ivanovitch (novelist, etc.), 1812-70.

Joukovski, Vassili Andréievitch (poet, translator, and miscellaneous writer), 1786-1852.

Kantémir, Antiochus Dmitriévitch (poet and satirist), 1708-44.

Karamzine, Nicholas Mikhaïlovitch (historian and novelist), 1766-1826.

Katkov, Michael (journalist and editor), 1820-87.

Khéraskov, Michael Matviéiévitch (epic poet), 1733-1807.

Khomiakov, Alexis Stéfanovitch (poet and theological writer), 1804-60.

Kiriéiévski, Ivan Vassiliévitch (miscellaneous writer and critic), 1806-56.

Koltsov, Alexis Vassiliévitch (poet), 1809-42.

Kostomarov, Nikolai Ivanovitch (historian), 1817-85.

Koukolnik (novelist and dramatist), 1809-68.

Kovalevsky, Sonya (novelist), 1840-1901.

Krylov (fabulist), 1768-1844.

Lermontov, Michael Iouriévitch (poet), 1811-41.

Liéskov, Nikolai Semenovitch (novelist), 1831-95.

Lomonossov, Michael Vassiliévitch (poet and prose writer), 1711-65.

Loukine, Vladimir Ignatiévitch (dramatist), 1757-1824.

Maïkov, Apollonius Nicolaiévitch (poet), 1821-98.

Nékrassov, Nicholas Alexiéiévitch (poet), 1821-76.

Nestor (historian), *cir.* 1050-*cir.* 1100.

Nikitine, Ivan Savitch (poet), 1826-61.

Novikov, Nicholas Ivanovitch (prose writer and social reformer), 1744-1818.

Ostrovski, Alexander Nicolaiévitch (dramatist), 1824-86.

R

RUSSIAN LITERATURE (*continued*)—

Oziérov, Ladislas Alexandrovitch (poet and dramatist), 1769-1816.

Pissemski, Alexis Féofilaktovitch (novelist and dramatist), 1820-81.

Polévoï, Nicholas Aléxiéiévitch (historian and miscellaneous writer), 1796-1846.

Polotski (poet and dramatist), *fl.* 17th century.

Possochkov, Ivan Tikhonovitch (reformer and miscellaneous writer), *cir.* 1673-1726.

Pouchkine, Alexander Serguiéiévitch (poet), 1799-1837.

Prokopovitch, Feofan (ecclesiastic, reformer, and controversialist, author of several prose works and some poems), 1681-1736.

Radichtchev, Alexander Nikolaiévitch (prose writer), 1749-1802.

Romanovna, Princess Dachkov (prose writer and editor, for some years president of the Academy of Science; her memoirs have been published in an English version), 1743-1810.

Saltykov (Chtchedrine), Michael Ievgrafovitch (novelist), 1826-89.

Saltykov, Michael Ievgrafovitch (miscellaneous writer), 1826-89.

Soloviov, Sergyei Mikhailovich (historian), 1820-79.

Soumarokov, Alexis Petrovitch (dramatist), 1718-77.

Tatichtchev, Vassili Nikititch (author of literary and scientific works), 1685-1750.

Tchadaïev, Pete Iakovlévitch (miscellaneous writer and critic), 1793-1855.

Tchéhoff, A. P. (novelist), 1860-1904.

Tchernichevski, Nicholas Gavrillovitch (critic, philosopher, and novelist), 1828-89.

Tioutchev, Fiodor Ivanovitch (poet), 1803-76.

Tolstoï, Alexis Constantinovitch (novelist, etc.), 1817-75.

Tolstoï, Leo Nicolaiévitch (novelist, etc.), 1828-1910.

Tourguéniev, Ivan Serguiéiévitch (novelist), 1818-83.

Trédiakovski, Vassili Kirillovitch (poet and prose writer), 1703-69.

Visine, Denis Ivanovitch von (dramatist), 1744-92.

Rye House Plot. A conspiracy formed during Charles II.'s reign in 1683; its aim was to assassinate the king and the Duke of York; the plot was frustrated soon after its origin. [Refer Burnet, *History of His Own Time.*]

Ryswick, Treaty of, 1697. Ended the war between France and the coalition composed of England, Spain, Brandenburg, Holland, and the Empire. [Refer Ranke, *History of England.*]

St. Albans, The Council of. Held Aug. 1213. It was a step in the progress of the representative system, as many of the people of the towns attended besides the barons. [Refer Low and Pulling, *Dicty. of English History.*]

St. Helena. *See* Helena, St.

St. John, Knights of. *See* Malta, Knights of.

St. Louis (U.S.A.). Named after Louis IX. of France and fd. in 1764 by Laclède. Possessed by Spain 1768; by U.S.A. 1803. [Refer Harper, *Encyclopædia of U.S. History.*]

St. Lucia (Windward Islands). Discovered by Columbus 1505. In French possession 1635. An English settlement estab. 1639; captured by British 1664; British evacuate 1667. Since this date it has several times changed hands, but in 1803 it was finally captured by the British. [Refer Martin, *History of British Colonies.*]

St. Petersburg. *See* Petersburg, St.

St. Sophia (Constantinople). Fd. by Justinian 531; Mahommedan mosque since 1453.

Salamanca (Spain). Captured by Hannibal 222 B.C.; Moors expelled from 1055; university fd. 1243; library of the university fd. 1254; defeat of French by Wellington 1812.

Salary Grab. The name given to the law passed by the U.S. Congress, Mar. 4, 1873, to increase the salaries of the senators; repealed Jan. 24, 1874. [Refer Harper, *Encyclopædia of U.S. History.*]

Salem (Mass. U.S.A.). Formerly *Naumkeag*. Fd. 1626; incorp. as a city 1836; settlement under Endicott, who gave the place its present name 1628; famous witchcraft trials 1692.

Salisbury (England). Cathedral commenced by Bishop Herman 1075; new building commenced 1220; dedicated 1260. [Refer Price, *Salisbury Cathedral.*]

Salisbury (England), **Councils held at.** (1) Summoned by William the Conqueror to take the oath of allegiance to himself 1086; (2) summoned by Henry I. to swear to the succession of the Etheling William 1116; (3) national councils 1296, 1328, 1384.

Salisbury Administrations. Robert Arthur Talbot Gascoyne-Cecil (1830-1903) at head. (1) June 24, 1885—Jan. 1886; (2) July 26, 1886—Aug. 11, 1892; (3) June 25, 1895 *et seq.*; (4) reconstructed Nov. 12, 1900, resigned 1902, but cabinet unchanged.

Salt Lake City (Utah, U.S.A.). Fd. by the Mormons (*q.v.*) 1847.

Salvador (S. America). Orig. *Cuscaltan*. Conquered by Pedro de Alvarado 1524-26; throws off Spanish yoke 1821; independent republic 1839. [Refer Bates, *Central America*.]

Salvation Army, The. Fd. by William Booth in 1865.

Samoan Isles (Pacific Ocean). Visited by Bougainville 1768; Christianity intro. 1830; independence recognised by European powers 1889. Treaty of 1899 divides Pacific Islands between England, Germany, and the U.S.; Samoa ceded to Germany.

San Francisco (California). Formerly *Yerba Buena*. Spanish mission arrived at, June 27, 1776; American settlement 1836; name changed to present one 1847; discovery of gold 1849; subject to U.S.A. 1850; disorder in and vigilance committee appointed 1851; earthquakes at 1868, 1872, and 1905.

Santa Cruz (Teneriffe). Spanish fleet destroyed by Blake 1657; attack on by Nelson, who here lost his arm, 1797.

Santiago (Spain). Sacked by Moors A.D. 995, who held it till taken by Ferdinand III. 1235; captured by French 1809; res. 1814.

Sardinia (Italy). Conquered by Carthaginians 512 B.C.; taken by Romans 238; Vandals, Goths, and Greeks were in turns later conquerors; first settlement of Saracens in early 8th century; given by Pope to King of Aragon 1323; after other changes of master it passed to the House of Savoy 1720, and the dukes thenceforth became kings; Victor Emmanuel king 1802; helped in liberation of the country, and proclaimed King of Italy 1861.

Sardinian Convention. Signed 1855 between the sovereigns of England and France and Sardinia, by which the King of Sardinia agreed to furnish troops for the Crimea. [Refer art. in Low and Pulling, *Dicty. of English History*.]

Savannah (Georgia, U.S.A.). Taken by English 1778; Americans and French repulsed 1779; evacuated by English 1782.

Savings Banks. First suggested by Defoe in 1697, but no practical scheme was carried out until 1799, when the Rev. J. Smith of Wendover, Bucks, instit. a bank for the use of his parishioners. Post Office Savings Bank estab. by Act of Parliament 1861. In the U.S.A. the first savings banks were estab. at Boston and Philadelphia 1816; New York 1819.

Savoy (Italy). Ceded to France by the King of Sardinia 1860.

Savoy Conference, The. For the purpose of discussing the proposed changes in the Liturgy of the Church of England; it was attended by the Church and Puritan parties, and sat from April 15—July 24, 1661. *See* Church of England.

Savoy Palace (London). Built by Peter of Savoy 1245; burnt by Wat Tyler 1381; res. by Henry VII.; used as a hospital till 18th century; finally taken down 1817.

Saxony (Germany). A kingdom since 1807. Entered by Prussians (Austro-Prussian war) 1866; peace with Prussia in Oct. of same year; Saxony was thereby forced to join the North German Confederation.

Schism Act, The. Passed by parliament in 1714 against the Oxford party; repealed by Occasional Conformity Act 1719. [Refer Stanhope, *Reign of Queen Anne*.]

Schleswig-Holstein. Former possession of Denmark, from whom it was several times wrested. After a long period of dispute and some sanguinary warfare between Denmark, Prussia and Austria it was settled at the Convention of Gastein 1865 that Holstein should be under Austrian government and Schleswig under Prussian; by the Treaty of Prague 1866, Austria resigned her rights; it was stipulated that North Schleswig should be re-united to Denmark if the people wished it; nothing was done, however, and the two countries were organised as a single Prussian province 1867.

Schools, Brothers of Christian. A Roman Catholic congregation for the education of the poor fd. by the Abbé de la Salle in France about 1684; Pope Benedict XIII. acknowledged the order 1725.

Scilly Islands (Cassiterides, Sillinæ) (England). Tin mines in known to Phœnicians and Greeks; conquered by Athelstan 938. Became Crown property on dissolution of monasteries 1539; leased to Sir Francis Godolphin 1593; present owner Mr. Dorrien Smith (1910). Sir Cloudesley Shovel and all his crew lost off 1707. [Refer Wren, *Scilly and the Scillonians*.]

Scotland (part known to the Romans as Caledonia). Name of Scotia originated in 11th century from a tribe of Scots. Macbeth murders Duncan and seizes crown 1056 or 1057; contention for throne between Balliol and Bruce 1292; country ravaged by Edward I. 1296; Wallace defeated at Falkirk 1298; Robert Bruce crowned 1306; b. of Bannockburn 1314; of Halidon Hill 1333; of Chevy Chase 1388; of Homildon Hill 1402; James I. captured by English 1406; James IV. slain at Flodden 1513; Mary Queen of Scots comes to the throne 1540; assassination of Cardinal Beaton 1546; defeat of Scots at Pinkie 1547; preaching of John Knox 1550 and following years; murder of Rizzio 1566; death of Darnley 1567; queen's marriage with Bothwell 1567; she is made prisoner at Carberry Hill 1567; resigns, and Regent Murray appointed 1567; Mary defeated at Langside and escapes to England 1568; Murray murdered 1570; Mary beheaded at Fotheringhay 1587; Gowrie conspiracy 1600; union of Scotland and England under James VI. 1603; Solemn League and Covenant subscribed 1638; Covenanters defeated at Bothwell Bridge 1679; Convention declares in favour of William III. 1689; massacre of Glencoe 1692; legislative union with England 1707: Jacobites defeated at Preston and Sheriffmuir 1715; victory of Charles Edward at Prestonpans 1745; defeated at Culloden 1746; dispute between Free Church and United Free Church 1902.

Seal of the United States, Great. Design adopted by Congress June 20, 1782. [Refer Harper, *Encyclopædia of U.S. History*, where the seal is reproduced.]

Sebastopol. A town in the Crimea built in 1784; famous for the eleven months' siege by the English and French in 1854-55.

Sedan. An old fortified city in the valley of the Meux; the scene of a desperate conflict in 1870 in the Franco-Prussian War. The carnage was so terrible that the French were compelled to abandon further resistance, and the capitulation of Sedan and the whole army therein took place on Sept. 2 of the same year.

Sedan Chairs. First used in England in 1581; came into general use in 1649.

Seditious Meetings Act. Intro. by Wm. Pitt in 1795. It prohibited the meeting of more than fifty persons (except county and borough meetings duly called) for the consideration of petitions or addresses for reform in Church or State. Seditious Meetings and Assemblies Bill 1817. [Refer Massey, *History of England.*]

Self-Denying Ordinance. A measure intro. into the Long Parliament on Dec. 9, 1644. It enacted "*that no member of either House of Parliament should during the war enjoy or execute any office or command, military or civil, and that an ordinance be brought in to that effect.*"

Servia. An independent kingdom south of Hungary; capital Belgrade, with a population of 80,000; total population of country nearly 3,000,000. Complete independence and frontier defined by Berlin Treaty 1878.

Shakespeare's Plays. S. was *b.* in 1564 and *d.* in 1616. First collected edition of his works 1623 in folio. The first plays produced about 1590, in which S. himself took part; the Globe Theatre, Southwark, was the scene of most of the early productions. Shakespeare's chief plays are:—" Titus Andronicus " and " Love's Labour's Lost," 1590; " Two Gentlemen of Verona," 1591; " Henry VI.," " Comedy of Errors," and " Romeo and Juliet," 1592; " Richard II.," " Richard III.," and " Venus and Adonis," 1593; " Lucrece," " King John," and " Midsummer Night's Dream," 1594; " Sonnets," 1594-1604; " Merchant of Venice " and " Taming of the Shrew," 1596; " Henry IV.," " Henry V.," and " Merry Wives of Windsor," 1598; " Much Ado About Nothing " and " As You Like It," 1599; " Twelfth Night," 1600; " All's Well that Ends Well " and " Julius Cæsar," 1601; " Hamlet," 1602; " Troilus and Cressida," 1603; " Othello " and " Measure for Measure," 1604; " Macbeth " and " King Lear," 1606; " Timon of Athens," 1607; " Pericles " and " Antony and Cleopatra," 1608; " Coriolanus," 1609; " Cymbeline," 1610; " The Winter's Tale " and " The Tempest," 1611; " Henry VIII.," 1612.

Sheerness. A royal dockyard in Kent, made by Charles II. in 1663; taken by the Dutch under De Ruyter in 1667; Nore mutiny here 1798; modern dockyard made in 1814, and covers 60 acres.

Siam. On the Burmese border of India; rediscovered by the Portuguese in 1511; area 200,000 square miles; population 7,500,000.

Siberia. In North Asia. Prisoners first sent there in 1710; population 7,100,000 (1908).

Sicily. So-called after its early inhabitants, the Siculi, who originally came from Spain. The Phœnicians fd. colonies here in 735 B.C. and the Greeks 200 years later; made a Roman dependency 210 B.C.; taken by Belisarius A.D. 536; by Saracens 832; in Norman possession 1061-90; made one kingdom with Naples 1131; Charles of Anjou King of the Two Sicilies 1266; " Sicilian Vespers," massacre of French at Palermo 1282; becomes a Spanish dependency 1501; revolution in 1848; Garibaldi lands at Marsala 1860; defeats Neapolitans at Melazzo 1860; annexation with Sardinia and arrival of King Victor Emmanuel 1860; annexation to Kingdom of Italy 1860; earthquake at Messina 1908.

Silk. The use of the silkworm was discovered by the Chinese about 2640 B.C., as far as can be ascertained, although it may be earlier; silkworms intro. into Europe in 552 by two Persian monks; manufactured in Italy, Spain, and S. France 1510; first S. mills in England 1604; formerly all S. was brought from abroad.

Slavery. Abolition of, in British colonies in 1833, and owners compensated; slavery in British possessions terminated following year; the abolition in U.S.A. announced 1862.

Soane Museum (13 Lincoln's Inn Fields). Formed by Sir John Soane; opened 1833.

Somaliland (Africa), British. Made a British protectorate 1885; Dr. Donaldson Smith's expeditions in 1894 and 1900; Mullah defeated by British at Berbera 1899; British and Abyssinian expedition 1902; further fighting in 1903 and 1904; withdrawal of British troops 1910.

Somerset House. Fd. 1549 on the site of some old churches. Its founder, Somerset, the Protector, was executed and his house fell to the Crown; demolished in 1775 and a new building erected. The east wing forms King's College, and was built in 1833.

South African War. Ultimatum sent 1899; Lord Roberts appointed commander-in-chief after severe British reverses, Dec. 23; relief of Kimberley, Feb. 15, 1900; Cronje's surrender at Paardeberg, Feb. 27; relief of Ladysmith, Feb. 28; relief of Mafeking, May 17 and 18; Transvaal Republic annexed to Great Britain, Sept. 1900; formally annexed, Oct. 1900; Peace Conference, May 1902.

Spain (Iberia, Hispania). Early settlements in by Carthaginians and Phœnicians; Carthaginians driven out by Romans 207 B.C.; Vandals, Alani, and Suevi take possession of country A.D. 409; Arabs enter Spain 709; Charlemagne's rearguard defeated at Roncesvaux, Aug. 15, 778; Saracen dominions seized by Moors from Africa 1091 and following years; kingdom of Granada estab. by them 1238; defeat of Moors at Tarifa 1340; their power annihilated by Ferdinand II. of Aragon 1479; destruction of Armada 1588; War of Succession 1701-13; English take Gibraltar 1704; b. of Trafalgar 1805; Carlist War in 1830-40; renewed 1872-76; war with America 1898; campaign in Melilla 1909; insurrectionary rising at Barcelona 1909. *See* Peninsular War.

Spanish Literature. The following are the principal Spanish writers:—

Alarcon, Pedro Antonio de (prose writer of tales, etc.), 1833-91.
Aleman, Mateo (prose writer, author of the popular *Guzman de Alfarache*), *fl.* last half of 16th century.
Alfonso the Learned (poet and patron of letters), 1226-84.
Alvarez Gato, Juan (poet), *fl.* 15th century.
Argote y Gongora, Luis (poet), 1561-1627.
Avila, Juan de (mystic and prose writer), 1502-69.
Balmes y Uspia, Jaime (controversial writer), 1810-48.
Becquer, Gustavo Adolfo (poet and tale-writer), 1836-70.
Berceo, Gonzalo de (poet), (?)1198-(?)1264.
Blanco, José Maria (Blanco White) (poet), 1775-1841.
Boscan Almogaver, Juan (poet and prose writer), (?)1490-1542.
Breton de los Herreros, Manuel (dramatist), 1796-1873.
Caballero Fernan (pseudonym of Cecilia Bôhl de Faber) (novelist), 1796-1877.
Cabanyes, Manuel de (poet), 1808-33.
Cadalso y Vazquez, José de (poet and dramatist), 1741-82.
Calderon de la Barca Henao de la Barreda y Riaño, Pedro (poet, dramatist, and prose writer), 1600-81.
Castillejo, Cristobal de (poet), *d.* 1556.
Castro y Bellvis, Guillén de (dramatist), 1569-1631.
Cervantes Saavedra, Miguel (author of *Don Quixote*, poet, dramatist, and prose writer), 1547-1616.
Cota de Maguaque, Rodrigo (poet), *fl.* late 15th century.
Cruz, San Juan de la (mystic, poet, and prose writer), 1542-91.
Cruz y Cano, Ramon de la (dramatist), 1731-95.
Diaz del Castillo, Bernal (historian of the conquest of Mexico), *fl.* second half 16th century.
Donoso Cortés, Juan (author of work on Catholicism, Liberalism, and Socialism), 1809-53.
Encina, Juan del (poet and dramatist), 1468-1534.
Ercilla y Zuñiga, Alonso de (poet), 1533-95.
Es-pronceda, José de (poet and miscellaneous writer), 1810-42.
Estebanez Calderon, Serafin (miscellaneous prose writer), 1799-1867.
Feijoo y Montenegro, Benito Geronimo (prose writer and critic), 1675-1764.
Fernandez de Moratin, Leandro (dramatist), 1760-1828.
Figueroa, Francisco de (poet), *d.* 1620.
Gallego, Juan Nicasio (poet), 1777-1853.
Garcia de la Huerta y Muñoz, Vicente Antonio (dramatist), 1734-87.
Garcia Gutierrez, Antonio (dramatist), 1813-84.
Gomez de Avellaneda, Gertrudis (poet, dramatist, and novelist), 1816-73.
Gomez de Quevedo y Villegas, Francisco (poet, dramatist, and prose writer), 1580-1645.
Gracian, Baltasar (prose writer), 1601-58.
Granada, Luis de (mystic and religious writer), 1504-88.

Dictionary of Dates

SPANISH LITERATURE (*continued*)—

Guevara, Antonio de (historical novel and letter writer, his *Dial of Princes* was translated by North), *d.* 1545.

Hartzenbusch, Juan Eugenio (dramatist), 1806-80.

Herrera, Fernando de (poet and critic), 1534-97.

Hervas y Cobo de la Torre, José Gerardo (poet and satirist), *d.* 1742.

Hurtado de Mendoza, Diego (poet and scholar), 1503-75.

Iriarte y Oropesa, Tomas de (fabulist), 1750-91.

Isla, José Francisco de (humorous prose writer), 1703-81.

Jáuregui y Aguilar, Juan de (poet and translator), 1570(?)-1650.

Jove-Llanos, Gaspar Melchior de (poet, dramatist, and prose writer), 1744-1811.

Juan Manuel, Infante (poet and miscellaneous writer; his chief prose work was *Conde Lucanor*, a collection of tales), 1282-1347.

Larra, Mariano José de (miscellaneous prose writer), 1809-37.

Léon, Luis Ponce de (poet and prose writer), 1529-91.

Leonardo de Argensolæ, Bartolomé (historian and poet),

Leonardo de Argensolæ, Lupercio (poet and dramatist), 1559-1613.

Lista, Alberto (poet), 1775-1848.

Lopez de Ayala, Adelardo (poet and dramatist), 1828-79.

Lopez de Ayala, Pero (poet and prose writer), 1332-1407.

Lopez de Gomara, Francisco (historian of the conquest of Mexico), 1519-60.

Lucena, Juan de (prose writer), *fl.* 15th century.

Luzan Claramunt de Suelves y Gurrea, Ignacio de (critic and poet), 1702-54.

Manrique, Gómez (poet), 1412-91.

Manrique, Jorge (poet), 1440-78.

Mariana, Juan de (historian), 1537-1624.

Martinez de la Rosa, Francisco (poet, dramatist, and novelist), 1788-1862.

Martinez de Toledo, Alfonso (prose writer and moralist), 1398-(?)1466.

Mayans y Siscar, Gregorio (miscellaneous prose writer), 1699-1781.

Melendez Valdis, Juan (poet and dramatist), 1754-1817.

Melo, Francisco Manuel de (prose writer), 1611-66.

Mena, Juan de (poet), 1411-56.

Mesonero Romanos, Ramon de (miscellaneous prose writer), 1803-82.

Molinos, Miguel de (author of the *Spiritual Guide*), 1627-97.

Montemayor, Jorge de (author of the prose pastoral, *Diana Enamorada*), *d.* 1561.

Montoro, Antón de (poet), *fl.* 15th century.

Morales, Ambrosio de (historian), 1513-91.

Moreto y Cavaña, Agustin (dramatist), 1618-69.

Naharro, Bartolomé Torres (dramatist), *fl.* early 16th century.

Nebrija, Antonio de (humanist), 1444-1522.

Ordoñez de Montaloo, Garcia (author of a version of Amadis de Gaula), *fl.* at close of 15th century.

SPANISH LITERATURE (*continued*)—

Padilla, Juan de (poet), 1468-(?)1522.

Paravicino y Arteaga, Hortensio Felix (poet), 1580-1633.

Perez, Andrés (Francisco Lopez de Ubeda) (picaresque novel writer), *fl.* early 17th century.

Pérez, Antonio (miscellaneous writer), 1540-1611.

Perez de Guzmán, Fernán (poet and historian), 1378-1460.

Perez de Hita, Ginés (historical novelist), *fl.* early 17th century.

Perez de Montalban, Juan (dramatist), 1602-38.

Pulgar, Hernando del (historian), 1436-(?)92.

Quintana, Manuel José (poet, dramatist, and prose writer), 1772-1857.

Rivas, Duque de (poet and dramatist), 1791-1865.

Rojas, Fernando de (author of *Celestina*, a romance in form of drama), *fl.* late 15th century.

Rojas Zorrilla, Francisco de (poet and dramatist), 1607(?)-61.

Rueda, Lope de (dramatist), *fl.* 16th century.

Ruiz de Alarcón, Juan (dramatist), 1581(?)-1639.

Ruiz, Juan (poet), *fl.* 14th century.

Samaniego, Felix Maria de (fabulist), 1745-1801.

Sancho IV. (author of *Castigos y Documentos*, and patron of letters), *d.* 1295.

Santillana, Marqués de (poet and prose writer), 1398-1458.

Sarmiento, Martin (prose writer and critic), 1695-1772.

Selgas y Carrasco, José (poet), 1824-82.

Sem Tob (author of a collection of proverbs and maxims in verse), *fl.* 14th century.

Silvestre, Gregorio (poet), 1520-70.

Solis y Rivadeneira, Antonio de (dramatist and historian) 1610-86.

Tamayo y Baus, Manuel (dramatist), 1829-98.

Teresa, Santa (poet and prose writer), 1515-82.

Tirso de Molina (poet, dramatist, and prose writer), 1571-1648.

Torre, Alfonso de la (didactic prose writer), *fl.* 15th century.

Torre, Francisco de la (poet), 1534(?)-94.

Urrea, Pedro Manuel de (poet), 1486-(?)1530.

Valdes, Juan de (mystic, scholar, and prose writer), *fl.* early half of 16th century.

Vega Carpio, Lope Félix (poet, novelist, dramatist, and miscellaneous writer), 1562-1635.

Vega, Garcilaso de la (poet), 1503-36.

Velez de Guevara, Luis (dramatist), 1570-1643.

Vicente, Gil (dramatist), 1470-1540.

Villamediana, Conde de (poet), 1582-1622.

Villegas, Esteban Manuel de (poet), 1596-1669.

Villena, Enrique de (poet, prose writer, and translator), 1384-1434.

Yañez, Rodrigo (author of an epic work known as the " Rhymed Chronicle," *Poema de Alfonso Onceno*), *fl.* 14th century.

Zorrilla, José (poet and dramatist), 1817-93.

Zurita, Jeromino de (historian), 1572-80.

Spanish Succession, War of, 1701-13. Grand Alliance of England with Holland, Austria, Prussia, and the German Empire, against Louis XIV. 1701.

Spectrum (solar). Treated of by Newton in his *Optics* 1704; chemical analysis by means of a spectrum invented by Bunsen and Kirchhoff in 1860.

Stamp Act. Passed 1765; opposition to in America; and repeal of act 1766. *See* Declaratory Act.

Star Chamber. Held in the Council Chamber at Westminster where the King's Council met from the time of Edward III. till it was abolished by parliament under Charles I. 1640.

Star of India, Order of the. Fd. by Queen Victoria 1861.

States General. Convocation of the three representative bodies in France, of nobles, clergy, and tiers état; in 1789 the last-named order constituted itself the National Assembly.

Stationers' Hall. Incorp. 1556; registration at, is necessary for securing copyright.

Steam Navigation. Watt's patents 1769, 1782; later experiments in America by Fitch, Rumsey, and Evans; screw-propeller by Stevens 1802; Robert Fulton's *Clermont* launched in America 1807; Henry Bell's *Comet* built 1811-12, and employed on the Clyde; first ocean-going steamer built by Fulton 1813.

Stoics. The disciples of Zeno, whose school was held in a portico (Greek *stoa*), hence the name. The system of the Stoics dates from the late 4th century B.C.

Strassburg. Capital of Alsace. Annexed by Germany 870; taken by France 1681; captured by Germany 1870. One of the most strongly fortified towns in the world, contains a fine Gothic cathedral and a celebrated university founded in 1621.

Submarines. *See* under Navy.

Sudan (N. Africa). French and English territory; revolt of Sudanese under the Mahdi 1882; annihilation of Hicks Pasha's forces 1883; Gordon killed at Khartoum 1885; b. of Omdurman 1898.

Suez Canal. Permission for its construction under M. de Lesseps 1854; company formed 1856; work begun 1859; opened to traffic 1869.

Sunday Schools. Originated in Milan under Borromeo 1580, and in England under Revs. D. Blair and J. Alleine in 1760. Exemption from rates of Sunday-school buildings 1869.

Suttee. Burning of the widow on the husband's funeral pile, a practice which prevailed in India and was forbidden by the English 1829.

"Sweating." A term applied to underpaid and overworked labour. Cradley Heath chainmakers' sufferings disclosed 1889; Anti-Sweating League formed 1889; Blue Book published 1890.

Sweden. Delivered from the Danish dominion by Gustavus Vasa 1521; Norway ceded to 1814; union with Norway dissolved 1905.

Swedenborgians. Disciples of Swedenborg (1688-1772), forming what is called the New Church or New Jerusalem Church.

Swiney Prize. Awarded every five years for a work on jurisprudence; Prof. Maitland and Sir. F. Pollock were the winners in 1904.

Switzerland. Struggle for independence against the Hapsburg dominion 13th-14th century; victories at Sempach and Näfels 1386 and 1388; overthrow of Burgundians at Granson and Morat 1476; defeated by French at Melegnano 1515; religious wars in during 16th century; Calvin at Geneva 1536 till his death; country declared independent at Peace of Westphalia 1648.

Synods. Convened formerly by the emperors, and afterwards by the Pope; they were rendered illegal in England except by royal permission 1533. The famous Synod of Dort was held from Nov. 1618 to May 1619.

T

Tadcaster. Town in West Riding of Yorkshire, nine miles south-west of York; b. of (fought at Towton), resulting in victory for Yorkists, May 29, 1461.

Tahiti. Chief island of Windward group of Society Islands situate mid-Pacific Ocean; discovered by Spaniard, De Quiros, in 1607; French protectorate 1842; French possession 1880.

Tai-Pings. Followers of Hung Hsinchwan, in the Chinese rebellion of 1851. Captured Nanking, Mar. 1853; Nanking retaken by the imperialists (under direction of Charles Gordon), July 19, 1864; and rebellion suppressed in 1865. [Refer Wilson, *Gordon's Chinese Campaign and the Tai-Ping Rebellion;* Hake's *Events of the Tai-Ping Rebellion.*]

Tairen. A Russian free port on the Pacific terminus of the Trans-Siberian railway. Opened to trade 1901; occupied by the Japanese in 1904.

Talavera de la Reina. B. of, between English and Spaniards under Sir Arthur Wellesley and French under Joseph Bonaparte and Marshals Jourdan and Victor, resulting in victory for English, July 27-28, 1809.

Talmud. The civil and religious code of the Jews. The Talmud dating from the 5th century is the one in use, an earlier one having become unintelligible. It is divided into the Mishna and Gemara. The first complete copy was published at Venice 1520.

Talmudists. Those of the Jewish faith who recognise the doctrines of the Talmud, as opposed to the Karaites, " followers of the Bible."

Tammany Society. A powerful democratic association of New York fd. in 1789; chartered 1805. Named after Tammany, a Delaware Indian chief; the name itself means " affable."

Tangier. Seaport of Morocco, and a city of great antiquity. Captured by Portuguese 1471; given to Charles II. on his marriage to Catherine of Braganza 1662; evacuated by English 1683; bombarded by French in 1844; terrorised by Rasuli in early years of 20th century; policed in 1906 as a result of Algeciras Convention.

Tantalum. A rare metal discovered by Hatchett in 1801.

Taoism. One of the three religions of China. The system was fd. by Laou-tsze in the 6th century.

Tapestry. Form of weaving of eastern origin known to exist at least as early as 1600 B.C. Intro. into Flanders during 10th century; Gobelin factory fd. in Paris about 1450; Arras chief centre during 14th and 15th centuries; famous tapestry factory fd. at Mortlake by Sir Francis Crane 1619; existed till 1703; another factory existed at Windsor 1872-88.

Tarentum. Seaport of southern Italy fd. about 710 B.C. by Spartans. Assisted by Pyrrhus in war against Romans 281 B.C.; captured by Romans 272 B.C.; became ally of Rome but went over to Hannibal 212 B.C., and on being recaptured by Fabius 209 B.C. was severely punished.

Tarifa. Most southern town of Europe, twenty miles south-west of Gibraltar. Captured from Moslems in 1292; defended by English against French 1811-12.

Tariff Reform League. Inaugurated July 1903.

Tarsus. City in Asia Minor occupied by the Assyrians in 850 B.C. Birthplace of Paul the Apostle. Captured by Arabs *circa* A.D. 660; taken by Tancred in First Crusade 1099; under Turks since about 1500.

Tasmania. Discovered in 1642 by Abel Jans Tasman. Penal settlement till 1852, when transportation to it was abolished. Granted local government 1855.

Tate Gallery. Opened July 21, 1897; enlarged Nov. 1899.

Tattersall's. Horse mart fd. by Richard Tattersall (1724-95) in 1766 at Hyde Park Corner; removed to Knightsbridge 1867.

Taunton. Castle first built by King Ine *circa* 710; rebuilt *circa* 1100; defended by Blake 1644-45; "Bloody Assize" opened by Judge Jeffreys 1685.

Tay Bridge. First bridge opened in 1877; partly destroyed by gale, Dec. 28, 1879 (nearly 90 people lost their lives); second bridge opened 1887.

Tea. First intro. into Europe in 16th century; when first brought to England in following century it cost from £5 to £10 a lb.

Telegraphy. Proposal to use electricity as means of communication made as early as 1753. Morse constructed an instrument in 1835, and Steinheil in 1837. Earliest trial made in 1837 on L. & N.W. Railway. First public line from Paddington to Slough opened 1843; London and Paris connected 1851. Post Office took over telegraph systems on Feb. 5, 1870. Wireless telegraphy proved practicable by Marconi 1896; first Transatlantic stations, Poldhu, Cornwall, and St. John's, Newfoundland, Dec. 1901; first applied to ships, Feb. 1902.

Telepathy. Transmission of thought, etc., otherwise than by the usual means of expression. Word first used by F. W. H. Myers 1882, though experiments in telepathy had been made as early as 1871.

Telephone. The apparatus for transmission of sounds to, and reception at, a distance from their origin. Wheatstone's "Magic Lyre" (one of the earliest experiments for reproducing sounds by means of sound boards connected by a rod) 1831. Philip Reis' experiments to reproduce human speech by means of electric pulsation 1861. Prof. Bell invents electric T. 1875, patented 1876.

Edison patented an invention of his, July 1877. The Telephone Company formed 1878; Edison Telephone Company formed 1879. Action by Postmaster-General against Edison for infringement of his rights 1879. National Telephone Company (amalgamation of various separate concerns) formed 1889; trunk wires transferred to Post Office 1896; government decide (1905) to buy out National Telephone Company in 1911.

Telescope. Roger Bacon, who *d.* 1294, describes principle of T. in his *Opus Magus*. Gambatista della Porta probably first to construct some form of instrument in 1558; Leonardo Digges is also said, in a book published in 1571 by his son, to have arranged glasses so as to obtain " miraculous effects." First practical instruments constructed by Lipperhey and Jansen in Middleburg 1608; Greenwich T. erected 1860.

Templars. Fd. by Baldwin II., King of Jerusalem, for the protection of pilgrims; reached England about 1185; they were much persecuted in the early years of the 14th century and abolished in 1312 by Pope Clement.

Temple (Lond.). Converted into Inns 1311; called after that date the Inner and Middle Temple. Middle Temple New Library built 1861.

Temple Bar. Earliest notice of, 1359; Wren's new gate built 1670-2; removed from Fleet Street 1878-9; new memorial, 1880.

Temple Church. Built *c.* 1250.

Territorials. Formed from Imperial Yeomanry as from April 1, 1908; composed of about 10,000 officers and 262,000 men on Jan. 1, 1910.

Test Act, 1673. All government officers thereby enforced to receive sacrament according to Church of England form, etc.; repealed 1828.

Teutonic Order. Order of Military Knights estab. 1191, for succouring the sick and wounded in the Holy Land; later they fought in parts of Germany for the Christianising of the country; their last remaining possessions were taken by Napoleon in 1809.

Thames. Conservation of the stream given to the Mayors of the City 1489; Twelve Conservators fixed by Act of Parliament 1857. Thames Tunnel opened 1843; closed 1866. Thames Conservancy Act 1894. County Council steamboat service opened 1905; discontinued 1909.

Thames Embankment. North side begun 1862; south (Albert 1866; north (Victoria), 1864; Chelsea 1871.

Theatres. Licence granted to Burbage 1574; the " Theatre " and the " Curtain," " Blackfriars " and " Globe," were among the T. extant in the time of Elizabeth, and were all used by Shakespeare. Old Drury Lane opened 1663; Haymarket 1702; His Majesty's 1705 (Sir H. Beerbohm Tree's new house built 1897); Covent Garden 1732; Sadler's Wells 1765; Adelphi 1806; Olympic 1806;

Lyceum 1809; St. James's 1835; Court 1871; Criterion 1874; Savoy 1881; Prince of Wales's 1883; Lyric 1888; Shaftesbury 1888; Wyndham's 1900; Waldorf 1905, re-titled Strand and reopened 1909.

Thermometer. Invention of attributed to Galileo. Three scales are used at the present day: Fahrenheit (used mainly in England), Réaumur, and Celsius or Centigrade (used chiefly on the Continent).

Thibet. An ancient kingdom in Central Asia; fd. 313 B.C.; ruled by Lamas. The country has always been shrouded in mystery, and several notable expeditions have been made with a vew to clearing up some much debated points. The most notable expeditions are those of Marco Polo in 1278, Dr. Sven Hedin 1899 and 1908, Colonel Younghusband 1904.

Thirty-nine Articles of Religion. Originally Henry VIII. decreed six articles of religion, and offenders against these articles were considered to be heretics and punished as such 1539. These articles were increased to forty-two in 1551 and reduced to thirty-two in 1563. Received the assent of parliament in 1571.

Thirty Years' War, 1618-48. Waged between the Protestants and Catholics of Germany; Gustavus Adolphus and Wallenstein are notable characters in this war. The war began in Bohemia and was terminated by the Peace of Westphalia.

Thistle, Order of. A Scottish order fd. by James V. in 1540; discontinued on James' death; revived by James VII. in 1687.

Thomas', St., Hospital. Fd. in 1213 as an almshouse; enlarged by the mayor of London in 1551; rebuilt 1693; and again in 1868.

Thomites. Followers of Thom (John Nicholls), who created a riot in May 1838 at Boughton (Kent) in opposition to Poor Law Act.

Thugs. Fanatics of India who sacrificed victims to Bhowain, a goddess; suppressed by the English in 1830.

Thundering Legion of the Roman Army. Gained their victories owing to severe storms which were supposed to be brought about by the prayers of the Christians in the legion, 174.

Tiber. A central Italian river on which Rome stands. Destructive floods have been frequent, the most recent being those of 1598, 1870, and 1900.

Tides. Theory of tides first made clear by Kepler in 1598, but had been studied by Posidonius of Apamea in 79 B.C.; completely explained by Sir Isaac Newton in 1683.

Tierra del Fuego. A group of islands in the S.W. of South America; discovered by Magellan in 1520.

Tilsit. A town in East Prussia which grew up around a castle; it is noted for the peace treaty between the Emperors Alexander and Napoleon in 1807.

" Times " Newspaper. First issued as the *Times* in 1788, but had been published as the *Daily Universal Register* since 1785. Fd. by Mr. John Walter; converted into a company in 1908 with Mr. A. F. Walter as first chairman of directors.

Tin. One of the earliest known metals, having been imported from England by the Phœnicians more than 1000 years B.C.

Tobacco. The origin of the name is doubtful. First observed in Cuba 1492; brought to England in 1565 or 1586 by Sir John Hawkins or Sir Walter Raleigh; cultivation in England was prohibited in 1684, and allowed in Ireland in 1779; permission to cultivate tobacco in England under certain conditions was granted in 1886.

Tolls. First estab. for vessels on the Elbe in 1109; the first tolls in England were collected in London in 1267; toll gates were instit. in 1663; from 1827 to 1893 toll gates were gradually abolished, and now very few remain in this country.

Tontines. Instit. by Tonti, a Neapolitan; first used in Paris in 1653; they were loans on life annuities; the last English public T. was in 1789.

Tories. A name applied to a political party; instit. in 1678.

Torpedoes. Invented by David Bushnell in 1777 in America; Fulton offered his invention to the British Government in 1805; first used in warfare in the war with the U.S. 1861-65.

Tower of London. Commenced in 1078 by William I.; completed by William Rufus in 1098; additions made in 1680-5; a portion was destroyed by fire in 1841.

Tractarianism. Arose from articles appearing in *Tracts for the Times*, a tract dealing with Church matters; published 1833-41, when all the tracts were condemned at Oxford.

Trades Unions. Instit. in 1825 to withstand the influence of capital and competition. A commission of inquiry into the working of T.U. was held in 1867; an act to protect the funds of T.U. was passed 1869. To counteract T.U. a Federation of Employers was fd. 1873. T.U. instit. in France 1884, and U.S.A. 1845.

Transvaal. Fd. by Dutch Boers in 1848; S. J. P. Krüger first president 1853; Kaffir War 1876; under British protection 1877; declared Crown colony 1879; Boers revolt and estab. republic 1880; b. of Majuba Hill, Feb. 26-27, 1881; Orange Free State proclaim neutrality, Feb. 1881; Peace, Mar. 24, 1881; Paul Krüger president 1883; Jameson Raid, Dec. 1895; ultimatum from Boers, Oct. 9, 1899; war declared, Oct. 11, 1899; annexation of Transvaal, Oct. 25, 1900; Sir A. Milner appointed High Commissioner, Mar. 4, 1901; new constitution on representative lines, Dec. 1906; Botha president 1907; establishment of Union of South Africa, May 31, 1910; Botha becomes Prime Minister, May 31, 1910. *See* South African War.

Trappists. Fd. in 1140 and named after the Abbey of La Trappe in Normandy. An order of monks whose rules are of the severest nature, absolute silence being insisted upon.

Treadmill. First used as an instrument for irrigation by the Chinese. Intro. into English prisons by Sir William Cubbit, and first used in Buxton prison in 1817; now very little used.

Trent (in Tyrol). The first Council of Trent sat in 1545, and continued to 1563; its decisions are the standard of the Roman Catholic faith.

Trial of the Seven Bishops. The Bishops of Bath, Bristol, Canterbury, Chichester, Ely, Peterborough, and St. Asaph were committed to the Tower because they refused to read the king's declaration for liberty of conscience 1688. They were acquitted in the same year.

Triennial Parliaments, *i.e.* parliaments meeting at least once in three years, were estab. by act in 1641. The Long Parliament of 1640-53 broke this act, and it was repealed in 1664. A further similar act in 1694 was repealed in 1716.

Trinity House. An institution for regulating pilots; fd. by Sir Thomas Spert, who was the first master in 1512. The maintenance of lighthouses and buoys is also one of the duties of the brethren of T.H.

Triple Alliance, 1668. Was ratified for the protection of the Spanish Netherlands, the contracting parties being the states general and England (Sweden joined later) against France. Other T.A. have been: 1717, England, France, and Holland, against Spain; 1795, England, Russia, and Austria; 1887, Germany, Austria, and Italy.

Troubadours. Poets of Southern France and Northern Spain in 12th-14th centuries. First troubadour poet, William Duke of Guienne, *fl. c.* 1096. Among the more celebrated were Pierre Vidal, *c.* 1160-*c.* 1215; Geoffroi Rudel, Bernard de Ventadour, and Bernard de Born, who *fl.* 12th, and Sordello 13th century.

Truce of God. Instit. in 1032 by the Bishop of Aquitaine for the abolition of private feuds in Europe. Decreed in 1027 that there should be truces from Saturday evenings to Monday mornings, the truce was decreed by a synod at Roussillon 1027; advocated by Bishop of Aquitaine 1032; adopted in England 1042, and confirmed 1123, 1139, and 1179 by the Lateran Councils.

Tuberculosis. The organism causing this disease was isolated by Dr. Koch of Berlin in 1881. Various commissions have been appointed to inquire into the causes of the origin and spread of the disease.

Tübingen School. Fd. in 1835 by Prof. F. C. Baur; deals with theology from an historical and philosophical point of view.

Tubular Bridges. The first T. B. was built over the Menai Straits in 1846-50.

Tuileries. The French imperial palace was built by Catherine de Medicis, Henry IV., and Louis XIV. Stormed in 1792; and ransacked in 1830 and 1848 during the revolutions. Now used as a museum.

Tunis. The largest city of N. Africa excluding Egypt; probably older than Carthage, and in 800-909 was a residence of the Aghlabite dynasty. Repeatedly pillaged during 10th century. French occupation 1881. At the present day T. consists of the native town and the European quarter.

Tunnels. The oldest T. is at Bezières; the first English T. was built on the Bridgewater Canal near Manchester in 1766. Channel Tunnel begun 1876; relinquished 1882-3. Mersey Tunnel opened 1886; Severn Tunnel 1886; Simplon Tunnel 1905; Hudson River 1908.

Turbines. The Hon. C. A. Parsons of Newcastle-on-Tyne built the first steam turbine in 1894; the first Atlantic passage turbine steamer was launched in 1904.

Turin. Capital of Italy till 1864. Besieged by the French in 1706; taken by French in 1798, but they were expelled by the Russians and Austrians in the following year; again surrendered to the French in 1800; res. to Sardinia in 1814.

Turkey. The Turkish Empire was fd. in 760, when a tribe of Tartars took possession of a portion of Armenia; in the 13th century they returned to Asia Minor; 1299 the Ottoman Empire was fd. by the Osmanlis under Othman at Prusa; Adrianople captured 1361; annexation of Macedonia 1430; termination of the E. Roman Empire by conquest of Constantinople by Turks under Mahomet II. 1453; Greece becomes subject to Turkey 1456; Egypt conquered 1516; Cyprus captured 1571; commercial treaty with England 1579; defeat by Persians 1585; defeat of Persians 1638; Crete taken after a siege of many years 1669; Belgrade lost 1717; retaken 1739; war with Austria and Russia 1787-91; in 1798 Turkey joined England and Russia against France owing to Napoleon's seizure of Egypt; Servian rising 1804; war with Russia 1807; revolt against Selim III. 1807; Mustafa put to death 1808; revolt of Greeks 1821; fleet destroyed by those of England, France, and Russia at Navarino 1827; treaty with Russia 1833; treaty with England 1838; Crimean War 1854; Russo-Turkish War 1877; Treaty of San Stefano 1878; Greek War 1897; Young Turks revolted at Résua 1908; new constitution promulgated 1909.

Turner's Legacies, *i.e.* the pictures which J. M. W. Turner, the great landscape painter, bequeathed to the nation. Turner was *b.* in 1775 and *d.* in 1851.

Tyburn. The place where evil doers were executed up to 1783. The gallows on which the executions took place were erected at a spot where Oxford Street, Edgware Road, and Bayswater Road join.

Tyler's Insurrection, 1380. Arose in consequence of the poll tax; raged chiefly in the eastern and southern counties, and was the direct result of an insult to Wat Tyler's daughter

U

Uganda (British Protectorate, Eastern Equatorial Africa). Boundaries defined by Protocol drawn up between Britain, Belgium, and Germany, signed May 14, 1910. First European to visit, Captain Speke, 1862. Anglo-German Treaty assigned Uganda to Britain 1890. Civil war 1891; rebellion 1897. [Refer Speke, *Discovery of Source of the Nile ;* Ashe, *Chronicles of Uganda ;* Tucker, *Eighteen Years in Uganda and East Africa*.]

Ulm (Würtemberg). Peace signed 1620; cathedral built 1377-1494; spire (reputed the highest there is), 530 feet high, completed 1894.

Ulster (North of Ireland). Colonisation of forfeited lands 1611; rebellion 1641; U. Convention in opposition to Home Rule met June 17, 1892; U. Convention League formed, Aug. 1892.

Ulundi, Battle of. Zulus defeated by Lord Chelmsford, July 6, 1879.

Umbrella. First person to use an umbrella generally in London said to be Jonas Hanway, who *d.* in 1786.

Unemployed Riots, 1886-87. Select Committee of the House of Commons appointed, Feb. 13, 1895; final report issued Feb. 1896; reappointed, April 17, 1896. London unemployed fund started by Lord Mayor, Dec. 1904; royal commission appointed, Nov. 28, 1905; Labour Exchanges Act 1909; Queen Alexandra's Unemployed Fund, Jan. 1906. *See also* Labour Exchanges.

Uniformity Acts. Jan. 15, 1549. Order of divine worship drawn up by Cranmer to be only one used. Confirmed in 1552; repealed 1554; re-enacted 1559. Act of U. of Charles II. obliging uniformity in matters of religion, all clergy to subscribe to XXXIX. Articles, etc., passed, Aug. 24, 1662 (Black Bartholomew's day). Act of U. Amendment Act passed, July 18, 1872.

Uniforms. In use in French army 1688; English naval uniforms in use 1748.

Union of England and Scotland. Mar. 24, 1603, on accession of James I. of England (James VI. of Scotland) to the throne. Act of Union passed, July 22, 1706; ratified by Scottish Parliament, Jan. 16, 1707.

Union Jack. English flag, originally red cross on white ground (banner of St. George); Scottish flag, white diagonal cross on blue ground incorp. April 1606; Irish flag, diagonal red cross on white ground (banner of St. Patrick), incorp. Jan. 1801.

Union Jack Club. Opened by King Edward VII. July 1, 1907, for soldiers and sailors, as memorial to men killed in wars in China and South Africa.

Unitarians. Sect fd. by Socinus in Italy in 1546; intro. in England about 1700. International Unit. Council, Geneva, 1905.

United Kingdom. England and Wales one kingdom 1283; union of England and Scotland 1707; union with Ireland 1801.

United States. First American Congress opposition to Stamp Act, Nov. 1765. Chests of tea destroyed at Boston and New York, Dec. 18, 1773. Declaration of Rights, Nov. 1774. First battle between British and Americans (Lexington), April 19, 1775. B. of Bunker Hill, June 17, 1775. Act of Perpetual Union of States, May 20, 1775. Declaration of Independence, July 4, 1776. Articles of Confederation proposed by John Dickinson 1776. Submitted to States, Nov. 1777. Alliance with France, Feb. 6, 1778; ratified, Mar. 1781. Lord Cornwallis surrendered with whole army at Yorktown, Oct. 19, 1781. Treaty of Peace signed at Paris, Sept. 3, 1783. New Constitution proposed by Convention of Philadelphia, Sept. 1787; ratified, May 23, 1788. George Washington elected first president (1789-97), April 6, 1789. John Adams elected 2nd president (1797-1801), 1797. Death of Washington, Dec. 14, 1799. Thomas Jefferson elected 3rd president (1801-09), 1801. Acquisition of Louisiana 1803. Ports closed to British ships, July 1807. Importation of slaves prohibited, Jan. 1, 1808. James Madison elected 4th president (1809-17), 1809. War with Great Britain declared, June 18, 1812. Peace Treaty with Great Britain signed, Dec. 24, 1814. James Monroe elected 5th president (1817-25), 1817. Missouri Compromise, defining boundaries of slave area, 1820. Monroe Doctrine proclaimed 1823. John Quincy Adams elected 6th president (1825-29), 1825. Andrew Jackson elected 7th president (1829-37), 1829. Martin Van Buren elected 8th president (1837-41), 1837. W. H. Harrison elected 9th president, March 4, 1841; d. April 4, 1841. John Tyler (vice-president) became 10th president (1841-45), April 1841. Texas annexed 1845. J. Knox Polk elected 11th president (1845-49), 1845. Mexican War over the annexation of Texas 1845-48. Mormons settle in Utah 1847. Zachary Taylor 12th president (1849-50), 1849; d. Mar. 31, 1850. Millard Fillmore (vice-president) 13th president (1850-53), 1850. Fugitive Slave Bill 1850. Fenimore Cooper d. 1851. Franklin Pierce, 14th president (1853-56), 1853. Commercial Treaty with Japan 1854. Civil War in Kansas 1856-57. James Buchanan 15th president (1856-60), Nov. 1856. Attack on Harper's Ferry by John Brown, Oct. 16, 1859. Execution of John Brown, Dec. 2, 1859. Republican convention at Chicago 1860. Abraham Lincoln elected 16th president, Nov. 6, 1860. South Carolina, State Convention of, passes ordinance of secession, Dec. 20, 1860. Admission of Kansas as a state, Jan. 21, 1861. Secession of Mississippi (Jan. 8), Florida

(Jan. 11), Alabama (Jan. 11), Texas (Feb. 1), Georgia (Jan. 19), and Louisiana (Jan. 26), Jan.—Feb. 1861. " Confederate " States' delegates meet at Montgomery, Alabama, elect Jefferson Davis president, Feb. 18, 1861, and form constitution, Mar. 11, 1861. Morrill Protection Tariff adopted, Mar. 1861. Civil War begins by an attack on Fort Sumter by the Confederates (South), April 13, 1861. Lincoln's call for troops, April 15, 1861. First blood spilt at Baltimore, April 19, 1861. Lincoln issues proclamation of blockade of southern ports, April 19, 1861. North Carolina and Arkansas secede, May 1861. B. of Bull's Run, July 21, 1861. B. of Ball's Bluff, Oct. 21, 1861. Jefferson Davis elected President of Southern Confederacy for six years, Nov. 1861. Paper currency (" Greenbacks ") adopted, Feb. 25, 1862. B. of Pea Ridge, March 6-8, 1862. B. of Winchester, Mar. 23, 1862. B. of Pittsburg, April 6-7, 1862. B. of Fredericksburg, Dec. 10, 1862. Homestead Act passed, Dec. 1862. B. of Chancellorsville, May 2, 1863. (" Stonewall " Jackson mortally wounded by his own troops in mistake at the b. of Chancellorsville; d. May 10, 1862.) British Consuls expelled from Southern States, Oct. 1863. Fugitive Slave Act repealed, June 13, 1864. Lincoln re-elected president, Nov. 8, 1864. Gen. Lee surrenders to Gen. Grant at Appomattox, April 9, 1865. President Lincoln assassinated, April 15, 1865. Gen. Johnston surrendered at Durham station, April 26, 1865. Andrew Johnson elevated to presidency, April 1865. Proclamation of Amnesty, May 29, 1865. Abolition of slavery proclaimed, Dec. 18, 1865. End of rebellion proclaimed by President Johnson, April 3, 1866. Civil Rights (of negroes) Bill passed, April 9, 1866. Bill of Impeachment of President Johnson carried in House of Representatives Feb. 25; sent up to Senate, Mar. 4, 1868. President Johnson acquitted by Senate, May 26, 1868. Gen. Grant elected 18th president, Nov. 1868. Civil War in Louisiana, Feb. 1873. Riots in Mississippi between whites and blacks, Aug. 1874. Negro insurrection in Tennessee, Aug. 1874. Reciprocity Treaty with Canada rejected by Senate, Feb. 4, 1875. Engagement with Indians at Little Horn River, June 25, 1876. Rutherford B. Hayes elected 19th president, Mar. 1877. Gen. James A. Garfield elected 20th president, Nov. 1880; assassinated July 1881. (Gen. Garfield d. from wounds, Sept. 19, 1881). Chester A. Arthur succeeds to presidency, Sept. 1881. Edmunds' Anti-Polygamy Act, Mar. 1882. Chinese Exclusion Act passed, April 1882. Revision of tariff, Mar. 1883. Grover Cleveland elected 21st president, Nov. 1884. Fiscal Reform: Mill's Bill reducing protection duties and placing many raw materials on free list passed 1888-89. Gen. Benj. Harrison elected president, Nov. 1888. Nicaragua Canal Bill passed, Feb. 1889. McKinley Tariff Bill (protectionist) passed, Oct. 1890. Grover Cleveland elected president, Nov. 1892. Railway strikes at Chicago, much rioting, June-July 1894. Income Tax declared by Supreme Court to be unconstitutional, May 20, 1895. Request to Spanish Government to recognise independence of Cuba, Mar. 2, 1896. Election of Mr. W. McKinley to presidency, Nov. 3, 1896. Arbitration

Treaty with Great Britain for five years signed at Washington, Jan. 11, 1897; Senate refuses to ratify it, May 5, 1897. Dingley Tariff Bill passed (highly protectionist), July 1897. Hawaii annexed, July 7, 1898. *Maine* explosion, Feb. 15, 1898. Ultimatum sent to Spain, April 19, 1898. War begins, April 21, 1898. Treaty of Paris between Spain and America, Dec. 10, 1898. McKinley re-elected president, Nov. 1900; assassinated at Buffalo, Sept. 6, 1901; *d.* Sept. 14, 1901. Theodore Roosevelt succeeds to presidency, Sept. 1901. Panama Canal Bill passed, June 26, 1902. Alaska Boundary Treaty, Feb. 11, 1903; Venezuela dispute settled by diplomacy of the U.S., Feb. 1903. St. Louis Exhibition opened, April 30, 1904. Arbitration Treaty with Great Britain, Dec. 12, 1904. Roosevelt re-elected, Nov. 1904. Riots in Chicago, May 1905. Asiatic Labourers Exclusion Bill, Feb. 1907. Arbitration Treaty with Great Britain, April 4, 1908. Canadian Fisheries Treaty, April 1908. Election of Mr. William H. Taft to presidency, Feb. 1909. Arbitration Treaty with Great Britain, July 1911.

Universities. Salerno, reputed to have been fd. in 9th century, is the earliest of which there is record; Bologna 1116, Paris 1200, Padua 1230, Salamanca 1240, Ingolstadt 1472 (transferred to Landshut 1800, to Munich 1826), Wittenberg 1502 (absorbed 1694 by Halle), Göttingen 1737. Oxford, the most ancient English U., was fd. in the early part of the 12th century, and Cambridge shortly afterwards. Earliest colleges were University College 1249, Balliol College 1263, Merton College 1264, Exeter 1314. Peterhouse College, Cambridge, was fd. in 1257, Pembroke College in 1347, Gonville and Caius 1348, and King's College 1352. Henry III. granted a charter to Cambridge in 1231 and to Oxford in 1248. The two U. were governed by the Elizabethan statutes of 1570 and the Laudian statutes of 1636 until 1858, when new codes came into force. Further changes were intro. by the Universities Act of 1877. The other U. of Great Britain are:—

Aberdeen	.	fd. 1494	Leeds	.	fd. 1904
Birmingham	. ,,	1900	Liverpool	. ,,	1881
Dublin (Trinity College) ,,		1591	Manchester	. ,,	1880
Durham .	. ,,	1831	St. Andrews	. ,,	1411
Edinburgh	. ,,	1562	Sheffield .	. ,,	1905
Glasgow	. ,,	1450	Wales:		
Ireland, Royal University of (formerly Queen's, 1850)	,,	1880	Aberystwyth Cardiff . Bangor .	. ,, . ,, . ,,	1872 1883 1884
London .	. ,,	1826			

Uranium. A metallic element, discovered in 1789 by Klaproth, contained in pitchblende.

Uranus. Planet discovered by Sir W. Herschel, Mar. 13, 1781.

Ursuline Nuns. Fd. orig. at Brescia by Angela Merci (St. Angela) about 1536.

Uruguay. South American Republic. First visited by Juan Diaz de Solis in 1512. Under Spanish power 1725-1825; Declaration of Independence, Aug. 25, 1825; republic formally constituted, July 18, 1830. Presidents:—

Pereyra 1856	Battle 1868	Obes 1890
Berro 1860	Varela 1875	Borda 1894
Aguirre 1864	Latorre 1876	Cuestas 1897
Flores 1865	Santa 1882	Batele 1903
Vidal 1866	Tages 1886	

Utopia. An imaginary commonwealth representing the most perfect conditions possible, described in book of that title by Sir Thomas More, published in 1548.

Utrecht, Treaty of. Between Great Britain, France, and the United Provinces, signed April 11, 1713, closing the European War of the Spanish Succession.

V

Vaccination. Protective inoculation against smallpox discovered by Sir Edward Jenner in 1798; V. was first made compulsory in the United Kingdom in 1853. "Anti-Vaccination" has been rabid in England of recent years, and the act of 1898 affords relief to parents who desire it.

Valentine's Day. Occurs on Feb. 14, and celebrates the martyrdom of a Roman priest and a bishop.

Vallombrosians. An order of Benedictine monks fd. by St. John Gualbert in 1038.

Valparaiso. A Chilian seaport. Fd. in 1536 by Juan de Saavedra; captured by Sir Francis Drake in 1578; sacked by the Dutch in 1600; suffered from severe earthquakes in 1730, 1822, 1839, 1873, and 1908.

Vatican. Named after a Roman hill, Mons Vaticanus. The palace, commenced in 1146, became the residence of the Pope in 1377; it is said to contain 7000 rooms. The Popes make the V. their voluntary prison.

Vauxhall Gardens. Laid out in 1661 on the south bank of the Thames. With George IV.'s permission called Royal in 1822. The gardens were closed in 1859.

Veddahs. The aborigines of Ceylon. Their habits were first studied in detail during the Dutch occupation in 1644-1796.

Vegetarianism. The practice of abstaining from a meat diet The word came into use about 1847.

Venezuela. A South American republic. Discovered by Columbus in 1498; remained under Spanish rule till the beginning of 19th century; revolted and proclaimed independence in 1811.

Venice. Fd. A.D. 452; first Doge 697; Rialto the seat of government 811; Bank of Venice 1157; first rite of "Wedding the Adriatic" 1177; Rialto Bridge and Piazza of St. Mark built 1592; annexed to Italy 1805; to Austria 1814; final transfer to Italy 1866.

Versailles. A town in N.W. France near Paris; here Louis III. built a hunting-box on the site of which Louis XIV. erected a palace 1661-87; Treaty of Versailles 1783; surrendered to Germans 1870.

Vesuvius. An Italian volcano on the shores of the Bay of Naples. An eruption in A.D. 79 totally destroyed Pompeii and Herculaneum; other disasters have taken place in 1631, 1759, 1794, 1822, 1855, 1858, 1868, 1892, 1906.

Veterinary Science. Practised by the Egyptians, but first definitely recorded by Hippocrates 460 B.C. Varro, 116 B.C., wrote three works on veterinary science, and Diocles of Corystus was the earliest recorded student of animal anatomy.

Vice-Chancellor of England. The first V.-C. was appointed in 1813, to assist the Master of the Rolls and the Chancellor; later, 1841, two additional V.-C. were formed, and in 1873 they became judges of the High Court of Justice; the last V.-C. was Sir J. Bacon.

Vichy. A town of Central France, celebrated for its mineral waters. Known to the Romans, but did not become famous till the 17th century.

Victoria and Albert Museum. Foundation stone laid in 1899 by Queen Victoria; opened in 1909 by King Edward and Queen Alexandra.

Victoria Cross. A reward for bravery to all ranks of the army and navy; instit. 1856. The Cross is manufactured out of the cannon taken from the Russians at Sebastopol, and is in the form of a Maltese Cross.

Victoria Falls (on the Zambesi, C. Africa). The greatest of the world's waterfalls; discovered by Livingstone in 1855; spanned by a bridge of the Cape and Cairo railway 1905.

Victoria Nyanza. An African lake; second largest fresh-water lake in the world, Lake Superior being the largest; discovered by Speke in 1858; Messrs. Wilson and Smith first voyaged across the lake 1877; divided between England and Germany 1890.

"Victory." Nelson's flagship at Trafalgar 1805, is preserved at Portsmouth.

Vienna, Congress of. Formed by Great Britain, Austria, Russia, and Prussia with a view to the disposition of the countries freed from French suzerainty after Napoleon's fall 1814-15. Did not secure the stability of Europe, in fact, territories were disposed of almost at random, and modern Europe owes little to its influence.

Vienne, Council of. A Roman Catholic Council under Pope Clement V. 1311-12. Its object was to decide as to the abolition of the Templars.

Vigilance Committee. A self-appointed judicial body of the U.S.A. organised in San Francisco 1851 for the protection of life and property.

Viking. A sea rover or pirate. The first V. fleet appeared off coasts of Britain A.D. 789; from this time onwards V. raids were common on the eastern shores of Britain.

Villefranche-de-Rouergue. A town in Aveyron, France. Fd. 1252; fell into the hands of the Black Prince 1348.

Villenage (serfdom). A Norman-French word first used in England in 11th century.

Virginia. One of the states of U.S.A. The first permanent English settlement in North America, 1607, by members of the London Company; John Smith was the first head of the company, whose object was to build a flourishing agricultural and commercial settlement; tobacco-growing was the great industry. Played a foremost part in the Civil War of 1812.

Virgin Islands (British). A group of about 100 small islands in W. Indies. Discovered by Columbus 1494; taken over by Britain 1666.

Vittoria. Capital of Alava, Spain. Fd. 581 by Leovigild, King of the Visigoths. A decisive victory, which freed Spain from France, was fought here during the Peninsular War 1813.

Vivisection, or experiments on living animals, had been carried out, from a physiological point of view, for many years, but in 1860 the matter was brought before the Society for Prevention of Cruelty to Animals by Mr. G. Macilwain. A bill to prevent V. was brought before parliament in 1883, but it failed to become law.

Volapük. The first artificial language of any note. Originated by J. M. Schleyer in 1880, based on the English language with a smattering of Latin and Romance. A Volapük Academy was formed in 1887, but in 1893 the academy was mainly concerned with the founding of Idiom Neutral, another international language.

Volsci. The greatest enemies of Rome during the first century of the Roman Republic; they lived in S. Latium.

Voltaic Pile. Invented by Volta *circa* 1793.

Volturno. A central Italian river of great military importance. The colony of Volturnum was fd. here 194 B.C. by the Romans. In 1860 the Neapolitans were defeated by Garibaldi's army, and as a result Capua fell.

Volunteers (English). Unpaid soldiers; granted a charter by Henry VIII. in 1537; organised on a larger scale 1757; English and Scottish V. were disbanded 1783, but raised again 1794; in 1900 V. supplied many service companies for the South African War; now converted into the Territorial force 1907-8.

Voronezh. A Russian town S.E. of Moscow. Fd. in 1586 to rebuff Tartar raids, but was burned by them 1590; here Peter the Great built his boats for the conquest of Azov; has been three times almost destroyed by fire 1703, 1748, 1773.

Vulgate. St. Jerome's Latin version of the Bible (4th century) 384; revised 1908 by the Benedictine order at the instigation of Pope Pius X. Gutenberg and Fust printed the earliest edition, *c.* 1457.

W

Wadai. A county in N. Central Africa. First made known to Europe by the Arabs, and later explored by Nachtigal 1873; notorious as a great slave raiding state; came under French influence in 1899, and annexed by France in 1909.

Wadi Halfa. A town in the Sudan. The British base in 1884 in the operation for the relief of General Gordon.

Wages. First fixed by Act of Parliament in 1350. In 1883 an act was passed to prohibit wages being paid in public-houses.

Wagner, W. R. German musician, dramatist, and poet, *b.* Leipzig 1813. Among his most celebrated works are Tannhäuser, Lohengrin, Tristan und Isolde, Parsifal, Die Meistersinger Von Nürnberg. Wagner died at Wahnfried 1883.

Wagram. A village N.E. of Vienna. Here Napoleon defeated the Austrians under the Archduke Charles in 1809.

Wahhabis. A Mahommedan sect; their chief was Ibn 'Abd ul-Wahhab, *b.* in 1691; the W. claimed to have returned to the earliest form of Islam.

Waits, or **Christmas Carol Singers.** Originally belonged to the king's court; night watchmen in 14th and 15th centuries; they were replaced as guardians of the peace by police in 1829.

Wake. A watching round a corpse before burial, custom now confined to Ireland; orig. religious services 1536.

Walcheren Expedition, 1809. Under Chatham and Sir R. Strachan. Flushing was taken, but there the army were overcome by ennui and disease; four months later the town was evacuated and the expedition returned to England.

Waldenses. A name given to a sect of Christian heretics in the south of France 1170; their modern name is Vaudois, and they are to be found at the present time in Piedmont. The earliest known document of the faith was written in 1218; in 1532 they were absorbed into Protestantism; the revocation of the Edict of Nantes had for its object the extermination of the sect.

Wales. A principality in the middle west of Great Britain. Occupied at the time of the Roman invasion 55 B.C. by five tribes, the Gangani and Decangi, the Ordovices, the Demetæ, and the Silures; Caractacus defeated by the Romans A.D. 43, taken prisoner to Rome 50; conquest of Silures and Ordovices by Julius Frontinus and Agricola 78; withdrawal of Romans, early 5th century; warfare with the Saxons: b. of Deorham 577; with the Angles: b. of Chester 616; b. of Hethfield and death of Edwin, king of the Angles, 633; Cadwallon slain soon after in battle; continued dissension among the Welsh princes; union under Rhodri the Great 844, and defeat of the Danes; peaceful reign of **Hywel the**

Good, who drew up a code of laws, 10th century; Gruffydd ap Llewelyn becomes king 1023; defeats English at Hereford, is surprised by Harold 1062, and slain by his own men 1063; gradual conquest of country by William the Conqueror and his son; expedition into under Henry I. 1121; general uprising under Ap Rhys 1135, and victory over English at Cardigan 1136; north and south divided between his sons and those of Ap Cynan; expedition into of Henry II. 1157, and peace concluded with princes of the north and south; later unsuccessful raid 1169; peace made with Rhys ap Gruffydd, the ruling lord of South Wales; Llewelyn becomes powerful in the north and marries King John's daughter 1206; joins the revolting barons, becomes Prince of All Wales, dies 1240; disputes between various claimants to the kingship, among them Prince Edward, Henry III.'s son; victory of Llewelyn over English at Dynevor 1255; peace concluded with Henry 1267; and Llewelyn declared Prince of Wales; Llewelyn refuses homage to Edward I.; invasion by the English king, and Llewelyn starved into submission, 1277; oppression of natives by English officers, and fresh rise under Llewelyn and Dafydd; English put to flight at the Menai Straits, and Llewelyn finally slain near Builth 1282; completion of conquest by Edward I. 1283; statute of Rhuddlan enacted 1284; Owain Glyndwr's rebellion 1400-15; Richmond (Henry VII.) lands in Pembroke 1485; Council of Wales under Bishop Rowland Lee, 1534; Wales incorporated into England, Act of 1535; Monmouthshire detached 1536; great sessions estab. 1542; Welsh Bible translated 1567-88; Council abolished 1689; circulating schools 1730; Intermediate Education Act 1889; Welsh Land Commission 1893-4; investiture of Prince of Wales at Carnarvon Castle 1911; Welsh National Library begun 1911. *See* Carnarvon.

Wales, Princes of—

British Princes :

Maelgwn Gwynedd	550
Rhun, son of Maelgwn	584
Cadwallon, son of Cadvan	630
Cadwaladr, son of Cadwallon	634
Idwal, son of Cadwaladr	661
Rhodri Molwynog	728
Cynan and Howel	755
Mervyn Frych	825
Rhodri the Great	844
Anarawd, Cadell, and Mervyn	877
{ Idwal Foel	915
{ Hywel Dda, the Good	943
Ieuan and Iago	948
Hywel ap Ieuan	972
Cadwallon	984
Meredith ap Owen	985
Idwal ap Meyric ap Idwal Foel	992
Aedan (usurper)	998

WALES, PRINCES OF (*continued*)—

Llewelyn ap Seisyll	1015
Griffith ap Llewelyn ap Seisyll	1023
Bleddyn, Rhiwallon, Meredith ap Owen	1067
Trahaiarn ap Caradoc ⎱ Meilir ⎰ Caradoc ⎰	1073
Griffith ap Cynan ⎱ Rhys ap Tewdwr ⎰ Cadogan ap Beddyn ⎰ Iorwerth ab Bleddyn ⎰	1079
Owen Gwynedd	1137
Howel ab Owen Gwynedd ⎱ David ap Owen Gwynedd ⎰	1169
Llewelyn ap Iorwerth, the Great	1194
David ap Llewelyn	1240
Llewelyn ap Griffith (" Llewelyn y Llyw Olaf ")	1246

English Princes :

Edward of Carnarvon (King Edward II.), *b.* 1284; created Prince of Wales	1301
Edward the Black Prince, son of Edward III.	1343
Richard (Richard II.), son of the Black Prince.	1377
Henry of Monmouth (Henry V.)	1399
Edward of Westminster, son of Henry VI.	1454
Edward of Westminster (Edward V.)	1472
Edward, son of Richard III. (*d.* 1484)	1483
Arthur Tudor, son of Henry VII.	1489
Henry Tudor (Henry VIII.), son of Henry VII.	1503
Henry F. Stuart, son of James I. (*d.* 1612)	1610
Charles Stuart (Charles I.), son of James I.	1616
Charles (Charles II.), son of Charles I.	1630
George Augustus (George II.), son of George I.	1714
Frederick Lewis, son of George II. (*d.* 1751)	1727
George William Frederick (George III.)	1751
George Augustus Frederick (George IV.)	1762
Albert Edward (Edward VII.)	1841
George Frederick Ernest Albert (George V.)	1901
Edward, son of George V., July 13	1911

Wales, University of. Received full charter in 1893; the university consists of three colleges, Aberystwith, 1872; Cardiff, 1883; and Bangor, 1884.

Wallace Collection. Opened to the public in June 1900; consists of art treasures collected by the third and fourth Marquesses of Hertford.

Walloons. Inhabitants of Hainault, Namur, Liege, Ardennes, etc.; their language is a separate branch of Romance, and was used as a literary language till 15th century.

Wallsend. A town in Northumberland famous for its coal. The colliery was opened in 1807.

Walpole's Administrations. *b.* 1676; War Secretary 1708; First Lord of Treasury and Chancellor of Exchequer 1715; resigned 1717, but resumed office 1721; *d.* 1745.

" Waltharius." A Latin poem relating the adventures of Walter of Aquitaine, written by Ekkehard *circa* 920.

Wampun. Shell money of N. American Indians, its value depending on colour; made by whites as well as Indians, and current in Connecticut in 1704.

Warden. A custodian or defender. The governor of Dover Castle is known as Lord Warden, and till 1870 the master of the mint was known as W.

War Game. A scientific game invented by Marshal Keith, but modernised by Von Reisswitz in 1824.

Warsaw. Capital of Poland and the chief stronghold of that country. The date of its foundation is unknown, but a castle was erected there as early as the 9th century; not mentioned in writings before 1224; passed through many stirring periods, being taken by Sweden in 1655; retaken by Poles 1656; taken again by Sweden 1702; by Russians 1764; and in 1806 was occupied by Napoleon's troops; taken finally by Russia 1813; an insurrection in favour of independence took place 1863; further insurrection 1905-6.

Wartburg. A castle in Saxe Weimar, built by Landgrave Louis *circa* 1120. In 1207 a celebrated minstrels' concert took place here, *vide* Wagner's *Tannhaüser*. Luther was brought here for safety in 1521, and here he completed his translation of the New Testament.

Washington. Capital of U.S.A. and one of the leading educational centres. The American Government was removed here in 1800; in 1814 the town was taken by the British, and the Capitol and president's house were burned; a centre of operations during the Civil War.

Washington, Treaties of, 1846, settled the boundary question between U.S.A. and British America; 1854, a trade treaty with Canada; 1871, a fishery treaty.

Waste Lands. Were first enclosed in England 1547; arising from this Ket's rebellion took place 1549; by an Act of Parliament in 1785 inclosures were once more promoted.

Watches. Portable timepieces invented in Germany in 15th century, when they were known as " Nuremberg eggs." The greatest advance in early watch-making was due to T. Tompion, an Englishman, who invented a dead-beat escapement (1639-1713).

Waterloo. Battle fought here in 1815 between the Allies (Prussians and British) under the Duke of Wellington and France under Napoleon; the French army was totally defeated, and Napoleon fled to Paris.

Waverley Novels, by Sir Walter Scott, were published between 1814 and 1831; the first of the series was *Waverley*.

Wazzan. A town in N. of Morocco celebrated for the manufacture of coarse woollen cloth and as the burial place of the Moorish saint, Idrisi Sharif, who lived there in 1727.

Weaving. First practised in China; the first mention of weaving in England is at York in 1331; early English centres of the industry were Canterbury, Colchester, and Norwich.

Weights and Measures. Invented by Pheidon of Ayos 895 B.C. A standard of English measure was made in 972 and kept at Winchester; the first official examination of weights and measures 1795; an act to enforce uniformity over the United Kingdom was passed in 1878; a metric system act was passed in 1897.

Weimar. Capital of Saxe-Weimar-Eisenach; earned the title of the German Athens owing to its association with classical German literature; its most flourishing period was from 1775-1828.

Wellington Administration. 1828 to 1830.

Wellington's Victories. Assaye, Argaum, and Gawalghur 1803; Vimiera 1808; Talavera 1809; Busaco and Torres Vedras 1810; Almeida 1811; Salamanca 1812; Vittoria 1813; Orthez and Toulouse 1814; Waterloo 1815.

Welsh Laws. Code drawn up by King Howel Dda *c.* 943. For Statute of Rhuddlan, and later English statutes, *see* Wales.

Welsh Literature. The following is a provisional list of Welsh authors (confined, with a *few* necessary exceptions, to those who have written in that tongue):—

Aneurin (poet), *c.* 560.
Taliesin (poet), *c.* 570 (*d.* 601).
Myrddin (poet), *c.* 570.
Llywarch Hen (poet), *c.* 580.
Meilyr (poet), *c.* 1137.
Gwalchmai (poet), *c.* 1157.
Owain Cyveiliog (poet), *c.* 1165.
Hywel ab Owain Gwynedd (poet), *c.* 1169.
Einion (poet), *c.* 1175.
Dafydd Benvras (poet), 1230 (?).
Elidir Sais (poet), 1230 (?).
Cynddelw (poet), 1250.
Llywarch ap Llewelyn (poet), 1250 (?).
Einion ap Gwgan (poet), 1260.
Phylip Brydydd (poet), 1250.
Einion Wann (poet), 1200-1250 (?).
Geoffrey of Monmouth (Latin chronicler and father of Arthurian romance), *d.* 1152.
Caradoc of Llancarvan (historian), *c.* 1150.
Authors of the *Mabinogion*, 1140-1200.
Edeyrn Dafod Aur (grammarian), *c.* 1270.
Llygad Gwr (poet), *c.* 1270.
Einion ap Madoc (poet), *c.* 1270.
Y Prydydd Bychan (poet), *c.* 1275.
Howel Voel (poet), *c.* 1280.

WELSH LITERATURE (*continued*)—

Bleddyn Fardd (poet), *c.* 1284.
Gruffydd ab yr Ynad Coch (poet), *c.* 1284.
Gwilym Ddu o Arfon (poet), *c.* 1300.
Gruffudd ab Meredydd (poet), *c.* 1380.
Hywel ap Einion Llygliw (poet), *c.* 1390.
Dafydd ap Gwilym (poet), 1340-1400.
Iolo Goch (poet), *c.* 1400.
Llywelyn Goch ab Meurig Hen (poet), *c.* 1400.
Gruffudd Llwyd ab Dafydd ab Einion Llygliw (poet), *c.* 1400.
Rhys Goch ap Rhiccert (poet), *c.* 1420 (?).
Rhys Goch Eryri (poet), *c.* 1410.
Sion Cent (poet), *c.* 1410.
Meredydd ap Rhys (poet), *c.* 1450.
Dafydd Nanmor (poet), *c.* 1460.
Howel Swrdwal (poet), *c.* 1460.
Ieuan ap Howel Swrdwal (poet), *c.* 1460.
Llawdden (poet and prosodist), *c.* 1460.
Ieuan Brydydd Hir Hynaf (poet), *c.* 1460.
Tudur Penllyn (poet).
Gutto'r Glyn (poet), wrote 1430-1460.
Dafydd ap Edmwnd (poet).
Gutyn Owain (poet and historian).
Ieuan Deulwyn (poet), 1460-1490.
Lewis Glyn Cothi (poet), 1440-1490.
Gruffudd ab Ieuan ab Llywelyn Fychan (poet).
Tudur Aled (poet).
Gruffudd Hiraethog (poet), 1530-1566.
Sion Brwynog (poet), 1550-1567.
Sir John Prys (historian and miscellaneous writer), 1502-1554.
Dr. Richard Davies (translator), 1501-1581.
Dr. Thomas Huet (translator), (?)-1591.
William Salesbury (translator and lexicographer), *c.* 1575.
Dr. William Morgan (translator), 1547-1604.
Maurice Kyffin (translator), *d.* 1598.
Henry Parry (grammarian), 1561-1617.
Huw Lewys (translator), 1562-1634.
Humphrey Llwyd (historian, etc.), 1527-1568.
William Llyn (poet), 1535-1580.
Dr. David Powel (historian, etc.), *d.* 1598.
Henry Salesbury (grammarian), *b.* 1561.
Dr. Morris Clynnog (catechist), *d.* 1580-1.
Dr. Gruffydd Roberts (grammarian and philosopher), *fl.* 1555-1595 (?).
Dr. Roger Smyth (translator), 1546-1625.
John Salisbury (translator), 1575-1625.
Owain Gwynedd (or Owain Ifan) (poet), *d.* 1590.
Simwnt Fychan (poet and grammarian), 1546-1606.
William Cynwal (poet), 1530-1600.
Sion Tudur (poet), 1535-1602.
Sion Phylip (poet), 1543-1620.

WELSH LITERATURE (*continued*)—

Rhys Cain (poet and painter), 1545-1614.
Edmwnd Prys (poet and translator), 1541-1623.
Dr. Sion Dafydd Rhys (poet, grammarian, etc.), 1534-161-(?).
William Myddelton, or Gwilym Canoldref (poet, translator, etc.), c. 1590.
Edward Kyffin (translator), (?)-1603.
Thomas Prys (poet), (?)-1634.
Vicar Prichard, or Rhys Prichard (religious poet), 1579-1644.
Edward James (translator), 1570-1610.
Dr. Richard Parry (translator), 1560-1623.
Dr. John Davies (grammarian), 1570(?)-1644.
Robert Llwyd (translator), c. 1640.
Rowland Vaughan (miscellaneous writer), (?)-1667.
Vavasor Powell (miscellaneous writer; wrote in English), 1617-1670.
Walter Cradoc (miscellaneous writer; wrote in English), 1606(?)-1659.
William Phylip (poet), 1577-1669.
Morgan Llwyd o Wynedd (miscellaneous writer), 1619-1659.
James Howell (miscellaneous and letter-writer; English), 1594-1666.
Richard Jones (translator), 1604-1673.
Thomas Gouge (educationist), 1605-1681.
Charles Edwards (religious writer), 1628-(?).
Stephen Hughes (translator, etc.), 1622-1688.
Edward Morus (poet), *d.* 1689.
Huw Morus (poet), 1622-1709.
Elis Wyn o Lasynys (author of the *Bardd Cwsg*), 1671-1734.
Edward Samuel (miscellaneous writer), 1674-1748.
David Lewis (philosopher), c. 1720.
Edward Lhuyd (philologist), 1660-1709.
Moses Williams (translator), 1686-1742.
Griffith Jones, Llanddowror (educationist, etc.), 1684-1761.
James Davies (Iago ab Dewi) (poet and translator), 1648-1722.
Theophilus Evans (historian), 1693-1767.
Simon Thomas (historian), c. 1730.
Joshua Thomas (historian), 1719-1797.
Goronwy Owen (poet), 1722-1769.
Lewis Morris (poet and miscellaneous writer), 1700-1779.
William Williams of Pantycelyn (hymn-writer), 1717-1791.
Thomas Edwards (Twm o'r Nant) (interlude-writer), 1739-1810.
Evan Evans (Ieuan Brydydd Hir) (poet, etc.), 1731-1781.
Daniel Rowland (religious writer, and translator [?]), 1713-1790.
Dr. Owen Pughe (lexicographer), 1759-1835.
Owen Jones (Owain Myfyr), 1741-1814.
Edward Williams (Iolo Morganwg), 1746-1826.
John Jones (Sion Glanygors), 1767-1821.
David Thomas (Dafydd Ddu Eryri), 1760-1822.
David Richards (Dafydd Ionawr), 1751-1827.
John Howel (Ioan ab Hywel), 1774-1830.

WELSH LITERATURE (*continued*)—

Reuben Davies (Prydydd y Coed), 1808-1833.
Robert Davies (Bardd Nantglyn), 1769-1835.
Edward Jones, Maesyplwm (religious poet), 1761-1836.
John Jones, LL.D. (historian, etc.), 1772-1837.
Griffith Williams (Gutyn Peris), 1769-1838.
Edward Williams (Iolo Fardd Glas), *fl.* 1839.
David Saunders, Merthyr (translator), 1769-1840.
David Owen (Dewi Wyn o Eifion), 1784-1841.
William Ellis Jones (Gwilym Cawrdaf), 1796-1848.
Ellin Evans (Elen Egryn), *fl.* 1850.
Robert Williams (Robert ap Gwilym Ddu), 1767-1850.
Evan Jones (Ieuan Gwynedd), 1820-1852.
Evan Davies (Myfyr Morganwg), *fl.* 1855.
Evan Evans (Ieuan Glan Geirionydd), 1795-1855.
John Williams (Ab Ithel), 1811-1862.
John Robert Pryse (Golyddan), 1841-1863.
Ebenezer Thomas (Eben Fardd), 1802-1863.
William Rowlands (Gwilym Lleyn), 1802-1865.
Thomas Jones (Glan Alun), 1811-1866.
David Owen (Brutus), 1794-1866.
Edward Roberts (Iorwerth Glan Aled), 1819-1867.
William Williams (Caledfryn), 1801-1869.
John Jones (Talhaiarn), 1810-1869.
Richard Foulkes Edwards (Rhisiart Ddu o Wynedd), 1836-
    1870.
Owen Wyn Jones (Glasynys), 1828-1870.
David Griffiths (Dewi Eifion), *d.* 1871.
William Roberts, LL.D. (Nefydd), 1813-1872.
Thomas Stephens, Merthyr, 1821-1875.
John Evans (I. D. Ffraid), 1814-1875.
Robert Ellis (Cynddelw), 1810-1875.
Rosser Beynon (Asaph Glan Taf), 1811-1876.
John Roberts (Ieuan Gwyllt), 1822-1877.
Richard Davies (Mynyddog), 1833-1877.
W. Thomas (Islwyn), 1832-1878).
Thomas Rowlands (grammarian), 1824-1884.
Jane Williams (Ysgafell), 1806-1885.
Roger Edwards (poet and miscellaneous writer), 1811-1886.
Edward Davies (Iolo Trefaldwyn), 1819-1887.
Robert John Pryse (Gweirydd ap Rhys), 1807-1889.
Thomas E. Davies (Dewi Wyn o Essyllt), 1820-1891.
John C. Hughes (Ceiriog), 1832-1887.
John Davies (Ossian Gwent), 1834-1892.
Mary Olwei Jones (novelist), 1858-1893.
Lady Charlotte E. Schreiber (Guest) (translator of the *Mabino-
    gion*), 1812-1895.
Daniel Owen (novelist), 1836-1895.

Wesleyans. One of the Methodist branches; fd. by John and
Charles Wesley 1727; for a time carried on their work in conjunction
with George Whitefield, but separated 1741. *See* Methodists.

Wessex. One of the three Anglo-Saxon kingdoms of Britain; fd. by Cerdic and Cynric in 494-95.

Westminster. A portion of London created a city 1899; it includes many of London's finest buildings.

Westminster Abbey. Supposed to have been built by St. Sebert in 7th century; rebuilt by Henry III. in 1220-69; converted into barracks for a short time 1643; new organ erected 1884.

Westminster Bridge. Old bridge opened 1750; new bridge 1862.

Westminster Confession of Faith. Drawn up at Westminster 1643-47, and from that time the standard of faith of Scotch Presbyterians.

Westminster Hall. Orig. William Rufus's banqueting hall 1097. Courts of Law estab. here by King John, where they remained till removed to the present buildings in the Strand in 1883.

Westminster School. One of the oldest English public schools. Fd. by monks, it was raised in status by Henry VIII.; it owes, however, much of its importance to Queen Elizabeth; it is the only London school of any standing occupying its original site.

Westminster, Statutes of. Became law during the reign of Edward I. Statute I. was passed in 1275, and Statute II. in 1285. Statute I. contains 51 clauses and covers the whole ground of legislation, " almost a code in itself." Statute II. is also a code; improves laws relating to trial of criminals, rights of commonage, dower, and advowson, also laws relating to manorial jurisdictions.

Westminster, Synods of. The more important London ecclesiastical councils; the first synod of note was held in 1075 by Lanfranc; in 1102 a national synod was held by Anselm; numberless synods have been held from this time onward, and the reader should consult larger works of reference.

Westphalia, Treaty of. Two treaties were signed in 1648 between Germany and France at Münster, and Germany and Sweden; by its means the Thirty Years' War was terminated.

Wheat, Importation of. In quantity into England first took place in 1347; had previously been intro. by Coll ap Coll Frewi.

Wheel, Breaking on the. A German and French form of torture first used in the former country 1535, and not abolished till 1827; used in Edinburgh in 1604.

Whigs. A term of reproach in the reign of Charles II. As the name of a political party the word Whig was first used during the Meal-tub Plot 1678.

Whisky Insurrection. A rising in 1794 in W. Pennsylvania against the enforcing of the excise law by the Federal Government.

Whiteboys. An Irish band of terrorists; their chief risings took place in 1761 and 1786-87; the Insurrection Act 1822 arose on their account.

Whitehall. The site of the chief British Government offices. York House, the residence of the Archbishop of York, stood on this site 1248. It was later acquired by Henry VIII. A new hall was designed for James I., but only partially completed, 1622; through this hall Charles I. passed on his way to execution 1649; it was also the death place of Henry VIII., Cromwell, and Charles II.

Whitsuntide. One of the chief feasts of the Christian Church, celebrated fifty days after Easter in commemoration of the descent of the Holy Spirit on the disciples. In Scotland Whitsun is a quarter day, and was fixed by Act of Parliament, 1693, for May 15.

Wickliffites. Followers of Wickliffe (*d.* 1384) in Church reform.

Wilhelmshaven. The chief naval station of Germany on the North Sea; fd. in 1853 at the time of the origin of the Prussian navy; the harbour was opened in 1869; many very important additions have been made to the naval station since 1900.

Winchester. A city in Hampshire. The first bishop was Hedda (*d.* 705), and legends attribute the construction of the cathedral to the 2nd century; signs of weakness manifested themselves in the cathedral in 1905, and restoration was at once put in hand. A celebrated public school fd. in 1387 by William of Wykeham is situated at W.

Window Tax, 1697. Brought in by William III. to atone for the deficiency on damaged coin; many bricked-up windows of the present day owe their origin to this tax; a door and window tax is in force in France at the present day.

Windsor Castle. The original building was started by William I.; it was enlarged 1110; in 1356 practically the whole castle was re-built by Edward III., who was *b.* there 1312; additions were made by Henry VIII., Elizabeth, and Charles II.

Witchcraft. A bull against W. was issued by Pope Innocent VIII. in 1484, whilst in England acts against it were passed in 1541, 1562, and 1603. As late as 1895 a woman was burned as a witch in Ireland.

Witena-gemot or **Witan.** The Anglo-Saxon National Council of England; in 7th and 8th centuries separate W. were possessed by Wessex, Kent, Mercia, and Northumbria; there was no fixed meeting-place, but the king was always present; meetings were held three times a year, at Easter, Whitsun, and Christmas; the most celebrated meetings were at Luton A.D. 931 and Winchester A.D. 934; died out after the Norman Conquest.

Witney. A market town in Oxfordshire, seat of blanket-making industry, which was estab. in the reign of King Edgar 909.

Wittenberg. A Saxon town on the Elbe. Mentioned in 1180; interesting in connection with Luther and the Reformation; here, in the Augustinian monastery, Luther dwelt, and in 1508 he was appointed professor of philosophy; bombarded by Austrians 1760; taken by France 1806; taken by Prussians 1814.

Wonders of the World. The seven Wonders of the World were: (1) the Egyptian pyramids; (2) the tomb of Mausolus; (3) the Ephesian temple of Diana; (4) the walls and hanging gardens of Babylon; (5) the Colossus of Rhodes; (6) the statue of Jupiter Olympus; (7) the pharos of Ptolemy Philadelphus.

Wood's Halfpence. Coined by patent in 1722; circulated in America and Ireland; the patent was withdrawn owing to the opposition of Jonathan Swift.

Woolsack. The seat of the Lord Chancellor in the House of Lords; placed there in the reign of Edward III. as a reminder of the importance of the wool industry; the earliest authentic mention of the W., however, is in the reign of Henry VIII.

Woolwich. A borough in S.E. London. Mentioned by King Edward the Confessor in 964; chief dockyard of navy till introduction of iron ships; closed as a dockyard in 1869; batteries erected against Dutch fleet in 1667; became the Royal Arsenal in 1805.

Works and Public Buildings. Placed under control of a Crown minister in 1832; a department of Public Works was instit. in 1851.

Worms, Edict of. Luther was summoned before the imperial diet. and was warned by Spalasin against entering Worms. His writings were recognised, yet he had to remain in hiding. Put under a ban May 1521.

Wrestling. One of the earliest of sports; bouts have been depicted on Egyptian tombs showing that the sport was known 3000 years B.C.; very much importance was given to wrestling by the Greeks, Milo of Crotona (*circa* 520 B.C.) being a celebrity; still largely practised in the country districts of Great Britain.

Writers to the Signet. Scottish law agents corresponding to English solicitors; by an act of 1868 they prepare all Crown writs.

Würtemburg. Part of Swabia. Noted for its opposition to Prussia in the war of 1866; however, the duchy sent a contingent to the war of 1870.

Wyatt's Insurrection, 1554. A futile riot led by Sir Thomas Wyatt in opposition to the marriage of Queen Mary with Philip of Spain; Wyatt was executed.

X

Xanthica. Named after Xanthicus, a month in the Macedonian calendar, corresponding to April; it was a military festival instit. in 392 B.C.

Xanthus (Asia Minor). Besieged by Brutus 42 B.C., when the inhabitants fired the town and perished in the flames rather than surrender.

Xenophon. A Greek historian *b.* at Athens 430 B.C.; the date of his death is unknown. His principal works are *The Anabasis, The Hellenica,* and *The Memorabilia.*

Xeres. A town in S.W. Spain and the seat of the Spanish wine trade; the word sherry is the English corruption of X. Roderic, the last Gothic king of Spain, was killed here by the Saracens in 711.

Xerxes, King of Persia. Led an enormous army into Greece 480 B.C.; but was defeated at Thermopylæ; his fleet was defeated at Artemisium and again at Salamis in the same year; X. was assassinated in 465 B.C.

X Rays. Discovered by Prof. W. C. Röntgen in 1895; used in surgery at the present time.

Y

Yachow-Fu. A city in the province of Szech'uen, China. An important tea-growing centre; first mentioned during the Chow dynasty (1122-255 B.C.).

Yachts. The first mention of a Y. in history is the one presented to Athelstan by the King of Norway; the word was first used in 1660, when Charles II. had a Y. named *Mary*; the first Y. Club was the Cork Harbour Water Club 1720.

Yakatsk. In Asiatic Russia. Celebrated for its theological seminary and for its great trade in furs; fd. in 1632.

Yakaud. Chief town of Chinese Turkestan. Noted for its leather ware; visited by Marco Polo 1271; little is known of the town till the 19th century when Adolph Schlagintweit visited it in 1857.

Yale University. The third oldest university in the U.S.; fd. in 1700 by ministers selected by the churches of New Haven county.

Yanaon. A French settlement in India; fd. 1750; after many vicissitudes it was res. to France in 1815.

Yankee. Slang for a citizen of the U.S. of America; used 1713 (*et circa*) as a term of excellency; probably first used in its present sense in 1765.

Yellow Fever. An infective tropical fever; ravages Mexico, Brazil, W. coast of Africa, and W. Indies; first authentic account from Barbadoes in 1647.

Yellowstone National Park. A public park in N.W. Wyoming, U.S.A., 3350 square miles in area; possesses several natural phenomena in the shape of hot springs, etc.; discovered in 1807.

Yeomanry. Mounted volunteers of Great Britain. Organised in 1794; served in the South African War; became merged in the Territorial force in 1907.

Yeomen of the Guard. A king's bodyguard instit. in 1485; the oldest military body in England; they were nicknamed " Beef-Eaters " in 1669; their services, originally most comprehensive, are now purely ceremonial.

Yezidis. Devil worshippers of the Caucasus; they regard the devil as a peacock, and never mention his name; their sacred book is Al-Yalvah (*circa* 1200).

Yokohama. A Japanese seaport on W. of Tokio Bay. Opened to foreigners in 1859—it was then little more than a village; silk and tea are the chief exports.

York. County town of Yorkshire and seat of an archbishop. The most important Roman station in North Britain; Hadrian visited York 120 A.D.; Severus *d.* there 211 A.D.; history of Y. is obscure from 410 to 627, when Paulinus was consecrated the first archbishop; burnt by William I. 1068; parliament held here 1175; Council of the North 1537; garrisoned by Royalists 1642, and surrendered after battle of Marston Moor; once a centre of weaving industry.

Yosemite. A celebrated valley on western slope of the Sierra Nevada, California; discovered in 1851.

Young Men's Christian Association. A social and religious organisation fd. in England by Sir George Williams 1821; the movement has spread to America, Germany, Denmark, Norway, Switzerland, and even China and Japan.

Yucatan. A Central American peninsula. Discovered in 1517; it has little commerce, and is thinly populated.

Z

Zaberu. A town in S. Germany. Many noted castles in neighbourhood, and a celebrated wood mentioned by Goethe in his *Dichtung* and *Wharheit*; occupied by insurgents in Peasants' War 1525; suffered from ravages in Thirty Years' War.

Zambesi. The largest African river flowing into the Indian Ocean, 2200 miles long. The river is naturally divided into three portions, the upper river from the source to the Victoria Falls, the middle river from the Victoria Falls to the Kebrabasa Rapids, hence to the sea is the lower river. The first European to explore the Zambesi was Dr. Livingstone in 1851-53.

Zante. An island of the Ionian group. A naval base for the Athenians in the Peloponnesian War; now celebrated as being the home of the " currant " of commerce.

Zanzibar. A British Protectorate in East Africa. Mentioned by Arab writers in 1328 as " The Land of the Zeuj; " fell into the hands of the Portuguese in the 15th century, and taken by the Turks in the 17th century; proclaimed a British Protectorate in 1890.

Zarhon. A Moorish mountain named after the founder of the Moorish empire, Mulai Idris I., who was buried there A.D. 791.

Zend-Avesta. The book of the religion of Zoroaster; the Avesta consists of five parts, and is still used by the Parsees as their Bible and prayer-book; mentioned by Hermippus in the 3rd century B.C.

Zinc. A metal used in early times as a component of brass (referred to by Pliny); the word Z. was first used by Paracelsus, and was described by Libavius in 1597.

Zindei. A town in N. of Central Sudan, and a great trade emporium; occupied by the French in 1899.

Znaim. A town in Moravia; fd. in 1226 by Ottacar I. of Bohemia. The armistice between Napoleon I. and the Archduke Charles was concluded here after the b. of Wagram 1809.

Zodiac, Signs of the. Twelve signs on an imaginary zone in the heavens suggested by the twelve full moons in the course of a year, 560 B.C.

Zollverein. A Customs Union, mainly used by German states between 1819 and 1871.

Zoological Nomenclature. First applied with any degree of accuracy by Linnæus in 1751.

Zouaves. French infantry serving in Africa. First corps was raised in Algeria 1831; saw service outside Africa for the first time in the Crimean War.

Zululand (in S.E. Africa). Inhabited by Zulus, who settled in the country in the 17th century; war with Britain in 1879 noted for the brave defence of a handful of the 24th Regiment against 4000 Zulus at Rorke's Drift, and for the massacre of British at Isandhlwana; annexed by Great Britain 1887.

Zutphen (in Gelderland, Holland). Scene of several battles, the most noted being that of 1586, when Sir Philip Sidney was killed; taken by the Spaniards 1587, and recovered by the Dutch 1591.

THE TEMPLE PRESS, PRINTERS, LETCHWORTH

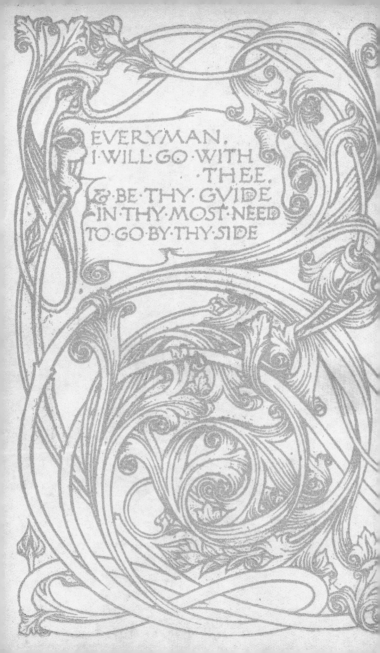

EVERYMAN,
I·WILL·GO·WITH
THEE,
&·BE·THY·GVIDE
IN·THY·MOST·NEED
TO·GO·BY·THY·SIDE